Roscoe Pound and Karl Llewellyn

N. E. H. Hull

Roscoe Pound and Karl Llewellyn

SEARCHING FOR AN AMERICAN JURISPRUDENCE

The University of Chicago Press / Chicago and London

Law in the Graduate Faculty in History at
and the author of a number of books on
eform," published in *Law and History*
American Society for Legal History.

The University of Chicago Press, Chicago 60637
The University of Chicago Press, Ltd., London
© 1997 by N. E. H. Hull
All rights reserved. Published 1997
Printed in the United States of America
06 05 04 03 02 01 00 99 98 97   1 2 3 4 5
ISBN: 0-226-36043-1 (cloth)

Library of Congress Cataloging-in-Publication Data

Hull, N. E. H., 1949–
    Roscoe Pound and Karl Llewellyn : searching for an American
jurisprudence / N. E. H. Hull.
        p.   cm.
    Includes bibliographical references and index.
    ISBN 0-226-36043-1 (cloth : alk. paper)
    1. Jurisprudence—United States—History.   2. Pound, Roscoe,
1870–1964.   3. Llewellyn, Karl N. (Karl Nickerson), 1893–1962.
4. Law teachers—United States—Biography.   I. Title.
KF380.H85   1997
349.73—dc21   97-2975
                                                        CIP

∞ The paper used in this publication meets the minimum requirements of the
American National Standard for Information Sciences—Permanence of Paper for
Printed Library Materials, ANSI Z39.48-1984.

For the men in my life, each of whom contributed in his own way to the making of this book:

Peter Charles Hoffer
Williamjames Branwell Paine Hull Hoffer
Louis Micah Gareth Hull Hoffer

CONTENTS

Photographs follow page 172

I started researching and writing this book in the fall of 1986. Any book that takes more than ten years from inception to publication will, unsurprisingly, accrue many debts for the author along the way; my debts are numerous indeed.

First, I must acknowledge and thank the following journals for permission to reprint parts of several articles that came out of my researches. Portions of the introduction first appeared in "Networks and Bricolage: A Prolegomenon to a History of Twentieth-Century American Academic Jurisprudence," 35 *American Journal of Legal History* 307 (1991), reprinted by permission of the American Journal of Legal History. Portions of chapter 1 first appeared in "Restatement and Reform: A New Perspective on the Origins of the American Law Institute," 8 *Law and History Review* 55 (1990), © 1990 by the Board of Trustees of the University of Illinois, used by permission of the University of Illinois Press. Portions of chapter 2 first appeared in "Vital Schools of Jurisprudence: Roscoe Pound, Wesley Newcomb Hohfeld, and the Promotion of an Academic Jurisprudential Agenda, 1910–1919," 45 *Journal of Legal Education* 239 (1995), reprinted by permission of the Journal of Legal Education. Portions of chapter 3 first appeared in "Reconstructing the Origins of Realistic Jurisprudence: A Prequel to the Llewellyn-Pound Exchange over Legal Realism," 1989 *Duke Law Journal* 1302, reprinted by permission of the Duke University Law Journal. Portions of chapter 4 first appeared in "Some Realism about the Llewellyn-Pound Exchange over Realism: The Newly Uncovered Private Correspondence, 1927–31," 1987 *Wisconsin Law Review*

921, © 1987 by The Board of Regents of the University of Wisconsin System, reprinted by permission of the Wisconsin Law Review. Other portions of chapter 4 and portions of chapter 5 first appeared in "The Romantic Realist: Art, Literature, and the Enduring Legacy of Karl Llewellyn's 'Jurisprudence,'" 40 *American Journal of Legal History* 115 (1996), reprinted by permission of the American Journal of Legal History.

Historical research requires funding for trips to archives and distant libraries. I was extremely fortunate to receive such support from many sources. First, and foremost, the entire project owes its inception to the yearlong resident fellowship I received from the Charles Warren Center for Studies in American History at Harvard University. I also benefited from the generosity of the American Council of Learned Societies, the American Bar Foundation, and the National Endowment for the Humanities. I am also immensely grateful to my own institution, Rutgers University; I doubt that any scholar ever received a greater level of support—in terms of both financial support and release time from teaching—than Rutgers University provided me over the past ten years. I must single out the deans of the law school, who always came to my aid—Richard Singer, Paul Robinson, and Roger Dennis. The Research Council of Rutgers University gave me the prestigious Henry Rutgers Fellowship for two years of support and summer research money as well; and the Rutgers University Center for the Critical Analysis of Contemporary Culture (CCACC) gave me a yearlong fellowship and stipend.

I spent a great deal of time in archives and libraries far from home. I want to thank the many individuals who assisted and befriended me. I am deeply in the debt of Judith Mellins, David DeLorenzo, and Pamela Ross of the Harvard Law School Library Special Collections; Judith Schiff and William Massa, Jr., of Sterling Library, Yale University; Charles Ten Brink of the University of Chicago Law School Library; Kevin Leonard of the Northwestern University Library Archives; and the many others on the staffs of those archives and libraries for all the help and especially their friendship.

I wish to thank the many libraries and archives that permitted me to use and quote from their collections: the Harvard Law School Library for permission to quote from the Roscoe Pound, Lon L. Fuller, Zechariah Chafee, Jr., and Felix Frankfurter Papers; the University of Chicago Law Library for the Karl Llewellyn Papers;

the Northwestern University Library for the John Henry Wigmore Papers; Sterling Library, Yale University, for the Jerome Frank, Thomas Swan, James Angell, and Charles E. Clark Papers; the University of Nebraska Archives, Lincoln, for the Roscoe Pound Papers and the University Collections; the Nebraska State Historical Society for the Pound Family Papers; the University of Iowa for the Paul Sayre Papers; the Mariam Coffin Canaday Library, Bryn Mawr College, for the Emma Corstvet Collection; the American Philosophical Society for the E. Adamson Hoebel Papers; the Seeley G. Mudd Library, Princeton University, for the American Civil Liberties Union Papers; the Federal Bureau of Investigation, Washington, D.C., for copies of the Roscoe Pound and Karl Llewellyn files; and the American Law Institute Archives, Philadelphia.

The present manuscript has benefited from the comments of colleagues who read or heard earlier versions of various parts of the book in conjunction with presentations to the Rutgers University School of Law–Camden Faculty Development Seminar, the American Society for Legal History, the University of Chicago Law School Karl Llewellyn Centennial Symposium, and the New York University Legal History Seminar. I was helped enormously by the comments of colleagues at each of those presentations. I would particularly like to acknowledge the suggestions and criticisms of Richard Helmholz, William Twining, Robert Summers, Daniel Ernst, Robert Gordon, William Nelson, Edward Purcell, William LaPiana, Eben Moglen, Craig Oren, Ann Freedman, Roger Dennis, Jay Feinman, Roger Clark, Michael Livingston, Patrick Ryan, Steven Friedell, and Stephen Conrad. I presented another part of the book at Union College, Schenectady, New York, as a Minerva Lecture; I am grateful to Byron Nichols and the Minerva Committee for providing a stimulating interdisciplinary forum in which I could test some of my ideas. I am also greatly indebted to Laura Kalman, Thomas A. Green, and Hendrik Hartog, who read the draft manuscript and provided enormously helpful comments. Finally, I would like to acknowledge the comments of successive generations of students in my legal history and jurisprudence courses, who allowed me to inflict early drafts of several chapters on them in the name of pedagogy.

The introduction, on networks and bricolage, was a direct outgrowth of the year I spent as a fellow at the Rutgers University Center for the Critical Analysis of Contemporary Culture. I am deeply indebted to Professors George Levine and Carolyn Williams, director and associate director, respectively, during the 1989–90 fellowship year; Beryle Chandler, coordinator; and the rest of the staff of the CCACC. I am grateful as well to the other fellows, who created a constructive and stimulating interdisciplinary atmosphere—Andrew Abbott, Norma Basch, Bob Beauregard, Ed Cohen, Edith Kurzweil, George Levine, Rajagopalan Radhakrishnan, Gordon Schochet, George Shulman, Neil Smith, Alan Williams, Carolyn Williams, and Eviatar Zerubavel. I am also indebted to George Levine for introducing me to Thomas Carlyle's Diogenes Teufelsdröckh.

My research assistants were splendid and performed above and beyond the call of duty: Williamjames B. P. H. Hoffer, William Deyerle, and Mathias Jaren, thank you. My husband, Peter Charles Hoffer, was a generous and devoted typist, go-fer, and line editor when health problems stalled my progress on this book.

I also want to thank the people at the University of Chicago Press who worked with me so tirelessly: John Tryneski, senior editor at the University of Chicago Press, for his faith and patience; Leslie Keros, my production editor; and Sherry Goldbecker, my copyeditor.

Although I have dedicated this book to others, I want to acknowledge here the inspiration of my father, William Hull (1907–92), who, despite ill health, listened with interest and encouragement to early drafts, but who died before I could share the final version with him; and my mother, Irene Gladys Gleicher Hull (1917–86), a woman of steel-like strength, who encouraged and supported me, and taught me not to give up in the face of pain and physical disability.

Discourse, Networks, and Bricolage

No mystery writer would tell an audience at the outset which clues are the ones to follow, much less the solution of the crime. Lawbook authors are a different breed. They are eager to limn out the lesson in the first sentence (and repeat the message periodically just in case the reader's mind wanders). Historians have a choice: to keep the reader in suspense or not. The subtitle of this book, "Searching for an American Jurisprudence," holds out the promise of a rousing chase after an elusive quarry. And the story herein told has its share of unexpected twists and sudden confrontations because it is a tale not just of ideas, but also of two engaging and powerful men. One was a gentle pedant with a will of iron whose happiest hours were spent at his desk at Harvard Law School. The other was a mercurial romantic whose joy and despair in the law spilled into pages of anguished poetry and exuberant lectures. Roscoe Pound and Karl Llewellyn were the most quoted and admired, the most disputed and abused jurisprudents of their day, and that day spanned the first sixty years of the twentieth century. They searched for an American jurisprudence in the criminal and the commercial law, at the gatherings of America's leading law teachers, and in the lecture halls of Peking, Leipzig, and Tokyo. This book is the story of what they found and what they did not find.

I am not the first detective to follow their trail. Pound had an admiring biographer in Paul Sayre.[1] Indeed, Roscoe's younger sister, Olivia, a high school teacher, had to scold Sayre: "I took you at

---

1. Paul Sayre, *The Life of Roscoe Pound* (Iowa City, 1948).

your word and tried to make such corrections, changes, and suggestions as I thought best. . . . Many of my suggestions as to choice of words are merely a matter of taste. It does seem, however, that the frequent repetition of certain words and phrases, such as 'honest,' 'true and worthy,' 'gallant,' [and] 'playfully,' . . . should be varied or left out entirely."[2] In 1974, David Wigdor gave Pound's life and writings a more critical review.[3] Since then, Pound has slipped into semi-obscurity. Llewellyn is still a cathartic figure for our generation of legal theorists, but William Twining's book remains the only full-length modern assessment of Llewellyn's life and contributions. It, too, is more than two decades old.[4]

Pound and Llewellyn have a secure place in the schools-and-movements literature of academic jurisprudence, but such mechanical treatments, to adopt one of the terms Pound used to criticize formalist jurisprudence, hardly do justice to either man.[5] True, sociological jurisprudence, the ideology associated with Roscoe Pound, and legal realism, the approach to law first given its name by Karl Llewellyn, have taken their place in the standard histories of jurisprudence, alongside John Austin's legal positivism and Immanuel Kant's metaphysics of law.[6] And, also true, in places in his writing, Pound delighted in imagining an orderly parade of schools and movements, each giving way to the next in an ever upward progress of jurisprudential acuity.[7] But privately Pound admitted that the American academic jurisprudent is too individualistic, fickle, and independent minded to line up as anyone's disciple and criticized those who spend their days in the "setting up and vigorous beating

2. Olivia Pound to Paul Sayre, Nov. 27, 1948, Paul Sayre Papers, University of Iowa (hereinafter Sayre Papers).

3. David Wigdor, *Roscoe Pound, Philosopher of Law* (Westport, Conn., 1974).

4. William Twining, *Karl Llewellyn and the Realist Movement* [1973] (Norman, Okla., 1985). The newer edition does not represent an alteration of the first edition, as Twining writes in the preface to the former: "I am prepared to stand by what I wrote" (xii).

5. The problem is fully explored in N. E. H. Hull, "Networks and Bricolage: A Prolegomenon to a History of Twentieth-Century American Academic Jurisprudence," 35 *American Journal of Legal History* 307–22 (1991).

6. See, e.g., Edgar Bodenhamer, *Jurisprudence: The Philosophy and Method of the Law* (rev. ed., Cambridge, Mass., 1974), 60–170.

7. Consider one such procession in his Storrs Lectures at Yale Law School in 1921: "Toward the end of the last century a positivist sociological thinking tended to supersede the metaphysical historical and the utilitarian analytical." Roscoe Pound, *An Introduction to the Philosophy of Law* (rev. ed., New Haven, Conn., 1953), 22.

of straw men, much wasted polemics, and refutation proceeding from misunderstanding."[8]

Llewellyn said as much in 1942: "[T]he concept of 'school' as applied to jurisprudence is prevalent but misleading. The heart of the actual contribution of the best writers is so little affected by the 'school' attributes ascribed to them by their opponents as to make it unwise to rely on any description of 'schools.'"[9] Of course, Llewellyn meant himself when he referred to the "best writers," and he spoke from painful personal experience when he recalled the attacks of opponents of legal realism, but modern scholarship bears him out. These thinkers, as Morton Horwitz astutely reminds us, were hostile to abstract concepts,[10] and the more recent work on the "realist controversy" of 1930–31 demonstrates that neither Llewellyn nor Pound (along with everyone else whom they tried to draw into the debate) thought that realism was a school with any bright-line boundaries.[11]

What, then, is left for a historian of jurisprudence to chronicle? We must apply Llewellyn's injunction: "'See it fresh,' 'See it whole,' 'See it as it works.'"[12] We need to come to the canonical texts of American jurisprudence determined to read them in a new way. The published works and the public discourse are vital sources of the story, but these documents are not as easily decipherable as we might wish. The plain meaning of public historical sources is rarely plain. We do not automatically know what the published word means by simply reading it. That is the kind of scholarly omniscience all too common in constitutional scholarship. The task of the historian is to try to recover past meanings, embedded in distant contexts.

What is more, in an academic setting, where the authors of the texts presumably think long and hard about what they are writing,

8. Roscoe Pound, Draft Introduction for Book on Jurisprudence, 1950, Roscoe Pound Papers, Harvard Law School (hereinafter RPP), 79-17.

9. Karl Llewellyn, Jurisprudence Lecture, Dec. 4, 1942, Karl Llewellyn Papers, University of Chicago Law School (hereinafter KLP), B.III.15, p. 3.

10. Morton Horwitz, *The Transformation of American Law, 1870–1960* (New York, 1992), 200.

11. N. E. H. Hull, "Some Realism about the Llewellyn-Pound Exchange over Realism: The Newly Uncovered Private Correspondence, 1927–1931," 1987 *Wisconsin Law Review* 921.

12. Karl Llewellyn, *The Common Law Tradition: Deciding Appeals* (Boston, 1960), 510.

the words that they use have a history of their own. Their meaning is not general, but special. Such internal histories of the language of intellectual exchanges reach out from the texts to the networks of intended readers in a kind of halfway code. Only those in the network can fully decode the many connotations and implications of every passage.

And if the latter notion of purposive relations between the texts and readers has any application to American academic jurisprudence at all, it cannot be enough to relate published works to the "life and times" of the authors. Such broad-stroked depictions of context—great events, sea changes in values, upheavals in politics, shifts in intellectual currents—are always useful, but academic jurisprudents rarely sit at the tables of power or report great events firsthand. Instead, most of the time their interest is focused on closer objects—what is going on in their schools, their discipline, and their circle of readers and friends. This is the intimate, human context in which academic jurisprudence is conceived and given voice.

Put in other terms: there are two contemporaneous, interlocking levels of discourse in twentieth-century American academic jurisprudence. There is the public discourse—the exchange of arguments in articles, speeches, and books—in which we see great thinkers explaining themselves to the world. This is the usual source material for the student of schools-and-movements. A scholar who limits herself to the public discourse may be able to group these articulations to fit preconceived categories, but the explication of the public text cannot be complete—that is, we cannot comprehend the entire meaning of that text—without taking into account what the jurisprudents themselves were doing at the time that they created the public discourse. To do this, we must recover a second, private level of discourse. This private discourse, carried on in the correspondence and informal discussion among jurisprudents, allows us to define fully the public discourse.[13]

Admittedly, seen from a distance over time, the public discourse comes to dominate the private discourse. Public exchanges sever

13. Peter Charles Hoffer, "Text, Translation, Context, Conversation: Preliminary Notes for Decoding the Deliberations of the Advisory Committee That Wrote the Federal Rules of Civil Procedure," 37 *American Journal of Legal History* 416–19, 431–38 (1993). A perfect and perplexing example of the converse—scholarship led astray by indifference to voluminous archival evidence or reliance on snippets quoted in secondary sources—is G. Edward White, "The American Law Institute and the Triumph of Modernist Jurisprudence," 15 *Law and History Review* 1 (1997).

themselves from private communications and take on a life of their own—an externally defined jurisprudential dialogue. Publications become the focus of later interpretation and analysis. The private conversation, so vital to the intellectual process—the social, intimate, interactive context of intellectual history—is lost. While later jurisprudents and legal scholars are entitled to abstract the public discourse from its original informing, nurturing private dialogue, the historian is not so free. Historians must rediscover the private discourse and use it to reinterpret the public discourse.

Once we have reintroduced the intimate discourse, we can see that American academic jurisprudence in the first half of the twentieth century is what American academic jurisprudents did as well as said. In *The Bramble Bush*, Llewellyn wrote that "this doing of something about disputes, this doing of it reasonably, is the business of the law. And the people who have the doing in charge, whether they be judges or sheriffs or clerks or jailers or lawyers, are officials of the law. *What these officials do about disputes is, to my mind, the law itself.*"[14] In later years, Llewellyn sanded smooth the rough edges of his insight (after all, there were rules, and lawyers had better know them), but what he said about law in general holds especially true for jurisprudence.[15] The constant overlapping of the public and private discourses of the jurisprudents reveals the pride, the ambition, the resentment, the need for approbation, and even (perhaps one should say especially) the yearning for professional standing that drove authors to emend the texts. Jurisprudence becomes human, which after all is not really news.

Academic jurisprudence is a quintessentially social act. Not only does it bring people together, but also it makes ideas inseparable from social concourse. Our focus thus shifts back and forth from the texts to the networks of academic writers reaching out from Pound and Llewellyn. At key intersections of these networks were not Nietzschean heroes working in isolation but *bricoleurs,* men who put together bits and pieces of existing theories to innovate a new American approach to legal thought.

Pound and Llewellyn did all of their jurisprudence within the framework of their institutional associations. What they wrote for

14. Karl Llewellyn, *The Bramble Bush* [1930] (New York, 1960), 3 (emphasis in original).

15. Llewellyn, *Common Law Tradition,* 511.

public consumption they first tested, often extensively, in private correspondence with other academics. Their commitment to networking changed what they thought and how they expressed those thoughts. Both men were very conscious of their audiences—Pound through a desire to please and a sense of insecurity, Llewellyn because he wanted attention and loved the romantic, outrageous gesture. By tracing the networks, we can recover the structure of the private discourse.

Networks are "set[s] of social relations which exist in reality"[16] and may encompass "any aspects of a social relation (kinship, information, economic exchange)."[17] Networks serve participants in multiple and reciprocal ways, but at bottom they are "essentially exchanges—both of material goods and services and of less tangible rewards such as advice, comfort, and praise."[18] Networks are fluid rather than static, reflecting "individual choices made within social constraints."[19] Individuals choose which relationships to pursue and decide when to discontinue them.

For American academic jurisprudents of the first half of the twentieth century, these "social relations" were, first and foremost, created by the jurisprudents' positions at particular law schools. Laura Kalman has described one such network of like-minded law teacher–jurisprudents at Yale.[20] Likewise, there was a strong Harvard Law School network of reformers that included Pound. Indeed, Pound was an intuitive networker—he loved to write to other scholars, offered his patronage to younger protégés, and worked to link the law school to other academic institutions. From 1906 to the middle 1930s, Pound made himself into the locus of a network of progressive-pragmatic law professors. Thereafter, as his views became more conservative, he attracted other admirers, including, for a time, China's Chiang Kai-shek. For his seminar in legal and political philosophy, Pound brought together and regularly networked with Harvard professors Gordon Allport (psychology), Talcott Parsons (sociology), B. F. Wright (government), and O. H. Taylor

16. A. R. Radcliffe-Brown, *Structure and Function in Primitive Societies* (Glencoe, Ill., 1968), 190.

17. Larissa Adler Lomnitz, *Networks and Marginality: Life in a Mexican Shantytown* (New York, 1986), 131.

18. Robert Max Jackson, Claude S. Fischer, and Lynne McCallister Jones, "The Dimensions of Social Networks," in Claude S. Fischer, ed., *Networks and Places: Social Relations in the Urban Setting* (New York, 1977), 43.

19. Ibid., 41.

20. Laura Kalman, *Legal Realism at Yale, 1927–1960* (Chapel Hill, N.C., 1986).

(economics). By so doing, Pound linked the law school to the rest of what was becoming the foremost research university in the country.[21]

While Pound served as an intellectual locus for the other early progressive pragmatists, joining their academic network helped Pound as well—taking him from the University of Nebraska to Northwestern to the University of Chicago to Harvard. Once Pound arrived at Harvard Law School, and particularly after he was appointed dean (1916–36), he used his powerful position to help numerous other law professors get grants, find jobs, and be awarded prizes or publishing contracts. But Pound's material assistance to these younger scholars (many of whom were his former students[22]) was motivated as much by Pound's desire to promote shared jurisprudential aims as by collegial largesse.

Llewellyn was an impulsive networker. He loved to write to other people and to be in their company. His teaching was a kind of networking, for there was no distance, literal or figurative, between him and his students. "He could be abrasive and demanding, but he was always there."[23] Young Llewellyn was by nature gregarious and hard working, which enabled him to keep the law journal going at Yale when most of the students went off to fight in World War I. A decade later, when he was challenged by Pound to define realism, he simply wrote to academics who might be classified as realists. Many replied. Llewellyn's correspondence with fellow realist Jerome Frank is a marvel of networking—in which the two enfants terribles planned their assaults on the citadels of legal orthodoxy.

Networks among academicians are not just institutional; they are personal as well. "Over time, people constantly choose whether to begin, continue, or cease exchanging with other people."[24] Long after he had left Nebraska, Pound continued to write to his old botany professor, Charles Bessey. Bessey reciprocated. The two men discussed plant ecology and the reform of the law. While Pound served as dean of the Nebraska College of Law, the sociologist Edward A. Ross joined the faculty of the university. The two men often lunched together and, over the food at "Jimmie's Lunch," began a

---

21. RPP, 62-2.

22. For example, Hessel Yntema, RPP, 54-7; Jerome Hall, RPP, 16-4.

23. Mary Ann Glendon, *A Nation under Lawyers* (New York, 1995), 6–7.

24. Jackson, Fischer, and Jones, "Social Networks," 43.

lifelong conversation.[25] Ross's work had an enormous impact on Pound's own ideas about law as a form of social control.[26]

Llewellyn's personal and professional ties to Frank were strong and fruitful. Between them, the two men carried the banner of legal realism. Llewellyn was skeptical of rules, and Frank worried that facts were little more than stories interested parties told, but between them they shook the legal heavens.[27] Later, Llewellyn would work closely with E. Adamson Hoebel on a study of Cheyenne legal customs and with Soia Mentschikoff (his third wife) on the Uniform Commercial Code. Collaboration and networking were Llewellyn's intellectual life blood.

Recognition of the importance of networking not only enables us to reconstitute the exact sequence and content of the private level of jurisprudential discourse, but also reveals to us the "play" of ideas among the crucial networkers. The interchange of ideas through a network of communicators initially served to invigorate Pound and encourage Llewellyn, and changed over time as differences of political commitment were amplified and refined in public discourse. The two worked hard to recruit other academic jurisprudents to share private expressions of opinion and take public stands on legal realism and sociological jurisprudence.

In their private and public discourse, Pound and Llewellyn displayed a marvelously far-ranging and free-thinking eclecticism. Pound's borrowing from biology,[28] sociology,[29] and comparative

25. "Jimmie was an old institution really much better known and patronized than one might have supposed from the outside. . . . Everything in the way of edibles was home cooked and strictly first class." Pound to Sayre, Sept. 14, 1945, Sayre Papers.

26. Michael R. Hill, "Roscoe Pound and American Sociology: A Study in Archival Frame Analysis, Sociobiography, and Sociological Jurisprudence" (Ph.D. diss., University of Nebraska, 1989), 387, 406, 421.

27. Hull, "Some Realism"; Robert Jerome Glennon, *The Iconoclast as Reformer: Jerome Frank's Impact on American Law* (Ithaca, N.Y., 1985), 54–55.

28. Pound did his graduate work in botany under Charles E. Bessey, the noted Nebraska ecological botanist. The two men continued to correspond up to Pound's appointment to the Harvard Law School faculty. See *Guide and Index to the Microfilm Edition of the Charles E. Bessey Papers (1865–1915)* (Lincoln, Neb., 1984), 151. On Bessey's important contributions to modern botany, see A. G. Morton, *History of Botanical Science: An Account of the Development of Botany from Ancient Times to the Present Day* (London, 1981), 456; Harry Baker Humphrey, *Makers of North American Botany* (New York, 1961), 27–29.

29. See, for example, Roscoe Pound, "Introduction" to Eugen Ehrlich, *Fundamental Principles of the Sociology of Law* [1936], trans. Walter L. Moll (New York, 1962).

law[30] was at times pedantic; Llewellyn was more poetic,[31] weaving together Icelandic sagas,[32] English novels,[33] and social science. Both men were inveterate borrowers. This feature of their methodology is a second essential and hitherto unexplored characteristic of the history of academic jurisprudence. They were bricoleurs.[34]

Bricoleurs? "In our own time the 'bricoleur' is still someone who works with his hands and uses devious means compared to those of a craftsman. . . . His universe of instruments is closed and the rules of his game are always to make do with 'whatever is at hand,' that is to say with a set of tools and materials which is always finite and is also heterogeneous because what it contains bears no relation to the current project, or indeed to any particular project, but is the contingent result of all the occasions there have been to renew or enrich the stock or to maintain it with the remains of previous constructions or destructions."[35] Like the bricoleur, American jurisprudents work within a fixed universe of legal forms and try to bring together its many fragments into satisfying wholes.

Since 1962, when Claude Lévi-Strauss used the colloquial French word "bricolage" in his now-classic *The Savage Mind* to explain the intellectual process of myth-making among primitive peoples,[36] the term has been adopted by numerous legal scholars in a variety of contexts.[37] Indeed, the extent of its popularity can be gauged by the

30. For example, see Pound's frequent references to Roman, German, and medieval legal systems and thought in his Storrs Lectures, published as *An Introduction to the Philosophy of Law.*

31. Llewellyn had two volumes of his poetry privately published in 1931: *Beach Plums* and *Put in His Thumb.*

32. Llewellyn used *Njal's Saga* as an illustration of the inadequacy of Pound's periodization of legal development. See Hull, "Some Realism," 929–31.

33. Llewellyn wrote several satirical jurisprudence articles under the pseudonym Diogenes Teufelsdröckh. He took the name from a character in Thomas Carlyle's 1831 novel, *Sartor Resartus.* I am grateful to George Levine for pointing out the origins of Llewellyn's pseudonym. For a discussion of these articles, see N. E. H. Hull, "The Romantic Realist: Art, Literature, and the Enduring Legacy of Karl Llewellyn's 'Jurisprudence,'" 40 *American Journal of Legal History* 115 (1996).

34. I am grateful to Professor Alan Williams of the Rutgers University French Department for introducing me to this term.

35. Claude Lévi-Strauss, *The Savage Mind* (Eng. trans., Chicago, 1966), 17.

36. Ibid., 16–33.

37. I have found six law review articles that employ the term. There are several others that cite Sidney Ulmer's article entitled "Bricolage and Assorted Thoughts on Working in the Papers of Supreme Court Justices," 35 *Journal of Politics* 286 (1973), but they do so for other reasons and never discuss bricolage. See Steven L. Winter, "The Cognitive Dimension of the *Agon* between Legal Power and Narrative Meaning," 87 *Michigan Law*

fact that the late Arthur Leff included "bricolage" and "bricoleur" in his unfinished "Dictionary of Law": "French word for a particular sort of handyman, one who fixes things by modifying whatever materials are at hand to serve his then purposes. [The term] has been taken over to a limited extent by legal writers to describe a similar process in law, by which judges and scholars bend concepts or rules to serve divers purposes rather than create new ones more particularly crafted to the job at hand." [38] Though Leff was skeptical of the general utility of the term, he did concede that one application of the notion of bricolage would be to explain the reasoning processes of judges who apply known and accepted legal theories or principles to new cases.

Shortly thereafter, Jack M. Balkin, reviewing William M. Landes and Richard A. Posner's *The Economic Structure of Tort Law,* argued that a neat economic theory of the evolutionary development of legal doctrines did not describe the reality of judicial reasoning. Instead, he insisted that doctrinal development must necessarily involve the concept of bricolage. Balkin suggested the "human conceptual structures—which include doctrines of law—are always makeshift to a large degree. They have no claim on being the best way of dealing with problems—they only represent a way that worked at a given time, given what had come before." [39] Judith Schelly has pronounced Ronald Dworkin a bricoleur, and James Boyle has likened the critical legal scholar to the bricoleur.[40]

The bricoleur collects castoffs and odd items with the idea that they may be useful. So, too, did Pound and Llewellyn collect ideas

---

Review 2231 (1989); "Administrative Law Symposium: Question & Answer with Professors Elliot, Strauss, and Sunstein," 1989 *Duke Law Journal* 551, 559 (in an answer by Dick Elliot); Murray Edelman, "The Construction of Social Problems as Buttresses of Inequalities," 42 *University of Miami Law Review* 711 (1987).

38. Arthur Leff, "The Leff Dictionary of Law: A Fragment," 94 *Yale Law Journal* 2212 (1985).

39. Jack M. Balkin, "Too Good to Be True: The Positive Economic Theory of Law," 87 *Columbia Law Review* 1487–88 (1987). Bricolage has not been used only to describe the reasoning processes of judges. Terry Fisher recently used the term to characterize the development of eighteenth-century political discourse. William W. Fisher III, "Ideology, Religion, and the Constitutional Protection of Private Property: 1760–1860," 39 *Emory Law Journal* 80 (1990).

40. Judith Schelly, "Interpretation in Law: The Dworkin-Fish Debate (Or, Soccer amongst the Gahuku-Gama)," 73 *California Law Review* 175–76 (1985); James Boyle, "The Politics of Reason: Critical Legal Theory and Local Social Thought," 133 *University of Pennsylvania Law Review* 779–80 (1985).

from their vast reading of their predecessors in jurisprudence as well as of economists, social psychologists, sociologists, and historians. They squirreled away ideas and then used them to construct their jurisprudential examinations of legal processes and the system of justice. Llewellyn, particularly in his early jurisprudential writings, publicly acknowledged various thinkers on whom he had drawn to compose his own view of jurisprudence.[41] The first list of acknowledgments appeared in an article Llewellyn published in the *American Economic Review,* in 1925.[42] The list included such diverse figures as conservative anthropologist William Graham Sumner, liberal economists John R. Commons and Thorstein Veblen, Justice Oliver Wendell Holmes, Jr., and fellow jurisprudent Roscoe Pound. Llewellyn included another eclectic list of thinkers in his contribution to the 1930 "Law and the Modern Mind" symposium in the *Columbia Law Review:*[43] Commons, Veblen, Sumner, and Holmes (Pound was notably omitted[44]) were joined by Max Weber as thinkers "to whom [Llewellyn is] particularly indebted." In addition, Llewellyn belatedly admitted that his "Realistic Jurisprudence" article,[45] which appeared earlier that year, had built not only on the thoughts of the sixteen jurisprudents he had listed on the occasion,[46] but also on the work of Arthur Corbin, Walter Wheeler Cook, Underhill Moore, Herman Oliphant, John Dewey, and "the Boas school" of anthropology.[47]

Once we reconceptualize Llewellyn as a bricoleur, not a devotee of social science, not a secret conservative defending custom against democratic regulation, not a theorist inspired by German neopositivist philosophy, we can begin to recover the motives of his academic enterprise. He wanted a sturdy, pragmatic method to

41. There is an evolutionary chronology of some of these lists in Hull, "Some Realism," 967.

42. Karl Llewellyn, "The Effect of Legal Institutions upon Economics" (1925), discussed in N. E. H. Hull, "Reconstructing the Origins of Realistic Jurisprudence: A Prequel to the Llewellyn-Pound Exchange over Legal Realism," 1989 *Duke Law Journal* 1311–12.

43. "*Law and the Modern Mind:* A Symposium," 30 *Columbia Law Review* 354 (1930) (contributions by Llewellyn, Mortimer Adler, and Walter Wheeler Cook).

44. See Hull, "Reconstructing the Origins of Realistic Jurisprudence."

45. Karl Llewellyn, "A Realistic Jurisprudence—The Next Step," 30 *Columbia Law Review* 431 (1930).

46. Ibid., 455.

47. Llewellyn, "Symposium," 356.

refashion and reform divorce, commercial law, and legal education. He was from start to finish an applied jurisprudent, cobbling together the bits and pieces in the universe of law and social science around him.

Pound, voraciously curious, with his ability to speed read, his command of nearly every European language, and his photographic memory,[48] had access to an enormous range of ideas. From personal contact as well as reading, Pound collected ideas from scholars in a variety of disciplines. Unlike Llewellyn, Pound did not directly include lists of acknowledgments in his jurisprudential writing. Rather, a great many of his writings themselves are summaries of others' scholarship on which he had implicitly drawn. In his three-part article in the *Harvard Law Review* on "Sociological Jurisprudence," for example, Pound reviewed the work of just about every important jurisprudent who preceded him in succinct and sharply etched summaries.[49]

Pound's bricolage was the heart not only of his method but also of the substance of his contributions. Like the primitive mythologist, Pound built a world from the bits and pieces of the many worlds he explored in his reading. Though criticized for not applying sociological jurisprudence—in effect, for not being another kind of jurisprudent entirely—Pound's formulations are an achievement in themselves because they made sense out of diversity and confusion. Llewellyn recognized this unique quality of Pound's work when he told his jurisprudence students "that of all the 20th century jurisprudents, Pound was the only one, the only one, who had sense enough to see that each of these outfits [jurisprudential approaches] had its contribution and to attempt to gather them into a whole—a great contribution indeed."[50]

Lévi-Strauss's bricoleur does not originate or invent new ideas of his/her own, but merely takes old ideas and puts them to new uses. This same criticism can be applied to Pound and Llewellyn and the rest of American academic jurisprudents in the twentieth century.

48. Pound's feats of speed reading and memory are documented in a series of articles by A. Lawrence MacKenzie in *Boston Sunday Post,* Mar. 14, 1926, at B11, col. 1; Mar. 21, 1926, at C6, col. 1 (copies in Pound scrapbook, Red Set, Harvard Law School Library).

49. Roscoe Pound, "The Scope and Purpose of Sociological Jurisprudence" (pt. 1), 24 *Harvard Law Review* 591 (1911), (pts. 2–3), 25 *Harvard Law Review* 140, 490 (1912).

50. Llewellyn, Harvard Jurisprudence Lecture IX, 1948, KLP, C.H.1–40.

Neither one developed brilliant, original theories of law. Their approach to law was only a bricolage of old ideas put together to form a new view. But despite the derivative nature of the thought processes of the "primitive" mythologist-bricoleur, Lévi-Strauss does not denigrate his accomplishment. "Like 'bricolage' on the technical plane, mythical reflection can reach brilliant unforeseen results on the intellectual plane."[51] Pound and Llewellyn—jurisprudential bricoleurs—were able to Jim-crack their storehouse of handy ideas in a brilliant fashion to create something innovative, if not inventive.

And the invention survived and prospered because it fit its place and time. Conceding all the valid criticisms of "consensus" history, it is clear that Pound and Llewellyn shared a cultural heritage. They were white, university-educated, middle-class, Protestant males, and this was not all that united them. Their bricolage was rooted in and based on the faith that good management and disinterested stewardship were basic principles of human nature. Thus, they expected to find in their tool kit the materials to reconstruct American law. Here I rely on the brilliant book by John A. Kouwenhoven, *Made in America*. Kouwenhoven begins by describing the process by which European tools and technology were adapted to the American environment by stripping them of their ornament to create an aesthetic of functionalism and simplicity.[52] Kouwenhoven's American aesthetic of the vernacular and practical exactly parallels Lévi-Strauss's bricolage in its emphasis on and appreciation of function over form and its clever adaptation of Old World forms to New World challenges. In 1948, Kouwenhoven did not have the term "bricolage" available to him, or he might have used it. Nor did he extend this American aesthetic to philosophy or jurisprudence, though he could have.

Pound and Llewellyn, like many other American academic jurisprudents in the first half of the twentieth century, used all the tools at hand—including European legal philosophies and American social scientific theories and methodologies—to search for a genuinely American jurisprudential approach. Nineteenth-century jurisprudential orthodoxies were crumbling under the weight of unprece-

51. Lévi-Strauss, *Savage Minds,* 17.
52. John A. Kouwenhoven, *Made in America: The Arts in Modern Civilization* (New York, 1948).

dented political and economic conditions and novel intellectual tides. It was high time for new voices to sing songs of law.

One might pause here, before the real story begins, to muse on the impact that such a reconceptualization not only of Pound and Llewellyn, but also of academic jurisprudence might have on scholarly accounts of legal realism. To be sure, this is not a book about legal realism per se, but one has to confront the fact that students of the history of realism in recent years, in the course of producing wonderful works of scholarship, have made their own search for a unifying theoretical theme. Laura Kalman, on whose study of realism at Yale we all rely, has identified functionalism as the credo of the realists. Charles E. Clark and William O. Douglas become the giants of realism.[53] John Henry Schlegel has bid us cast off the mantle of intellectual history and look at what the realists "did." Thus, with Schlegel in the van, we follow the trail of Walter Wheeler Cook and a handful of other pioneers into the legal institute movement. At the Johns Hopkins University Institute, law professors like Walter Wheeler Cook and Hessel Yntema, and their assistants, set out to use social science methods and models to penetrate to the hidden springs of the law. Schlegel's realists are social scientists, which makes Pound nearly irrelevant, Llewellyn a marginal character, and ineffective social inquirers like Charles Clark of Yale failures.[54] Morton Horwitz has reckoned correctly that the realists opposed categories and abstract reasoning, but finds in their quest for truth a new science, a neo-objectivism based on their own reading of facts. The realist (excepting Jerome Frank) was a rule skeptic but a fact lover. Thus, a theory of the power of facts replaced a theory of the power of rules for the true realist.[55]

Students of modern legal theory are even more active in trying to unravel the mysterious allure of realism and claim for their own movements the mantle of "inheritor" of or successor to the realists. Are we all realists? Perhaps. No one can teach law or jurisprudence today without at least listening to the claims of functionalism and instrumentalism. The law and society movement, with its social sci-

53. Kalman, *Legal Realism*, 28–30, 231.

54. John Henry Schlegel, *American Legal Realism and Empirical Social Science* (Chapel Hill, N.C., 1995), 20, 252.

55. Horwitz, *Transformation*, 200–1.

ence orientation, must be the heir at law to the empirical realists, but the "law and" movements can enter caveats. The first "law and economics" texts were not those produced by Judge (then Professor) Richard Posner, but those written by realists like Llewellyn, Douglas, and Wesley Sturges in the 1920s. So, too, the first work of the "law and literature" movement was not James Boyd White's *The Legal Imagination* (1973) but Karl Llewellyn's poetics. But if my argument about the importance of the private world is correct for Pound and Llewellyn, might it not be so for the rival camps of inheritors of realism? Might our student of law and economics be incomplete without knowing more about the internal dynamics of private discourse at the University of Chicago in the 1960s? And who can doubt that the internal conversations of the leaders of the Critical Legal Studies movement throw wonderful light on their many publications, illuminating them in ways that might draw a more sympathetic response from their critics? When the histories of these movements are written, investigators must capture both levels of discourse.[56]

If the essence of twentieth-century American jurisprudence is not a set body of doctrine (or anti-doctrine), but a search based on the latitude of the bricoleurs and the proclivities of networkers, then we must stop looking for the core of realist thought or any other persuasion's thought and try to follow the human story. Forget theory. As usual, Llewellyn himself said it best. Llewellyn regularly decried philosophers and philosophy. He told his students that "[j]urisprudence ought to be for lawyers and not for philosophers."[57] Philosophizing in general terms was the antithesis of Llewellyn's method. "I take no ideas as ideas. This is a course which is a course in Jurisprudence. And Jurisprudence, for my money, is of the nature of law; and law has no purposes, generalities, or other

---

56. One example: Andrew Altman makes a generous and thoughtful attempt to see the differences and similarities in modern liberal jurisprudence and Critical Legal Studies in his *Critical Legal Studies: A Liberal Critique* (Princeton, N.J., 1990), but his sources are drawn entirely from the public discourse. Thus, when he wants to explain the shifts (or apparent shifts) in Roberto Unger's thought, Altman must either fall back on supposition ("I believe that Unger would respond to this criticism by making two related points." [174]) or simply repeat what Unger says ("What led Unger to change his mind . . . ? In his later work, Unger comes to the conclusion that human history has generated certain 'surprises' that, when fully appreciated, defeat the two main ideas of deep culture theory. . . ." [159]). Why not ask Unger instead?

57. Llewellyn, Jurisprudence Lecture 1, Mar. 31, 1959, KLP, C.P.1-5, p. 27.

things unconnected with measures and with the concrete."[58] He neither admired nor participated in legal philosophizing.

> I shall attempt to keep away from the more than three syllable words. "ology" is three syllables and is meaningless without a fourth. It is obvious, therefore, that I shall attempt to keep away from "ologies." I wish for this purpose that "ism" were a three-syllable. But I shall treat it as if it were. . . . In other words, I regard the vocabulary of professional philosophy as curiously inept to our purposes. . . . And I say, therefore, that everyone of these "ology" boys in the Jurisprudence field, has fallen completely down on his work as a lawyer. He may be a grand philosopher—and peace be with him—in that capacity, but he isn't my bird. I want fellows who talk Jurisprudence to lawyers, not to philosophers and leave the philosophers to do their own work.[59]

In his last statement on the subject, *The Common Law Tradition* (1960), he maintained that "[r]ealism was never a philosophy."[60]

So what was it? In the answer to that question lies the solution to our mystery. The legacy of Pound's and Llewellyn's search for an American jurisprudence lay not in theory but in experience. That experience began in a time of great travail for the law and its expositors.

58. Ibid., p. 15.
59. Ibid., pp. 27–28.
60. Llewellyn, *Common Law Tradition*, 509.

The Crisis of American Jurisprudence

The project of fashioning an American jurisprudence for the twentieth century was as much an act of political faith as it was one of intellectual creativity. Law had been the first casualty in the Civil War, for before any shots were fired, secession challenged the viability of the federal Constitution and exalted slave law over free labor. When hostilities began, President Abraham Lincoln, a lawyer, cast the South's act as one of individual lawlessness, rather than collective nation-making. The war itself tested the police powers of the federal government as well as its ability to make war. Without much precedent to guide them and with much at stake, federal officials and lawgivers had to frame rules for freeing former bondsmen and bondswomen, confiscating private property, and repatriating former rebels.[1]

There was much law but little jurisprudence, save that of legal positivism: the law is the command of the state.[2] That command might imagine and implement a new kind of society, one in which government enabled all Americans, regardless of race or gender, to fulfill themselves, or it might lead to massive resistance rooted in covert unwillingness to accept the verdict of arms. The challenge to the nation's lawmakers was manifest, and they bore it with grim dedication, writing new kinds of civil statutes that reached deep

1. Harold Hyman and William Wiecek, *Equal Justice under Law: Constitutional Development, 1835–1875* (New York, 1982), 101 ff.
2. Ervin H. Pollak, ed., *Jurisprudence: Principles and Applications* (Columbus, Ohio, 1979), 533. The doctrine of legal positivism was fully formulated by John Austin in his lectures in the first half of the nineteenth century. Edwin W. Patterson, *Jurisprudence: Men and Ideas of the Law* (Brooklyn, N.Y., 1953), 125–26.

into the everyday intercourse of men and women. The burden re-construction of the nation's laws laid on jurisprudence was just as heavy, if not so visible. The old certitudes of natural law on which the first federal and state constitutions rested were blown away by the cannons. Both sides had cited Jefferson's formulation of life, lib-erty, and the pursuit of happiness in their cause. So, too, the ro-mantic idylls of reform of schools, prisons, and asylums that had spread through the North and the South in the antebellum period proved no more durable than the tattered flags of the combatants. A newer, more tough-minded law replaced the sentimentality of the first American Victorians.[3]

The new mood of the law suited the mood of the nation. In 1870, the fighting had been over for five years, but the animus still ran deep. The Union army had gone back to its peacetime status, except in the states of the old Confederacy, where troops continued to watch over Reconstruction, the Freedmen's Bureau, and the new railroad tracks. The United States, still recovering from the effects of its disastrous Civil War, struggled to heal its wounds and recon-cile its sections under the president who, as general, had com-manded the Union army to victory. Out of the ruin of the war, a new nation was emerging—but what kind of nation, and what role would law play in its growth? Too soon the initial commitment to civil rights for the freedmen and freedwomen seemed to founder on the victors' unwillingness to fully articulate and vigorously pursue the enforcement of their own laws and the elimination of the plague of racial animus. The federal courts, charged with oversight of the civil rights of minorities, seemed unable to comprehend how deeply racial prejudice had sunk its roots, and where the courts were will-ing, violence by unreconstructed whites did what rebellion could not—maintain two nations.[4]

3. William E. Nelson, *The Roots of American Bureaucracy, 1830–1900* (Cambridge, Mass., 1983), 41–61; James M. McPherson, *The Struggle for Equality: Abolitionism and the Negro in the Civil War and Reconstruction* (Princeton, N.J., 1964), 99–133 ff.

4. William Gillette, *Retreat from Reconstruction, 1869–1879* (Baton Rouge, La., 1979), 42–55; Michael Perman, *Reunion without Compromise: The South and Recon-struction, 1865–1869* (Baton Rouge, La., 1973), 27–34 ff.; Eric Foner, *Reconstruction: America's Unfinished Revolution, 1863–1877* (New York, 1987), 469–88; Robert J. Kaczorowski, *The Politics of Judicial Interpretation: The Federal Courts, Department of Justice and Civil Rights, 1866–1876* (New York, 1985), 158 ff.; Peter Charles Hoffer, *The Law's Conscience: Equitable Constitutionalism in America* (Chapel Hill, N.C., 1990), 123–37.

But the plight of the lowest classes was not just the product of prejudice—it was also a necessary component of industrialization, according to some legal thinkers. A lower class was a working class that could be exploited—and was, both in the fields and in the factories. For business was booming in the city and the countryside. Large corporations were just starting to coalesce. The giant trusts were embryonic, but the accumulation of capital and the rise of middle-level bureaucracies were already at hand. On the two coasts, banks and industry worked hand in hand to exploit vast natural reserves of land, oil, coal, and iron ore. The first railroad trains ran from the Pacific coast to New York City, signaling the beginning of a truly national economy and culture.[5]

It was an era of nearly unbridled expansionism and optimism, prompting Ralph Waldo Emerson to look at "Civilization" and counsel the young to "Hitch your wagon to a star" and Horace Greeley to advise young men to "Go West." The law bent to the will of the avid and the daring. Corporations no longer needed to claim a public purpose; new state laws allowed them to come into being by registering with the state's secretary. Land whose use had been restricted by old rules of access to air and light could be built over with tenements and foundries.[6]

To the west stretched the mixed prairie grasses of the Great Plains. The region was sometimes called "The Great American Desert" because of its lack of trees. Indeed, white settlement of the region had been impeded and postponed by the mistaken belief that land without trees must be soil incapable of sustaining farming. Early-nineteenth-century settlers foolishly passed through some of the richest farmland in the country, preferring to brave the dangerous overland trek to the more familiar forest landscape of the Oregon territory. The rhythms of drought and rainfall would alternately curse and bless the plains, but their bounty unfolded in waves of corn and wheat. Again, the law bowed to the speculator and the developer. Land grants to railroads, mining concerns, and timber

---

5. Alfred Chandler, *The Visible Hand: The Managerial Revolution in American Business* (Cambridge, Mass., 1977), 79–206; Richard Wiebe, *The Search for Order, 1877–1920* (New York, 1967), 23–25; Olivier Zunz, *Making America Corporate, 1870–1920* (Chicago, 1990), 11–36.

6. Morton Horwitz, *The Transformation of American Law, 1870–1960* (New York, 1992), 73–74; Hoffer, *Law's Conscience*, 147–74.

companies violated Indian treaties and natural boundaries alike. The land was there for the taking, and the law aided the taker.[7]

Lincoln, Nebraska, in the heartland of the restored nation, was a fairly new city in 1870, the year Nathan Roscoe Pound was born. Starting out in 1856 as an antebellum settlement to work salt deposits, it was quickly transformed after the war into the capital of the new state (1867) and renamed for the still-mourned wartime president. Two years later, in 1869, the state legislature founded in Lincoln the University of Nebraska, an institution that would play a major role in Pound's intellectual development. In the very same year that Judge Stephen Pound's only son was brought into the world, Lincoln got its first rail connection, an event that signaled the future transformation of the city into a railroad center, with nineteen different rail lines converging there before the end of the century. It was only natural that railroad car repair would become its major industry, though Lincoln would also attract more than thirty insurance companies; manufacturers of agricultural (and later telephone) equipment, cement, and bricks; meat and dairy producers; and printing and publishing plants. But Lincoln was an island in a sea of grain, and Nebraska farmers did not trust the railroads and the grain elevator owners. The family farmers organized granges and talked politics. The legislature listened and curbed freight and storage rates by law, setting the stage for challenges to the power of the state to regulate the economy.[8]

The farmers knew that events far from home influenced their lives. It was not just a matter of the price of wheat on the world markets either. They shared a Victorian world with European monarchs. Wilhelm I of Prussia reigned in Germany with the aid of his iron chancellor, Otto von Bismarck; in France, the Emperor Napoleon III was in the process of losing a throne and inadvertently aiding Prussian plans to unify Germany; Czar Alexander II, who would be killed by a nihilist's bomb eleven years later, wisely kept Russia out of the war and held onto his throne for another decade; and Victoria herself reigned in Great Britain over an expanding empire guided by the counsel of her prime minister, the colorful Benjamin

---

7. Lauren Brown, *Grasslands* (New York, 1985), 45–56; Patricia Nelson Limerick, *The Legacy of Conquest: The Unbroken Past of the American West* (New York, 1987).

8. "Nebraska," *Compton's Interactive Encyclopedia* (New York, 1994); Robert C. McMath, Jr., *American Populism, A Social History* (New York, 1993), 20 ff.

Disraeli. The "Old World" gloried in the last decades of its dominance over world events and culture.

From this brilliant, self-confident milieu came all manner of theories of how civilized people ought to govern themselves. No Englishman thought it odd that Thomas Babington Macaulay, an English scholar turned bureaucrat, had prepared a code of laws for the entire subcontinent of India. In France and Germany, advocates of Roman Law and defenders of national custom bickered in royally appointed councils and on university faculties, even as their nations prepared for war. The law was the pronouncement of the state; that much everyone of any substance in Europe already knew.[9]

Not only was the world monarchical and European-centered, but also it was much emptier, harsher, and more poorly educated than it is now. Fewer than thirty-nine million people inhabited the United States of America according to the 1870 census; the world population was less than one and a half billion. Life expectancy at birth was around forty years. And only 2 percent of Americans seventeen years of age and older graduated from high school. Here, too, the law had made its presence felt. In the United States, a new kind of law had emerged, a law that required young men and women to go to public schools. In these schools, rough farm children and bewildered immigrants were to learn how to behave. The school was to be a melting pot from which would flow Americans. State law also created "land grant" universities dedicated to the twin goals of a liberal arts education and a more efficient economy.[10]

In the decade following Pound's birth, scientific and technological discoveries signaled the advent of a new, more sophisticated and complex world. Russian chemist Dimitri Mendeléev published *The Principles of Chemistry* (1870), which contained the first periodic table of elements; in the same year, Tübingen chemistry student Friedreich Miescher discovered deoxyribonucleic acid (DNA), though several decades would pass before it was identified as the basic genetic material. One year later, Charles Darwin published *The Descent of Man*, setting off a controversy that would rock

9. Peter J. Hugill, *World Trade since 1431: Geography, Technology, and Capitalism* (Baltimore, 1993), passim; James Trager, *The People's Chronology* (New York, 1994), passim.

10. *Historical Statistics of the United States, Colonial Times to 1970, Part II* (Washington, D.C., 1975), 55, 56; David Tyack and Elisabeth Hansot, *Managers of Virtue: Public School Leadership in America, 1820–1980* (New York, 1982), 28–104.

science, religion, and law for more than a century. Technological developments that would revolutionize business and commerce included the introduction of the Remington typewriter in 1874; Alexander Graham Bell's invention of the telephone in 1875 (perfected and demonstrated a year later at the Centennial Exhibition in Philadelphia); Thomas Alva Edison's development, in 1878, of a carbon-filament light bulb that could burn forty-five hours or more; and Dayton, Ohio, saloon keeper James Ritty's invention of the first cash register that same year. The law took note of invention—the number of patents rose exponentially, and so did the litigation over patent infringement. Patent law was a monopoly of the federal government, and more than civil rights litigation (almost a dead letter by the 1890s), patent law kept the federal courts busy.[11]

A person could take pride in the belief that science and technology could and would transform the world—it was the birth of the "modern"—but no one could be sure that the upward course of civilization would be perfectly linear. Economic and technological developments did not avert crisis and collapse. Railroad speculation led to a financial crisis in 1873 and a depression that would last five years. A major railroad strike by workers on the Baltimore and Ohio Railroad in 1877 was ended only when President Hayes sent federal troops. That same year, the militant Molly Maguires were crushed with the hanging of eleven of their leaders for the murder of mine officials and police. The courts readily provided aid to the owners and managers of the mines and factories, issuing injunctions against union organizing and strikes. The law was hardly neutral in the struggle between capital and labor. At the same time, many state legislatures tried to regulate health and safety, as well as wages and hours, in the workplace. Most of these regulations passed muster in the federal courts on appeal, though some were struck down because they failed to connect the law to the health or welfare of the workers.[12]

The cultural world was also changing. The last decades of the century enjoyed much of the same sentimental and moralistic pap that had long dominated American culture, like Horatio Alger's

11. Lawrence Friedman, *A History of American Law* (2nd ed., New York, 1985), 435–37; Thomas J. Schlereth, *Victorian America: Transformations in Everyday Life, 1876–1915* (New York, 1991), 177–208.

12. Charles O. Gregory and Harold A. Katz, *Labor and the Law* (3rd ed., New York, 1979), 52–104; Friedman, *American Law,* 556–60.

best-selling hortatory juvenalia and P. T. Barnum's elaborate and popular circus and sideshow entertainments. Yet the same years saw a flowering of American literary talent—novels by Henry James, Mark Twain, Henry Adams, and "realist" pioneer William Dean Howells—and the emergence of innovative artists like Winslow Homer, Thomas Eakins, and American émigrés Mary Cassatt and James McNeill Whistler. The highbrow and the lowbrow met, of course, at the department store, where all that glittered was for sale.[13]

By 1893, the profound intellectual, social, and economic changes that had begun around the time of Roscoe Pound's birth had already left their imprint on the world, in particular on America. Huge manufacturing trusts and conglomerates challenged the Old World's industrial dominance and altered the very nature of the workplace. The disparity between the richest and the poorest in society had grown exponentially, falling hardest on the newest Americans—the blacks, Asians, and Hispanics who labored in the fields—and poor women. The population of the United States had mushroomed to nearly sixty-three million, and more than twenty-five urban centers across the nation could claim population in excess of one hundred thousand. Cities like Pittsburgh and Detroit were immensely energetic but increasingly dark places, beclouded with soot and the smell of sulfur. Hundreds of railroads crisscrossed America, linking markets and people in every town, city, and region and bringing the products of industrial labor to an increasingly selective body of consumers. They could even order by mail from catalogues—so modern was consumerism. While 1870 had marked the first transcontinental rail line, by 1893 six railroads linked the two coasts. One of these had its western terminus in Seattle, Washington.[14]

Before the railroads completed their two-mile tunnel through the Cascades, linking Puget Sound to the Northern Pacific transcontinental route in 1888, the inland saltwater sea had been the primary

13. Eric Cheyfitz, "A Hazard of New Fortunes: The Romance of Self-Realization," in Eric J. Sundquist, ed., *American Realism: New Essays* (Baltimore, 1982), 42–65; William Leach, *Land of Desire: Merchants, Power, and the Rise of a New American Culture* (New York, 1993), 15–70; Daniel Boorstin, *The Americans: The Democratic Experience* (New York, 1973), 101–9.

14. Alan Dawley, *Struggles for Justice: Social Responsibility and the Liberal State* (Cambridge, Mass., 1991), 1–62; Boorstin, *The Democratic Experience*, 109–29.

means of reaching the city. Even though it lies near the northwestern edge of the country, Seattle boasts a temperate marine climate, with cool summers and mild winters. Despite its moderate climate, majestic mountain vistas, and serene bays, its latitude brings sixteen hours of darkness in winter and a moist, dreary sky much of the year. But the phenomenal growth of the nation was outdistanced by the growth of Seattle in the late nineteenth century. With a population of little more than thirty-five hundred in 1880, a decade later the city had grown more than tenfold. It was a bustling metropolis in 1893 when the *Seattle Telegraph* announced the birth of a "baby boy . . . at the home of Mr. and Mrs. W.H. Llewellyn of West Seattle," an area of the city undergoing heavy residential development according to real estate advertisements of the time.[15]

The changes roiling the rest of the country were not overlooked by Seattlites. The front-page headline of the *Telegraph* the day immediately before the issue that recorded Karl Llewellyn's birth announced the creation of "A League of Labor . . . Which Will Include All Railway Employees" headed by Eugene V. Debs. Another story with local basis reported "[a]n anti-Chinese meeting . . . held in the Knights of Labor hall," at which the speakers delivered "stirring remarks about the evils resultant upon the hordes of Mongolians in and coming to this country." Ethnic, particularly anti-Asian, strife was not new to the city. The Chinese, who had helped bring the railroads to the region and were thus partly responsible for its economic expansion, had been targets of violent outbursts in 1885 and 1886, leading many Asian immigrants to flee the city.[16]

Industrialism, urbanization, and scientific and technological advancement came at a price—rapid social and economic change challenging and testing the capacity of the young nation to adapt. Two years after Llewellyn was born, his family relocated to a city at the opposite end of the continent. New York, a busy harbor for the Atlantic trade, just as Seattle had been for the Pacific, was the largest and most diverse city in the country. It was also expanding—in 1894, the year before Llewellyn arrived, the citizens of Brooklyn, Queens, the Bronx, and Staten Island had voted and approved by a narrow margin their consolidation into five boroughs of one city called New York.[17]

15. *Seattle Telegraph*, May 23, 1893.
16. *Seattle Telegraph*, May 22, 1893, at 1.
17. William Twining, *Karl Llewellyn and the Realist Movement* [1973] (Norman, Okla., 1985), 89.

In 1895, New York was a teeming metropolis of more than three million, already plagued by tenement slums crowded with immigrants. The Ellis Island immigrant-receiving station opened in 1892, replacing Castle Garden. Jacob Riis's tenement photographs and his 1890 book, *How the Other Half Lives,* roused civic conscience and progressive reformers, but tenement reform laws passed in 1879, 1887, and 1895 seemed to have little effect on overcrowding and unsanitary conditions. Conditions might have been worse, however, but for the opening in 1892 of the $24 million New Croton Aqueduct, which, after seven years of construction, brought clean drinking water to the city. Nevertheless, physicians estimated that the death rate in the tenements was the highest in the world.

Despite, or perhaps because of, the city's immense growth in population and its prominence as a port for immigration, New York experienced rapid physical modernization in the years encompassing Karl Llewellyn's boyhood in Brooklyn. Mass transit in the city in 1890, measured by total mileage, exceeded that of London, though the city's greatest subway-building era was just arriving. The Brooklyn Bridge, opened in 1883, was the longest suspension bridge in the world. By the time Llewellyn graduated from Boys High School in 1909, the Manhattan, the Williamsburg, the Queensboro, and several smaller bridges would be completed. Until 1892, the tallest building in New York was the 284-foot spire of Trinity Church, but the age of skyscrapers was beginning—the term "skyscraper" was, in fact, coined in 1891.

New York was also a bustling retail center. The commercialization and consumerization of American culture had begun, probably affecting the young Karl's later choice of legal specialization. The large retail emporiums, including A. T. Stewart, Stern's, B. Altman, Lord & Taylor, Brooks Brothers, and R. H. Macy's, with their various specialized "departments" (the term "department store" only came into vogue in the 1890s), had already opened and pioneered retail sales techniques such as the "annual clearance sale." But in the late 1890s and the first decade of the twentieth century, these stores would move uptown and expand into consumer palaces with sophisticated window and floor displays and easy-credit charge accounts. This was the dawn of the great consumer age, and New York was its hub.[18]

18. Eric Homberger, *The Historical Atlas of New York City* (New York, 1994), 90–111; Leach, *Land of Desire,* 29–30.

All of the technological innovation, corporate expansion, and consumer growth required a response from the law and its guardians. The law and the legal profession had changed greatly between 1870 and 1893, accommodating themselves to a changing society. The law greeted the business corporation as a welcome new member of the family, but ostensibly warned out the giant trust. The legislatures churned out regulatory statutes, and the courts manufactured opinions on a vast array of subjects other than business, but law and the economy were the objects of the most fascinating and rapidly growing body of legal treatises.[19]

In part, the whole of these laws relied on outmoded economic concepts of fair markets and small entrepreneurs competing freely—the stuff of Adam Smith's *Wealth of Nations*—but newer ideas of the functioning of business had also found their way into the law, and in these as well implicit moral understandings were borne aloft by "scientific" facts. The new conservatism that replaced the old liberalism (for in such cycles ideas invariably go) stressed the need for efficiency and productivity. "The best management is a true science, resting upon clearly defined laws, rules, and principles, as a foundation," according to Frederick Taylor. Taylor raised this program to the level of universal truth in his *Principles of Scientific Management:* "The principal object of management should be to secure the maximum prosperity for the employer, coupled with the maximum prosperity for each employee."[20] And even if employees did not see immediate gains, large enterprises were justified by great returns, presumably to the new legions of stockholders and the expanding work force, though, in fact, more often to an emerging elite of corporate moguls. The titans of industry were not the only beneficiaries of this new ideal of big business. A legion of middle-level managers and servants of the wealthy, including large numbers of lawyers, gained from the growth of business "combinations."[21]

And lawyers benefited, too. The typical lawyer in the middle of the nineteenth century was a sole practitioner or worked in a two-man partnership. Even the leaders of the bar employed only a hand-

19. See generally Friedman, *American Law,* 337–70, 439–66; Martin J. Sklar, *The Corporate Reconstruction of American Capitalism, 1890–1916: The Market, the Law, and Politics* (Cambridge, England, 1988) 86–127.

20. Frederick Winslow Taylor, *The Principles of Scientific Management* [1911] (New York, 1967), 7, 9.

21. Herbert Hovenkamp, "The Sherman Act and the Classical Theory of Competition," 74 *Iowa Law Review* 1019 (1989).

ful of clerks. The needs of the new business culture transformed the practice of law at the top. By 1900, the sole practitioner remained the norm in rural areas and small towns, but in the great centers of industry—starting with New York City—a new phenomenon had emerged: the large law firm. The firm had a number of partners and, under them, younger associates who hoped to one day become partners. The largest of these firms would seem anemic by modern standards, but the way in which they had begun to specialize transformed the elite bar.[22]

To service the expanding economy's business clientele and represent the corporations in federal courts, the firms recruited the best and brightest of the law school crop. Bright young men from the best university law schools turned their sights to the financial centers and their new, large, specialized corporate law firms. The transformation of the university law schools had as much to do with the demands of the new legal labor market as with the case method ideology of Harvard's dean, Christopher Columbus Langdell. Rapid economic growth fueled the demand for increasing numbers of sophisticated lawyers. The law school replaced law office apprenticeship for two reasons: the law schools could meet the increased market demand for lawyers by a kind of mass production of lawyers that the former and time-honored method of training could not begin to approach, and the abstract analytical approach of Langdell's case and Socratic methods of teaching encouraged the kind of rational reasoning that could create legal innovation for the new business environment. The writ-copying apprenticeship had encouraged rote and simplistic legal practice.[23]

The new national economy also inspired a new type of bar association. Local bar associations were a feature of American law practice from the middle of the eighteenth century, and by the 1870s, state and local bars were well-established social and economic institutions. In 1878, a new, voluntary, by-invitation-only

22. Wayne K. Hobson, "Symbol of the New Profession: Emergence of the Large Law Firm 1870–1915," in Gerard W. Gawalt, ed., *The New High Priests: Lawyers in Post–Civil War America* (Westport, Conn., 1984), 3–28; Jerold Auerbach, *Unequal Justice: Lawyers and Social Change in Modern America* (New York, 1976), 14–73; Marc Galanter and Thomas Palay, *Tournament of Lawyers: The Transformation of the Big Law Firm* (Chicago, 1991), 4–15.

23. Robert W. Gordon, "Legal Thought and Legal Practice in the Age of American Enterprise, 1870–1920," in Gerald L. Geison, ed., *Professions and Professional Ideologies in America* (New York, 1983), 75; Auerbach, *Unequal Justice,* 74–101.

association appeared, called into being by Simeon Baldwin of Connecticut. Baldwin was old stock, a scion of one of Connecticut's leading families and a former law professor—and soon to be governor. In an age when the country was inundated with eastern European and Asian immigrants, he saw himself and those like him (including Pound's father, a founding member of the new association) as the savants of an American legal tradition. They would uphold the purity of the Anglo-Saxon, English, New England common law against the tide of foreignness. The American Bar Association (ABA), which Baldwin and his stalwart 100 allies created in Saratoga, New York, was thus as much a moral as an economic institution. The ABA would grow, but in its first years, slowly, taking care to reflect the high ideals and social predilections of its members.[24]

In the meantime, the corporate bar found itself facing a new challenge. It did not come from the huddled masses, though they were visible in the begrimed alleys of the great cities and some of the leaders of the bar were eager to restrict immigration from southern and eastern Europe. No—the first threat came from a new political movement calling itself progressivism. It had risen in the cities, among the same middle-class professionals that spawned the new generation of lawyers, but its roots were as old as the Republic. The progressives wanted many reforms, but all of them depended on an end to corruption. Some favored large business if it could be regulated in the public interest. Theodore Roosevelt would speak for this group in coming years, although when the Congress proved unsympathetic to some of his regulatory schemes, he was willing to "bust" trusts. Others, for whom Louis Brandeis and Woodrow Wilson came to be leaders, wanted a return to a more competitive economic system—one that would be fair to both business and organized labor.[25]

Brandeis did not see reform of the economy as a form of redistribution of wealth, unlike the socialist and other radical movements with whose leaders he sometimes conversed. Instead, he saw eco-

24. John A. Matzko, "'The Best Men of the Bar': The Founding of the American Bar Association," in Gawalt, *New High Priests*, 75–96.

25. Arthus S. Link, *Woodrow Wilson and the Progressive Era, 1910–1917* (New York, 1954), 1–53; George Mowry, *The Era of Theodore Roosevelt* (New York, 1958), 131–34; Page Smith, *America Enters the World: A People's History of the Progressive Era and World War I* (New York, 1985), 345–47.

nomic reform as a redress of the illicit concentration of wealth that had perverted true American capitalism, destroying competition and denying the workers their fair share of the fruits of their labors. The Brandeisians saw the distribution question not as a continuum, with conservatism at one pole and communism at the other, but as a dichotomy, with their position—a level playing field—in a separate category from the socialist and communist theories of taking from the rich to give to the poor. Thus, Brandeis, and those who modeled themselves on him, like the young Felix Frankfurter, believed in bringing labor and capital to the negotiating table as equals and using government to facilitate the dialogue between opposing interests. All the progressives shared this commitment to a basic regime of reason, in which rational men could work out their differences. What was needed was facts and good faith (a creed that differentiated the progressives from their more radical cousins in the ideological spectrum of the day).[26]

One of the weapons that Brandeis deployed in the battle against misuse of public funds by crooked utilities, rate gouging by the railroads, abusive labor conditions in factories, and attacks on labor unions was what came to be called "the Brandeis brief." In bringing to his formal legal presentations vast arrays of information about actual conditions in the mill and the foundry, he wedded law to the emerging social sciences. Brandeis employed young social scientists to gather and, even more important, to interpret the data, uniting in the service of legal advocacy social science and progressive policy.[27]

The social scientists' rise had paralleled that of the lawyers. University educated, with postgraduate degrees, like the college-trained, university law school bar, the sociologists, economists, and political scientists worked in state, academic, and private capacities to investigate and expose. The University of Wisconsin (the great laboratory of democracy under Governor Robert M. La Follette), Columbia University, and other centers of learning employed the social scientists as teachers. In turn, they served on public commissions and as consultants to lawyers like Brandeis. The appearance

26. John W. Johnson, *American Legal Culture, 1908–1940* (Westport, Conn., 1981), 29–51; Phillipa Strum, *Louis D. Brandeis: Justice for the People* (New York, 1984), 114–31; Clyde Spillenger, "Elusive Advocate: Reconsidering Brandeis as People's Lawyer," 105 *Yale Law Journal* 1461–62 (1996).

27. Leonard Baker, *Brandeis and Frankfurter: A Dual Biography* (New York, 1984), 7–17.

of national social science organizations like the American Economic Association and the American Sociological Association not only marked the academic coming of age of these disciplines, but also allowed the social scientists to weigh into current policy debates with the strength of numbers. The results could be electrifying—for the new partnership of law and social inquiry had exciting possibilities.[28]

Standing behind the progressive urge and the heightened influence of the social investigator was a belief in the power of people to transform their world that accorded neatly with the new science and technology. The American reformer was first and foremost an optimist, a believer in the plasticity of nature and the malleability of the human spirit. Consciously, academic philosopher-reformers like John Dewey set about applying new ideas to old problems. The cornerstone of the effort was the first purely American theory of meaning—pragmatism. Pragmatism originated in the work of Charles Sanders Peirce and his circle of friends at Harvard, though after a brief stint at Johns Hopkins, Peirce ("Poor Peirce" to his friends) never held a formal teaching position. Peirce concerned himself with the truth of scientific propositions and decided that all truth was really a matter of probability (anticipating quantum mechanics, it may be noted). Thus, the only measure of truth was the applicability—the effect or consequence—of a scientific statement. Extended to common language, pragmatism assigned meaning to practical consequences. This was not the same as assigning value or worth to applicability (the essence of utilitarianism). There were no metaphysical entities, no shadows on the cave of our understanding.[29]

It may be that pragmatism was not very new (Peirce did not think it so) and that the fundamental notion of meaning coming from action broadly supported a regime of competitive, even ruthless, concentration of wealth. After all, if concepts like wealth and power were not bounded by ethical standards whose meaning lay not in action, but in a separate moral realm, then who could criticize the successful robber baron? Peirce did not see this as the consequence of his theory, however, for he had set out to banish the idols of meta-

28. See, e.g., Thomas Haskell, *The Emergence of Professional Social Science* (Urbana, Ill., 1977), 203–10.

29. H. S. Thayer, *Meaning and Action: A Study of American Pragmatism* (Indianapolis, 1973), 7, 31, 65; Morton White, *Pragmatism and the American Mind* (New York, 1973), 97.

physics and open the door to the investigation of how things actually worked.[30] Neither did the philosophers who picked up his banner, notably William James and John Dewey, regard pragmatism as a defense of uncontrolled individualism.[31]

In these terms, the application to law and jurisprudence was clear, though it would take a generation for Peirce's ideas to filter across disciplinary boundaries. If truth lay in use, then no one—not even the best-trained corporate lawyer—could argue that the iron laws of economic life—never seen but always assumed to be there—should dictate public policy or the outcome of private lawsuits. Gone would be the old ideas of economic morality that still dominated judges' views of labor unions and other "unnatural" combinations. Gone would be the brooding omnipresence of free markets and their invisible, unerring power over human economic activity. Peirce's work was adapted by William James and John Dewey to argue for a more democratic workplace and reforms in the political arena. The social sciences need not have been progressive and reformist—William Graham Sumner's folkways were not, and some who misread Darwin as a brief for the survival of the fittest were hardly friendly to the masses of huddled émigrés from Europe and Asia.[32] But much of the newest social science did seek to ameliorate the excesses of industrial capitalism in the name of pragmatic reform and progressive ideals.

So much had changed in society and in the law that today one would assume someone would put two and two together and arrive at a "law and society" jurisprudence. It had happened already in Europe. German-speaking philosophers of law had laid out the argument that law should be a study of social inputs, for it was rooted in social and economic interests.[33] There were more than a

30. Charles S. Peirce, "What Pragmatism Is," in Philip P. Wiener, ed., *Charles S. Peirce: Selected Writings* (New York, 1958), 192.

31. Henry F. May, *The End of American Innocence: A Study of the First Years of Our Own Time, 1912–1917* (Chicago, 1964), 145–53; William James, *Pragmatism,* ed. H. S. Thayer (Cambridge, Mass., 1975), 44; Morton White, *Social Thought in America: The Revolt against Formalism* (Boston, 1957), 142–46; Edward C. Moore, *American Pragmatism: Peirce, James, and Dewey* (New York, 1961), 245.

32. Richard Hofstadter, *Social Darwinism in American Thought* (rev. ed., Boston, 1955), 51–66.

33. Roscoe Pound, *Jurisprudence* (St. Paul, Minn., 1959), 1:3335–36; James E. Herget and Stephen Wallace, "The German Free Law Movement as the Source of American Legal Realism," 73 *Virginia Law Review* 399 (1987).

few hints that the old paradigm of freestanding natural law was in trouble. Populists who refused to obey the laws and progressives who wanted to reform the laws were restless with the idea that law could rest on unshakable first principles. Economists like Henry Carter Adams attacked the notion that both land and markets were embodiments of immutable principles. State policies favored some and not others; the idea that pure law, like pure laissez-faire, was natural had to be discarded and a franker view of the state's role adopted. The hint was there that laws were products of policy choices and that regulation of the economy was not merely a matter of allowing natural forces to work their way clean. But Adams was not really interested in jurisprudence, and his arguments read like a combination of liberal reformism and social science special pleading.[34]

Adams was not alone in seeing the frailty of the pre–Civil War paradigm. Oliver Wendell Holmes, Jr., in his lectures on the common law at Lowell Institute, later revised and expanded as *The Common Law* (1881), recognized that the life of the law was change and that logical formalism of the Langdellian sort only obscured the changes.[35] Holmes knew Peirce's work slightly, but was not very much taken with pragmatism. Instead, he offered a "grab-bag of other 'forces' that shaped the law": necessity, history, public policy, moral consensus, and even the prejudices of particular judges, yes— logic, no.[36] Holmes did not assay any jurisprudence—certainly nothing more original than a combination of John Austin's positivism (the law is the command of the state) and Jeremy Bentham's instrumentalism (the command of the state should better the condition of the people)—though later in life, Holmes decided that he was sympathetic to Dewey's social pragmatism.[37]

Holmes's contribution to jurisprudence was to couple historical subjects to instrumental objects, a feat of scholarship that made Holmes the patron saint of the next generation of modernists, but

34. Herbert Hovenkamp, "The First Great Law and Economics Movement," 42 *Stanford Law Review* 998 (1990), 998.

35. See, e.g., Thomas C. Grey, "Langdell's Orthodoxy," 45 *University of Pittsburgh Law Review* 1–53 (1983).

36. G. Edward White, *Justice Oliver Wendell Holmes: Law and the Inner Self* (New York, 1993), 151, 153.

37. Oliver Wendell Holmes, Jr., *The Common Law* (Boston, 1881), 1; Thomas C. Grey, "Holmes and Legal Pragmatism," 41 *Stanford Law Review* 793 (1989); Patrick J. Kelley, "Was Holmes a Pragmatist," 14 *Southern Illinois Law Journal* 430 (1990).

did not really move formalism from its pedestal. Indeed, as Morton Horwitz has written, in the same decades that Holmes's *The Common Law* was read and admired, the style of legal reasoning of most courts became more, not less, abstract, formal, and inflexible. Categories like "tort" had taken the place of a congeries of discrete subject matters, and references to immutable principles of law replaced open advocacy of policy in judicial opinions. William LaPiana has called this jurisprudence "an appeal to absolutes." Although, as Peter Karsten has demonstrated, these abstractions might not have reached the ears of every trial judge, most of whom (particularly in the midwestern and western states) continued to apply what Llewellyn would later call a "situation sense" to particular cases, academic jurisprudence still reflected the iron laws of "formalism."[38]

Writing near the end of his career, in 1960, Llewellyn caricatured formalism in what is now a classic summary: "The formal style is of particular interest to us because it set the picture against which all modern thinking has played. . . . [T]hat picture is clean and clear: the rules of law are to decide the cases; policy is for the legislature, not for the courts, and so is change even in pure common law. Opinions run in deductive form with an air or expression of single line inevitability." Llewellyn's pose was studied in its neutrality, but his point was evident: "'Principle' is a generalization producing order which can and should be used to prune away those 'anomalous' cases or rules which do not fit, such cases or rules having no function except, in places where the supposed 'principle' [because, of course, principle was always malleable] does not work well, to accomplish sense—but sense is no official concern of a formal-style court."[39]

Llewellyn did not believe that formalistic courts were without resources when it came to rigging precedent; he was describing a style of reasoning. He knew well that all courts were sensitive to politics, despite the formalists' proclaimed aversion to politics (law and poli-

---

38. Horwitz, *Transformation*, 9–32; Peter Karsten, "Explaining the Fight over Attractive Nuisance Doctrine," 10 *Law and History Review* 45–92 (1992); William LaPiana, "Jurisprudence of History and Truth," 23 *Rutgers Law Journal* 559 (1992). The formalism of the second half of the century is discussed in William LaPiana, *Logic and Experience: The Origin of Modern Legal Education* (New York, 1994). Pound anticipated much of this in his "Mechanical Jurisprudence," 8 *Columbia Law Review* 605–6 ff. (1908).

39. Karl Llewellyn, *The Common Law Tradition: Deciding Appeals* (Boston, 1960), 38.

tics were supposed to be separated by a high wall, as was the private from the public sphere) as well as to wealth and social standing. There was no neutrality, though again the formalists insisted that the courts were merely neutral arbiters.[40]

The problem for the student of law who dwelt in the land of formalism was that formalism as an ideology had no room for change. The very nature of the formalist argument—that law was discovered, not made, and that each discovery was rooted in an absolute—denied lawmakers the flexibility to respond to a new world of demands. Of course, the lawgivers did respond, but adherence to formalism required that they deny what they knew they were doing. Consider James C. Carter of New York, one of the leading expositors of formalism. In 1890, he told the American Bar Association, which he served as president, that lawyers ought to long for "a higher condition and a higher life which we nowhere see realized." Such ideals in the mortal breasts of lawyers (including well-to-do corporate counsel like Carter) were reflected in the ideals of the law. Legislatures did not make law. Judges did not make law (if they admitted as much, they were acting in an impeachable fashion)—no, to Carter, "the law reveals itself in its true character as in Inductive Science engaged in the observation and classification of facts. The naturalist observes the plants and animals of the globe and arranges them in classes according to some common features which they exhibit, the higher and more general including the lower and narrower. . . . The judge and jurist perform a precisely similar function in the domain of the law. They observe the transactions of men and arrange them in orders, families, genera and species according to their proper description from a jural point of view."[41]

Carter proposed a Linnaean system of jural relations, a static science of the law. True, its contents were custom and opinion; to that extent, he seemed to agree with Holmes, but such a system could hardly accommodate change. Law was always found, never made, for customs and opinions were fixed by history, culture, and (although Carter never used the term) blood. Perhaps such jurisprudents as Carter fooled themselves. Perhaps they intended to fool

40. Judicial supremacy, laissez faire doctrine, and the conservatives' triumph went hand in hand. Arnold M. Paul, *Conservative Crisis and the Rule of Law: Attitudes of Bar and Bench, 1887–1895* (Ithaca, N.Y., 1960), 235.

41. James C. Carter, "The Ideal and the Actual in Law," 24 *American Law Review* 752, 764–65 (1890).

everyone else. The root problem remains, however, that a system of legal reasoning based on fixed principles could hardly declare that these principles had suddenly changed.

Against the bedrock of formalism flowed higher and higher tides of social and economic controversy. It was a perfect Kuhnian situation of a paradigm under assault—the paradigm still stands, but more and more observations contradict its central tenets.[42] A court that denied political and social reality would (and did) have a hard time dealing with new forms of political and social organization and new ideas of political and social right. The purpose of jurisprudence is to aid lawmakers in understanding what they do, but the old jurisprudence was helpless, and when the forces of reaction in the courts came to light, formalist jurisprudence changed from a bumbling anachronism to a sinister co-conspirator in the eyes of reformers.

42. Thomas S. Kuhn, *The Structure of Scientific Revolutions* (2nd ed., Chicago, 1970), 52–91.

CHAPTER ONE

Pound Discovers Sociology
and Leaves the Prairie

Jurisprudential thinking in nineteenth-century America failed both to keep pace with changing social, political, and economic conditions and to develop original ways, commensurate with American experience, to look at law and the legal system. In part, this was because the expositors of jurisprudential ideas in the nineteenth century were busy attorneys and judges.[1] The Thomas Cooleys and Christopher Tiedemans whose treatises dominated post–Civil War thinking were concerned with practical law, not theory.[2] Reformers like John Norton Pomeroy and David Dudley Field had narrow objectives. They did not try to reconceptualize the law, merely to make it more efficient.[3] The classics of jurisprudence, like John Austin's lectures, were still widely read, supplemented by German historical writers like Friedrich von Savigny and Rudolph von Ihering, who debated endlessly the relative value of Roman Law and Germanic customs. The younger German writers seemed to appreciate the role of social and economic context, but they made little impression here.[4] Our own lawyer-jurisprudents were out of touch with the new academic disciplines that were coming to dominate the

1. Gary J. Aichele, *Legal Realism and Twentieth Century American Jurisprudence* (New York, 1990), 7–8; John W. Johnson, *American Legal Culture, 1908–1940* (Westport, Conn., 1981), 20–21.

2. Lawrence Friedman, *A History of American Law* (2nd ed., New York, 1985), 628–29.

3. Robert G. Bone, "Mapping the Boundaries of a Dispute: Conceptions of Ideal Law Suit Structure from the Field Code to the Federal Rules," 89 *Columbia Law Review* 1011 (1989).

4. Roscoe Pound, *Jurisprudence* (St. Paul, Minn., 1959), 1:121–91.

curriculums at the elite universities.[5] They still clung to a natural law order, colored with the idea of progress, in which the Great War was only a misstep.[6]

Christopher Columbus Langdell, Harvard Law School's path-breaking dean from 1870 to 1895, may be best remembered today as the promulgator of the casebook method of law study. But perhaps equally important to his impact on legal education and jurisprudence in America well into the twentieth century was his innovation in appointing and arguing for a professional academic law professor class—the single most important precondition of the new jurisprudence. Though exogenous anomalies were daily shaking the old jurisprudential verities, only a new kind of insider, a new cadre of professional academics, could refashion jurisprudence in any profound and thoroughgoing way.

Langdell's persistence, in the face of dwindling classes and puzzled students, was remarkable.[7] But in the end, he triumphed.[8] Full-time professors of law were to have no allegiance to a particular client's perspective; they were to be intellectually free to explore and

5. Laurence R. Veysey, *The Emergence of the American University* (Chicago, 1965), 121–79.

6. Howard Mumford Jones argues that European ideas had a profound impact on American intellectuals. The flow of information from the eighteenth through the nineteenth centuries was from east to west, from Europe to America. America, in the nineteenth century, looked to Europe for philosophical ideas. America was the student, and Europe was the teacher. The United States was still a colony in an intellectual and cultural sense, if not in a political sense. Howard Mumford Jones, "The Influence of European Ideas in Nineteenth-Century America," 7 *American Literature* (1935), reprinted in The Bobbs-Merrill Reprint Series in History. Take James C. Carter, again. He was a lawyer-scholar whose lectures collected as *Law: Its Origin, Growth, and Function* (New York, 1907) concluded: "I hope, at least, that I have done something to convince my hearers, that while legislation is a command of the sovereign, the unwritten Law is not a command at all; thus it is not the dictate of Force but an emanation from Order; that it is that form of conduct which social action necessarily exhibits, something which men can neither enact nor repeal, and which advances and becomes perfect with the advance and improvement of society" (344–45).

7. Franklin G. Fessenden, "The Rebirth of the Harvard Law School," 33 *Harvard Law Review* 502–3, 513 (1920).

8. Pound was happy to celebrate the victory: "In 1913, the Carnegie Foundation for the Advancement of Teaching in the course of its pending investigation of the teaching of law in the United States invited Dr. Josef Redlich, professor of law in the University of Vienna, to examine into the mode of instruction originated at Harvard under Langdell and now general in this country. . . . It is most gratifying, therefore, to those who believe in Langdell's mode of teaching law to read Professor Redlich's report recently published . . . in which he pronounces the method not merely practically successful but eminently scientific and worthy of study by Continental teachers of law." RPP, 156-2.

argue the rules of law as they saw fit. As members of a university community, they were also encouraged to apply emerging academic disciplines and ideas to fundamental questions about law. Finally, as academics, freed from court-imposed deadlines, client meetings, and other practical chores, they were to have more time to simply think about the law, its problems, and its place in American society. Roscoe Pound was not the first of these, but he studied under them and saw, as practitioner-professors did not, where academic jurisprudence might go. And he was determined to take it there.

Pound's father, Stephen, and mother, Laura Biddlecombe, were not children of the plains themselves (they were New Yorkers) and, unimpressed with the quality of late-nineteenth-century plains education, schooled Nathan Roscoe and his two sisters at home until they were old enough to attend the preparatory department of the University of Nebraska.[9] Memoirs of the girls' childhood recalled a loving and supportive family whose intellectual curiosity was sated by trips and play. Neither sister married. Louise, the elder, became a professor at Nebraska. Olivia was a high school teacher and principal.[10] At fourteen, Pound entered the University of Nebraska, where he studied botany; he received his bachelor's degree in the subject in 1888 and completed a master's degree the following year. Then he succumbed to his father's importuning to study law, but he convinced his father that he should do so at Harvard Law School. While Pound's enthusiasm for law study may have been only lukewarm at the time he left for Harvard,[11] his experience during his year there converted and transformed him. He never really intended to stay the course and loved the theater, symphony, opera, and Har-

9. Details of Pound's early life can be found in Paul Sayre, *The Life of Roscoe Pound* (Iowa City, 1948), 5–46. On Pound's father, see Nebraska State Historical Society (hereinafter NSHS), MS 910, box 1, folder 3, describing a plains emigrant who gained legislative and judicial office through his merits. It is a typical (almost iconographic) portrait of the middle-class professional. Pound's mother is profiled in the *Lincoln Star* on February 5, 1922. She died six years later, on December 10, 1928, at the age of eighty-seven. Today she would have been a university provost. Then she home schooled her children and took a vital interest in their professional achievements. NSHS, MS 910, box 1, folder 4.

10. Olivia Pound, Home Life of the Pound Family, typescript, NSHS, MS 911, box 2.

11. Sayre points out that, when Pound convinced his father to let him go to Harvard to study law, Pound was not yet committed to the subject, but thought he might continue his scientific study in Cambridge as well. Sayre, *Pound*, 58–59. Pound cooperated with Sayre in the writing of his biography, and Sayre's insights into the young Pound's motivations came directly from Pound himself.

vard football as much as his legal studies, but he did reveal to his father that he admired the law as taught there.[12] From his first moment in Cambridge, he virtually moved into the law library.[13]

More than sixty years later, Pound reminisced about his brief sojourn as a Harvard Law School student. As throughout his life, Pound had no hesitation about reinventing himself to suit his audience. In that later account, one incident stood out in his memory, an encounter with Professor John Chipman Gray in the law school library during the Christmas recess. (He "didn't have money enough to go back . . . home during the recess. In those days, to go from Boston to Lincoln, Nebraska by train took a little better than four days in sixteen different cars, and it didn't lend itself to charity."[14])

> Well, I was sitting there working on the first volume of Gray's *Cases on Property,* which dealt with personal property, and in front of every section he had an extract from the Institutes of Justinian in the original Latin. . . . Well, I was there trying to find out what the text of the Roman Law meant, and what that had to do with what we were studying, and it occurred to me I might do something about Roman Law. So I came over here to the delivery desk . . . and asked for a book on Roman Law . . . when I heard a gruff voice behind me saying "Don't read that." I looked up and saw that it was Professor Gray. I said, "Mr. Gray"—I don't know how it is now but in my day anybody from the President of the University to the janitor was Mr.—I said, "Mr. Gray, what should I read?" "Do you read German?" "Oh, yes," I said. "I can read German." He took Lord Mackenzie's book away from me and walked back to the stacks here, put away Lord Mackenzie, came back with Sohm's *Institutionen des Römischen Rechts*—the great book on Roman Law in those days—which hadn't been translated—"Read that." and then walked off.[15]

Pound was truthful to this extent: the later story indicates how earnest he was in his search for intellectual fulfillment, his awe of Harvard's great professors, his own sense of himself as outsider—the distance from Lincoln to Cambridge—and the inspiration he found

12. Roscoe Pound to Stephen Pound, Mar. 3, 1890, NSHS, MS 911, box 1, folder S.1, vol. F.1.

13. Roscoe Pound to Laura Biddlecombe Pound, Sept. 29, 1889, NSHS, MS 911, box 1, folder S.1, vol. F.1.

14. Roscoe Pound, "Threescore and Ten Years of the Harvard Law School" (privately printed from an address Pound gave in 1960).

15. Ibid., 7–8.

at Harvard.[16] The professors at Harvard showed him that the law could be a great intellectual enterprise, not just the day-to-day practice he had seen in his father's office in Lincoln.

Pound did not admit the fact that he had planned from the outset to do as much of the three-year curriculum in one year as he could and return to Lincoln. Instead, he wrote that he had intended to stay in Cambridge to pursue his studies, but pressure from his father to return home and stop wasting his time curtailed his idyll, at least for the time being. Parson Mason Weems would have been proud of Pound's dramatic invention. When Pound's father received his son's grade for his first year's study, he supposedly told Roscoe: "This is ridiculous . . . if you can't do better than 75 or over, there's no reason why you should go east to law school."[17] Pound remained in Lincoln—and studied in his father's firm. He was admitted to the bar in the year 1890.[18]

Whatever the facts behind his return to his hometown, Pound was not happy in Lincoln. Two years after leaving Cambridge, he confided to Omer Hershey, a friend from his Harvard days who would become a Baltimore attorney, that "[i]f it wasn't for the fact that I am tied down here in Lincoln in a thousand ways I should like to get out. I don't like the state or its prospects, or mine if I stay here." Writing on his father's "Pound & Burr" legal stationery, he told Hershey that "I think I could pull away from everything and everyone but father—I can't do anything so long as he is determined to take my pulling out as a personal matter. I can't do that. Otherwise I don't think I would have very much pain or regret at parting from the land of my birth as I really don't think very much of a good many features of it." Anger at being cut off from Harvard, Cambridge, and Boston was welling up within him. His father—cum

16. John Chipman Gray was a commanding presence in the school, authoritative (even authoritarian), yet much loved by the students, as two of them, Samuel Williston and Joseph Beale, recalled in 1915. "John Chipman Gray," 28 *Harvard Law Review* 545 (1915) (Williston repeating the Pound story as "an anecdote told me by a colleague"— Pound himself, of course); ibid., 548 (Beale recalling his own experiences with Gray).

17. Ibid., 548.

18. Pound's reasoning here smacks of rationalization, since he admits that he was admitted to the bar in the same year that he left Harvard, without extra years of apprenticeship. Ibid., 11. It should be noted that Pound offered a different reason for his failure to finish at Harvard in a 1915 letter to a recent graduate who was practicing law, but who expressed a desire to enter law teaching. "As you know I was not able to finish at law school for want of money and was compelled to go into a law office as a stenographer." Pound to George K. Gardner, Jan. 5, 1915, RPP, 156-11.

employer—had started to criticize him for the time he spent on his academic fripperies. There were too many books on "impractical" subjects (something like eighty) that young Pound had purchased or borrowed.[19] But Roscoe had no interest in practice—a position that would later influence his view of legal education at Nebraska and Harvard.[20] He told Hershey, "There is no use building any hopes on what I have said, but at the same time there is liable to be an eruption here someday and if I lose my temper there is no accounting for what I may do." In pique, he had even written out his "first last will and testament" and had designated Hershey the beneficiary for his hundred or more books and pamphlets on jurisprudence.[21]

Pound's attitude toward Hershey was warm and confessional, but hinted at Pound's burning ambition for intellectual reputation.[22] A mere novice, Pound still could not help pontificating. He advised his friend that jurisprudence could act as an "antidote" for the intellectual stultification of law practice. "It is a great subject—at least it is to me—and just closely enough connected with the practical end of law to keep one from running too far astray. I really find it an inspiration."[23] He devoted two nights a week to his study of jurisprudence, stealing time from a "long and tedious" law practice.[24] In 1915, he recalled: "I shall always remember the years in which I was a combined collector of bad debts, messenger boy and stenographer in a big law office as the most irksome of my existence."[25]

It may have been the drudgery of practice in these early years that inspired him to go on with his botanical studies (he earned a Ph.D. in botany in 1897) and join the Nebraska Botanical Survey.[26] He

19. Pound to Omer Hershey, Feb. 20, 1893, and Mar. 5, 1893, Sayre Papers. Pound allowed Sayre to use these letters, but tried to convince Sayre to "use your good judgment" to prune his quotations from them. Pound to Sayre, Nov. 13, 1946, Sayre Papers.

20. See N. E. H. Hull, "Vital Schools of Jurisprudence: Roscoe Pound, Wesley Newcomb Hohfeld, and the Promotion of an Academic Jurisprudential Agenda, 1910–1919," 45 *Journal of Legal Education* 239 ff. (1995).

21. Pound to Hershey, Jan. 24, 1892, University of Nebraska Archives, Lincoln. Pound later recalled that his letters to Hershey were written with candor and fullness. Pound to Paul Sayre, NSHS, MS 911, box 1, folder S.1, vol. F.20.

22. Roscoe Pound to Stephen Pound, Nov. 10, 1889, NSHS, MS 911, box 1, folder S.1, vol. F.1.

23. Pound to Hershey, Sept. 1, 1892, Sayre Papers.

24. Pound to Hershey, Sept. 11, 1892, Sayre Papers.

25. Pound to Gardner, Jan. 5, 1915, RPP, 156-11.

26. Pound complained about practice incessantly, but he continued to practice law throughout the time he lived in Lincoln, even when he taught and then led the University

wrote Hershey during this time that "I can't get up any where near as much enthusiasm over legal subjects. A fungus is a living thing and one can get acquainted with him and understand him and his ways and so arouse some interest. When I see some of the forms I worked with back in '88 they seem quite like old friends."[27] Yet even as he waxed eloquent on the intimate joys of fungi, he told Hershey about how impressed he was by books the Harvard faculty wrote: "I really am getting a great deal out of them." He still loved the law. Even after he graduated to the more interesting work of trying cases in magistrate's court, he spent his spare time searching for the intellectual stimulation he had found, but had to give up, at Harvard. "I was trying to supply the defect in my legal education not only by studying the Harvard case books as they came out—for most of them were just appearing at that time—but also by building up a library of my own on the subject of jurisprudence and Roman law, buying new books only after I had read thoroughly those already on my small shelf."[28]

Pound's autodidacticism during this period inspired no brilliant insights, nor was there evidence of the anti-formalist rebel that would emerge a decade later. Immersion in the classics of law may have remedied a gap in his education, but it also mired him in the inadequacies of classic jurisprudence. He wrote to Hershey of his disdain for the "violent" innovations of Lord Mansfield, though he accorded him some credit for his "work as a founder—though he was *not* the founder—of commercial law." It was fashionable to laud Mansfield's contributions, but the adulation left Pound cold: "[S]o much is said in extravagant and unmerited praise of him, that

---

of Nebraska Law School. Indeed, he wrote briefs for his old firm after he had left Lincoln for Chicago. Pound to Sayre, Feb. 13, 1946, Sayre Papers. I suppose it was simply a matter of money—with Pound, money was always an important consideration, even at the end of his life. "One cannot exist on a Harvard retiring allowance, and I have had in the immediate past to be very busy eking out my income," he wrote on February 3, 1958, to Anton-Hermann Chroust. RPP, 39-2.

27. Pound to Hershey, Jan. 21, 1893 (on Nebraska Botanical Survey stationery), Sayre Papers.

28. Pound to Gardner, Jan. 5, 1915, RPP, 156-11. Pound apparently used his friend Omer Hershey as a purchasing agent for his library. Throughout the Pound-Hershey correspondence during the early 1890s are references to books Pound wished Hershey to purchase for him. Indeed, we can get a fairly good idea of exactly what Pound was buying and reading during this period from reading his letters to Hershey. Omer Hershey Correspondence, Sayre Papers.

his defects need showing up badly. It makes me swearing mad to read panegyrics on him with the usual tirade against all England's really great lawyers. . . ."[29]

Who deserved Pound's praise? Surprisingly, considering Pound's ardent progressivism in the next two decades, Pound expressed admiration for the conservative, formalist undoer of Mansfield's reforms: Lord Eldon. During this period, in Pound's early twenties, one hears ominous echoes of his later jurisprudential and political conservatism. As a self-declared "infernal Tory," he told Hershey that he admired Eldon because "[h]e didn't make any loudly advertised changes—but he took disjointed materials and made a great system what it has been since." Eldon's great contribution, and what Pound would aspire to for himself, he told Hershey, was as "not the founder of the modern system—he is rather what Linnaeus is to Botany—the man who gave permanent direction to the system."[30]

Actually, Pound's conservatism was part of a dual strain in his jurisprudential nature. It is clear from the early letters to Hershey that Pound always despised violent change and lauded systemization and classification, and he would continue to hold these views throughout his life. The conundrum is that Pound would spend three or more decades espousing a progressive-pragmatic doctrine of jurisprudence that seems at odds with these fussy taxonomies. Pound disdained John Austin's positivism and the work of his "neo-Austinian" followers.

There must be something that went beyond mere classification or explanation of law. Pound experimented in these letters with what would become one of his favorite analytical styles: definition by negation. His own views would peek out of the interstices of his attack on another writer's arguments. His target this time was Sir Thomas Erskine Holland's *Elements of Jurisprudence* (1880), a book Pound later described as "the most widely used" textbook in "the common law world in the last decade of the nineteenth century."[31] In a letter to Hershey at the end of 1892, Pound relied on a biological analogy to explain his objections to Holland and the tradition for which he seemed to stand. "Holland and others I might name are compara-

29. Pound to Hershey, Sept. 21, 1892, Sayre Papers.
30. Ibid.
31. Pound, *Jurisprudence*, 5:40–41.

tive Histologists of Modern Law."[32] Histology is the clinical examination of tissue structures, sometimes taken directly from the body
of the subject. Others had misused biological comparisons—not
Pound. "'The Scientific system under which the final word is said
where all the parts or elements are properly labeled and classified'—
That is exactly the layman's idea of science—and is about as far
from the biologist idea of science as it possibly can be. . . . The fact
is that systematic work, if I may quote myself, is the remnant of
scholastics in biology. . . . Holland . . . is comparable to the histolo-
gist. He takes law as it now exists and dissects it with little regard
to what it was or what it will be. Of course this procedure fails to
tell really what it is, though it purports to do so . . . but enough."[33]
It was late in the evening, again, and Pound admitted that his "head
was duller than a stub pen," but he had put his finger on the problem. Neither academic jurisprudence nor popular jurisprudence
worked in his America. It was classificatory or purely philosophical.
It explained little and predicted nothing. Even the current version of
a science of law was inadequate, for surely the purpose of science
was not merely Linnaean but predictive.

Pound was formulating a new view of law and of science out of
old materials, a bricolage, seeking an American jurisprudence by
pruning away the errors of European thinkers and their American
acolytes. He knew biology as well as he knew scholastic jurisprudence and hoped that concepts taken from the former could fill in
the gaps left after he had stripped the latter. He told Hershey, "Law
like every super organic thing is essentially organic—I mean when I
think of it I am tempted to think of it that way and I believe it can
best be handled that way." Pound meant not an organism already
evolved and now fixed in its morphology, but rather a living organism, changing and adapting: "The study of Jurisprudence on the
strict lines laid down by Holland without going further is as un-
profitable morally as the study of comparative anatomy of vertebrates without having in mind that vertebrates have not always been
vertebrates and that life is a *living* thing." The organic, evolutionary
analogy thus refuted the positivist philosophy: "Such conception

---

32. Pound to Hershey, Nov. 2, 1892, Sayre Papers. On the popular neo-Austinians,
see Stephen A. Siegel, "Joel Bishop's Orthodoxy," 13 *Law and History Review* 215–60
(1995); Edwin W. Patterson, *Jurisprudence: Men and Ideas of the Law* (Brooklyn, N.Y.,
1953), 388.
33. Pound to Hershey, Nov. 14, 1892, Sayre Papers.

does put a sort of life into it—whether or not it puts spirit into it. Law may as it now exists be 'the command of' a sovereign—but it hasn't always been that by any means. And for that reason it isn't *essentially* that now!" He continued, "Law is a living developing thing and when studied as such must be intensely interesting to one who can get interested in a living thing."[34]

It was Pound's old teacher, John Chipman Gray, who led Pound to contemplate the next step toward an American jurisprudence. Again, Pound advanced his argument by refuting Gray's. "You may have seen a note by Prof. Gray in the *Harvard Law Review* last year in which he doubted whether there was such a thing as Jurisprudence at all. It is singular that no one can agree with anyone else as to what Jurisprudence is and as no one agrees with anyone else at the outset, of course the contradiction and confusion becomes appalling as one proceeds. There really are no *recognized fundamenta Jurisprudentiae.*" Gray's dismissal of jurisprudence had awakened Pound from his slumber. But how to answer Gray? "I think the solution lies in the recognition of the organic character of law," Pound offered. Again, biological analogy was the key: "All super organic phenomena are now being treated as organic."[35]

The organic model was the "in" thing, and Pound's recourse to biology in an age when Darwinian models of human progress were all the rage could hardly be called original, but his gift was to catch the academic tide as it surged, not to anticipate it.[36] "Language has been for years, and Politics, and Political science now is, theology, and I see [illegible] now comes out with a book on the organic character of literature. Why not treat law the same way?" Pound, an omnivorous and voracious reader, was also the bricoleur—and why not? "Jurisprudence as Austin and Holland understand it, then becomes the histology and anatomy of modern law, and only a part, though a very necessary part, of Jurisprudence. . . . So if I were to write on Jurisprudence, I should begin with the anatomy and histology of law as we know it now in civilized communities. . . . *It would not be necessary to define law.* Nothing organic can be defined. . . . It is like tying a string around a tree. The tree will grow and break the string. The law, too, will grow, and all the strings tied

---

34. Pound to Hershey, Nov. 2, 1892, Sayre Papers.
35. Ibid.
36. Edward J. Larson, *Trial and Error: The American Controversy over Creation and Evolution* (New York, 1985), 7–27.

about it by way of definition by past students and learned writers, have not availed to stop it."[37] In 1959, at the age of eighty-nine, Pound published his last great work, the four-volume *Jurisprudence*. It brought together his many earlier writings, but its structure, its anatomy as it were, closely followed the plan he laid out in 1893.[38]

In a later missive to Hershey, Pound summed up: "The only thing to be insisted on is the futility of defining law or contending over a definition of it. . . . We are dealing with phenomena, not with 'immutable' 'eternal' etc. facts. But it should be borne in mind always that the biological jurisprudence is a figure—and in some respects an imperfect one. It can be abused so as to produce results as bad as those once produced by the analogy of 'the law of God.' "[39] Pound's facility with analogy, here the analogy of law to biology, was typical of an age in which metaphors drawn from the natural sciences guided the infancy of the social sciences. Yet Pound had gone beyond the conventional wisdom that law was "a science" in a rather clever way. He admitted that he was borrowing and that his analogy was imperfect. He cautioned against the sort of thinking that might make a study of jurisprudence as dogmatic or fixed as theology. He was already the bricoleur. And this from a twenty-two-year-old man who had read everything—everything worth reading—in Latin and German as well as English (for his mother had insisted on languages for him and he took to them like a duck to water when he went to college) and who wanted to make a difference in the world of ideas.[40]

37. Pound to Hershey, Jan. 29, 1893, Sayre Papers.

38. Pound, in *Jurisprudence,* 1:7–60, defines jurisprudence by what jurisprudents have said.

39. Pound to Hershey, Feb. 9, 1983, Sayre Papers.

40. Near the end of his life, he still remembered the foreign language teachers he had had for Greek, Latin, German, and French at Nebraska. Oral history interview of Pound by Dr. Robert N. Manley, July 12, 1962, Cambridge, Mass., Transcription in University Archives of University of Nebraska, Lincoln (hereinafter Pound, Oral History). R. Pound Bio Bib file. According to Pound's sister Olivia, the Pound family had a German maid, and Roscoe and his mother used to converse with the maid in German all the time. Olivia Pound to Sayre, Mar. 18, 1946, NSHS, MS 913, box 1, folder 1. Before America's entry into World War I, Pound was still defending the Germans against the Anglo-American propaganda machine. See Pound to W. G. Langworth Taylor, Jan. 28, 1915, RPP, 156-16: "As near as I can make out he [the Anglo-American] thinks of the United States as simply a British colony and anyone who ventures to suggest that there may be two sides to many matters which are not in dispute is regarded as little, if anything, short of a traitor."

Pound's intellectual ambition must have been widely known around Lincoln, for "[a]t the end of nine years I was unexpectedly called upon to teach jurisprudence and Roman law at the University of Nebraska." This was in 1895. Whether the call to academia was as great a surprise as Pound later portrayed it or whether he had, in fact, been soliciting an offer to teach is an open question. Indeed, Willa Cather, a close friend of Pound's sister Louise, recalled how Pound would hang around the university: "He stood around the halls button-holing old acquaintances and showing the University to them. He exhibited the campus, buildings and faculty with an air of proprietorship and pleased condescension. . . . He seemed very enthusiastic about University matters, but it seemed rather boyish and immature in a man of his age. It was not a large kind of enthusiasm, that could take in principles and beliefs, it was a petty traditionary sort of enthusiasm that was confined to a few people and incidents. He is liberal to all University enterprises, but it seems to be rather to perpetuate his own name and fame among the students. He has no particular business except hanging around the University in order that people may ask who he is and be told what fine marks he used to get in his classes." Cather's final assessment of Pound's talent and prospects was pretty dim: "He has ability enough but he just seemed to quit growing when he graduated. He has never got past the blue ribbon, sheepskin, 'vos salutamus' stage. He is a University graduate, and that's all he ever will be in this world or that to come." [41]

Cather's scathing critique of her friend's brother appeared in 1894, five years before Pound was offered an assistant professorship. We have no record of Roscoe's reaction to Cather's profile, although they must have known one another well. [42] The truth is that Pound was already consumed with ambition to join the faculty and chafed at his temporary exile from academia. When combined with the distaste for the life he was leading in Nebraska, the ap-

41. Willa Cather, "Pastels in Prose," 23 *Hesperian* 4 (1894). The unsigned piece did not identify Pound by name, though other details of description leave no doubt about whom she wrote. It was also identified as such by noted Willa Cather scholar James Woodress. In a chapter entitled "The Lincoln Years: 1890–1896," he wrote: "If her circle of friends was small, it was select . . . among them were the Pounds. . . ." "The Pounds, however, were early casualties, for she satirized Roscoe in her column in the Hesperian and alienated the entire family, a break that was not healed, if it ever was, for many years." James Woodress, *Willa Cather: Her Life and Art* (New York, 1970), 63.

42. Phyllis C. Robinson, *Willa: The Life of Willa Cather* (New York, 1983), 60–61.

pointment must have been a bittersweet victory. Others he had known were progressing farther faster. Pound was auditioning for something better; indeed, he had his eye on Harvard all along, but Harvard hardly noticed him. He grieved, but did not despair.[43]

Cather's criticism hints at one reason Pound pursued the Ph.D. in botany—he sought academic legitimation, even though he was a practicing member of the bar. Pound's Ph.D. was the first in the subject granted at Nebraska (and the second Ph.D. given there). Pound explored a forerunner of ecological methodologies in use today— plant geography. Indeed, Pound had seen that plants lived in communities, a key concept in modern ecology.[44] The possibility of a career in botany kept Pound from despair. "Until I was four years old, I lived at the foot of J Street. And I can remember when mother could lift me up and I could look out the window across to where the salt basins were and the hills just beyond it. And see the buffalo grazing on the hills there. I got interested, mother was interested in botany, and I used to go out and collect plants. I had a pretty good herbarium as a small boy, and I had some pretty good books on entomology."[45] Pound's relationship with his parents was powerful, but Stephen and Laura Pound were not the only parental influences in Roscoe's life.

Charles Bessey, who taught Pound botany at Nebraska, was a second intellectual father. Bessey had come to Nebraska only a short time before Pound matriculated, opened his lab and his thoughts to Pound and other young botanists, and formed the members of his "seminar" into a closely knit, energetic cadre that used to "haze" the "lits" unmercifully.[46] "Dr. Bessey gave [Pound] infinite time to tell him where to look, how and why. I don't suppose I could measure it," Pound recalled in 1962. "What I owe to him is the training I got from him in how to go about finding out about things. I would rate him as one of the few men to whom I think I owe more than anyone else. Of course what I owe mainly is to my father and mother, but as for teachers, Bessey."[47] For Bessey was

43. Pound to Hershey, Feb. 20, 1893, Sayre Papers.

44. Michael R. Hill, "Roscoe Pound and American Sociology: A Study in Archival Frame Analysis, Sociobiography, and Sociological Jurisprudence" (Ph.D. diss., University of Nebraska, 1989), 219–26.

45. Pound, Oral History.

46. Ernest Bessey, Random Notes on the Early Days of the University of Nebraska with Reference to Roscoe Pound, enclosed in Ernest Bessey to Sayre, July 10, 1946, Sayre Papers.

47. Pound, Oral History.

more than Pound's undergraduate inspiration and graduate mentor; he was an important sounding board for Pound's legal thinking. Well after Pound had left botany and Lincoln behind (despite Bessey's efforts to keep Pound in the fold), Pound sent Bessey articles on the law and took Bessey's replies to heart. His work with Bessey had been on the frontier of a new discipline—ecological mapping—and what Pound seemed to see in law was an ecological process, a contextualized growth fostered and hindered by the cultures that surrounded law. But this may be flying too high. Pound, with all the chances in the world to do so, never called his views ecological.

Pound and Bessey continued to appreciate each other after Pound left Lincoln. Bessey urged Pound to publish his thoughts on the wider implications of law, and Pound promised to do as much. Indeed, it was to Bessey that Pound revealed his plan for a sociological jurisprudence: "I have for some time felt that there is need of work along the lines suggested in your letter and have been engaged upon a series of articles with the view possibly to a book ultimately to be entitled 'Sociological Jurisprudence.' Between you and me, overtures have been made to me by the MacMillan Company with reference to such a book." [48]

It was a near thing, the choice of law over botany, and well into the next decade Pound continued to think of jurisprudence in biological terms. For the rest of the 1890s, Pound divided his time equally between botany work and legal study. In 1893, his name was on the masthead of the Nebraska Botanical Survey (and he was writing to Omer Hershey about his friendly fungi), and in 1897, after receiving his doctorate, he was named director of the survey. Nevertheless, his study of intellectual legal subjects continued. But as Paul Sayre recognized in his adoring biography of Pound, by the late 1890s the law was winning Pound's primary attention. In 1895, he became an instructor at the law school. Four years later he was appointed an assistant professor. By 1903, he was dean. [49]

Behind his rise was ambition, but not for power or wealth. He wanted to be an authority. As early as 1892, he had written to Her-

48. "My dear Pound (I am going to call you that altho you are learned associate dean and ex-judge and professor and all that)," Bessey wrote to Pound on December 3, 1908. "I hope you will never forswear botany. I am sure that you will live longer and be happier if you keep a little botanical den into which you can retire when you are worn out with business of state." Charles Bessey to Pound, Apr. 30, 1908, and Pound to Bessey, May 11, 1908, Bessey Papers, University of Nebraska.

49. Sayre, *Pound*, 137–46.

shey, "I am full of schemes now I have little else to do, and some of them I may be able to work. I have two or three legal articles and possibly a book, which I am evolving mentally . . . whether any of them will ever see light is more than I can tell yet."[50] The plan brought together Pound's reading and teaching. "Although I had not studied [Roman law and jurisprudence] in courses anywhere I found myself tolerably well prepared to deal with them and kept this work up while practicing and afterwards while on the bench until I was made dean of the law school at Nebraska and had to put my energies purely into *dogmatic* subjects."[51]

Pound kept active, of course, and his activities went far beyond a survey of his state's flora. By 1901, he was elevated to the Nebraska Supreme Court as a commissioner—an auxiliary judge to handle the overflow of cases. Pound's father had been a judge, for the prairie bar often converted its practitioners into judges.[52] By 1900, the court was far in arrears, Pound recalled, and Populist farmers would not vote for any judges. The outcomes of the cases that commissioners decided were binding, but the opinions delivered by the commissioners had no precedential force. Pound admitted that he left the post because he only made a third of what he made in practice (and he was not the most effective of rainmakers in practice). "Anyhow, I resigned from the commission and was going back into practice. And Dr. Andrews insisted that I should take the deanship of the law school with a promise that I could do private practice. Well I soon found it couldn't be done. Practice is a whole man's job and being head of a respectable school is a full man's job."[53] Another reason that Pound's career as a judge was so short lived (lasting only from 1901 through 1903) was his recognition that he did not have the judicial temperament. Nearly a decade before, he told Hershey, "I hope I may never be a judge! The strain of being fair is a fearful one to a man naturally partisan—bitterly and uncompromisingly partisan, as you know."[54]

But Pound aspired to more than teaching or administration; he wanted to change the law, as some of his opinions demonstrated.

50. Pound to Hershey, Oct. 24, 1892, Sayre Papers.
51. Pound to Gardner, Jan. 5, 1915, RPP, 156-11 (emphasis added).
52. C. Robert Haywood, *Cowtown Lawyers: Dodge City and Its Attorneys, 1876–1886* (Norman, Okla., 1989), 46–68.
53. Pound, Oral History.
54. Pound to Hershey, Oct. 24, 1892, Sayre Papers.

"His sympathies," a college companion and later colleague recalled, "were mostly with the 'under dog.'"[55] In the main, he relied on simple rules and well-known sources of law. Pound was never a wholesale innovator. But in a small corner of the many cases that came to him, he found a place to move the law forward. He was a believer in a balance of interests when a private landholder sought an injunction against a public utility or some other legal entity acting in the public interest.[56] Other courts had balanced the equities (that is, looked beyond the pleadings in the case to examine the effect of the sought remedy on the community) when a private party sought an injunction against a business or public utility.[57] Pound had proved himself willing to receive new tides of opinion in his court.[58]

In 1903, as the newly appointed dean of the college of law at the university, Pound gave an inaugural lecture, in which he propounded his views of legal education and made his case for a curriculum beyond the "dogmatic subjects." He began with an analogy to Roman law (all his reading—and his tendency to pedantry—on display, and after all, he had taught the subject for nearly a decade at Lincoln): "The stage of development which our common law system has now reached is strikingly analogous to the close of the classical period of Roman law." He took the analogy seriously, for then in Rome "the old *ius civile* broke down and became obsolete," just as part of the common law "has done with us." The problem lay not alone in law, however, for then, as in 1903, the root of the problem was the teaching of law. In Rome, as in the American republic, law had gone from private instruction to public schools, but in America, the "scientific character" of law had outstripped the ability of practitioner teachers, even at the best schools, like Pound's beloved (and here much praised) Harvard. "What shall be the next step," he mused, and then answered himself: "I believe it may be asserted boldly that a university law school can and should do more."[59]

55. Bessey, Random Notes.

56. E.g., Bronson v. Albion Telephone Company, 67 Nebraska 111 (1903).

57. Peter Charles Hoffer, *The Law's Conscience: Equitable Constitutionalism in America* (Chapel Hill, N.C., 1990), 157–67.

58. The judgment of Harold Gill Reuschlein, "Roscoe Pound—The Judge," 90 *University of Pennsylvania Law Review* 292–329 (1942).

59. Roscoe Pound, "The Evolution of Legal Education: An Inaugural Lecture Delivered September 19, 1903" (privately printed, 1903), 3, 4, 5, 9, 11, 14, 15.

Pound had in mind the great project of uniting law studies with allied fields of study already taught in great universities—anticipating one of the major contributions of the legal realists to the curriculum of law schools.[60] Pound specifically wanted legal history and jurisprudence, two subjects practitioner-teachers shunned, added to the required course list. With these comparative subjects, taught by professional teachers, the law schools might begin to function as engines of law reform, leading to an "overhauling of our unwieldy case law and formal improvement of the whole body of substantive law." The times were critical, and "[i]f the law schools fail us here, whither shall we look?"[61]

His ideals of legal education brought to Lincoln the fashions of Cambridge. In particular, Pound immediately overhauled the curriculum at Nebraska, introducing elective courses in analytical jurisprudence and the Harvard system classroom dialectic. As he wrote to the chancellor in 1906, "[T]he system [of teaching] that I use, which has fought its way to recognition as the best system of teaching law and has revolutionized its study, has placed the Harvard Law School in its well recognized position as the leading institution in the world for the teaching of the Common Law. . . . [T]he system substitutes thinking, criticism, analysis, for memorizing; and the student is thrown more than ever before upon his own resources and feeling a weakness somewhere, ascribes it at first to the method, rather than to himself. Afterward, if he is honest with himself, he knows better. . . . [T]he method, so far as class-room work is concerned, might be likened to the Socratic method applied to the teaching of law, and the students having the same class of mind as those who opposed Socrates are likely to oppose it."[62]

Pound also pressed (as he would later at Harvard) for greater use in the law school of the faculties of the other colleges, for "one of the advantages of a law school connected with a university is that such connection makes it possible for the faculty of law to make use of the resources of other faculties in this way. It would seem that the

60. Laura Kalman, *Legal Realism at Yale, 1927–1960* (Chapel Hill, N.C., 1986), 71–72.

61. Pound, "Evolution," 20.

62. University of Nebraska College of Law Schedule for the First Semester, RPP, Paige box 4; Pound to Benjamin [Chancellor E. B.] Andrews, July 13, 1906, University Archives, University of Nebraska, box 19, folder 147. But Pound did not like the case law system at first. Pound to Laura Biddlecombe Pound, Sept. 29, 1889, NSHS, MS 911, box 1, folder S.1, vol. F.1.

College of Law should have the advantage of the other colleges of this University in this respect."[63] Pound argued for another Harvard rule—that students admitted to the law school have bachelor's degrees from colleges. "The Student must come to the law school with a foundation in history, in economics, in politics, and in sociology which general college training alone can supply," for "the universities have the right and the duty of insisting upon the value of their law degree."[64] And Pound did not hide his own light under a bushel. When the combination of American history and jurisprudence in one chair proved awkward—Pound held the jurisprudence side of the chair—Pound offered, with fellow member of the law faculty Walter Wheeler Cook, to assume a new chair in "Jurisprudence and Public Law."[65]

Cook had come to Nebraska in 1901 to teach in the history department, after training in law and political science at Columbia and studying mathematics and physics in Germany. He did not have a law degree, but neither did Pound. He was as intellectually active and varied in his interests as Pound, and the two evidently hit it off. When Pound became dean, he moved immediately to bring Cook into the college of law. Cook did not stay long, however, moving to Missouri's new law school in 1904, to Wisconsin in 1906, and to Chicago in 1910, replacing there Roscoe Pound, who had just left to go to Harvard. Two years later, Cook went to Yale. The two men's paths would cross again and again.[66] They should have been fast friends. Both aspired to change the law and use the legal academy to do it. Both were progressives, and both were ambitious for professional advancement. Both were regarded highly, and their leaving Lincoln was regretted by students and alumni. Yet something happened at Nebraska that made them wary of each other.

Pound was close to his faculty and fought for them tenaciously. He defended their rights of free speech, a position he reprised when Felix Frankfurter and Zechariah Chafee, Jr., came under fire at Harvard during the first Red Scare. When Pound himself was accused

63. Pound to Andrews, Dec. 11, 1905, University Archives, University of Nebraska, box 18, folder 143.

64. Pound, Report of the Dean of the College of Law, 1906–1907, University Archives, University of Nebraska.

65. Pound to Andrews, Nov. 20, 1903, University Archives, University of Nebraska, box 17, folder 133.

66. John Henry Schlegel, *American Legal Realism and Empirical Social Science* (Chapel Hill, N.C., 1995), 28–35, 40, 41, 52 ff.

of expressing to the students "political opinions" on imperialism, the tariff, the ownership of railroads and other public service agencies, the suppression or control of the liquor traffic, political organizations, and the fitness of candidates for public office, he huffed that he was falsely accused. He admitted having such opinions and expressing them privately, and he would "never renounce" the right to hold and express such opinions on appropriate occasions. These included short talks at club meetings and professional gatherings, but not student political meetings. He reminded the chancellor that he had even backed out of teaching a course in corporations because the subject, in his opinion, had taken on a political hue, and he did not wish to communicate his views to the students.[67] The students sided with Pound, as did a large segment of public opinion.[68] He did not leave, however, until he received an offer from Northwestern, by which time Cook had already departed.

That Pound had tried to mentor Cook, and the project had gone awry, seems obvious. Cook was acting secretary of the law faculty before Pound became dean.[69] Cook's academic credentials were more impressive than Pound's at the time; perhaps Cook was jealous of Pound for getting the deanship when he might have had it; after all, Cook departed a little hastily, in 1904. Perhaps Pound accused Cook of jumping ship too soon, when Pound needed him, for Pound regretted that Cook's replacement could not in reason "do all that Mr. Cook did."[70] Perhaps Pound was jealous, for so far, no one courted him. Too many perhapses, but the fact remains that Cook and Pound never did sort out their relationship. In later years, Cook would undermine Pound's influence in the profession and yet turn to Pound for help in finding jobs. Pound would try over and over again to help younger protégés wherever he taught and could claim much success—in later years, for example, Sam Bass Warner, Rollin Perkins, and Edward A. Ross, on behalf of his son Frank, sent letters thanking Pound for his mentoring.[71] Indeed, when he finally

67. Pound to Andrews, June 11, 1905, University Archives, University of Nebraska, box 18, folder 141.

68. "Pound Out of Law School," *Nebraska State Journal*, Mar. 2, 1905, at 1. One of Pound's many resignations, but it was not accepted by Chancellor Andrews.

69. See, e.g., Walter Wheeler Cook to Andrews, May 11, 1903 (a month before Dean M. B. Reese resigned), University Archives, University of Nebraska, MS 1.

70. Pound to Andrews, July 18, 1904, University Archives, University of Nebraska, MS 1, box 17, folder 135.

71. Rollin Perkins to Pound, May 5, 1920, RPP, 31-12; Sam Bass Warner to Pound, Jan. 31, 1921, RPP, 34-17; Edward A. Ross to Pound, Dec. 24, 1919, RPP, 32-7.

did leave Nebraska, there was "an uprising at the university." Students genuinely appreciated the personal attention he gave them, during and after their stay at the college.[72]

In the meantime, Pound was again thinking hard and publishing frequently on jurisprudence, an outgrowth of his teaching analytical jurisprudence. He had not forgotten his botany, but a new organizing principle had energized his writing. As he told Bessey, he was planning a "sociology of the law." The rising social sciences had swept through American higher education and came to Nebraska in the person of Ross. One of the country's first and foremost sociologists, Ross spent the years 1901–1906 at Nebraska, and Pound, always on the lookout for interdisciplinary connections, was soon a friend and collaborator. Ross, an academic maverick and supporter of radical causes, was also an engaging man, tall, rangy, and energetic, a westerner who galvanized the teaching of the social sciences at Nebraska. Ross was the sociologist of the progressive movement, much respected and often quoted. He was a combination of elitist and democrat (common among the progressives to be sure)—strongly believing in the power of the average man to improve the world when tutored by the best minds. Pound agreed. Like Pound, Ross was no friend to populism, but he did advocate legislative remedies to social evils, including the passage of health and safety regulations for factories, limitations of working hours, minimum wage provisions, and prohibitions on child labor. Pound was coming around to the same positions and would strongly support a constitutional amendment barring child labor. Like Pound, Ross believed strongly in freedom of the press and of speech.[73]

Thirty years later, Ross took credit for tutoring Pound in a sociological view of the operation of courts, just as a decade before Bessey had mentored a younger Pound.[74] Pound had said as much to Ross in 1906, thanking Ross for starting Pound "on the path he is moving in."[75] Ross would later lobby to get Pound named president of the University of Wisconsin, where Ross went in 1906, joining Cook. Here were two obvious and compelling examples of the way

72. *Nebraska State Journal,* May 28, 1907, at 1.

73. Julius Weinberg, *Edward Alsworth Ross and the Sociology of Progressivism* (Madison, Wis., 1972), 123, 126–27, 131, 134.

74. Hill, "Roscoe Pound and American Sociology," 274–82; on Pound as mentor, see chapter 2.

75. Pound to Ross, Nov. 2, 1906, quoted in Weinberg, *Ross,* 136.

in which academic networking affected Pound. In Bessey, Cook, and Ross, he had found a circle of admiring friends whose ideas influenced his own.[76]

Pound's gradually growing circle, in which private conversations about the nature of law and society circulated, became the beginning of a public discourse. As dean, Pound was solicited to give talks, which were then published. His first, in which he expressed many ideas that he would later expand, is in some ways his most striking. Though later students of Pound (and legal realism) have either overlooked it or not given it enough attention, Pound's first sally into sociological jurisprudence demonstrated its and his strengths and limits. Like so many of Pound's later articles, "A New School of Jurists" (1904) began with a genealogy of jurisprudents. Pound would rework and restate his analysis and classification many times over the next fifty years. Perhaps in part it was mere pedantry, a defensive reflex meant to display his learning to his Nebraska colleagues. But his purpose went beyond mere preening. As Karl Llewellyn acknowledged fifty years later, Pound was the first legal academic to try to weave all the strands of Western jurisprudential thought together as a coherent tapestry.[77] Llewellyn was right: Pound's strength lay in the fact that he could see the relationships between disparate schools of jurisprudents. The final reason that Pound dwelt on the history of jurisprudential schools was that he wanted to show the evolution of these ideas, supporting his own proposition that the time was ripe for a "new school of jurists."

The first point he made was that the boundaries of the recognized jurisprudential schools of the nineteenth century—philosophical, historical, and analytical—had gradually dissolved, "bring[ing] these formerly divergent schools into something like accord." He perceived "jurists are coming together upon a new ground from many starting points . . . but there is much to indicate that, instead of a further variation of one of the old creeds, an entirely new creed is to be looked for." He foresaw this leading to "the rising and still

76. The fact is that Pound changed his thinking over time in quite distinct ways. Despite Edward B. McLean, *Law and Civilization: The Legal Thought of Roscoe Pound* (Lanham, Md., 1992), 301, there was no consistent underlying legal philosophy in Pound, although there always was a disposition to piece together, to listen, to reflect, and, at his best, to see deeper meanings. Pound changed from conservative to liberal to conservative. Period.

77. Karl Llewellyn, "Review of Roscoe Pound, *Jurisprudence*," 28 *University of Chicago Law Review* 174 (1960).

formative school to which we must look hence forth for advance in juristic thought, [that] may be styled the Sociological School."[78] Evidently, regular lunch with Ross had changed Pound's thinking dramatically.

But Pound was cautious—a personality trait that became the hallmark of his jurisprudence. Rather than breaking new ground, he detoured through a bibliography of European—primarily German—pioneers of sociological jurisprudence, once again displaying his expertise, but only indirectly promoting his own, American, enterprise. Pound had returned to comfortable territory in discussing the philology of terms to describe law and the history of the sources of law. Eleven pages later, after a sound analysis of positive law, legislation, and judicial discretion from the Romans through Jeremy Bentham, Austin, and everyone else, he asserted that the progress of the law was cyclical. "In the history of jurisprudence periods of legislation and codification, in which the imperative theory of law has been predominant, have always been periods of stagnation. The law has lived and grown through juristic activity under the influence of ideas of natural right and justice or of reasonableness, not force, as the ultimate source of authority."[79]

Thus far, there was nothing radical—indeed, little reformatory—in what he had written. The new school looked pretty much like the old schools. But Pound was not finished. Indeed, the article may be said to have ended where it should have begun. In the last few sentences, Pound staked out the new ground. "Realizing that a final answer to the question, 'What is Law?' is impossible, since the thing to be defined [as he had proved in the preceding pages, and echoing ideas that he had shared with Hershey a decade before] is living and growing, and therefore subject to change, the most conspicuous representative of the new school abandons that question and goes behind it to define the legal order (*Rechtsordnung*) in which law results and for which it exists. . . . Law is not an end, but a means." Here was the realist program in embryonic form. Let jurisprudence describe how law actually worked, for any attempt to find the hidden meaning or natural structure was deluded.[80]

What was missing was any conception of why law changed when and how it did. There was no real sense of what contribution soci-

78. Roscoe Pound, "A New School of Jurists," 4 *University Studies* 249 (July 1904).
79. Ibid., 250, 265.
80. Ibid., 266.

ology made to the inquiry into the nature of law. But Pound was working on it. In the meantime, he had found a new venue for his scholarship—the law review. Not at the *Harvard Law Review*, whose pages were graced with the wisdom of its own faculty and students, but at competing newer law reviews, like Yale's and Columbia's, whose editorial boards were urged to solicit the articles of leading outside practitioners and scholars.[81] At Columbia, Pound found a home for his next major piece on jurisprudence, "Do We Need a Philosophy of Law?" (1905).

Pound was willing to admit to a gnawing dismay in this essay, for his audience was different. Now he spoke to the law professors. In America, the common law was everywhere, and everywhere that it had gone, its "triumph seems assured." Even the growing tide of legislation was checked by common law, for each piece of legislation and codification was but "a fresh starting point for a new body of case law." The enshrinement of common law ensured that "radical legislative innovations" were impossible. But all was not well, not in 1905, for "there is a growing popular dissatisfaction with our legal system. There is a feeling that it prevents everything and does nothing. . . . [T]he common law finds itself arrayed against the people. . . . Commissions and boards, with summary administrative and inquisitorial powers are called for, and courts are distrusted." And "in large part this dissatisfaction had a real basis and is well founded." The root problem was that the common law, and the legal system, "exhibits too great a respect for the individual, and . . . too little respect for the needs of society."[82] This was vintage Ross, just as Pound's earlier ecology of law was vintage Bessey. Indeed, Ross later recalled pummeling Pound with indictments of the courts, which, at the time, Pound had withstood in silence.[83]

In case after case, Pound judged, the courts had struck down the very legislation the people wanted to protect workers from the worst abuses of large employers. Pound was cautious. He did not (and never would) attack the judges as judges, for "[a]s the law stands, I do not doubt they were rightly determined. But they serve

81. Michael I. Swygert and Jon W. Bruce, "The Historical Origins, Founding, and Early Development of Student-Edited Law Reviews," 36 *Hastings Law Journal* 780, 782 (1985).

82. Roscoe Pound, "Do We Need a Philosophy of Law?," 5 *Columbia Law Review* 342, 343, 344 (1905).

83. Hill, "Roscoe Pound and American Sociology," 387.

to show that the right of the individual to contract as he pleases is upheld by our legal system at the expense of the right of society to stand between our laboring population and oppression." The common law gave to judges the power (and, Pound implied, the duty) to uphold the property rights of individuals, no matter how bent by reality (for the workers who "bargained" for longer hours and accepted jobs with dangerous working conditions had little choice in reality), and that made the common law the defender of an old and now dangerous view of society. "Today we no longer hold that society exists entirely for the sake of the individual. We recognize that society is in some wise a co-worker with each in what he is and in what he does, and that what he does is quite as much wrought through him by society as wrought by himself alone." The common law assumed a level playing field, in which its officers and rules might act the role of neutral referee, but in 1905, there was no such equality. In litigation, the powerful party won, whatever the merits of the case might be. Indeed, the courts allowed "a fortified monopoly to shake its fist in the face of a people and defy investigation or regulation."[84]

But there was a remedy within the law itself. Just as once upon a time, in England, when the common law gave no relief, the king allowed equity to remedy wrongs, so in America, this "residuary authority [within the state] has given us the police power." This source of remedy "is furnishing the antidote for the intense regard for the individual which our legal system exhibits." Pound spoke here as never before—the progressive pragmatist, finding in the bits and pieces of existing law (the pragmatist as a bricoleur) the materials for its reform. "In fact a progressive liberalizing of our constitutional law is noticeable already, and to all appearance, a slow but sure change of front is in progress." But the way was still hard, for the common law (note that Pound did not say the interests or parties whom the common law benefited) "is jealous of all indefinite power." The victory must come from outside the courts then. At this moment, when a conventional progressive would call for a reform of the courts, a more radical critic would argue for a restructuring of the economy, and a socialist would call for a redistribution of power and wealth, Pound hesitated. He wanted a "balance between individualism and socialism." So what was the remedy? For a law

84. Pound, "Philosophy of Law," 345, 346, 347.

school dean, the answer was simple: "To my mind, the remedy is in our law schools. It is in training the rising generation of lawyers in a social, political, and legal philosophy abreast of our time." Law school should require that students immerse themselves in a philosophy of law, but not one that revisited the classics. No—instead, the new philosophy would rest on "the elements of the social and political science of today."[85]

In the *Columbia Law Review* article, Pound used the phrase "popular dissatisfaction," anticipating his most powerful sally into the controversy over the law. Pound often recycled phrases, indeed, repeated entire passages, from older pieces in newer ones. As he grew older and had to give talks and symposia all over this country and elsewhere in the world, such repetition may have been inevitable, but for Pound, it was also a way of refining ideas and reflecting on what he had said. It became, alongside definition by negation and categorization, a hallmark of his style. Pound was always mindful, as well, of his audience. He had been fierce in his ambition to be taken seriously, betraying perhaps a lack of confidence that never left him. After all, he never did finish at Harvard. But the desire to impress and to please audiences went hand in glove with a growing sophistication in knowing what to say to whom. It might seem like disingenuousness, cunning, or even moral cowardice, but it was always there.

Six months after "Do We Need a Philosophy of Law?" was published, Pound gave a talk entitled "The Spirit of the Common Law" at a 1906 Nebraska State Bar Association meeting. It was published in *The Green Bag* in January 1906, and it repeated portions of his *Columbia Law Review* piece. But it differed in important ways as well. The implicit defense of progressive political programs and the condemnation of monopolies and the unequal bargaining position of laborers were gone. Pound was talking to Nebraska judges and lawyers, and he wanted to please them. So he said, "Hence, this same obstinate individualism of the common law, which makes it fit so ill in many a modern niche, may yet prove a necessary bulwark against an exaggerated and enfeebling collectivism." And the lawyers, whose "obstinate conservatism in refusing to take the burden of upholding right from the concrete each, and put it on the abstract all, may yet save for us a valuable—nay an indispensable—element

85. Ibid., 350, 351, 352, 353.

in our institutions." Perhaps Pound had received criticism on the *Columbia Law Review* piece and wished, as the dean of Nebraska's College of Law, to demonstrate his loyalty to the status quo. Perhaps after-dinner speakers are not allowed to be Cassandras. Above all, he knew his audience. On his home ground, Pound dissociated himself from any radical plan of reform.[86]

Nevertheless, running alongside the platitudes was an embryonic political jurisprudence, an analysis of the relationship between law and politics that reached out beyond Nebraska's legal elite to another legal elite, whose reformist bent Pound had seen and pooh-poohed at Harvard. Pound's intellectual reputation, and his chance to leave the Nebraska judges and lawyers behind, depended on a bolder critique than the state bar talk. Pound was hardly the first to assay the larger problems of the courts—indeed, the political reformers of his day had an ongoing argument with the self-congratulatory view of law of the large firms, the ABA, and the highest courts of the land. But Pound decided to take a chance. After all, in 1906, political progressivism was no longer radical. President Theodore Roosevelt was a progressive Republican, and under his prodding, Congress had passed and he had signed acts regulating industries.[87]

Not so long before, Pound had not particularly cared for Roosevelt's bully reformism. When Roosevelt came to Harvard in 1889, Pound wrote to his parents, "Tuesday night Theodore Roosevelt addressed a crowded hall on the subject of Public Life. He talked very virtuously and gave us considerable rot. The latter article as applied to politics is very fashionable here. Everything is to be 'reformed.' The list of reforms upon which we have been lectured here this Winter would fill this sheet. Whatever mugwumpery ideas I may have had before I came have been thoroughly dispelled and I shall be content to be an offensive partisan the rest of my days." In those days, he had no love for the polite reformism of the genteel Democrats, whose mugs were on one side of the political fence and whose wumps occupied the other. As a youth, he later recalled, he flirted with populism. "As I look back now on many performances of my junior and senior year which seemed to me at the time highly creditable, I am persuaded that we were essentially a pack of populists

---

86. Roscoe Pound, "The Spirit of the Common Law," 18 *Green Bag* 17–25 (1906).
87. George Mowry, *The Era of Theodore Roosevelt* (New York, 1958), 207–12.

who took for granted bad motives in everything which the administration [of the University of Nebraska] did because the administration was [he now realized] proceeding on higher lines of which we had no conception." He later thought the populists a little suspect, and though he knew William Jennings Bryan, he was later unmoved by the populist creed.[88]

Pound told Hershey that he was apolitical and in the next sentence gave ample evidence that he was no man of the people. He did not like or trust populism or the antics of the state legislature.[89] As dean of the country's premier legal college, his later dealings with the board of regents and the chancellor were equally disheartening. As he commented on the story of a member of the Harvard Corporation who had spent $250,000 to buy the seat, "I believed such a bargain is much more advantageous to a university than the political bargains that determine such things in some state universities."[90] Pound always opposed the great populist legal program of recall of judges.[91]

But Pound had loyalties. Despite his disclaimers to Hershey, Pound was a diehard Republican, just like his father.[92] The son became chairman of the Republican Party in Lincoln in 1896 and remained active in politics until after the 1906 election. In a time of partisanship, he steered the Republican Party to local victories. More important for his later scholarship, Pound became attracted to the moderate progressive wing of the Republican Party in the early 1900s. Within the party, he favored liberal candidates, but he was opposed to splinter groups, and his views moved to the right when the progressives bolted the Republican Party in 1912.[93] Still, in 1906, some form of progressivism appears to have been more to his liking; in many ways, it was elitist, was pro-business, recognized the value of expertise, and was supported by some members of the

88. Pound to Stephen Pound and Laura Biddlecombe Pound, Sept. 24, 1889, NSHS, MS 911, box 1, folder S.1, vol. F.1; Pound to Olivia Pound, Dec. 17, 1918, NSHS, MS 911, box 1, folder S.1, vol. F.4. By 1918, Pound had been a dean at Nebraska and Harvard for over five years and saw the issues from the other side.

89. Pound to Hershey, Feb. 10, 1895, Sayre Papers.

90. Pound to Laura Biddlecombe Pound, Aug. 16, 1914, NSHS, MS 911, box 1, folder S.1, vol. F.2.

91. Pound to Stephen Pound, Mar. 21, 1911, NSHS, MS 911, box 1, folder S.1, vol. F.2.

92. *Stephen Bosworth Pound* (New York, 1940), n.p.

93. Sayre, *Pound*, 101–5.

legal fraternity. He campaigned hard for progressive candidates in Nebraska. True, Pound had already gone on record as opposing sweeping reforms via the legislature, and he wrote in 1904 that periods of legislative action were periods when the state acted by command and not times when jurisprudence progressed, but these views were subject to change. Might not legislative action be necessary in times when justice demanded immediate relief to the people?

Pound finally got the chance for which he had longed to put personal ambition together with his jurisprudential thinking in 1906 at the ABA convention. While unrest and reform played themselves out in the arena of politics, a large proportion of the elite bar who attended the annual summer outing called the convention of the American Bar Association tried very hard to ignore the turmoil and believed they could hold the line against the ferment. The hall where they met for the closing dinner was decorated with a "lavish" display of "palms, flowers, and bunting."[94] They invited Pound, the Pound who boasted of the spirit of the common law, to give an opening address. What they got was the Pound of "Do We Need a Philosophy of Law?"

Pound's talk, "The Causes of Popular Dissatisfaction with the Administration of Justice," began almost apologetically. For dissatisfaction "with the administration of justice is as old as law. . . . In other words, as long as there have been laws and lawyers, conscientious and well-meaning men have believed that laws were mere arbitrary technicalities, and that the attempt to regulate the relations of mankind in accordance with them resulted largely in injustice." Pound was not one of these good men (a bone he threw to the reform everything faction, however), but he did believe that something more was at stake than inevitable carping by the masses. Again, like the mugwumps, whose posturing (and posture) he derided, Pound hedged his bets. He would not prescribe for the ills, only diagnose them.[95]

94. John A. Matzko, "The ABA," in Gerard W. Gawalt, ed., *The New High Priests: Lawyers in Post–Civil War America* (Westport, Conn., 1984), 75 ff.; "Meetings of the American Bar Association and the Association of American Law Schools—1906," 2 *American Law School Review* 17 (1906).

95. 29 *American Bar Association Reports* 395, 396 (1906). Aichele attributes Pound's unwillingness to condemn the courts and the lawyers directly to his "Midwestern roots," which taught him that "ignorance rather than malice" was the cause of the problem. Aichele, *Legal Realism*, 32. But midwestern roots did not stop William Jennings Bryan and the Populists from accusing the judges of malice.

The diagnosis was a sharp one. "The most important and most constant cause of dissatisfaction with all law at all times is to be found in the necessarily mechanical operation of legal rules." If the courts were to make law uniform (today we would say uphold expectations of parties at law), the rules must be strictly applied. But change had made old rules unjust, for example in employment contracts. The answer was not more discretion, for that led to greater uncertainty, the rationale for mechanical law in the first place. A better answer was to take into account the clash of groups and interests "when a community is divided and diversified, and groups and classes and interests, understanding each other none too well, have conflicting ideas of justice." Law, lawyers, and courts had to be aware of the needs of the many, Pound implied, but as he had promised, he offered no practical way this might be done.[96]

Such gaps between law and "public opinion" (Pound might have said public interest) were common, for "law is often in very truth a government of the living by the dead." It was slow to change, which led people to demand extreme solutions. Indeed, most people assumed that law could be made and changed by anyone, a fact Pound disputed. "Laws may be compared to the formulas of engineers." Only "trained minds" could see the problems and come up with solutions. Pound's critique was thoroughly progressivist, in that he believed in the importance of expertise. His elitism also manifested itself—he was still no democrat. But it was a "collectivist age" in which he and his fellow jurisprudents lived, and law must rise above individual demands to comprehend the good of the whole. No more "sporting" rules of litigation that actually favored the wealthier or more powerful party against the weaker party. No more reliance on individual initiative in bringing suit to protect the public against corrupt or self-seeking public service companies and common carriers. But what was to be done?[97]

Pound rejected the enhanced role of courts as expanders of legal doctrine. That way had brought *Lochner v. New York*[98] and its cousins, as federal courts used substantive due process and freedom of contract to bring down popular legislative enactments. "Such interpretation," Pound opined, "is spurious. It is legislation. And

96. 29 *American Bar Association Reports* 398–417 (1906).
97. Ibid.
98. 198 U.S. 45 (1905).

to interpret an obnoxious rule out of existence rather than to meet it fairly and squarely by legislation is a fruitful source of confusion." Pound wanted courts to steer clear of "the work of the legislature," not to act as miniature legislatures, an attack on the judicial activism (to use a modern term) of the Fuller and White courts. Yet Pound did not lose faith in the power of the courts to reform themselves: "[O]ur administration of justice is not decadent. It is simply behind the times." [99]

A furor erupted at the ABA meeting over a resolution to have Pound's talk reprinted and distributed in advance of its publication in the annual report of the organization.[100] Pound's admirers, led by Dean William Draper Lewis of the University of Pennsylvania School of Law and Dean John Henry Wigmore of Northwestern University (the audience for Pound's *Columbia Law Review* essay, not his addresses to the Nebraska bench and bar), wanted his scathing critique disseminated as quickly as possible to all members of the bench and bar who had not had the opportunity to hear it for themselves. The ABA's conservative old guard responded by condemning Pound's "drastic attack" and defending the orderly, formalistic system of justice that had prevailed for nearly half a century. James D. Andrews found fault with Pound's formulation, claiming that it would undermine the common law as the lawyers knew it. Pound demurred; he did not say that. The progressives retreated in the face of the "repressed indignation of the assemblage," but the altercation signaled a new generation's open break with the old formalist jurisprudence. More important to Pound, he had found a cadre of supporters among the other legal academics. They were active in the ABA and the fledgling Association of American Law Schools (AALS), and they had already begun to think about reform of the law. More important, they placed its center in the law schools. They recognized a kindred spirit in Pound's *Columbia Law Review* piece.[101]

99. 29 *American Bar Association Reports* 398–417 (1906).

100. The account of what happened at the meeting is taken from John Henry Wigmore, "Roscoe Pound's St. Paul Address of 1906: The Spark That Kindled the White Flame of Progress," 20 *Journal of the American Judicature Society* 176 (1937). See also N. E. H. Hull, "Restatement and Reform: A New Perspective on the Origins of the American Law Institute," 8 *Law and History Review* 56–58 (1990), for an analysis of what happened in St. Paul and after among the insurgent law professors.

101. 29 *American Bar Association Reports* 55–65 (1906); Albert Kocourek, "Roscoe Pound as a Former Colleague Knew Him," in *Interpretations of Modern Legal Philoso-*

Wigmore was so impressed that he offered Pound a job at Northwestern, and Pound accepted.[102] After all, as he wrote a decade later to his sister Olivia, "I learned long ago that when anything is going on in the country[,] Nebraska can be relied upon to make it ridiculous."[103] He might be a son of the plains born and bred, but he wanted no part of the plains. Of course, at Northwestern he would still be in the Midwest, and Northwestern was not quite the leading law school that Wigmore hoped to make it, but the call was irresistible. Chicago, where the law school lay, was a major center of learning.

Before he departed Lincoln, Pound wrote one more piece on "spurious interpretation," the theme that closed his ABA address. Again, Pound thought in overlapping linear terms. He used each article as the springboard for the next, reviewing what he had said previously and then going on a little further. Again, he inveighed against "tying down future generations by" a futile longing for perfect expressions of law. Instead, the purpose of judicial interpretation should be to determine the intention of the lawmakers.[104] Spurious interpretation used the courts as a screen to make new law. Pound was hopeful (here he inched forward) that "[a]s legislation becomes stronger and more frequent, examples of this type of [judicial] so-called interpretation will finally become less common. . . . Spurious interpretation is an anachronism in an age of legislation. It is a fiction." Such fictions were common in past times, but now "[p]opular feeling that courts make law, and hence that judges are political officers to be elected as such," was the inevitable end of judicial legislation comporting itself as mere interpretation. The courts and the judges opened themselves to attack in this manner, and the people suspected, with or without reason, that such interpretations merely reflected the political opinions of the judges. Pound's authority for this warning was none other than "Mr. Dooley," the newspaper persona

---

phy: Essays in Honor of Roscoe Pound (New York, 1947), 431 n.27; Wigmore, "Roscoe Pound's St. Paul Address"; William R. Roalfe, *John Henry Wigmore: Scholar and Reformer* (Evanston, Ill., 1977), 107–8; George Wharton Pepper, "William Draper Lewis," 98 *University of Pennsylvania Law Review* 6 (1949); Hull, "Restatement and Reform," 83–85.

102. Roalfe, *Wigmore*, 50–51.

103. Pound to Olivia Pound, June 4, 1918, NSHS, MS 911, box 1, folder S.1, vol. F.4.

104. Pound had taken sides in an ongoing controversy over the use of legislative histories in courts. See Johnson, *American Legal Culture*, 78–79.

of Peter Finley Dunne, whose famous aphorism, "the coort follows th' iliction rethurns," had become common wisdom.[105]

Pound also pushed ahead with the sociological jurisprudence project, again building on an earlier piece. He placed "The Need of a Sociology of Jurisprudence" in *The Green Bag*. He began with the message of the ABA address: "[I]t must be admitted that the law of the land has not the real hold upon the American people that law should have." The cause was not lawlessness per se, but "the fault must be laid largely to the law and to the manner in which law is taught and expounded." Teachers of law could no longer dismiss "sociological principles," but were to apply them "to the problems of state and municipal life." Data must be collected on the actual administration of law (a project that legal academics like Charles E. Clark, William O. Douglas, and Underhill Moore of Yale thought they invented in the 1920s[106]). What was more, "pseudo-philosophies" of law should be cast off and replaced with the solid social sciences that had remade European science of the law. Pound had by now read Eugen Ehrlich and was greatly impressed with the Austrian's theory of sociological causation of law. This was the missing portion of Pound's 1904 call for a sociology of law. Once more, Pound inched ahead. "We must reinvestigate the theories of justice, of law, and of rights. We must seek the basis of doctrines, not in Blackstone's wisdom of our ancestors, not in the apocryphal reasons of the beginnings of legal science, not in their history, useful as that is in enabling us to appraise doctrines at their true value, but in a scientific apprehension of the relations of law to society and of the needs and interests and opinions of society of to-day."

Pound did not sound the charge against the courts—they must still be respected. His adversaries were the law school professors. Yes, he admitted, they had to train their charges to make a living, but this was only a weak excuse for the law professors' indifference to the flaws in "traditional legal pseudo-science." Instead, "the modern teacher of law should be a student of sociology, economics, and politics as well [as formal rules of law]." For "law is a means, not an end," and Pound judged that end to be "away from the older individualism" and "property rights" toward a larger goal. Modern

105. Roscoe Pound, "Spurious Interpretation," 7 *Columbia Law Review* 381–85 (1907).

106. Schlegel, *American Legal Realism*, 81–146.

legislation limiting the independence of large employers, providing insurance to workers, and repudiating contributory negligence doctrines showed that way. Pound quoted as his authority Theodore Roosevelt, the latter demanding that the financial burden of accidents be shifted from the shoulders of the poor working person and be shared by the employer. Pound verged on the creed that whoever would be a teacher of law must be its critic, for he concluded that "if in so doing [a social and economic analysis] they must often take issue with courts and practitioners and books of authority as to the nature of justice and of rights and the basis of current legal conceptions and of received principles," then so be it.[107]

Pound sent his piece to Ross, by then at Wisconsin, and Ross knew a convert when he saw one and continued to encourage Pound. After reading the 1907 packet of Pound's offprints, Ross reported, "Your distinction between the civil and the criminal liability of the members of a corporate aggregate is splendid, and if that is a sample of your discussion of the relation of law to the current needs of society, your book will be of very great aid to all of us." Two years later, Ross again flattered Pound: "I am glad to get your letter and to learn how near you are to the completion of your studies in sociological jurisprudence. I will bet a million the book will make far more of a splash than any law book could have created."[108] Pound's cover letters must have promised the imminent completion of the same book on sociological jurisprudence that Pound described to Bessey in 1904. In fact, that book was never written, though Pound did make another start on it at Harvard in the following decade and continued to talk about it until his final years.[109]

107. Roscoe Pound, "The Need of a Sociology of Jurisprudence," 19 *Green Bag* 608, 609, 610, 611, 612, 613, 614, 615 (1907). Pound was later angry at Roosevelt for quoting, without attribution and almost verbatim, Pound's attack on *Lochner* in his Yale piece on "Liberty of Contract." See Pound to Stephen Pound, Mar. 21, 1911, NSHS, MS 911, box 1, folder S.1, vol. F.2: "He has merely transposed sentences, like a boy writing a theme out of the cyclopedia. . . . A busy man has to do such things, I suppose, but really our great statesmen show very badly alongside the English statesmen who manage to be scholars."

108. Ross to Pound, Dec. 19, 1907, and Jan. 7, 1909, RPP, 227–28.

109. Roscoe Pound, in "The Scope and Purpose of Sociological Jurisprudence," a three-part article appearing in 24 *Harvard Law Review* 591–619 (1911) and 25 *Harvard Law Review* 140–68, 489–516 (1912), made the case for a book without mentioning its prospects. Roscoe Pound, "The End of Law as Developed in Juristic Thought," 27 *Harvard Law Review* 605 (1914), has the following "Note": "[T]he substance of this paper

Pound's progressivism was in full flower in these pieces, however—witness his bow to Roosevelt (whose talk at Harvard years before Pound had dismissed as rubbish). But Pound was ever the bricoleur, using the materials at hand. His tactic of pressing for reform of legal education perfectly suited his own station. As a legal educator, he was an insider, and one of increasing reputation and influence. As bricoleur, he had used botany and sociology; he could also deploy pragmatism. What was meant by a science of law? Pound the progressive pragmatist answered in a fashion that would have done any pragmatist proud. For a science was nothing more than a body of actual knowledge, a set of working behaviors. There should be no mystery and no metaphysics to it. Such a law "has the practical function of adjusting everyday relations so as to meet current ideas of fair play." [110]

Pound did not cite Charles Sanders Peirce, but he did refer to William James's attack on metaphysics in philosophy. The analogy to law was so obvious to Pound as to cause genuine pain. "The nadir of mechanical jurisprudence is reached when conceptions are used, not as premises from which to reason, but as ultimate solutions. So used, they become empty words. . . . Current decisions and discussions are full of such solving words: estoppel, malice, privity, implied, intention of the testator, vested and contingent—when we arrive at these we are assumed to be at the end of our juristic search. Like Habib in the Arabian Nights, we wave aloft our scimitar and pronounce the talismanic word." Pound's deconstruction of the mechanical words of law, and the formalism that made such words into the end products of deductive reasoning, was far ahead of its time in the legal academy. What was more, Pound was giving this lecture to the bar of North Dakota. He had thrown his mincing caution to the winds and firmly aligned himself with the pragmatists. The claim to a jurisprudence based on absolute scientific truths of law was a sham. "In truth it is not a science at all. . . . In the philosophy of today, theories are 'instruments, not answers to enigmas.'" Pound was certain that "we have to rid ourselves of this sort of legal-

---

will appear in a book to be entitled 'Sociological Jurisprudence.'" The article was continued in 30 *Harvard Law Review* 201–25 (1917), but the book never appeared. Pound later claimed to Sayre that his eyes had given out in 1928. Pound to Sayre, Oct. 1, 1946, NSHS, box 1, folder S.1, vol. F.20.

110. Roscoe Pound, "Mechanical Jurisprudence," 8 *Columbia Law Review* 101–16 (1908).

ity and to attain a pragmatic, a sociological legal science." In fact, the two concepts were not necessarily united, yet for Pound they were, for his pragmatism was not a philosophical game but a way to progressive reform of the law. Pragmatic jurisprudence was not a jurisprudence of endless self-doubt but a "jurisprudence of ends." [111]

In rejecting a jurisprudence of conceptions, a critique that Pound developed and that remains current with leading historians of jurisprudence, as one of ends, Pound's aim was to attack the current status of "our case law," for it had failed "to respond to vital needs of present day life." And Pound was ready at least to limn out those areas of case law wherein courts and lawyers had failed the needs of the people. In the law of partnerships, the courts' insistence on deducing the rules of partnership from an abstract theory of joint obligation instead of "ascertaining and giving effect to the actual situation as understood and practiced by merchants" was an obvious case of conceptualism holding back businessmen. The idea of looking at the actual practice of merchants was at least as old as Mansfield's use of juries of merchants in the 1760s, and Pound admitted as much, but Pound updated Mansfield even while praising the great jurist's contributions.[112] It was not the rigidity of the common law per se that Pound criticized, but the formalism of Gilded Age judges. He bewailed the failure of courts to find a way to extend employer liability for injuries to workers, the inability to prevent discrimination by public utility companies, and the incapacity of the courts to pierce the corporate veil to protect the interests of investors against corrupt or mismanaged corporate enterprises—"all these failures, and many more might be adduced, speak for themselves." [113]

Worse still was the deathlike grasp of doctrines like "[Herbert] Spencer's Social Statics" on the United States Supreme Court, within whose precincts "rules that have been deduced . . . obstruct the way of social progress." The Court had failed in its duty to "inquire what the effect of such a deduction [of freedom of contract]

111. Ibid.
112. This was the central theme of Karl Llewellyn's draftsmanship in the Uniform Commercial Code (UCC), on which see chapter 6, and Llewellyn privately (that private discourse again) admitted that Pound might had been ahead of him in this. He sent a picture of himself to Pound in the late 1930s, inscribed "To Roscoe Pound, Who Still Leads the Way." On Llewellyn and the custom of merchants in the UCC, see pages 295–300 below. Pound had changed his mind on Mansfield.
113. Pound, "Mechanical Jurisprudence."

will be, when applied to the actual situation." Using formal, instead of instrumental, reasoning, the majority failed to grasp that setting aside a New York statute limiting the hours bakers might labor did not give bakers more freedom to bargain with their employers, but gave employers more power to oppress the bakers. "Deductions from this and like conceptions, assumed to express the meaning and the sole meaning of the [due process] clause [of the Fourteenth Amendment,] have given us rules which, when applied to the existing commercial and industrial situation, are wholly inadequate."[114]

The answer was legislation. Pound had finally slipped the bonds that prevented him from fully adopting a pro-legislative stance. Here, he insisted, "[w]e must soon have a new starting point that only legislation can afford. That we must put the sociological, the pragmatic theory behind legislation, is demonstrated every day. Legislative reference bureaus, the Conference of Commissioners on Uniform State Laws, such hearings as the one before the Interstate Commerce Commission . . . hearings before legislative committees, such conferences as the one held recently with respect to the Sherman Anti-Trust Law, bar-association discussions of reforms in procedure—all these are furnishing abundant material for legislation of the best type." The future was one of legislation, in which "common-law lawyers will some day abandon their traditional attitude toward legislation; will welcome legislation and make it what it should be." In this effort, the jurists, as in the days of the Roman republic, would again become leading interpreters of the law.[115] Here was the Pound who might justly be called the founder of progressive pragmatism in the law school, for it would be the new generation of law students—his students—and law professors who would bring the millennium on.

To his side in this quest he summoned philosophy, sociology, history, and the more traditional sources of legal study—a bricolage of disciplines. With him stood Oliver Wendell Holmes, Jr. (whose dissent in *Lochner* Pound had quoted with approval), Mansfield, Bentham, William James, and the characters of the Arabian Nights—a fictive network of right-thinking men. Pound had fabricated from the bits and pieces of old jurisprudence and modern case law a powerful restatement of what was wrong with American jurisprudence.

114. Ibid., 108–9. Pound expanded on these views in his "Liberty of Contract," 18 *Yale Law Journal* 454–87 (1909).
115. Pound, "Mechanical Jurisprudence," 112.

And in his last footnote, he offered it and himself to the audience he had always wanted to impress. Note 70 of "Mechanical Jurisprudence" read: "The restating and rationalizing of our law of partnership upon which Professor Ames is engaged for the Commission on Uniform State Laws is a striking example [in text: of the opportunity to "lay sure foundations for the ultimate legislative restatement of the law"]."[116] Eyes still on the prize: Ames's Harvard.

But first, three years in Chicago—two at Northwestern, under the aegis of Wigmore, and one at the University of Chicago School of Law. Both schools were in the city, and Northwestern offered to match Chicago on salary, but Pound was ambitious, and Chicago was a better school than Northwestern. In the city, in those three years, Pound came to know the learned progressivism of Chicago's Ernst Freund, the empiricism of sociologist Albion Small, and through Ross, with whom Pound regularly corresponded, the reformist energy of the Social Science Club at the University of Chicago. His former student Edith Abbott introduced Pound to the circle of Jane Addams at Hull House. There Pound became interested in social work and joined the Juvenile Court Committee. Pound had longed for such interdisciplinary companionship since he left Harvard in 1891, and it gave vitality to his jurisprudence. At Chicago, Pound found a clique of pragmatists and progressives whose agenda included free speech and social science research. He felt right at home.[117]

It was during his Chicago sojourn that he wrote his most scathing indictment of the old jurisprudence, his attack on the doctrine of "Liberty of Contract." The doctrine underlay a series of cases in which appellate courts had struck down legislative provisions for hours, wages, and safety conditions in the workplace. Pound's attack was direct, learned, composed, and compelling. He quoted from the United States Supreme Court's opinion in *Adair v. United States*[118] written by Justice John Marshall Harlan: "'In all such particulars [as terms of labor, conditions of labor, and termination of labor] the employer and the employee have equality of right, and

116. Ibid., 116 n.70, 112.
117. Paul D. Carrington, "The Missionary Diocese of Chicago," 44 *Journal of Legal Education* 503–13 (1994); David Wigdor, *Roscoe Pound, Philosopher of Law* (Westport, Conn., 1974), 133–59; David M. Rabban, "Free Speech in Progressive Social Thought," 74 *Texas Law Review* 989–90 (1996).
118. 208 U.S. 161 (1908).

any legislation that disturbs that equality is an arbitrary interference with the liberty of contract, which no government can legally justify in a free land.'" Pound had little sympathy for the fact that free labor had been a liberating doctrine in the antebellum political world or that for Harlan, a former slaveholder, to espouse it was not entirely illiberal. Pound, whose intellectual pleasure in ideological developments was elsewhere, apparently had no patience for the ideology behind this distortion of simple facts. "With this positive declaration of a lawyer [in this context almost a derogatory reference, and about the only occasion Pound used it so], the culmination of a line of decisions now nearly twenty-five years old, a statement which a recent writer on the science of jurisprudence has deemed so fundamental as to deserve quotation and exposition at an unusual length, as compared with his treatment of other points, let us compare the equally positive statement of a sociologist: 'Much of the discussion about "equal rights" is utterly hollow. All the ado made over the system of contract is surcharged with fallacy' [Ward's *Applied Sociology*]." For Pound, it was not merely a matter of preferring sociological observation to legal doctrine, for "[t]o everyone acquainted at first hand with actual industrial conditions the latter statement goes without saying. Why, then, do courts persist in the fallacy?" Pound could have stopped here, but his indignation (and the plaudits of his social science comrades in Chicago) bid him continue in what was perhaps his finest rhetorical writing. "Why do so many of them force upon legislation an academic theory of equality in the face of practical conditions of inequality? Why do we find a great and learned court in 1908 taking the long step into the past of dealing with the relation between employer and employee in railway transportation, as if the parties were individuals—as if they were farmers haggling over the sale of a horse? Why is the legal conception of the relation of employer and employee so at variance with the common knowledge of mankind?"[119]

Pound rejected the easy answers—the bias of the judges, the politics of law. The root causes of the malady were as deep as its injustices. He had a little list: the court "exaggerates the importance of property and of contract, exaggerates private right at the expense

---

119. Pound, "Liberty of Contract," 454, 455. Lester Frank Ward was a democratic sociologist and federal civil servant who believed in liberal social planning. Paul F. Boller, Jr., *American Thought in Transition* (Chicago, 1969), 65–69.

of public right, and is hostile to legislation." The court was the prisoner of mechanical jurisprudence, "in which deduction from conceptions has produced a cloud of rules that obscures the principles from which they were drawn . . . and in which the artificiality characteristic of legal reasoning is exaggerated. . . . Purely juristic notions of the state and of economics and politics" trumped "social conceptions of the present." The judges were still trained in eighteenth-century philosophy "because it is to be found in law-sheep bindings." The formal equality of the natural law language of the Bill of Rights obscured the reality of the human condition. The comparative youth of labor law made it prey to misconception. And finally, and "by no means least, [there was] the sharp line between law and fact in our legal system which requires constitutionality, as a legal question, to be tried by artificial criteria of general application and prevents effective judicial investigation or consideration of the situations of fact behind or bearing upon the statutes."[120]

The last was the kicker—for Pound was attacking the intentional blindness of appellate courts of law to the facts of the case. Appellate courts heard cases on grounds of legal error. Courts of equity (separate from federal courts of law until 1938) could call for additional factual investigations; law courts could not. But Pound reminded the courts that they worked in an age of bewildering factual complexity. They needed to come closer to the reality of that world, not move away from it. "As it is, in the ordinary case involving constitutionality, the [appellate] court has no machinery for getting at the facts. It must decide on the basis of matters of general knowledge and on accepted principles of uniform application. It cannot have the advantage of legislative reference bureaus, of hearing before committee, of the testimony of specialists who have conducted detailed investigations, as the legislature can and does. The court is driven to deal with problems artificially or not at all, unless it is willing to assume that the legislature did its duty and to keep its hands off on that ground." But this is what the High Court was refusing to do in *Lochner, Adair,* and other "liberty of contract" cases. And the result was "lost respect for courts and law. . . . The evil of those cases will live after them in impaired authority of the courts long after the decisions themselves are forgotten."[121]

120. Pound, "Liberty of Contract," 469–70.
121. Ibid., 487.

For Pound, the search for an American jurisprudence had led through the European schools to the home shore, to a combination of progressive political advocacy and pragmatic social insight. But Pound was a careful man, and his jurisprudential ventures never outreached his grasp. As committed as he was to reform, it was a muted commitment, muted by his legalism, by his native caution, and by his ambition for a prize beyond the Midwest.[122] In 1910, Dean Ezra Ripley Thayer of Harvard offered Pound what he wanted—Harvard Law School—and Pound eagerly accepted.

122. But consider how far Pound had outdistanced the pack. Jerome Frank, of whom more later, credited Joseph W. Bingham of Stanford Law School with the initial destruction of what Frank called "Rule Fetishism" in the law, thus being the precursor of legal realism. Jerome Frank, *Law and the Modern Mind* (New York, 1930), 295. In 1911, Bingham wrote that the positivist creed, that law is an authoritative system of rules and principles, was rubbish. Instead, the rules of law were mental constructs, and they had the same status as "rules and principles of biology or of architecture or of any other science or art." Joseph W. Bingham, "What Is the Law," 11 *Michigan Law Review* 22 (1912). He repeated his point in the face of opposition from more conservative thinkers; see, e.g., Joseph W. Bingham, "Science and the Law," 25 *Green Bag* 165 (1913); Joseph W. Bingham, "Legal Philosophy and the Law," 9 *Illinois Law Review* 99 (1914). Bingham did not ask where such mental constructs arose, however; nor did he argue that they were imbedded in culture; nor did he apply his argument to current cases. Pound was far ahead of Bingham.

Note that Pound did not believe that law was a "science." Here, again, G. Edward White, "The American Law Institute and the Triumph of Modernist Jurisprudence," 15 *Law and History Review* 26 (1997) ("even the most adventurous twentieth-century juristic reformers were deeply committed to the proposition that law was a science"), is totally misleading.

CHAPTER TWO

Pound Finds Joy and Heartache at Harvard

Pound taught summer school at Chicago in 1910 and then went off to Cambridge. He was ecstatic at what he found. "The library is the best in the country," he wrote to his mother. "My office has been fitted up luxuriously by the school. I have plenty of stenographic assistance without expense to me. Then the students are better than I supposed could be anywhere." [1] And then there was Cambridge. The greater Boston area may no longer have been the Athens of America, but it was home to two great Solons of the law: Oliver Wendell Holmes, Jr., and Louis Brandeis. Both were Harvard men and remained intimately involved in the operation of the law school. Both were also men of liberal politics, though Holmes could blow hot and cold. Both men supported Pound's appointment to the faculty. Holmes wrote in 1911, "I was rejoiced that Harvard should have got Pound," and Brandeis thought Pound an invaluable ally. In return, Pound strongly supported Brandeis when the latter's appointment to the United States Supreme Court was under fire from members of the Boston legal community and defended Holmes's dissents in *Lochner* and *Abrams v. United States*.[2]

1. Roscoe Pound to Laura Biddlecombe Pound, Dec. 12, 1910, NSHS, MS 911, box 1, folder S.1, vol. F.2.
2. Oliver Wendell Holmes, Jr., to Frederick Pollock, Dec. 31, 1911, in Mark DeWolfe Howe, ed., *The Holmes-Pollock Letters: The Correspondence of Mr. Justice Holmes and Sir Frederick Pollock* (2nd ed., Cambridge, Mass., 1961), 1:187; Harold Laski to Holmes, Nov. 27, 1919, in Mark DeWolfe Howe, ed., *The Holmes-Laski Letters, The Correspondence of Mr. Justice Holmes and Harold J. Laski, 1916–1935* (Cambridge, Mass., 1953), 1:223; Leonard Baker, *Brandeis and Frankfurter, A Dual Biography* (New York, 1986), 72, 108; Pound to Louis Brandeis, Nov. 30, 1914, RPP, 156-2; 250 U.S. 616 (1919).

John Henry Wigmore, too, had reconciled himself to the loss of Pound. On March 29, 1910, Wigmore wrote to Pound to congratulate him on his appointment as Story Professor of Law at Harvard Law School.[3] Wigmore had gotten over his mixed feelings about Chicago's raid that carried off Pound, but he knew that he had lost a rising star.[4] Wigmore confided to Pound that he had not been surprised by Harvard's announcement of Pound's appointment, for "[s]ome weeks ago [Harvard University] President [A. Lawrence] Lowell wrote to ask my opinion; and I replied sincerely that I considered you the most eligible man in the United States for the place, and that the Harvard Law School could do itself no greater service than to acquire you."[5] Despite any disappointment he might have felt the year before when Pound had abandoned him for Chicago,[6] Wigmore still believed in Pound's talent and vision. Wigmore enclosed a short poem he had penned in his colleague's honor:

> All hail the newest star, now fixed amidst our constellation!
> A brilliant varied spectrum marks your lofty stellar station.
> As sociologic jurist, may the message of your pen
> Widely spread a mighty influence, from your editorial den!
> When Pharaoh set the Israelites to make bricks without straw,
> He didn't know how harder 'twould be to reform the law;
> But Pharaoh had his Moses; *you*'re the Moses by whose hand
> Our Common law will pass from bondage to the promised
>   land.[7]

Leaving aside Wigmore's obvious limitations as a poet, the symbolism he employed is striking. At first, Wigmore saluted Pound as a new star among the constellation of stars within the legal academy, the equal of Wigmore and other law professors of the first rank. Not satisfied with his encomium, in the second half of the poem Wigmore anointed Pound prophet of that elite. Likening Pound to Moses, Wigmore placed on the shoulders of the not quite forty-

---

3. John Henry Wigmore to Pound, Mar. 29, 1910, RPP, 231-10.

4. William R. Roalfe, *John Henry Wigmore: Scholar and Reformer* (Evanston, Ill., 1977), 51; Paul Sayre, *The Life of Roscoe Pound* (Iowa City, 1948), 154.

5. Sayre, *Pound*, 154.

6. Wigmore could not help but opine again about Pound's defection the year before even as he congratulated him on the Harvard appointment: "But after all, isn't it a pity now that you didn't wait just a year before abandoning our letter-heads? That would have spared us the regrets of seeing you encamped just across the street from us." Wigmore to Pound, Mar. 29, 1910, RPP, 231-10.

7. Poem handwritten on card enclosed with letter of March 29, 1910, cited in the previous note.

year-old Nebraskan the mantle of prophet and leader of a people in the wilderness. Pound's task, according to Wigmore, was even greater than that of Moses: to reform the common law, freeing it from the shackles of nineteenth-century formalist legal thought and bringing it to the promised land of progressive jurisprudence. His appointment to Harvard would therefore provide Pound the most prominent pulpit from which to propound and effectively indoctrinate the elite and future elite of the profession.

Even as Wigmore enthusiastically congratulated Pound and Harvard on their alliance, he expressed a reservation about the appointment that was prophetic (and as in all good prophecy, rooted in experience; after all, Wigmore was a dean and a Harvard alumnus). Pound's senior by only seven years, Wigmore counseled Pound, "Being older than you, I can take liberty and express the hope that you will not allow the traditions and inertia and complacency of an age-honoured institution to congeal or ossify your living zeal or any of your well-defined views. You know what the usual fate of the opposition is when it accepts office as the Party in Power." [8] The danger was as real as the opportunity. Led by Pound, Harvard Law School could become the fount of reforming jurisprudence, but slowed by the conservatism of Harvard alumni and the temptations of corporate contributions to the school, Pound's reformism might wither. The prophet might become a priest. But not yet—indeed, Wigmore's reputation would wither among the reformers long before Pound's.

To Harvard Pound carried with him the reputation of being the most energetic and forceful of the new American school of jurisprudents. Frederick Pollock, in a letter to Holmes, described Pound as "monstrously learned." [9] But as we have seen, Pound was a bricoleur, not an inventor. By borrowing from Edward Ross and Charles Bessey, incorporating pragmatic and instrumentalist impulses, rereading Jeremy Bentham and the German social theorists, and drawing on his law school teaching and administrative experience, he had made sociological jurisprudence American. But he had not found an American jurisprudence. He had issued the call and explained the need for such a jurisprudence; he had offered sociology as its organizing principle; he had diagnosed the ills of mechanical

8. Wigmore to Pound, Mar. 29, 1910, RPP, 231-10.
9. Frederick Pollock to Holmes, Dec. 9, 1915, in Howe, *Holmes-Pollock Letters,* 1:228.

jurisprudence and formalistic judging; but he had not fully articulated an alternative. Still, at forty, he was at the height of his powers,
and in the coming years, he would assay two approaches to that
alternative. First, he rummaged through the cupboard of European
jurisprudence once again and found there (to mix a metaphor) two
heros—Rudolph von Ihering and Eugen Ehrlich. He became their
advocate, but advocacy of the German social school did not quite
solve the American problem in a world that was edging toward class
war and dynastic carnage on a scale never before seen. Second,
Pound sought younger acolytes, whose careers he supported and
whose ideas he encouraged. Perhaps they could find a way if he
could not.

But old business first: who belonged in the pantheon of European jurisprudents? Pound again defined his position by negation.
In the fall of 1910, Pound was serving on Wigmore's Association of
American Law Schools Committee on the Study of Jurisprudence
and Philosophy of Law, which had undertaken to sponsor the publication of translations of important European works of legal philosophy.[10] The publication project was another way the law professors sought to promote broad jurisprudential thinking about law
among practicing lawyers and law students.

The first order of business for the AALS committee was to agree
on those works for inclusion in the series—the consecration of the
canon of legal philosophy. One might have expected intellectual
consensus among the five members of the committee, for all represented the progressive wing of legal academia. In addition to Wigmore and Pound, the committee included Ernst Freund from Chicago; Ernest Lorenzen, then at George Washington University; and
Charles Huberich at Stanford University. A dispute between Pound
and Wigmore disrupted the concordance. Wigmore strongly felt
that one of the "necessary books"[11] was an essay by French legal
philosopher Alphonse Boistel.[12] According to Wigmore, Boistel's

10. The Modern Legal Philosophy Series was initiated by the AALS in 1910.

11. Wigmore, Memorandum to Members of the Committee on the Study of Jurisprudence and Philosophy of Law, Nov. 10, 1910, RPP, 231-10.

12. Alphonse Bartolome Martin Boistel (1836–1908) was a professor of jurisprudence at the universities of Grenoble and Paris. He wrote several books about family law
and commercial law as well as legal theory. His notable jurisprudential works included
De l'Indivisibilite Solutionee (1866) and *Cours Elementaire de droit naturel* (1870). The
book that Wigmore probably intended to include was Boistel's *Théorie Juridique de*

tome was "the only book which I have seen (except Kohler,[13] and he does it better than Kohler) which discusses the moral, ethical and social reasons for particular legal rules and institutions."[14] Pound strongly objected. As Wigmore summarized Pound's objections, "Brother Pound says that 'Boistel, in common with all French men, is much behind the time in the matter of so called natural law.'"[15]

Pound had taken exception to the promulgation of what he believed was an outmoded nineteenth-century natural law philosophy—the very sort of thinking that he was fighting. Why should the committee canonize and promulgate those very ideas that its members, as progressive legal philosophers and educators, were trying to replace? In contrast, Wigmore believed that the series should "give a hearing to all leading schools if possible and let our people have the benefit of thinking it out for themselves."[16]

The controversy between Wigmore and Pound over the inclusion of Boistel was more than a question of whether the series should serve as a partisan forum for the new jurisprudence. It was also a controversy over what the new jurisprudence was. Wigmore was a complex combination of progressive legal academic and moralistic legal philosopher whose innate conservatism would make him less and less responsive to reform in the coming years. Long before his World War I display of jingoistic conservatism,[17] Wigmore revealed himself in this controversy as an advocate of nineteenth-century moralistic, natural law philosophy and polled the rest of the committee for their "various choices and views on all these matters."[18]

---

compte courant (1883). My thanks to my research assistant, William Deyerle, for his diligent work in finding a biographical entry for Boistel in *Enciclopedia universal ilustrada,* Tomo VIII, 1370 (Barcelona, Spain).

13. Josef Kohler's (1849–1919) *The Philosophy of Law* was later published at volume 12 of the Modern Legal Philosophy Series. *The Philosophy of Law,* trans. Adolbert Albrecht (Boston, 1914). It is not surprising that Kohler rather than Boistel was included in the series. Kohler, a professor at the University of Berlin, was considered "an early representative of the sociological school of jurisprudence, which focused on the social purpose of law." *New Encyclopaedia Britannica* (15th ed., Chicago, 1990), 6:932.

14. Wigmore, Memorandum to Members of the Committee on the Study of Jurisprudence and Philosophy of Law, Nov. 10, 1910, RPP, 231-10.

15. Ibid.

16. Ibid.

17. Wigmore was fiercely patriotic and opposed pacifism and radical reform during the World War I era. His intolerance of dissent during and after the war estranged him from many progressives. See Roalfe, *Wigmore,* 144–54.

18. Wigmore, Memorandum, Nov. 10, 1910.

Pound apparently reiterated his strong views in a letter to Wigmore,[19] and Wigmore, failing to muster support from the rest of the committee, yielded Boistel for a substitute, Luigi Miraglia's *Comparative Legal Philosophy*.[20] Wigmore commended Miraglia's approach to Pound in terms designed to gain Pound's support. "The author's general attitude seems to be an open minded one, and upon a very cursory inspection of the first part of the book, I conclude that he himself favors the positivist attitude."[21] Pound did not easily acquiesce in Wigmore's compromise, however.[22] Wigmore replied with his own complaint that "I think I have done most of the proposing, and anyone who for the third time votes against my proposal, is in duty bound to bring up a proposal of his own."[23] Pound relented, and Miraglia's *Philosophy* was issued as the third volume in the Modern Legal Philosophy Series. Boistel disappeared from American jurisprudential consciousness.[24]

The next year, Pound proposed his own pantheon of essential European writings in his three-part "The Scope and Purpose of Sociological Jurisprudence," published in the *Harvard Law Review*. In one sense, it was a disappointing performance, for it ended where it might have begun, with a call for a new kind of jurisprudence. Critics have noted the whimper at the end of Pound's essay.[25] Were

---

19. Wigmore refers to Pound's letter (no copy remains) in a letter he wrote to Pound. Wigmore to Pound, Jan. 12, 1911, RPP, 231-10.

20. Luigi Miraglia (1846–1903) was a professor of the philosophy of law at the University of Naples.

21. Wigmore to Pound, Jan. 12, 1911, RPP, 231-10.

22. There is no copy of Pound's letter to Wigmore, but a letter from Wigmore to Pound refers to Pound's letter and its contents. Wigmore to Pound, Mar. 6, 1911, RPP, 231-10.

23. Ibid.

24. Luigi Miraglia, *Comparative Legal Philosophy Applied to Legal Institutions*, trans. John Lisle (Boston, 1912). A search in the card catalogues of the Rutgers main and law libraries, Columbia Law Library, and New York University Law Library; the *Encyclopedia of Philosophy*; and John Arthur Passmore's book on the history of philosophy, *A Hundred Years of Philosophy* (New York, 1967), did not reveal any trace of Boistel. Whether his obscurity vindicates Pound's judgment of his work or whether it is an indication of the power of canonization (or lack thereof) through great books series like the Modern Legal Philosophy Series would be difficult to gauge.

25. See, e.g., Richard A. Cosgrove, *Our Lady the Common Law: An Anglo-American Legal Community, 1870–1930* (New York, 1987), 205, 206 (Pound had abandoned "the legal radicalism of his youth"); Alan Hunt, *The Sociological Movement in Law* (Philadelphia, 1978), 33–36 (Pound's theory clever and insightful but without an adequate or consistent theoretic basis); G. Edward White, "From Sociological Jurisprudence to Realism," 58 *Virginia Law Review* 1013 (1972) (Pound's sociological ideas, rooted in pro-

expectations not so high, Pound's literate, readable, and insightful survey of European schools would have been taken as proof of his scholarly powers. From our distance, it is hard to credit the extent to which Pound made these theorists available to a broad lawyerly reading audience. Nor was he a mere popularizer, as he demonstrated over and over (albeit covertly). Those philosophers who defended individual rights (like Boistel) he denigrated, and those who celebrated the collective and purposive nature of law, its instrumentalism, he praised.[26]

Foremost among the latter was Rudolph von Ihering. "A great Romanist, von Ihering saw, none the less, the futility of the jurisprudence of conceptions which the historical school had built upon the classical Roman law, and stood for a jurisprudence of actualities. Moreover, legislation was developing steadily in Germany as a living organ of the law, and this development was refuting a fundamental position of the orthodox historical jurisprudence." Pound did not mention that the discarded tenet was one he himself held until recently: that legislation, as the command of the state, could not but retard the growth of jurisprudence. But von Ihering knew (Pound knew at least and gave the words to von Ihering) that the jurist "must not merely perceive how it [law] has developed, but for what purpose and to what end. He is not to draw the conclusion that legal doctrines and legal institutions are to be left to work themselves out blindly in their own way. They have not so worked themselves out in the past, but have been fashioned by human minds to meet human ends." In this, as in other crucial respects, "all exposition of the doctrines and achievements of the social utilitarians must take account of Ihering's personality." For von Ihering badgered and bullied modern jurisprudence into focusing on "the interests which the legal system secures rather than upon the rights by which it secures them." In time, von Ihering saw that one could not divorce the "is" from the "ought" in law. Pound advocated von Ihering's theory that law grew out of the struggle of interest groups

---

gressive impulses, supplanted by newer set of ideas); David Wigdor, *Roscoe Pound, Philosopher of Law* (Westport, Conn., 1979), 209 (Pound's larger loyalties to the common law and to the ideal of an organic growth of society prevented him from exploring the implications of sociological jurisprudence).

26. Pound, "The Scope and Purpose of Sociological Jurisprudence" (pt. 2), 25 *Harvard Law Review* 160 (1912).

to vindicate themselves and the law ought to favor those interests that promoted the social good.[27]

That interest groups struggled for control of American government was hardly intellectual news. James Madison had suggested as much in *The Federalist Number 10,* but Madison saw such groups as fixed in nature: there were commercial interests and agrarian interests. Pound had already argued that interests were products of history; thus, the groups that contested for the law at any one time were products of that time. For example, the battle of capital and organized labor that was endemic in Pound's time was only a cloud no bigger than a man's hand on Madison's horizon. Pound's achievement was real, for it led him to a powerful conclusion not in *The Federalist:* "[T]o one who thinks of society as recognizing interests and creating rights to secure them, law is very likely to be something made rather than found." So much for formalism or a jurisprudence of concepts, as Pound derisively termed the old paradigm.[28]

The inference led Pound to a powerful social insight: "[T]he conception of law as a means toward social ends, the doctrine that law exists to secure interests, social, public, and private, requires the jurist to keep in touch with life." The teacher of law, the treatise writer, and the judge (cum jurisprudent) must all take a big bite of reality. No more hiding oneself or one's opinions in the mysterious cloak of "wholly abstract considerations"—a challenge to every judge who did so and every teacher who was not "up" on the latest newspaper reports and sociological data. But Pound stopped short of prescribing. He was still the diagnostician, and he had little patience for the jurisprudence that argued law was nothing more than the "manifestation of the will of the dominant social class, determined by economic motives." Such analysis was nothing more than a variant of the Austinian school, for it had no room for historical context; that is, it was unreal, prescriptive, and uncompromising. Indeed, "the doctrine, which purports to rest on history, is refuted by history."[29]

One would expect that, following this powerful exegesis of the sociological method, Pound would offer some concrete suggestions.

27. Ibid., 140, 141, 143; Edgar Bodenhamer, *Jurisprudence, the Philosophy and Method of the Law* (rev. ed., Cambridge, Mass., 1974), 88–90.

28. Pound, "Scope and Purpose," 145.

29. Ibid., 146, 147, 166, 167.

Not so. The concluding part of the article offered a taxonomy of the various "stages" of sociology of law. They were the mechanical or positivist stage, the biological or evolutionary stage, and the psychological or group-based stage. Again, the analysis was clever and clear, bringing together a vast body of reading and making it accessible to the lawyers and judges (and perhaps even the few students who cared to follow it). Pound did throw in barbs—against, for example, judges and legislators who assumed that innovation in law could never change society—but he could only lament that there was no book by lawyers for lawyers comparable to Ross's *Social Psychology* (1908). Presumably (or so Pound informed more than one correspondent), he was writing such a work, and his lament may have been advertising promotion for the book to come, but it did not come.

Pound did have a program. The sociological jurisprudents had overcome their differences, Pound boasted, and now agreed that law must "take more account, and more intelligent account, of the social facts upon which law must proceed and to which it is to be applied." In particular, the agenda included social scientific studies of the "actual social effects" of legal doctrines. Students of later realists like Underhill Moore take note. Pound said it first: gather data, look at outcomes. But Pound did not say it; he quoted Herman Kantorowicz and praised Eugen Ehrlich. He noted the work of American sociologists of crime and empirical students of civil litigation. He cited with approval Holmes's views in his *Harvard Law Review* piece "The Path of the Law" (1896): the law must come to terms with reality. Pound himself vanished behind so many other bodies, emerging only at the end of the article to remind his readers that "a pragmatist philosophy of law is yet to come. When it is promulgated it may expect many adherents from the sociological jurists." Pound teased instead of satisfying.[30]

Perhaps "teasing" is not the right word. For Pound actually had misgivings about calling his approach sociological jurisprudence. In 1919, he told Thomas Reed Powell, whom he would shortly recruit as a colleague at Harvard Law School, that "[v]ery likely the word 'sociological' is unfortunate. Certainly it is unfortunate philologically. On the other hand, I should think it a mistake to abandon it.

30. Ibid., 507, 513, 516.

The very fact that it is a challenge is of importance . . . [it suggests] the radical contrast between the methods that must obtain in the present and the future and those which obtained in the nineteenth century. The word 'sociological' seems to me important because it necessarily associates itself in men's minds with this element of change."[31] Sociology was then the most progressive and innovative of the emerging social sciences, and this was the "pioneering" era of American sociology.[32] "Sociology in the United States—and in Europe as well—emerged as an intellectual response to the consequences of industrialism."[33] As Pound's friend and former Nebraska colleague Edward A. Ross put it, sociology in these early years rebelled against "abstract political economy, . . . unhistorical jurisprudence, . . . *a priori* ethics and the 'speculative politics' of nineteenth-century scholarship."[34] To align himself with sociology, then, was for Pound to liberalize and politicize early-twentieth-century jurisprudence.

Pound was just as self-conscious about the uses to which he put his political jurisprudence, as he demonstrated in an address to the American Political Science Association's annual meeting on December 28, 1911. His topic was "Courts and Legislation." No coyness here; it was the burning topic of the day. "Under one name or another, juridical method has become a chief subject of discussion." It was false that courts could apply ideal principles of law, a belief that was a relic of eighteenth-century assumptions about the existence of an "unchangeable and independent" universe of legal rights and wrongs. John Austin had demolished that conceit (though Pound was no Austinian, as he had already made abundantly clear). And a "fiction" it remained. Here Pound used the book learning well, for he was not really wedded to any theory, even sociological jurisprudence. He manipulated the classic writers and the canon to demolish targets far closer to home. If he needed someone as a target for the argument that natural law principles were a smokescreen, then

31. Pound to Thomas Reed Powell, Mar. 15, 1919, RPP, 78-6.

32. See, e.g., the essays in Paul Buck, ed., *Social Sciences at Harvard, 1860–1920* (Cambridge, Mass., 1965).

33. Julius Weinberg, *Edward Alsworth Ross and the Sociology of Progressivism* (Madison, Wis., 1972), 56.

34. Ibid., 57 (quoting Ross).

he blasted Sir William Blackstone, not one of the justices who joined the majority opinion in *Lochner*.[35] When Pound needed to show the vacuousness of the conventional reliance on common law principles, he fabricated the "American lawyer," a mannikin who never questioned the notion that "the principles of law are absolute, eternal, and of universal validity, and that law is found, not made, [and that] the state enforces law because it is law," never imagining that the people buy none of that.[36]

Better to face the fact that "hard and fast rules soon defeat the purpose for which law exists." Courts had to be "free to deal with the individual case so as to meet the demands of justice between the parties." Pound believed there were two answers: One, on which Pound had written extensively, was equity. The other was legislation to "provide new and better premises" from which the courts would begin—a more realistic base line.[37] Legislation, Pound implied, rested on the popular American ideal that sovereignty lay in the representative branch. With this the lawyer might not be in full accord, but when the courts seemed to transgress it, the people suspected the courts. Pound did not make it clear here whether he was attacking the courts for their loyalty to an old logic or for their ill policy (though elsewhere he did the latter—so putting the two kinds of attacks together, one might get a powerful indictment of judicial conservatism). One does not have to read between the lines to see where Pound was going: "More careful legislation, proceeding upon better understanding of what legislation may achieve and should attempt on the one hand and the disappearance on the other hand of the notion of the finality of the common law are now things, if not of the present, certainly of the immediate future." Even the courts were becoming more liberal in their willingness to allow "social legislation" its day. Pound urged the courts to obey his injunction against spurious interpretation, that is, to try to find and follow the intention of the legislature, rather than referring back to some "prescriptive constitution, of principles running back of all govern-

35. The United States Supreme Court's opinion striking down a New York state law regulating the hours a baker might work caused a great stir among progressive academics. See Paul Kens, *Judicial Power and Reform Politics: The Anatomy of Lochner v. New York* (Lawrence, Kans., 1990).

36. Roscoe Pound, "Courts and Legislation," 77 *Central Law Journal* 220, 221, 222, 227 (1913).

37. Ibid., 225.

ments." That was only the backdoor to natural law. Instead (here he put his prescription in the mouth of Kohler, by quoting Kohler), "'the lawmaker is a man of his time, thoroughly saturated with the thoughts of his time . . . hence the principle: rules of law . . . are to be interpreted as products of the whole people, whose organ the lawmaker has become.'"[38]

The same almost prissy care to mask a reform program with a forest of scholarship was evident in Pound's talk before the Allegheny (Pa.) Bar Association on April 5, 1912. The title was "Social Justice and Legal Justice," which should have heralded a full-scale indictment of the judicial system. But Pound was trying to preserve the system, while attacking its narrow-minded and out-of-date productions. Not an easy task. Now Pound found other allies in history—this time the founding fathers. They had claimed the inalienable right to pursue happiness. Today, he told the lawyers, "the idea of justice as a mere unshackling of men's energies, and giving the fullest room for development to each man's individual powers of achievement . . . is no longer accepted as the conclusion of the whole matter." Individualism, which assumed a level playing field, or as Pound put it, playing the game without fraud, "has become an anachronism." At the end of the nineteenth century and into the twentieth, legislation bespoke a new goal: "The watchword is not freedom of will, freedom of individual activity, but satisfaction of human wants." The new justice was utilitarian. It limited the use of private property in the common good, prevented outrageous claims of liberty of contract, established the duties of public utilities, and protected the virtuous debtor. The new justice even pointed to a return to strict liability. Overall, social interests were now being recognized, according to Pound. In fact, these visions of the future were still contested in the courts, but Pound was not above characterizing a prediction as a reality. The conclusion was obvious: "The courts, then may not in reason be asked to lead in the present transition . . . it is no ill sign that economists and sociologists are ahead of the law, provided the law knows it." And he threw down the gauntlet to the judges: "In the hands even of zealous and friendly courts—and most judges have yet to learn of any theory of justice other than that they read as students—the adjustment must be tedious and painful." But Pound did not blame the judges. "Instead of recall of judgements

38. Ibid., 229–30.

[which Pound genuinely opposed—though he understood the need for judges to be sensitive to public opinion], recall of law teachers would be a useful institution."[39] After all, they were his primary audience now.

But coyness and camouflage were no help. Conservative judges and intellectuals saw the danger implicit in Pound's logic.[40] The assault began in earnest in 1914, at the hands of New York Judge Robert Ludlow Fowler. The New York courts had long had a reputation for judicial conservatism, beating off procedural reforms and resisting attacks on the common law as the judges were used to it.[41] Fowler took Pound to task, though not by name. Fowler began, "There is a visible tendency at the moment to subject this country to an alien philosophy of law."[42] Given the nativism that marked the early years of the twentieth century, the use of the word "alien" could hardly have been accidental. Fowler knew it called up nativist horror of the hordes of babbling, dirty poor entering the country from eastern and southern Europe. Movements to restrict immigration were well under way in 1914.[43] The bearers of the alien ideas were "politicians and philosophers" (not lawyers or judges themselves, note), and the ideas themselves were the philosophy of the "German socialists." This was nonsense on stilts, for von Ihering was hardly a socialist (quite the opposite, in fact), and the others that Pound cited were from a variety of camps, but not socialism. Fowler spoke with the venom of a man insulted, however, and the insult was plain: "Many of us [the hardworking, right-thinking common law judges of America, one presumes—Fowler never spelled it out] are apt to think that a technical subject is beyond our comprehension if it is couched in unfamiliar language." But a patriotic judge should not worry about this, for "[o]urs is the greatest of republics, with an already long history and an unlimited future. The

39. Roscoe Pound, "Social Justice and Legal Justice," 77 *Central Law Journal* 459, 460, 461, 462 (1912). On Pound's general support for sensitive judging, see Stephen Stagner, "The Recall of Judicial Decisions and the Due Process Debate," 24 *American Journal of Legal History* 271–72 (1980).

40. Wigdor, *Pound*, 202–3.

41. See Charles E. Clark, "A Modern Procedure for New York," 30 *New York University Law Review* 1194–95 (1955).

42. Robert Ludlow Fowler, "The New Philosophies of Law," 27 *Harvard Law Review* 718 (1914).

43. Page Smith, *America Enters the World: A People's History of the Progressive Era and World War I* (New York, 1985), 137–40, 411–12.

final philosophy of the law of this great country should find its inspiration here, and not in alien civilizations." In the spring of 1914,
Fowler had already taken sides in the coming European war. For
Fowler appealed to the good sense of "English-speaking men" and
the ideas of "English-speaking races."[44]

For Fowler, German philosophy was different from English philosophy. "The German" (typical in this age of "blood" and race,
Fowler regarded the Germans as a racial type) philosophy was a
search for the transcendental, and it was as different from the English philosophy as the cultures of the two nations were different.
Fowler assumed that America was English and that its philosophy
was English. No melting pot, much less pluralism, for him. "Law
is one thing in Germany, and another in the countries subject to
the common law." The common law as framed by Blackstone and
Chancellor James Kent "is concrete and adapted to law-men." In
their discussion of rights, they "avoid the sophism and equivocation
so apparent in the transcendental discussions of 'right' by the scientific jurists of some other countries."

In a way, Fowler and Pound were like ships passing in the night,
but Fowler strewed citations to German jurists throughout the essay to prove that a sitting judge could be just as learned in Continental law as a Harvard law professor. That is, he wanted to join
combat with Pound on the latter's own ground. Historical inaccu-
racy did not deter Fowler. "It has been well said [no authority given
in the notes or elsewhere, however] that these people [the "Italian
Aryans"—Fowler's depiction of the Romans, for he could hardly
credit the achievement of Roman law to swarthy Mediterranean
types—and the "English"] only have combined the moral force and
analytical acuteness indispensable for the creation of a great system
of law. The peculiar gifts of the Germans, their incomparable fancy,
their creative passion and scientific depth, are correctly stated [again
not clearly by whom or where] to be hindrances in the formation
of law." German writers were too influenced by "modern economic life." They were generally ignored by the rulers of Germany,
but taken seriously, "they are more apt to take root and to spread
their pernicious influences among incompetent or shallow thinkers." Here is where Pound entered the story, presumably one of the
shallow thinkers. "This is the serious side of the Germanomania of

44. Fowler, "Philosophies of Law," 719, 720, 721, 723.

some American professors of law, educated in Germany or imbued with German thought and theory." A more stable English approach prevented such enthusiasms. The newer German philosophies had a destructive and subversive economic program, along the "lines marked out" by the "economic and philosophical thinkers of the socialistic schools." And here was the nub of Fowler's concern—the danger was not German ideas, but Pound and other progressives' plan for limitations on private property and liberty of contract. Fowler played on growing Germanophobia to enhance his argument. It was very able propaganda.[45]

Criticism never rolled off Pound's back.[46] He replied in a carefully worded note that the editors of the *Harvard Law Review* allowed him at the end of Fowler's piece. Pound cited Wigmore's *Cases on Torts* to demonstrate that the law had to rest on the experience of that day, rather than common law canon. It was the same argument that Judge Benjamin Cardozo would make with even more power in his Storrs Lectures at Yale Law School in 1920, and for which Cardozo thanked Pound at the time.[47] By bringing in Wigmore, Pound protected himself from the charge of being alone in his ideas and too far ahead of his time. He also used Wigmore's arguments as he used the arguments of other, more distant jurisprudents—to make his own points. And his own point here was a critical histori-

45. Ibid., 724, 728, 729, 730.

46. He was still angry at Fowler five years later, when he wrote to Thomas Reed Powell of Columbia (and shortly thereafter of Harvard): "Whether . . . Judge Fowler will or not, Anglo-American law is going to keep on in a process of expressing the civilization of the time and furthering the civilization of the future, which has shocked orthodox lawyers at least from the 14th century to the present." Pound to Thomas Reed Powell, Jan. 27, 1919, RPP, 78-6.

47. Roscoe Pound, "Reply," 27 *Harvard Law Review* 732 (1914); Benjamin Cardozo, *The Nature of the Judicial Process* (New Haven, Conn., 1921), 22–23: "The Common Law does not work from pre-established truths of universal and inflexible validity to conclusions derived from them deductively. Its method is inductive, and it draws its generalizations from particulars," and the common law judge did not look to a heaven of formal rules, for "[w]e are tending more and more toward an appreciation of the truth that, after all, there are few rules; there are chiefly standards and degrees." Ibid., 161. On July 31, 1920, Cardozo thanked Pound for sending "your interesting articles on the Progress of the Law. During the Summer I have been working on one or two lectures which in a rash moment I undertook to write upon the Nature of the Judicial Process. They are without importance as a contribution to jurisprudence; and I mention them only to make acknowledgment of the debt I owe you. Of course, I have known your work more or less intimately for years. The writing of these little lectures, however, has made me know it even better. I do not see how I should have made any progress if you had not shown the way." Benjamin Cardozo to Pound, July 31, 1920, RPP, 182-11.

cal one: the common law had prospered by being incorporative. Fowler was simply wrong. "No one in speech or writing at least had proposed that we subscribe offhand to every detail of the system of any philosopher, German or otherwise. What is urged is that now as in the past we look to what the leaders in the philosophical thought of to-day are thinking and saying and ask ourselves what use we may make of it." Fowler used "socialist" and "socialism" as epithets, not as precise terms, and precision was what was Pound loved.[48] It was time to get rid of such "childish fictions" (Pound quoting Austin, of course, hiding as usual behind authority to bash authority) as Fowler proposed. What was more, common law judges had always concerned themselves with "interests," whatever Fowler, a common law judge, said. For law to grow, it must be in touch with philosophical ideas. The contact of lawyer (and judge) with philosopher (here Pound meant Pound) was as American as the Enlightenment philosophy of the founding fathers. Finally, Pound denied that he relied on misconceptions of economics or sociology. He never claimed they were exact. Indeed, he agreed with Fowler that the law must be pragmatic and had said so himself. In fact, "some of our most promising American students of philosophy of law are to be found in the camp of the *neo-realists* and there seems no reason to suppose that it would be possible or desirable to have all American jurists in the same philosophical camp [as Fowler]." And the parting shot: "It may be suspected that ten years hence most of what is dubbed socialism because it is a bit unfamiliar to those steeped in the Anglo-American law reports will appear quite commonplace."[49]

Pound was wrong about the acceptance of socialism; it was American by 1914 but was never fully accepted.[50] But far more important, he had foreseen the rise of a realist (he even used a variant of the term) philosophy of law. The term was ready to hand and easy for a bricoleur to borrow. Pound was familiar with the rise of realism in literature. In the post–Civil War novel, fiction had turned to depiction of the realm of the senses and the everyday world. Realism empowered the imagination to enter new territories of urban back

48. Pound, "Reply," 733; Pound to Olivia Pound, Dec. 17, 1918, NSHS, MS 911, box 1, folder S.1, vol F.4. Pound had learned at an early age to read texts with great care and to be precise in his interpretations of them.

49. Pound, "Reply," 732, 733, 734, 735.

50. See, e.g., Warren I. Susman, *Culture as History: The Transformation of American Society in the Twentieth Century* (New York, 1984), 75–85.

streets and impoverished valleys and see things not as they actually were, but as they might be beneath the surface. It was American in its themes—war, property, commerce, the conflict between the new and the old, the power of technology and the effect of space, the insights of the new science of psychology, and the impact of the myriad of detail that data gatherers in other professions made public—all these went into the new genre. And there was the beast— the Octopus—that lurked in the cornfield or behind the factory wall. No longer a natural force like Moby Dick onto whose whiteness men projected their own daemons, the realist beast was a genuine destroyer of the human spirit. Slice-of-life novels were inherently reformist, like their journalistic cousin, the muckraking investigative report.[51]

In his reply to Fowler, Pound had made the claim for the preeminence of professors as interpreters of the laws over judges. He did it quietly, using all his marvelously devious and indirect methods of argument, but he made the claim nonetheless. When E. R. A. Seligman, a reform-minded economist at Columbia and the first secretary of the newly established American Association of University Professors, approached Pound a short time after the exchange with Fowler with a draft of the association's plan for tenuring faculty, Pound made the argument for a public professorate more firmly.[52] Seligman wanted to protect the freedom of discourse among academics, but Pound wanted to continue his reply to Fowler. Pound agreed with the sentiments of the draft but found it tepid. Seligman and his committee wanted professors to abjure advocacy in the classroom, and Pound concurred, but in the public arena, the professor had a higher duty:

> The public is filled everyday with a volume of nonsense of every subject in magazine articles and newspapers proceeding from charlatans of all degrees. That the specialist [read university professor] has got to keep quiet or confine himself to classroom discussion on such subjects seems to me distinctly against the public interest. I suspect one reason why the specialist does not have the influence he ought to have in this country is because

51. Eric J. Sundquist, "Introduction," in Eric J. Sundquist, ed., *American Realism: New Essays* (Baltimore, 1982), 3–23; David M. Chalmers, "Law, Justice, and the Muckrakers," in John M. Harrison and Harry H. Stein, eds., *Muckraking: Past, Present and Future* (University Park, Pa., 1973), 65–80.

52. Ellen W. Schrecker, *No Ivory Tower: McCarthyism and the Universities* (Oxford, England, 1986), 17–18.

he has kept still too much. . . . What makes me somewhat insistent upon this point is that the matter is very acute in connection with law reform and the law schools. The member of the bar who knows only the practice and adjudications of his own jurisdiction and often assumes that they were dictated by nature is apt to resent intrusion of the law teacher into discussions of law reform. [This was an error, as Fowler had proved.] But usually the law teacher has made some survey of the legal institutions of the rest of the world [a swipe at Fowler] and is in a position to render a distinct service to the public if he has the boldness to stand out against professional pressure. I do not see why the university professor should be restrained in any way in the discussion of any subject of public interest which comes within the scope of his studies. . . . If he conducts his discussion as a scholar should, the fact that at the same time he makes a vigorous and possibly effective presentation of his views to the public ought not to be taken against him. . . . In short, I think the scholars in this country have been altogether too meek.[53]

Pound had company in this program for university professors. From the days of Robert La Follette's "laboratory of democracy" at the University of Wisconsin, professors and Progressive politicians had formed alliances to gather data and rewrite social policy into law.[54] At Seligman's own institution, as Thomas Bender has demonstrated, professors were staking out the ground for the connection between academic expertise and influence in the real world. But as at Columbia under President Nicholas Murray Butler and at Harvard during and after World War I, the more the university professor spoke out, the more the professor, and the faculty as a whole, became vulnerable to attacks from influential alumni and administrators who feared the failure of their institutional programs.[55]

And Fowler was right if he suspected that Pound did not favor liberty of contract and unregulated capitalism in the real world. Pound could be an awesome proponent of reform in arenas outside of academe. One of his crusades was against child labor. He was one of the signers of the petition for a child labor ban in the United States Constitution.[56] In 1917, Pound journeyed to Greensboro,

53. Pound to E. R. A. Seligman, Dec. 9, 1914, RPP, 156-6.
54. Lawrence R. Veysey, *The Emergence of the American University* (Chicago, 1965), 107–9.
55. Thomas Bender, *New York Intellect* (Baltimore, 1987), 294–318. In general, on the danger to the professor/advocate in the universities and colleges before tenure, see Schrecker, *No Ivory Tower*, 14–23.
56. *New York Times*, Dec. 15, 1924, at 19, col. 5.

North Carolina, to argue for enforcement of the federal child labor law. "The judge was a confederate veteran. So Dixie was sung and the Rebel yell shouted from the start. The other side declaimed against Massachusetts, supposing that would irritate me, and were rather chagrined presently to find that I was not from the Bay State and didn't care. The judge asked me if the government's argument that people with social consciences abhorred the product of child labor and wanted to be protected against using it [the federal stat- ute, eventually declared unconstitutional, put a tax on goods pro- duced using child labor] and thus giving aid to an institution ab- horrent to their moral sense wasn't chimerical. To this I said that exactly such a situation existed in my grandfather's time when su- gar produced by slave labor was not used by many conscientious people." Of course, by raising the parallel between child labor and slavery, Pound was rubbing salt (or sugar) in the wounds of the "lost cause" borne by one of its veterans. He did not mention that his grandfather, in New York, had been an abolitionist. "The judge suggested to me that 'you people in Massachusetts don't understand the poverty that faces people here to put their children to work.' I told him that I grew up in the plains and could remember grasshop- pers and drought that made the prosperous poverty of North Caro- lina seem plenty. That shut off talk about Massachusetts."[57]

Pound was not an egalitarian, however—not about the law itself. He was an elitist, a top-down reformer. He did not favor supporting the night schools, despite the fact that they were the only avenue for legal education for many poorer people. "I think we ought to jerk up the poorer schools in the Association [of American Law Schools] and throw some of them out bodily. Also I think we ought to go after the matter of bar examinations and inferior substitutes for le- gal education vigorously. I am afraid that the Carnegie Institution in its fear that the poor man will not have an opportunity to be swindled by paying a cheap price for a worthless education will give aid and comfort to night schools on the theory that there must al- ways be cheap lawyers and that the cheap product must be pro- duced cheaply."[58]

Nor was Pound an eager sponsor of legal education for women. "I suppose the only way to determine the possibilities of law as a

57. Pound to Laura Biddlecombe Pound, Sept. 2, 1917, NSHS, MS 911, box 1, folder S.1, vol. F.4.
58. Pound to Henry M. Bates, Dec. 5, 1914, RPP, 156-2.

profession for women is for some women to undertake it and see what they can accomplish," he wrote to Margaret Cairns in March 1917. "Most if not all of the women who have been admitted to the bar in the past have not devoted themselves seriously and thoroughly to the profession for a sufficient number of years to give the matter a test. The law as a profession demands and amply rewards unremitting devotion over a long period of time, but nothing short of that will enable one to go far in the profession."[59] Of course, Pound had gone far with only minimal and desultory attention to "the profession," choosing to follow teaching, rather than practice. His admonition to Cairns was thus inapplicable to himself. Harvard Law School did not admit women, and Pound may have been defensive, but few law schools did, and his views reflected those of the majority of his elite peers. One can sense in his reluctance to admit equality of opportunity, much less equality of potential, to women a stuffiness that hardly fit his regard for his mother and his sisters. Louise was already a professor at Nebraska; Pound would hardly have made the same arguments to her.

But what might have seemed to others to be Pound's "Limits of Effective Legal Action," the limits he imposed on his own reforming social jurisprudence, could have double and triple meanings. On June 27, 1916, he told the Pennsylvania Bar Association, "When men demand much of law, when they seek to devolve upon it the whole burden of social control, when they seek to make it do the work of the home and of the church, enforcement of law comes to involve many difficulties . . . in the wake of ambitious social programs calling for more and more interference with every relation of life, dissatisfaction with law, criticism of legal and judicial institutions, and suspicion as to the purposes of the lawyer become universal."[60] The blanket warning sounds like a condemnation of the progressive agenda, which would have been a genuine *volte-face* for Pound and was read that way in the 1920s by those who suspected him of harboring strongly conservative tendencies.

Pound did fear "over-ambitious plans to regulate every phase of human action by law . . . of things which in their nature do not admit of objective treatment and external coercion." He was concerned about the "turn to all manner of new enforcing agencies,"

59. Pound to Margaret J. Cairns, Mar. 2, 1917, RPP, 175-7.
60. Roscoe Pound, "The Limits of Effective Legal Action," 3 *American Bar Association Journal* 56 (1917).

and he worried that the attempt to legislate morals would lead, and was leading, to the breakdown of the agencies of enforcement. Yes, indeed, "[e]xperiments of all sorts are in the air, and all manner of administrative tribunals, proceeding summarily upon principles yet to be defined are acquiring jurisdiction at the expense of the courts."[61] Pound was no friend to the new strict liability standard, which imposed penalties on guiltless parties. Nor did he believe in an insurance-like program wherein everyone paid for the injuries of a few.[62] But he had more fish to fry than those caught by the shift from contract theories of liability to tort theories. He was also after "extravagant translations of Puritanical ideas of conduct into penal codes, known as blue laws, and the voluminous social legislation of today." For it could not be denied that "[m]any still think of law after the Puritan fashion," as the coercer of human conscience.[63] What appeared on its face as a condemnation of rate making and regulation of the economy that would have done a David Brewer proud was also a rather clever, and entirely disingenuous, attack on the new social morality—the morality of prohibition and blue laws. One wonders how many of the Pennsylvania lawyers in the audience recognized that Pound's criticism was double edged.

Whatever his private reservations and his occasional public cautions, Pound's consistent defense of a social jurisprudence had made him the leading academic advocate of law reform. As Albert Kocourek wrote him, "Judge Fowler's amateurish paper on 'The Philosophies of Law' and your dispositive comment, I think makes this issue res judicata. It is evident that he was camping principally on your trail; but after Judge Fowler has extracted the literary buckshot from his epidermis, he will probably pause to reflect that philosophy of law is a good deal more dangerous for him than for his country."[64] Pound had been cautious and careful but had achieved much. He had made himself an idol of the progressive jurisprudents and drawn them to him and to Harvard. He had an international reputation, for Cambridge was a center of legal thought. But Pound needed help, and as the man who recruited him, Dean Ezra Thayer,

61. Ibid., 56, 60, 64.
62. As he repeated at some length in his *Introduction to the Philosophy of Law* (rev. ed., New Haven, Conn., 1953), 102–3.
63. Pound, "Limits," 69.
64. Albert Kocourek to Pound, June 9, 1914, RPP, 225-1.

wrote to Felix Frankfurter, Pound needed someone to keep him going.[65]

Pound had found one younger scholar whose career he patronized already. At Chicago, in the summer of 1910, he met and befriended thirty-one-year-old Wesley Newcomb Hohfeld. Despite the fact that the two men had shared only a summer session together, an immediate bond was struck between them, and they started to correspond regularly.[66] Hohfeld was born in Oakland, California, in 1879 into an artistic and intellectual family circle.[67] A brilliant student in high school in San Francisco and at the University of California, Berkeley, where he received the gold medal for scholarly achievement, Hohfeld early demonstrated an intensity and acuity that would mark his entire career. He went directly from college to Harvard Law School, entering in 1901. He graduated cum laude in 1904, after serving on the editorial board of the *Harvard Law Review*. After a year of practice in San Francisco, at the end of which he was proffered but refused a partnership, he accepted appointment to the faculty of Stanford Law School. He loved music, never married, and walked for recreation.[68]

By the summer of 1910, when he met Pound, Hohfeld was already thinking about the reform of legal education, but he had not

65. Joseph P. Lash, ed., *From the Diaries of Felix Frankfurter* (New York, 1975), 11.

66. A substantial amount of the Pound-Hohfeld correspondence is missing. Most of Pound's letters to Hohfeld are lost and some of Hohfeld's to Pound as well. Pound recalled that "the Hohfeld letters are purely concerned with his ideas about fundamental legal conceptions. I kept no copies of mine and what he did with them after his death I have no idea. I have his put away somewhere, but they are very long, and concerned simply with the details of his analysis." Pound to Paul Sayre, Oct. 1, 1945, NSHS, MS 911, box 1, folder S.1, vol. F.20. The Hohfeld Papers, which according to his family were donated to Stanford for a Hohfeld archive, cannot be found by the Stanford archivists. There are few copies of Pound letters to Hohfeld in the RPP. A few carbon copies can be found in RPP, 156-11. An inference about the extent of their correspondence can be made, however, from references in the extant Hohfeld letters to Pound in the RPP. See RPP, 223-7. The first Hohfeld letter, dated March 15, 1912, clearly indicates that a considerable correspondence had already taken place between the two. Hohfeld wrote, "It is good to hear from you once again!" A fuller exploration of this relationship, tracing its implications for the recent debate on accreditation of law schools, is N. E. H. Hull, "Vital Schools of Jurisprudence: Roscoe Pound, Wesley Newcomb Hohfeld, and the Promotion of an Academic Jurisprudential Agenda, 1910–1919," 45 *Journal of Legal Education* 235–82 (1995).

67. George W. Goble, "Wesley Newcomb Hohfeld," in *Dictionary of American Biography* (New York, 1932), 9:124–25.

68. Ibid.

published anything on it. Pound's prompting and Hohfeld's own ambition for place (indeed a specific place—Yale) were to remedy that
fault. The outline for that proposed reform existed in the cocoon of
his first article, a long-forgotten four-part piece in the *Columbia
Law Review* on stockholders' individual liability for corporation
debts.[69] While the primary object of Hohfeld's first published effort
was to challenge an English court's refusal to hold English shareholders liable for debts incurred in California, portions of his text
announced an abiding interest in the way in which judges' and lawyers' language obscured essential jural relationships. He charged
that "[t]he law is constantly suffering from a loose, undiscriminat-
ing, and misleading terminology."[70] It was critical to Hohfeld's ultimate objective—to prove that shareholders should be liable for
the debts of the corporation—to explode the fiction that the corporation is anything more than or independent of the people who own
it. In the process, however, he made the kind of point later legal
realists, like his future student, Karl Llewellyn, would adopt as one
of their fundamental tenets. As Hohfeld put it, "The real nature of
this transaction can be adequately understood only if [we look] beneath the ordinary language and forms."[71]

Pound had undoubtedly read the article—he read everything in
the law reviews—after he met Hohfeld, if not before, and Hohfeld's nascent pragmatic, realistic approach to legal analysis appealed to the older scholar. They shared, it appeared, a commitment to that progressive-pragmatic jurisprudence developed by
Pound.[72] But Hohfeld's attraction to Pound's educational program
was prompted as much by personal experience as by ideological or
pedagogical motives. Hohfeld's visit in Chicago during the fall of
1911 may have been an audition for an offer to join the permanent
faculty, but the offer did not materialize. His uncompromising ap-

69. Wesley Newcomb Hohfeld, "Nature of Stockholders' Individual Liability for Corporation Debts" (pt. 1), 9 *Columbia Law Review* 285 (1909); subsequent parts of the
article were published under a slightly different title, "The Individual Liability of Stockholders and the Conflict of Laws" (pts. 2–4), 9 *Columbia Law Review* 492 (1909), 10
Columbia Law Review 283, 520 (1910).

70. Hohfeld, "Stockholders' Individual Liability," 290 n.14.

71. Ibid.

72. On progressive pragmatism, see N. E. H. Hull, "Reconstructing the Origins of
Realistic Jurisprudence: A Prequel to the Llewellyn-Pound Exchange over Legal Realism," 1989 *Duke Law Journal* 1302; N. E. H. Hull, "Restatement and Reform: A New
Perspective on the Origins of the American Law Institute," 8 *Law and History Review*
55 (1990).

proach to law teaching turned off the Chicago faculty and students, and their criticisms had stung him deeply. He became defensive in describing his approach to Pound: "I feel sure that in the course of a somewhat [illegible] adequate interval of time (as distinguished from a single quarter) every student in the class would, in connection with the totality of his law studies and work, have come to see the genuine 'practical' importance of the jurisprudential analysis that I interwove with the discussion of the concrete legal problems presented by the cases." [73]

Thus far, only Hohfeld's students and a few colleagues knew what this "practical" analytical jurisprudence of his might be. Pound was one of them. Another was Walter Wheeler Cook. Cook was then a professor at Chicago, and he and Hohfeld hit it off at once. [74] Cook would play a recurring role in Hohfeld's career during Hohfeld's life and even more so as the administrator of his intellectual estate after Hohfeld's death. [75] "[I]ndeed, we were lively 'companions-in-law.'" A year later, in 1912, Hohfeld expressed his attachment to Cook in effusive terms. He urged Pound to regard Cook as another strong supporter of the reform program. "I know that he is in full sympathy with my own views," Hohfeld told Pound. "He [Cook] is an *exceptionally* strong man in every way, and he has a very genuine enthusiasm for the deeper analysis of legal problems commonly dealt with in works on 'analytical jurisprudence.' He is a very clear thinker." [76] Of course, Pound knew Cook at Nebraska, but Hohfeld had not made the connection.

To promote Hohfeld's reputation within the profession, Pound, the outgoing president and a member of the executive committee of the AALS, arranged for Hohfeld to present a paper following his own president's address at the organization's annual meeting that August. Pound's patronage was founded in admiration as well as the desire to have younger acolytes among the academics. He wrote privately of Hohfeld, "[H]e is more likely to produce work of the first magnitude . . . than any of the men who are coming forward." [77] Hohfeld was grateful for Pound's efforts and wanted to accept, but

73. Wesley Newcomb Hohfeld to Pound, Mar. 15, 1912, RPP, 223-7.
74. John Henry Schlegel, *American Legal Realism and Empirical Social Science* (Chapel Hill, N.C., 1995), 27–29, 40, 42.
75. Cook was Hohfeld's heir both figuratively and literally. Hohfeld left all of his books and teaching notes to Cook in his will.
76. Hohfeld to Pound, Mar. 15, 1912, RPP, 223-7 (emphasis in original).
77. Pound to William Mikell, Feb. 12, 1915, RPP, 156-13.

had long-standing plans to go to Europe that summer. Hohfeld generously and enthusiastically recommended a substitute: "Cook is the man for you!"[78]

There is some naïveté or even arrogance (of an innocent but thoroughly characteristic sort) in Hohfeld's advocacy of Cook. It may have been Cook's admiration for things German that spurred Hohfeld to travel there, but favored protégés are not supposed to turn down such offers in order to travel abroad, and even if Hohfeld did not know that Cook had served under Pound, Hohfeld ought to have noticed that Cook was already secretary-treasurer of the AALS and served on its executive committee with Pound.[79] While Hohfeld's suggestion may have prompted Pound to offer the honor to Cook, Cook did not really need Hohfeld's endorsement.[80] Cook gave the address on the need for a union of law and equity and, as was his wont, offended some. Hohfeld was among them and chided Cook for the latter's views of equity. Hohfeld had the gift of offending even those whose support he sought and whose patronage he enjoyed.[81]

When Hohfeld returned from Europe, he wrote to his "friend Pound" to again express his thanks for Pound's "courtesy and kindness" in recommending him for the AALS address. He then commented that, although he had not seen the text of Pound's address, he was sure that "it has struck the right note as regards the future development of the common law in the United States, and the demands concomitantly made upon law teaching in university law schools."[82]

Hohfeld was right about Pound's AALS presidential address. It was an outspoken and valiant plea for the activist role of law professors in promulgating the new progressive-pragmatic jurisprudence. As he had called the lawyers and judges to task in his 1906 ABA address, Pound now tried to awaken the law professors to

78. Hohfeld to Pound, Mar. 15, 1912, RPP, 223-7.
79. For biographical detail on Cook, see Schlegel, *American Legal Realism*; obituary in the *New York Times*, Nov. 9, 1943, at 21. He is listed as secretary of the AALS and member of the executive committee in "Proceedings of the Twelfth Annual Meeting of the Association of American Law Schools," in 12 *Handbook of the Association of American Law Schools* 3 (1912).
80. Cook did, in fact, deliver the address at the 1912 AALS meeting. See "Proceedings," 77.
81. Schlegel, *American Legal Realism*, 42.
82. Hohfeld to Pound, Sept. 24, 1912, RPP, 223-7.

"new ideas." From the opening paragraphs, Pound took on the complacency of his fellow law teachers, who ought to be, but probably were not, "dissatisfied with themselves," and argued that "they should be so dissatisfied and that it will be a healthy symptom when such dissatisfaction becomes acute." And why should they be dissatisfied with themselves? The answer was the "defect[ ] . . . in our law, as it is taught . . . [t]he attitude of the law as a whole still in large part accepted by lawyer and by judge, and handed down by the teacher, toward the policy of modern lawmaking and the relation of law to social progress." The grave consequence of this defect in law teaching, according to Pound, was that an ever-widening schism was opening "between the law as it is taught and received and administered, and those who are working for social progress." The role of the law teacher was crucial to making law schools leaders in promoting progressive ideas, and yet the university law schools were still dominated by traditionalist professors "imbued chiefly with threshing over old straw" in an "attitude of indifference which has prevailed in the immediate past toward the social ends, to which law and laws are but means." Pound was outspoken about the consequences he hoped would result from reforming the jurisprudence of law teaching, "[i]n the same way the work of the law teacher must win its way, not merely in the lecture room, but in the courts. . . ." The ultimate objective of the law professor was to reform and serve the law through both scholarship and teaching. Pound's vision for the legal profession went beyond the mere practice of law, and the law schools were crucial to effecting that vision. "If lawyers are to be of service in the community as well as to clients, teaching of law must take account of this." [83]

For Hohfeld, as for Pound, the cause of progressive jurisprudence and the course of legal education were closely linked. Hohfeld held markedly strong and intellectually elitist views of the role of the university law school. [84] Like Pound, he believed that the university law school should be populated by professional law teachers who could advance both the depth and breadth of legal education and, through deeper and broader training for its graduates, the cause of progres-

83. Pound, "Taught Law," 3 *American Law School Review* 165, 164, 172, 171 (1912).

84. Such sentiments are evidenced throughout the Hohfeld-Pound correspondence and are also represented in Hohfeld's AALS address "A Vital School of Jurisprudence and Law," in 14 *Handbook of the Association of American Law Schools* 76 ff. (1914).

sive legal thought.[85] As he wrote to Pound in September 1912, "Surely university law schools must take the lead in endeavoring to develop a *system* as distinguished from the present unwieldy and imperfect mass of case law; and to accomplish this purpose it would seem necessary that the law schools worthy of the name begin by building up a body of men who shall be real jurists comparable to those of Germany,—not merely a body of money-making lawyers with wits sharpened by mere dialectic based upon the acute and subtle distinguishing of the judicial instances to be found in the Harvard case-books."[86] He also linked these views to Pound's own by pronouncing his views as congruent with Pound's. He told Pound that "I agree heartily with every word that you had already uttered, in relation to the same important matters, in your 'Inaugural Address,' (now in my volume entitled 'Legal Essays' by Pound)."[87]

Hohfeld was already writing his seminal article, "Some Fundamental Legal Conceptions as Applied in Judicial Reasoning,"[88] and this singular piece of scholarship turned out to be a watershed for the Yale Law School, legal education, and American jurisprudence. Pound's "sociological" approach differed considerably from Hohfeld's analytical one, but in the same fashion as David Hume's philosophical works stirred Immanuel Kant from his repose, so Hohfeld was stimulated by Pound's work and acknowledged his leadership in legal reform.[89] Three Hohfeld articles,[90] the most important of which was his *Yale Law Journal* article on jural relations, appeared shortly thereafter.

85. Ibid. See also John Henry Schlegel, "American Legal Realism and Empirical Social Science: From the Yale Experience," 28 *University of Buffalo Law Review* 475 n.86 (1979), and Hull, "Restatement and Reform," 58–60, on the way in which Hohfeld's talk contributed to the founding of the American Law Institute.

86. Hohfeld to Pound, Sept. 24, 1912, RPP, 223-7 (emphasis in original).

87. Ibid.

88. Wesley Newcomb Hohfeld, "Some Fundamental Legal Conceptions as Applied in Judicial Reasoning," 23 *Yale Law Journal* 16 (1913).

89. Hohfeld to Pound, May 20, 1913, RPP, 223-7.

90. The first of the three articles, appearing in May 1913, was "The Need of Remedial Legislation in the California Law of Trusts and Perpetuities," 1 *California Law Review* 305 (1913). The second appeared only a month later, in June 1913. In "The Relations between Equity and Law," 11 *Michigan Law Review* 537 (1913), Hohfeld expanded on Cook's comments at the AALS meeting that he had not attended. Hohfeld took exception to Cook's claim that no American law school's course on equity jurisdiction adequately addressed the explicit differences between equitable rights and duties and legal ones. Hohfeld may have had a very high opinion of Cook, but clearly thought he had something more to contribute than Cook in this area. The last article, appearing in November 1913, was "Some Fundamental Legal Conceptions."

"Some Fundamental Legal Conceptions as Applied in Judicial Reasoning" is one of the most often cited law review articles.[91] Its influence today may be less than it once was, but its significance for the history of mid-twentieth-century jurisprudence is inestimable, and it cemented Hohfeld's position at Yale. As Arthur Corbin wrote to Yale Law School's Dean Eugene Rostow in 1957, the article and Hohfeld's career path were joined, and Corbin was "the only living person to whom these facts (or most of them) are known."[92] According to Corbin's recollection, "In 1913, Hoh submitted his first article on 'Fundamental Legal Conceptions' to the Yale Law Journal. Whether this was in response to an invitation to contribute, I do not know." It is clear, at least, that Corbin had not played a part in soliciting the article, but Corbin, as faculty advisor to the *Journal*, was asked to evaluate the article for possible publication. "I was at once much interested; and I advised publication."[93]

Hohfeld's article was not intended as a revolutionary theoretical contribution to analytical jurisprudence. His objectives for the piece were actually pedagogical, or at least he wanted to demonstrate that improvements in jurisprudence and legal pedagogy must be tied together. In this, he was forwarding the agenda he shared with Pound. As Hohfeld himself wrote, the article was "intended more for law school students than for any other class of readers."[94] Hohfeld's idea was to demonstrate the educational implications of clear ana-

91. Hohfeld's article is hailed by Fred R. Shapiro as one of "The Most-Cited Articles from The Yale Law Journal," 100 *Yale Law Journal* 1449 (1991). Joseph Singer includes a bibliography of articles that discuss Hohfeld's schema of jural opposites and correlatives in his 1982 article "The Legal Rights Debate in Analytical Jurisprudence from Bentham to Hohfeld," 1982 *Wisconsin Law Review* 975, 989–91. My own search has turned up a couple of dozen new articles citing Hohfeld since Singer published his bibliography.

92. The Corbin letter suggests that the story of legal realism at Yale begins not in 1927 but in 1913. It adds to the story many details, events, and perceptions that suggest a new interpretation of Yale's realist origins. I am deeply grateful to William R. Massa, Jr., public services archivist in the Manuscripts and Archives Division of the Yale University Library, for digging up this letter in response to my request for any extant material on Hohfeld at Yale. Arthur Corbin to E. V. Rostow, Aug. 10, 1957, Thomas Swan Papers, Yale University Library, box 1, folder 12. For another account of these events, generally consistent with Corbin's detailed memoir, see Laura Kalman, *Legal Realism at Yale, 1927–1960* (Chapel Hill, N.C., 1986), 261–62 nn.8–11. Kalman bases her account of Hohfeld and Corbin's relationship and Hohfeld's career at Yale on a much briefer and less candid published memoir by Corbin, correspondence in the Arthur Hadley Papers, and the law school faculty minutes.

93. Corbin to Rostow, Aug. 10, 1957, Thomas Swan Papers, Yale University Library, box 1, folder 12.

94. Hohfeld, "Some Fundamental Legal Conceptions," 20.

lytical thinking about legal problems, and he denied that the article, as its title might "suggest[ ][, was] a merely philosophical inquiry as to the nature of law and legal relations." [95]

Some of the language of the *Yale Law Journal* piece reprised complaints he had made much earlier in his 1909 *Columbia Law Review* article, specifically his condemnation of "the ambiguity and looseness of our legal terminology." [96] The jurisprudential contribution of Hohfeld's "Some Fundamental Legal Conceptions" was, in its essence, a pragmatist exercise and thus close to Pound's heart. Hohfeld's analytical schema of jural relations was pragmatic to the extent that he tried to connect legal symbols to the human relationships they described. He did not believe in abstractions called "rights" and "duties." He insisted that they be defined in relation to human beings. By juxtaposing these terms with their "jural opposites" and "jural correlatives," he made clear that no person held a right without that right having a legal impact on someone else and that two different types of legal impact flowed from that right. He also argued that legal relations were far too varied and complex to be explained by using only the two terms, "right" and "duty." "One of the greatest hindrances to the clear understanding, the incisive statement, and the true solution of legal problems frequently arises from the express or tacit assumption that all legal relations may be reduced to 'rights' and 'duties,' and that these latter categories are therefore adequate for the purpose of analyzing even the most complex legal interests." [97] He looked at the practical effect of legal relationships to distinguish many types of relationships and tried to apply more descriptive terms to label them.

To the extent that Hohfeld stressed underlying relationships and practical context for his analysis of jural relations, his article furthered Pound's program, but there were clear divergences from realism in Hohfeld's piece that would haunt even his most devoted realist followers in later years. "Incisive statement" and "clear understanding" were pragmatic and realistic goals, to be sure, but Hohfeld did not stop there. He believed his rigorous analysis would also yield "a true solution of legal problems." [98] This "true solution" harkens back to classical-formalist legal thinking, which argued

95. Ibid.
96. Ibid., 21.
97. Ibid., 28.
98. Ibid.

that the law was a closed analytical system in which logic would yield the correct answer to every legal problem. This was just the kind of thought anti-formalists like Pound rejected. Even Corbin, who enthusiastically approved the article for publication, would later criticize Hohfeld's dogmatic faith in the power of analytical jurisprudence to discern "true solutions" or correct rules. In his memoir of Hohfeld, he commented that "it was Hoh's belief that there is a 'positive law,' to be determined by logical analysis. He certainly handled his materials with positiveness and vigor and reached definite results. At the age of 36, he might not have approved of my notion that *all* legal rules are merely tentative working rules, drawn out of and changing with the customs and mores of men." But so devoted was Corbin, in 1957, to the genius of his departed friend that he tried to excuse him by suggesting that "I would expect him, in the course of time [had he lived], either to agree with me or to convince me of error." [99]

Hohfeld concluded his article by reiterating "the great practical importance of a clear appreciation of the distinctions and discriminations set forth." [100] He likened the application of his schema to finding the "lowest common denominator of the law" through which "comparison becomes easy, and fundamental similarity may be discovered." [101] But what was the ultimate practical purpose of finding those comparisons and similarities? How was this more than an academic exercise? Hohfeld hinted at a deeper purpose in a singular sentence near the end of his article. "By such a process it becomes possible not only to discover essential similarities and illuminating analogies in the midst of what appears superficially to be infinite and hopeless variety, but also *to discern common principles of justice and policy underlying the various jural problems solved.*" [102]

While this lone statement may lack the force of Pound's "Taught Law" rhetoric in its endorsement of policy and social justice as the engine behind jurisprudential reform, nevertheless Hohfeld was admitting the progressive motivation behind all his analytical schematization. This progressive strain to Hohfeld's jurisprudence has always been overlooked, even by his closest allies. His great friend

---

99. Corbin to Rostow, Aug. 10, 1957, Thomas Swan Papers, Yale University Library, box 1, folder 12 (emphasis in original).
100. Hohfeld, "Some Fundamental Legal Conceptions," 58.
101. Ibid.
102. Ibid., 59 (emphasis added).

and mentor Arthur Corbin later observed that, "so far as I ever knew, his interests were analytical and logical, rather than sociological. He spoke of the 'positive law.' [In a faculty meeting, Cook and I once, *in exact unison,* asked him 'Where is it?'].["][103] Thus, like Pound's, Hohfeld's search for an American jurisprudence returned again and again to the practical. A jurisprudence must not merely describe or theorize; it must also leave its mark on the future.

The article and Corbin's patronage led to the Yale job for Hohfeld, but once there, he antagonized colleagues and students. "He in turn was lonesome and felt isolated, both socially and intellectually."[104] Hohfeld was an exacting and exacerbating personality, "not patient with what he regarded as incompetence; and he often gave offense, both socially and intellectually. He was at times so frank in his criticisms that it was painful to his associates who were present."[105] Pound commented that he "had heard it said that [Hohfeld] is not sometimes the easiest colleague to get along with," but, trying to mitigate such reports, claimed that "from pretty close association with him in several summer quarters at Chicago I should not be alarmed by this."[106] Llewellyn, Hohfeld's most enthusiastic devotee, candidly admitted in the tribute he wrote for the *Yale Law Journal* at the time of Hohfeld's death that Hohfeld "had little of that grace in putting forth his thoughts—or meeting men—which makes for general popularity."[107] Llewellyn also remarked on the intellectual intolerance Hohfeld exhibited in the classroom. "'Hoh' was no believer in the royal road. He had scant sympathy for mental laziness or physical, for scattered energies or surface-thought, for what he used to call the small and common coin of legal learning."[108] Llewellyn painted a very explicit picture of Hohfeld in the classroom, a figure that Llewellyn admired, but one capable of generating dislike among students.

Yet Hohfeld not only survived the complaints of students, but also prospered at Yale. With Corbin, he convinced Dean Thomas

103. Corbin to Rostow, Aug. 10, 1957, Thomas Swan Papers, Yale University Library, box 1, folder 12 (emphasis in original).

104. Ibid. Corbin was not alone in discerning Hohfeld's isolation and loneliness. Llewellyn noted, "He was a lonely man." Karl Llewellyn, "Wesley Newcomb Hohfeld—Teacher," 28 *Yale Law Journal* 797 (1919).

105. Corbin to Rostow, Aug. 10, 1957, Thomas Swan Papers, Yale University Library, box 1, folder 12.

106. Pound to Mikell, Feb. 12, 1915, RPP, 156-13.

107. Llewellyn, "Wesley Newcomb Hohfeld," 786.

108. Ibid., 796–97.

Swan to hire Cook. The three musketeers then imposed the Hohfeldian categories on the Yale students. One of these was Llewellyn, who never forgot the intellectual excitement of sitting at Hohfeld's feet. "There he sits, crouched somewhat forward on the desk; his black-haired eagle-face seems set with anticipation of the clash of views, his heavy shoulders tense, for all their student's stoop,— there he sits, silent through several seconds."[109] Corbin's description agrees with Llewellyn's: "Hoh's manner (except to a close friend) was cold, his face was *very* pale and inexpressive of emotion, and his voice was keen and penetrating."[110]

With Hohfeld working his wonders at Yale, Pound had time to nurture another academic friendship, this time with Frankfurter. Frankfurter had come to New York as a boy of eleven in 1893 and had graduated at the top of his class from both the City College of New York and Harvard Law School. He worked for a time for Henry Stimson, the liberal Republican federal attorney for the Southern District of New York, and stayed on when Taft lost, Wilson was elected, and Stimson returned to private practice. At Frankfurter's rooming house, "the House of Truth," a band of brilliant and ambitious young men thought about the connections among law, government, and ideas. Frankfurter was the brightest and most indefatigable of them and had developed as well an attachment to older mentors like Stimson, Brandeis, and Holmes.[111]

Like Pound, Frankfurter had his eyes on the greatest meritocracy in the world, Harvard Law School. Unlike Pound, Frankfurter was a Jew, and that raised the question of anti-Semitism. At first, it did not matter, for Pound became Frankfurter's mentor. Indeed, Frankfurter, who was capable of great loyalty (sometimes amounting to adulation), seemed to feel as strongly about Pound. Louis Brandeis wrote to Frankfurter urging the latter to accept a teaching position at Harvard Law School: "You have probably heard of the progressive law work which the Harvard Law School is undertaking, and

109. Ibid., 798. Llewellyn never lost his fascination with Hohfeld, but he grew out of the infatuation. "Now had Hohfeld lived another twenty years, he and I would have been at war." Llewellyn, Lecture on Jurisprudence, Apr. 26, 1955, KLP, C.M.10, p. 11. Nothing in Hohfeld's jural schema dictated results. Nothing in it captured the legal interests that lie beneath the surface. Nothing in it recognized the reciprocity, or the reversibility, of rights and duties, according to Llewellyn in 1955.

110. Corbin to Rostow, Aug. 10, 1957, Thomas Swan Papers, Yale University Library, box 1, folder 12 (emphasis in original).

111. Michael E. Parrish, *Felix Frankfurter and His Times: The Reform Years* (New York, 1982), 59–61.

in which Professor Pound is particularly interested." [112] Frankfurter
later wrote to his friend Stimson that, though he had reservations
about taking an academic post at Harvard, " 'I am struck with the
big public aspect of what should be done by our law schools, and
the kind of thing that surely is capable of being done with Pound at
Cambridge.' " [113]

Pound's attempts to reinvent (or at least invert) the European jurisprudential canon and to nurture progressive-pragmatic academic
jurisprudents at home were profoundly altered by the onset of war
in Europe. Not only did the outbreak of hostilities there undermine
the claims of Continental jurisprudential thinkers, but also it sun-
dered the ties that Pound had tried to make between American jurisprudential reform and German legal theory. Pound did not quit
easily, however. In December 1914, Pound again selected a speaker
for the annual meeting of the AALS. Again, the choice was a jurisprudent who would, Pound hoped, further his program. The invitee
was preeminent European legal sociologist Eugen Ehrlich. [114] Ehrlich's trip to America was eagerly anticipated not only by Pound but
also by the entire progressive jurisprudential community. Ehrlich's
sociology of law showed "that it is not enough to be conscious that
the law is living and growing, we must rather be conscious that it is
a part of human life. It is not merely that it should look upon noth-

112. Brandeis to Felix Frankfurter, Jan. 24, 1913, in Melvin I. Urofsky and David W.
Levy, eds., *Half Brother, Half Son: The Letters of Louis D. Brandeis to Felix Frankfurter*
(Norman, Okla., 1991), 21.

113. H. N. Hirsch, *The Enigma of Felix Frankfurter* (New York, 1981), 38. It is interesting that Hirsch identifies Pound in an asterisked footnote as "a leading legal 'realist'." See also Parrish, *Frankfurter*, 59.

114. Ehrlich was born in Czernowitz, the capital of the province of Bukovina (at that
time part of Austria-Hungary), in 1862. There is some disagreement about the date of his
death; various sources suggest he died in 1918, in 1919, or as late as 1922. Walter Moll
gives no date, but seems to support the idea that Ehrlich died at the end of 1918 or early
in 1919. In his "Translator's Preface" to his English translation of Ehrlich's *Fundamental
Principles of the Sociology of Law*, Moll said, "He died shortly after the close of the war."
Eugen Ehrlich, *Fundamental Principles of the Sociology of Law* [1936], trans. Walter L.
Moll (New York, 1962), 3. I cannot pinpoint with precision the date of Ehrlich's death,
but I can show that he was alive as late as March 24, 1921. There is a letter from and
signed by Ehrlich sent to Pound from Bucharest, Romania, with that date. RPP, 62-20.
Biographical entries about Ehrlich can be found in N. S. Timasheff, "Eugen Ehrlich," in
International Encyclopedia of the Social Sciences (New York, 1968), 540; *New Encyclopaedia Britannica* (15th ed., Chicago, 1990), 4:394; and *Encyclopaedia Judaica* (Jeru-
salem, Israel, 1971), 6:514.

ing human as foreign to it, in a sense everything human is a part of it."[115] Ehrlich's translator, Walter Moll, characterized Ehrlich's contribution to legal thought in similar terms. He praised Ehrlich for recognizing "that the phenomena of legal life arise in society, and in turn exercise a profound influence upon society."[116] Ehrlich was an empiricist, and his philosophy represented strong European support for the progressive pragmatism that underlay Pound's sociological jurisprudence.

Pound's respect for Ehrlich was expressed privately as well as publicly. John Chipman Gray, at seventy-six still Hohfeld's favorite professor from his student years at Harvard and one of Pound's first teachers, aided the career of both men but still clung to the traditional jurisprudence.[117] Gray apparently had written to Pound a stinging memorandum in which he criticized Pound's views.[118] Pound, in response, generously conceded that he may have mischaracterized analytical jurisprudence in his zeal to promote his own views, but argued that Gray was guilty of the same intellectual error. "I submit, however, in your memorandum you do the same thing with respect to those who are seeking a sociological jurisprudence." Gray suspected Pound of being a progressive, which was true, but Pound retorted that it was the analytical jurisprudence of Gray and his generation that had brought the law into disrepute and had driven people to adopt an activist progressive agenda. Pound argued that "it is because exclusively analytical and historical study of the law have brought about a situation that drives the impulsive but enlightened layman to such views that I think we need something more than we have had in the past." After assaulting Gray's jurisprudence, Pound recommended that Gray read Ehrlich's recently published book, which Pound thought Gray might find en-

115. Pound to Holmes, July 22, 1915, RPP, 156-11. Pound waxed eloquent about Ehrlich to Holmes in this letter, in which Pound was replying to Holmes's request for Ehrlich's address.

116. Walter Moll, "Translator's Preface," in Ehrlich, *Fundamental Principles,* ix. Even critics, like Paul Vinogradoff, "The Crisis of Modern Jurisprudence," 28 *Yale Law Journal* 320 (1919), conceded that Ehrlich led "the onslaught on the barren symbolism of legal mathematicians."

117. H. W. Howard Knott, "John Chipman Gray," in *Dictionary of American Biography* (New York, 1932), 7:520–21; Samuel Williston, "John Chipman Gray," 28 *Harvard Law Review* 546 (1915).

118. Again, we have no copy of Gray's original memorandum, but only Pound's reference to it in his responsive letter. Pound to John Chipman Gray, Feb. 3, 1915, RPP, 156-11.

lightening.[119] "If you have not seen it, Professor Ehrlich's *Gundlagen der Sociologie des Rechts* would be well worth looking at. I think it is the best thing that has been written recently."[120]

Pound saw Ehrlich's work as one of the strongest forces at work in contemporary legal thought tearing down the analytical approach. In his "Introduction" to the English translation of Ehrlich's book, Pound extolled Ehrlich for rejecting "the metaphysical-analytical-historical jurisprudence of the last century"[121] and for substituting for it a jurisprudence concerned with "relations and groups and associations, rather than abstract individuals."[122] Pound also commented on Ehrlich's contribution to the demise of analytical jurisprudence in a private letter to Justice Holmes: Ehrlich punctured "our specialization of the nineteenth century which tried to put everything in its water-tight compartment as a whole complete in itself—something that has been breaking down in many things less practical than the law—[and] is quite out of place in a matter which is so intimately a part of life as the law."[123]

In the fall of 1914, Ehrlich was scheduled to give a series of lectures at the Lowell Institute as well as the featured address to the AALS. But Ehrlich's plans to travel to the United States hit a snag at Sarajevo. As late as October, Ehrlich still expected to make the trip. Pound wrote to a political science professor at the University of Chicago that "I have a letter from Professor Ehrlich . . . saying that he will come to this country in December . . . we had been fearing that the war would interfere with his coming," but Pound's optimism was short lived. An ocean crossing by a subject of the Central Powers became nearly impossible with virtual British control of the North Atlantic. In early December 1914, Ehrlich wrote to Pound to tell him that he would have to cancel his trip because the American embassy in Vienna backed off from giving him a safe conduct. He feared that his American ship would be stopped by British warships and that, when he was discovered on board, he would be removed and imprisoned as a hostile.[124]

119. Ibid.
120. Ibid. Pound knew that Gray could read German. It must have given Pound an ego boost to be able to recommend a German text to the professor who had done the same for him twenty-five years before.
121. Roscoe Pound, "Introduction," in Ehrlich, *Fundamental Principles*, xxx.
122. Ibid., xxxi.
123. Pound to Holmes, July 22, 1915, RPP, 156-11.
124. Pound to James H. Tufts, Oct. 26, 1914, RPP, 156-6; Pound to Brandeis, Dec. 7, 1914, RPP, 156-2.

Pound enlisted Brandeis's assistance. Pound complained that it "does seem most unfortunate that a scholar of his standing, a well-known pacifist, a man whose whole interest for years has been in making the law an efficient agent of social improvement should be accused by our embassy at Vienna of intending a political propaganda." Pound asked Brandeis if there was anything Brandeis could do to "induc[e] the authorities at Washington to do something for Ehrlich" and concluded bitterly that "[w]e must indeed be in a state of decadence in this country if we cannot protect on an American ship a scholar whose interests are purely of a scholarly nature who is coming to this country by our invitation for the sole purpose of lecturing before our institutions of learning."[125] A week later, Pound wrote to Brandeis that he had received a telegram from a Mr. Phillips (in the State Department or at the American embassy) requesting Ehrlich's full name, and so he thought Brandeis might have managed to move the government to help Ehrlich.[126] Pound's optimism was premature. Only three days later, Pound was "advised that the state department hesitates to do anything on the ground 'that the British might object.'"[127]

Pound's experience with the United States government in trying to bring Ehrlich to speak at the AALS meeting in the fall of 1914 was the beginning of his skepticism and cynicism about popular opinion against combatants in wartime that would color his views for decades to come. Pound had always been partial to German culture and legal philosophy, and this episode did little to change his opinions. Amid the Ehrlich debacle, Pound wrote to the eminent German jurisprudent Rudolf Leonhard that "[p]ersonally I am of purely English descent on both sides and moreover [illegible] mothers-in-law one is domiciled in London and the other at Cape Town. Nevertheless I hope I am liberal minded enough to appreciate the German side of the present war and to hope that it may terminate somehow in such a way that the greatest force for idealism and for culture in the modern world may not be impaired. Unhappily in this country we have heard and still hear in general only what comes through English and French channels. What comes through from Germany is often grossly mistranslated."[128]

125. Pound to Brandeis, Dec. 7, 1914, RPP, 156-2.
126. Pound to Brandeis, Dec. 14, 1914, RPP, 156-2.
127. Pound to Miss S. P. Breckinridge, Dec. 17, 1914, RPP, 156-2.
128. Pound to Rudolf Leonhard, Dec. 14, 1914, RPP, 156-4.

The episode of Ehrlich's proposed visit to the United States seems to have exacerbated Pound's antipathies and pushed him toward outright prejudice against the English and French. One month after Ehrlich would have spoken to the AALS, Pound wrote to an old acquaintance in Nebraska defending the Germans and attacking rabid Anglophiles who seemed to dominate American culture and policy. "With respect to the hyphenated Americans of whom you speak, may I not suggest that our German friends are just now in evidence? In this part of the country at least an Anglo-American is extremely conspicuous. As near as I can make out he thinks of the United States as simply a British colony and anyone who ventures to suggest that there may be two sides to many matters which are now in dispute is regarded as little, if anything, short of a traitor. . . . Possibly where you live the German-American is making the most noise. I hope he is making some somewhere because if we are to have neutrality in this country, there has got to be something to set over against the din which is making here by those whose ideas and trousers are manufactured in London."[129]

Pound found himself under attack for his defense of German views and his efforts to bring over Ehrlich. He wrote to Leonhard that "I, myself, who have every reason to be sympathetic with the English, because I insist upon looking fairly, as nearly as possible, at the German side of things am generally denounced as 'a rabid pro-German.'"[130] Harold Laski commented on Pound's prejudices in favor of German over French and English culture to Justice Holmes in 1916: "I am often bewildered at things like Pound's conviction that the typical French institution is the *Folies Bergères*—that learning is confined to Germany, that England's day is past and so forth."[131]

Stung by Ehrlich's mistreatment and the onset of anti-German propaganda, Pound called on Hohfeld (not by accident a German-American who respected German thought and had just returned from Germany) to carry the banner of the new jurisprudence at the AALS meeting. He would regret the offer. Hohfeld lacked Ehrlich's stature and, more galling to the delegates, did not seemed cowed by the comparison. Instead, Hohfeld treated the law professors as he treated his students—he simultaneously bored and infuriated them. It was a shame because the text of Hohfeld's address—entitled "A

129. Pound to W. G. Langworth Taylor, Jan. 28, 1915, RPP, 156-16.
130. Pound to Leonhard, Feb. 15, 1915, RPP, 156-13.
131. Harold Laski to Holmes, Dec. 21, 1916, in Howe, *Holmes-Laski Letters*, 1:45.

Vital School of Jurisprudence and Law: Have American Universities Awakened to the Enlarged Opportunities and Responsibilities of the Present Day?"—was a genuinely original contribution to the small but growing corpus of American jurisprudential writings. On one level, Hohfeld echoed Pound's messages of 1906 and 1912. Hohfeld claimed that "our leading lawyers and judges have been awakened to such of our juridical defects as are real and substantial" by Pound's early critique. Time and events had made reform of the law and legal thinking increasingly urgent: "Men's minds have been stirred to the point of conscious and definite struggle for change, and matters of law and justice have become great political issues both in the nation at large and in the various states." [132]

Hohfeld's solution was a radical program to transform professional law schools at certain universities into national academic juristic centers to foster genuine academic training in law and jurisprudence and promote research that would lead to the needed reform of the law. Again, Hohfeld, with Pound behind him, had captured the essential program of progressive-pragmatic jurisprudence: thought should lead to action; critique should stimulate reform. Hohfeld did not include in this center judges and practicing lawyers. The essence of his plan was the newfound self-importance of the legal academic. At present, Hohfeld complained, "[t]he majority of the universities have . . . been content to offer purely professional or vocational courses in law along conventional lines— what is commonly called general jurisprudence being entirely, or almost entirely, ignored." [133] Hohfeld argued, as he had for years to Pound, Corbin, and his hapless students, that without law-school-sponsored training and research in jurisprudence, there could never be the kind of reform of the law everyone agreed was necessary. While Hohfeld's plan may have gone beyond anything Pound might have recommended—for Pound, as Harvard dean, never endorsed a wholesale restructuring of the law school—his criticisms of, vision

132. Hohfeld, "Vital School," 76, 77, 136. Over the years, Hohfeld's reputation has been defined by and limited to his contribution to abstract, analytical jurisprudence through his schema of jural relations. As the following analysis of his address to the AALS points out, Hohfeld was actively concerned with reform of the law, and no doubt, had he lived, he would have translated his jurisprudential ideas into a reformist program, very probably through the ALI. Hohfeld's reputation as an abstract theorist has led subsequent scholars to overlook the strong, practical reformist objective of Hohfeld's AALS plan. See Schlegel, *American Legal Realism*, 475 n.86.

133. Hohfeld, "Vital School," 81–82.

of, and basic goals for university law schools in the larger scheme of juristic renewal and reform were the same.

Hohfeld reassured his colleagues that the graduate jurispruden-tial centers he proposed were not meant to supplant *ordinary* law schools entirely. "I am not thinking specially of the needs of the or-dinary professional law students. On the contrary . . . I have in mind primarily the gradual building up of a class of university jurists— legal pathologists and surgeons, we might call them—who shall have a far greater share and influence than at present in prescribing for our ills. . . ." [134] Hohfeld's endorsement of the academics' role in promoting clarification of the law was not unequivocal, for there was a subtle criticism of existing legal education and law profes-sors in his program to rework major university law schools into na-tional juristic centers. Hohfeld's criticisms and recommendations prompted no immediate response from his AALS audience, and his plan for a drastic recasting of the major law schools spurred little discussion. [135] Hohfeld's attempt to communicate his vision to his academic colleagues, in fact, fell distinctly flat—a shame indeed, for he had envisioned the American Law Institute. [136]

Pound lamented that Hohfeld's tendency to pedantry displayed itself to his disadvantage at his AALS talk. He wrote to Mikell less than two months after Hohfeld's performance that "it must be said that his German grnst der ins Ganze geht [*sic*] has sometimes led him to bear down with equal emphasis on all sorts of unimportant details so that, for instance, at the meeting of the Law School Asso-ciation in Chicago he occupied an unconscionably long time with a paper in which he tried to deal thoroughly with every nook and corner of a subject when the rest of us would have touched the high places and stopped." Pound reflected that "I suspect this may have given rise to an erroneous impression about Hohfeld in many quar-ters." [137] The unfortunate limitations of Hohfeld's overly ambitious presentation thwarted his goal of converting the law professors to

134. Ibid., 88.
135. Ordinarily, after a speaker finished his talk, the president of the association would ask for questions and comments, and the minutes often indicated some lively re-action to the preceding address. After Hohfeld's talk, President Beale asked in vain for questions and comments; there being none, he went on to other business. 14 *Handbook of the Association of American Law Schools* 5 (1914).
136. Hull, "Restatement and Reform," 59–60.
137. Pound to Mikell, Feb. 12, 1915, RPP, 156-13.

his standard. His consecration as prophet outside of Yale would elude him for the rest of his short life.

Hohfeld died after a prolonged struggle against a viral infection of the heart, but in death, Hohfeld's influence grew,[138] for his ideas, grounded in a passing stage of deductive, analytical faith, fell into Cook's hands.[139] Cook made Hohfeld into the first legal realist; Pound was left behind. Corbin never cared much for realism, despite his later patronage of the Yale realists, but he cared less for Pound and was happy to ignore the latter's relationship with Hohfeld.[140] The loss to Pound was more than public recognition of his sponsorship of Hohfeld. The Yale coup was a slap, but Hohfeld's death took from Pound a sounding board, goad, and critic. Pound, stung by Cook's end run and weighed down by administrative duties, soon lost some of his enthusiasm for reform of legal education. To students at the University of West Virginia, in 1923, he admitted that "there are many signs that our law is entering upon a new stage of development" and that "already there is a call for juristic creative activity," but now there was in his mind "no gulf between academic teaching of law and the law of the tribunals." Instead, like the framers of our first laws, and the treatise writers of the mid-nineteenth century, the makers of law in the 1920s could be proud of their

138. Apparently, Hohfeld's analytical system became so popular in the years after his death that it was adopted even by some students at Harvard, though it is not clear whether that can be attributed to Pound's influence. Edwin Patterson wrote to Pound in 1923 decrying the spread of such analytical systems among law students, implying that Pound had expressed similar views (if Pound had expressed such sentiments to Patterson, we have no copy of it). Patterson wrote: "I am heartily in accord with your views as to the utility of a mechanical apparatus for analyzing legal problems. I am surprised that this insidious error *i.e. the Hohfeldian apparatus* has found its way into the Harvard student body." Edwin Patterson to Pound, Mar. 3, 1923, RPP, 31-8 (italicized material appears as a handwritten insert in Patterson's typewritten letter).

139. So did Hohfeld's unfinished manuscripts. Llewellyn remembered: "Immediately after Hohfeld died, Cook left Yale and went to Columbia and all of us students at Yale knew what he was going to do—he was going to steal Hohfeld, the owner. . . . [A]fter Hohfeld's death, I got a key and got into his office before Cook got there, and dug out his copy of [Joseph] Story [on Conflict of Laws] and went through it with the greatest of care, it was all full of notes, all full of cards, the book was this big as it was with the cards stuck in it . . . the trouble was I couldn't understand what the notes were about . . . and in due course, Cook, without one slightest acknowledgment to Hohfeld, brought out his logical and legal bases of the Conflict of Law—one of the dirtiest things that was ever done in the history of American jurisprudence." Llewellyn, Lecture on Jurisprudence, Apr. 26, 1955, KLP, C.M.10, pp. 13–14.

140. Schlegel, *American Legal Realism*, 52; Corbin to Karl Llewellyn, Dec. 1, 1960, KLP, R.III.15.

achievements.[141] Two years later, addressing University of Michigan Law School students, honoring the school's new graduate program in research, he praised the "work of research which is urgently required by the condition of the administration of justice in America today," but insisted on an equally important search for "a means of reconstructing the professional tradition, and professionalizing the lawyers of our great cities." Only then would the "old-time effective teaching of law" be adapted for a new century.[142]

Pound's greatest test between 1915 and 1920 was not the seduction and defection of Hohfeld. Europe was engulfed in war, a terrible war, not the least because it undermined all of Europe's conceits that technology and civilization in the West had found a way to progress without war. Pound had been educated at a German private school in Lincoln, had a German housemaid, spoke German, loved German culture, venerated German jurisprudence, and fought hard to bring Eugen Ehrlich (though not a German, but an Austro-Hungarian Jew) to Harvard. In the way, at every turn, was the growing semi-official Germanophobia. In part, it was the triumph of an English propaganda machine. In part, it was the aggressiveness of Kaiser Wilhelm. Pound was furious. As he told private correspondents, the expression of any pro-German sentiment was viewed as anti-patriotic. To a German friend in mid-1915, Pound held out hope that, "[a]s the war progresses and the truth gradually filters through to this country, which has been flooded with books, pamphlets and leaflets of every sort giving the British side, a change in American opinion becomes evident and I do not believe in the end your countrymen will have much to complain of, all circumstances considered, with respect to the attitude of the American people at large."[143]

As was often the case, Pound was either too optimistic or (more likely) simply did not give credit to what he knew was true—that President Woodrow Wilson led the attack on "hyphenated Americans" that was aimed at Germans.[144] In general, Pound kept his

141. Roscoe Pound, "The Work of the American Law School," 30 *West Virginia Law Quarterly* 20 (1923).

142. Roscoe Pound, "The Law School and the Professional Tradition," 24 *Michigan Law Review* 164 (1925).

143. Pound to Leonhard, June 25, 1915, RPP, 156-13.

144. David M. Kennedy, *Over Here: The First World War and American Society* (New York, 1980), 24.

opinions to himself, for good reason. In 1916, the Harvard Corporation intended to appoint him dean. On the eve of the appointment, he wrote to Olivia Pound that the appointment would go through "unless the combination of a non-Harvard man, pro-German (for everyone is dubbed pro-German here if he is not for going to War with Germany tomorrow morning) and pro-Brandeis man is more than the traffic will bear." He added, unnecessarily, that "this is confidential."[145] Pound was trimming, but to him, the deanship was worth his silence.

When the war came to the United States, the lot of German-Americans and any who sympathized with them or their homeland became worse.[146] Pound seethed, but gallantly turned his own private anger at the treatment of Germany in a positive direction. He had always believed in free speech, had nearly lost his job at Nebraska in its defense (though to be sure he was defending his own rights), spoke for it in Chicago, and now found the oppressive measures of the wartime administration morally bankrupt. But Harvard and Cambridge were spared the worst excesses of the persecution. As he wrote to Olivia in June 1918, "There are a good many here who will get in the front rank to lick the blacking off the boots of even a Cockney Englishman when he heaves in sight, but at least they do not prosecute those who do not like the taste of shoe blacking. Some of us still conceive that as Americans we are born free if not equal, and that one of our prescriptive rights is, as long as we refrain from incendiary public speeches, to believe what our consciences teach us in private life."[147] Pound, as usual, was circumspect in public but given to fury in private. Not so cautious were two of his younger faculty, and he rushed to their aid. The first was Zechariah Chafee, Jr.; the second was Felix Frankfurter.

Chafee was a Rhode Islander who had come to Harvard in 1916 after graduating from the law school and spending time in private practice.[148] From a long line of successful merchants (some of whom had engaged in the slave trade), Chafee was no radical. Indeed, he taught the commercial law courses at Harvard in a most conven-

145. Pound to Olivia Pound, Feb. 2, 1916, NSHS, MS 911, box 1, folder S.1, vol. F.4.
146. Kennedy, *Over Here,* 67–68.
147. Pound to Olivia Pound, June 4, 1918, NSHS, MS 911, box 1, folder S.1, vol F.4. See also David M. Rabban, "Free Speech in Progressive Social Thought," 74 *Texas Law Review* 997–1001 (1996).
148. I have drawn my account of Chafee's life from Donald L. Smith, *Zechariah Chafee, Jr.: Defender of Liberty and Law* (Cambridge, Mass., 1986), 16–76.

tional way. But in 1918, in the process of teaching about equitable injunctions, he decided to lecture on prior censorship of the press. It was hardly a propitious time for a quiet man to engage in such an inquiry. Wilson's administration was not so quietly suppressing "seditious" speech, a practice going back to the English prosecutions of critics of the government for "seditious libel." In theory, the First Amendment prevented prior censorship, but the possibility of prosecution after publication was still alive and well.[149] The Espionage Act of 1917 made it a federal offense to send through the mails false reports on military events and to attempt to interfere with the armed forces or recruitment to the latter. The last was like the Salvo to the Treason Act of 1325 in England, which made any action leading to the endangerment of the crown a treason. Such "constructive" treasons led to the indictment of any opponent of the crown and gave to the king the power to suppress all dissent.[150] The Espionage Act, construed broadly, did the same for the wartime government of the United States.

Chafee, publishing by invitation in Herbert Croly's *New Republic* (one sees the hand of Frankfurter and Laski in the invitation), concluded that the framers of the First Amendment had meant freedom of the press to extend beyond the ban on prior censorship, to a license to publish all manner of political views. He based his conclusions in part on the Jeffersonian reaction to the Seditious Libel Act of 1798, and although he was probably wrong (in fact, the Jeffersonians, when they gained power, did not repeal the Seditious Libel Act), he had gained powerful allies. Learned Hand and Holmes, for their respective courts, had reached the same conclusions. Hand, in the summer of 1917, had enunciated a direct action test that protected dissenting speech and press. The words uttered had to be "triggers of action" before they could be grounds for an indictment. In *Schenck v. United States*, Holmes applied a less rigorous, but still limiting, test: the words had to present a clear and present danger.[151]

Pound had decided to support Chafee. He was already angry at the treatment given dissenters within the faculty at Harvard. "I doubt if an intellectually honest man can justify himself in teach-

---

149. Leonard L. Levy, *The Emergence of a Free Press* (New York, 1985).

150. Bradley Chapin, *The Law of Treason* (Eugene, Oreg., 1964).

151. Masses Publishing Company v. Patten, 244 F. 535 (S.D.N.Y. 1917); Schenck v. United States, 249 U.S. 47 (1919) (Holmes, J.). See generally Richard Polenberg, *Fighting Faiths: The Abrams Case, the Supreme Court, and Free Speech* (New York, 1987), 154–96.

ing in this country by the next decade," he wrote to his mother in April 1918. By September, his despondency and his ire had grown. "I know a man who is paid $30,000 a year to denounce anyone who shows a sign of liberal thinking, and he is earning his money. I refuse to submit to this sort of thing. If it is patriotic for these people to use the war as a cloak for advancing their own interests and undoing the work of the last generation's social improvement, it is patriotic for me stand up in my right to expose them and discuss the real interest of the public. Any way, I refuse to have my ideas made to order for me by businessmen." [152]

Pound had put his finger on the underlying issue. It was not free speech itself that was under fire, but certain kinds of free speech. Not only was anti-war speech attacked, but also anti-business and anti-capitalism sentiments were unacceptable to the government. Thus, the prosecutions fell on the anarchists and other political radicals of the day. Among these, a small group of émigré Russian Jews in New York City became the target of the entire federal Espionage Act enforcement team. Jacob Abrams, Mollie Steimer, Hyman Lachowsky, Samuel Lipman, and Jacob Schwartz were anarchists. In the Yiddish language, they agitated against the war, the conditions of laborers in New York City, and the allies' attempts to undo the Russian Revolution through military intervention. They scattered leaflets from tenement windows, demanding in Yiddish and English that "the people" awake to Wilson's hypocrisy and come to the aid of the Russian Revolution. Workers were to seek the truth but not overthrow anything. The five were arrested, confessed, and were tried in federal courts in the fall of 1918, soon after Chafee had gone on record in favor of a broad reading of the First Amendment. The trial was something of a travesty, with the judge, Henry DeLamar Clayton, Jr., an Alabaman sitting by assignment, acting as a prosecutor. The convictions were appealed to the United States Supreme Court, where Holmes and Brandeis—the former influenced by Hand and others and the latter convinced from the start of the government's mistake—dissented from the majority of their brethren. Holmes found the leaflets expressions of opinion, exhortations, not likely to cause an upheaval, and so protected. Brandeis joined, and in other free speech cases that term he went further. [153]

---

152. Pound to Laura Biddlecombe Pound, Apr. 27, 1918, and Sept. 3, 1918, NSHS, MS 911, box 1, folder S.1, vol. F.4.

153. Polenberg, *Fighting Faiths*, passim.

Chafee was not entirely happy with the dissent, but praised it in an article for the *Harvard Law Review* in 1919 and then used it as the centerpiece for his 1920 book *Freedom of Speech*. In April, before the publication of the book, he signed an amnesty petition, which brought him to the notice of the Department of Justice, and that not for the first time. The surveillance of dissidents had already turned up Chafee's name after he praised Holmes's dissent in 1919. In part, the Department of Justice was responding to perceived criticisms of its own conduct, a matter that Chafee reiterated in a 1920 *Harvard Law Review* piece on the Abrams trial. In the meantime, influential law school alumnus Austin G. Fox had joined with federal prosecutors from the Abrams team to have Chafee fired. He then threw fuel on the fire by testifying before a Senate committee hearing on the Red Scare. Chafee opined that the Department of Justice had used illegal and unconstitutional means to arrest and try suspected critics of the government (and of the Department of Justice). Fox rounded up his allies, met them at the Harvard Club in New York City, and asked J. Edgar Hoover for documents that would prove Chafee's association with "Reds," which Hoover happily sent. Harvard President A. Lawrence Lowell now intervened, in part because Pound (who had himself signed the amnesty petition), Frankfurter, Holmes, and Brandeis were all lobbying him, and arranged for a hearing before the Visitors of the Law School instead of a lynching. Pound sat with Chafee and strongly supported him. When the committee of Visitors deliberated on the evidence, they found no conscious errors in Chafee's writings, but only voted six to five not to censure him, Cardozo casting the deciding vote. There were some technical mistakes, which Chafee conceded in print shortly thereafter.[154]

Chafee was grateful to Pound and said so. "I was very sorry not to see you before leaving Cambridge, for I wanted to wish you the best kind of a year abroad, and also to thank you heartily for the unfailing support you have given me through the late unpleasantness," Chafee wrote to Pound on August 17, 1921. "It is all of a piece with the encouragement which it has been such a great pleasure to me to receive from you ever since I came to the school to teach. . . . I think of myself as just a sentry whom they hoped to pick

154. Ibid., 272–84; Smith, *Chafee*, 36–57.

off before assaulting the main positions." Chafee was less than contrite in this private letter, for he knew that his errors were not the issue: "Of course, they wouldn't have bothered about my 'inaccuracies' if it hadn't been for my opinions."[155]

Frankfurter had been on leave from Harvard for most of this. Although he had never been a strong supporter of Wilson, he served as a labor mediator at Wilson's request. Frankfurter's style was part jawboning and part Brandeisian faith that good men, forced to sit at a table and listen to each other's troubles, could find a solution to them. In case after case, however, Frankfurter faced not personal troubles but the conflict of radical labor and entrenched capital. In general, he settled disputes, prevented or ended strikes, and averted the violence that had plagued such confrontations in the past. It was a test of his endurance, and sometimes, notably in the case of the Arizona miners, he failed. But even his failures he used, for when he was named chairman of the War Labor Policies Board on May 7, 1917, he glimpsed a new kind of government, led by experts, using their discretion, in administrative agencies.[156]

Pound had already expressed his reservations about such agencies, and he and Frankfurter could not have been more at odds than on this question, but in the matter of free speech at Harvard, they were in hearty accord. Returned to the school in the fall of 1919, Frankfurter told a rally at Fanueil Hall in Boston that Wilson should reverse his policies on Russia. Accused by a member of the Corporation of consorting with Communists, Frankfurter took umbrage. He joined the amnesty petition, helped Chafee defend radicals, and aided Pound in defense of Chafee at the "trial" in May 1921. He had probably urged Stimson and Augustus Hand, among the Visitors, to "acquit," but there is no evidence to prove it.[157] His mentor, Pound (though the relationship between the two men was more symmetrical now), had to threaten to resign unless Frankfurter got the new chair in constitutional law (which Brandeis's efforts had helped create).[158]

Pound did not hesitate here to make the private discourse of his support for Chafee and Frankfurter into a public statement. In

155. Zechariah Chafee, Jr., to Pound, Aug. 17, 1921, RPP, 182-12.
156. Parrish, *Frankfurter*, 81–117.
157. Ibid., 118–28.
158. Urofsky and Levy, *Half-Brother, Half-Son*, 44 n.2.

1920, the ABA polled its members on the following highly charged referendum:

> WHEREAS, The Constitution of the United States and the Constitutions of the several States contemplate government by and for all the people and not by or for any particular class, group or interest:
> *Now be it Therefore Resolved,* That the liberties of the people and the preservation of their institutions depend upon the control and exercise by the Federal, State and municipal governments of whatever force is necessary to maintain at all hazards the supremacy of the law and to suppress disorder and punish crime.[159]

The preliminary results of the voting, as reported in the *American Bar Association Journal,* showed overwhelming support for governmental force "to suppress disorder": 4,950 voting in the affirmative and only 58 voting against the resolution.[160] With the majority of the bar solidly and publicly supporting the use of extreme measures, United States Attorney General A. Mitchell Palmer carried on with impunity a brutal crusade against dissidents—mass arrests and deportations—that wreaked havoc with Bill of Rights guarantees of free expression and due process of law.[161] While the elite bar as a whole either supported or condoned the attorney general's assault on dissent, Pound made his own views public. In May 1920, twelve prominent attorneys and law professors published a scathing, documented denunciation, *Report upon the Illegal Practices of the United States Department of Justice.*[162] Among the twelve protesters were Chafee, Frankfurter, and Roscoe Pound.[163]

And Pound used his networks to help himself. Pound praised Holmes to Laski, knowing that Laski reported to Holmes. Laski did not need to be prompted much, as he wrote to Holmes in June 1917: "Pound and I have had some great talks—and his plans for the Law School strike me as splendid."[164] Pound's defense of Chafee and

---

159. *6 American Bar Association Journal* 3 (1920).

160. Ibid.

161. Robert Murray, *Red Scare: A Study of National Hysteria, 1919–1920* (Minneapolis, 1955), passim.

162. National Popular Government League, facsimile reprinted in Richard E. Rubenstein and Robert Fogelson, eds., *Mass Violence in America* (New York, 1969).

163. Freund, Pound, and Chafee, as well as lawyers Alfred S. Niles and Tyrrell Williams, were all ALI members and founders.

164. Laski to Holmes, June 4, 1917, in Howe, *Holmes-Laski Letters,* 1:89.

Frankfurter had made his own tenure in office shaky. Laski and Holmes rode to his rescue. Laski to Holmes, May 11, 1919: "The real truth is that there's a great fight on as to the future of the [Law] School and the older Tories are eager to make the place unbearable by Pound [in the wake of Pound's defense of Frankfurter and Chafee for their pro–free speech articles]. He is a very great dean and the students worship him and sooner or later the Law School Alumni Association has to step in and tell the world what Pound is counting for in scholarship and prevent this idle insistence on a *status quo* that has already lost its status." Holmes reciprocated. Holmes to Laski, a week later: "Following your suggestion I have just written this note to Grinnell. . . . 'I have a very strong conviction of the value and importance of Pound who I think has done much to maintain the superlative reputation of the School.'" Laski to Holmes: "That is a most generous letter of yours about Pound and on his account, as well as my own, I am very grateful. It will give exactly the kind of help that is needed." "[O]n his account" indeed—Laski no doubt shared this exchange with Pound.[165] Pound joined with Holmes and Laski in deriding Wigmore's attack on Holmes's dissent. Wigmore had called Abrams and his friends thugs—hardly appropriate, of course, but Wigmore had been called back to the colors and enjoyed helping the war effort.[166]

Privately, Pound was less than grateful for all this newfound help. He confided to his mother that he was coming to resent the complacency, arrogance, and passivity of the Brahmins, matched only by the reckless radicalism of the intellectual populists.[167] He was equally ill at ease with "[t]he technical progressive on any subject connected with law . . . [where] zeal and enthusiasm will take the place habitually of critical investigation and hard thought."[168] But he was still Pound, who led the way, and he believed, still, that jurisprudence made a difference. In his jurisprudence seminar notes for January 28, 1919, he wrote, "XIX century social science held that

165. Laski to Holmes, May 11, 1919, Holmes to Laski, May 18, 1919, and Laski to Holmes, May 20, 1919, in Howe, *Holmes-Laski Letters* 1:201, 204, 205.

166. Laski to Holmes, Apr. 2, 1920, in Howe, *Holmes-Laski Letters,* 1:257; John Henry Wigmore, Abrams v. United States: Freedom of Speech and Freedom of Thuggery in War-Time and Peace Time, 1920, John Henry Wigmore Papers, Northwestern University; Roalfe, *Wigmore,* 120–43, 148–50.

167. Pound to Laura Biddlecombe Pound, Dec. 1, 1914, NSHS, MS 911, box 1, folder S.1, vol. F.2.

168. Pound to Henry M. Bates, Nov. 21, 1914, RPP, 156-2.

we could only observe. Now we are confident that we can do things—that we can create." It was the old progressive faith, but what was to be done with it? The key was "this notion of the efficacy of effort in jurisprudence." Such jurisprudence, like all modern social science, must do more than sit back, observe, and describe. It must be an active aid to the improvement of law. "It is intelligent effort, not blind, blundering effort, that is efficacious. We must study the interests to be secured and discover the ends to be met by law. We must arrive at ethical principles for valuing these conflicting ends." [169]

Indeed, the very essence of litigation in the common law, Pound opined, was balancing the claims of contending interests. The stakes were not just individual interests, that is, individuals trying to vindicate their rights, but also social interests, groups, organizations, and classes, vying for a piece of the social and economic pie. Public policy decisions, not abstract notions of individual duty and obligation, were required to settle these disputes.[170] Social psychology helped to probe the instincts behind the claims. Groups' needs gave more insights. An inventory of social instincts allowed the jurist to see into the conduct of entire institutions. Pound assumed that the goal was to harmonize these demands, for everyone wanted safety, a decent standard of living, and moral conduct. To these, Pound added his own concern for the conservation of material resources and the progress of learning and technology. A good progressive, no matter how pragmatic, always abhorred waste.[171]

---

169. Pound, Jurisprudence Seminar Notes, 1918–19, RPP, 198-4.
170. Roscoe Pound, "A Theory of Social Interests," 15 *Proceedings of the American Sociological Society* 17, 22 (May 1921).
171. Ibid., 29–41.

CHAPTER THREE

Pound Expounds and Llewellyn Has a New Idea

In 1920, Roscoe Pound turned fifty. He stood at the pinnacle of his profession. Harvard graduates like Walter Lippmann, emerging as major journalists and interpreters of ideas, continued to view Pound as the great critic of illiberal courts, even though Pound had always been careful to exonerate the person of the judge.[1] Contemporary book reviewers readily gave Pound credit for originating the attack on "mechanical jurisprudence."[2] Nathan Isaacs wrote from the University of Pittsburgh School of Law, "Perhaps you will be amused to learn how you are passing down into history . . . one of [my] students asked whether [John] Selden was the same one who wrote *Uxor Ebraica* and similar works. I answered, 'Oh. Yes. His scholarship embraced everything. He was the Dean Pound of his day.'"[3] Sam Bass Warner, a former Pound student then teaching at the University of Oregon Law School and soon be to Pound's colleague, did not want to take his visiting year at Harvard "if you are not there."[4] Peers later recalled that "[u]nder his administration the [Harvard Law School] reached the highest enrollment in its history and the Common Law survived with various changes in the direc-

1. Walter Lippmann, *Drift and Mastery: An Attempt to Diagnose the Current Unrest* (New York, 1917), 157.

2. R. F. Alfred Hoernlé, "Review of *Science of Legal Method*," 31 *Harvard Law Review* 807 (1917–18).

3. Nathan Isaacs to Roscoe Pound, Apr. 1, 1921, RPP, 21-1.

4. Sam Bass Warner to Pound, Oct. 15, 1920, RPP, 34-17.

tion of socialization." Pound himself "represents what is the soundest and most workable in our legal system."[5]

Pound had achieved the status of foremost American academic jurisprudent of his day. Benjamin Cardozo, whose judicial rulings and thoughtful essays had made him Pound's counterpart on the bench, saw Pound as a liberal ally. Critics of the Taft Court's reversion to the jurisprudence of the Gilded Age called on Pound's essays as one would invoke a sacred relic in a time of danger.[6] Pound was not the patron saint of political radicalism, or even structural reform of the courts. He was the spokesman (though he would have raised an eyebrow at the appellation) of one interest group among the many providing remedies for the ills of the age. This was the liberal legal academic community. As he wrote at the end of his Dartmouth Alumni Lectures in 1921, "The right course is not to tinker with our courts and with our judicial organization in the hope of bringing about particular results in particular kinds of cases at a sacrifice of all that we have learned or ought to have learned from legal and judicial history. It is rather to provide a new set of premises, a new order of ideas in such form that the courts may use them and help them into a modern system by judicial experience of actual causes. . . . It is an infusion of social ideas into the traditional element of our law that we must bring about." The "we" referred to the law professors, and the "social ideas" were the program of the pragmatic progressives.[7]

The study of law could no longer be restricted to internal concerns and developments. It must be a study also of the "actual social facts upon which law must proceed and to which it is to be applied. Where the last century studied law in the abstract, [modern jurisprudents] insist upon study of the actual social effects of legal institutions and legal doctrines." Law, then, must entertain the findings

5. Albert Kocourek, "Roscoe Pound as a Former Colleague Knew Him," in *Interpretations of Modern Legal Philosophy: Essays in Honor of Roscoe Pound* (New York, 1947), 428.

6. Benjamin Cardozo, "A Ministry of Justice," 35 *Harvard Law Review* 114 (1921) (Pound a leading advocate of a watchdog agency over the actions of the Department of Justice); Maurice Finkelstein, "From Munn v. Illinois to Tyson v. Banton: A Study in the Judicial Process," 27 *Columbia Law Review* 772 (1927) (quoting from Pound's "Liberty of Contract" to prove that judicial assertions of the equality of bargaining power of individual laborers and large businesses were ludicrous).

7. Roscoe Pound, *The Spirit of the Common Law* (Francestown, N.H., 1921), 190, 189.

of the economists and sociologists (even to admitting these scholars to law faculties) and must incorporate their findings into its own required readings. "Before we can have sound theories here we need facts on which to build them. Even after we get sound theories, we shall need facts to enable us to apply them."[8]

Pound's faith in the law and its teaching was the faith of the progressive generation, a faith in salvation by ability, pluck, and facts. Although he no longer espoused the radical restructuring of the law school—with the passing of Hohfeld, Pound's interest in that project dissipated—he still believed that empirical studies were the ticket to the future. As he told Sam Bass Warner: "An intelligent study of the output of the judicial mill, say in San Francisco [Warner taught at the University of Oregon Law School] made by one who could appreciate the important points to investigate, and give us not merely conventional statistics, but a real study, would have a value far outside the limits of California."[9] And no one was better suited to such a study than the academic—indeed, than the legal academic. "A well trained man with a clear head and a reasonable amount of determination is certain to make a place for himself in the law teaching profession," he believed, because there was such work to do.[10]

It helped to be at Harvard, where faculty like Felix Frankfurter and Zechariah Chafee, Jr. were just such men, and whose regular academic departments included social scientists of note, but the message was not lost on law faculties at Yale, Columbia, and elsewhere, whose younger scholars interested in the social sciences looked to Pound as an inspiration. Pound had made himself into the central figure in a network of academic study of law. The network was open ended; anyone with the right credentials could apply for admission to Pound's circle.

But Pound was a man out of place when he stepped beyond that circle. Others might not notice, but he surely did. He was physically exhausted and had been for a number of years. As he had written to his mother in 1918, "As long as the war lasts, I must stick to this job and pull it through somehow. It would be cowardly to quit. When it is over, I think I shall quit and let some one else make bricks

8. Ibid., 212, 213–14.
9. Pound to Warner, Mar. 1, 1919, RPP, 84-5.
10. Pound to Edward A. Ross, Feb. 14, 1919, RPP, 80-19.

without straw." Teaching a progressive-pragmatic line seemed futile. "Reaction will have things its own way for a generation," he moaned.[11] Pound was more hopeful when the war ended: "For a season the reactionaries are going to have things their own way," he predicted to Ross early in 1919. "But it cannot be a long season, Reaction cannot wrap itself in the American flag and shriek much longer." But Pound was wrong, and the Great Fear grew worse.[12]

He had opposed President Woodrow Wilson's "War to Make the World Safe for Democracy," with its suppression of dissent, and now watched with horror the Red Scare that followed the peace. "The general attitude about 'radicals' here is that of 17th-century Salem toward witches. Accusation carries condemnation with it."[13] Intellectuals like Pound were aghast, in part at the treason of their own kind, for many reputable university scholars had joined in the propaganda effort of the Committee on Public Information.[14] As Randolph Bourne wrote shortly before the end of the war (the flu epidemic of 1918 took him, as it had Hohfeld), "The herd-coalescence of opinion which became inevitable the moment the state had set flowing war-attitudes became interpreted as a pre-war popular decision."[15] What else could Pound have felt when he read A. Mitchell Palmer, the attorney general of the United States, its highest legal officer, fulminate: "Like a prairie fire the blaze of revolution was seeping over every American institution of law and order a year ago. It was eating its way into the homes of the American workman, its sharp tongues of revolutionary heat were licking the alters of the churches, leaping into the belfry of the school bell, crawling into the sacred corners of American homes, seeking to replace marriage vows with libertine laws, burning up the foundations of society."[16]

The irony was that Wilson's own country could not live up to the ideals of Wilson's grand Fourteen Points, not after the president caved in at the Versailles Treaty sessions and allowed the victors to

11. Pound to Laura Biddlecombe Pound, Apr. 27, 1918, NSHS, MS 911, box 1, folder S.1, vol. F.4.

12. Pound to Ross, Feb. 14, 1919, RPP, 80-19.

13. Pound to Laura Biddlecombe Pound, June 19, 1919, NSHS, MS 911, box 1, folder S.1, vol. F.2.

14. The notorious "Creel Committee." Page Smith, *America Enters the World: A People's History of the Progressive Era and World War I* (New York, 1985), 558.

15. Randolph Bourne, "The State" (1918), in Carl Resek, ed., *War and the Intellectuals: Essays by Randolph S. Bourne, 1915–1919* (New York, 1964), 84.

16. A. Mitchell Palmer, "The Case against the 'Reds,'" 63 *Forum* 173 (Feb. 1920).

carve their initials on the face of Europe; not after Wilson fell to a stroke trying, vainly, to get the United States Senate to ratify America's participation in the League of Nations.[17] Again, Pound was a man out of place, for he supported humane causes even in the beleaguered Soviet territories. While Wilson agreed to aid the "White Russian" revolt against the Bolsheviks, Pound gave money to rebuild Russia's farms and retool its farmers.[18]

Instead of a new birth of civic virtue at home, the war gave way to the "Roaring Twenties," an age of artificially regulated morality that bred immorality. Prohibition and the Ku Klux Klan walked hand in hand. As John Dewey had warned in response to William Jennings Bryan and his campaign against the theory of evolution, "We have been so taught to respect the beliefs of our neighbors that few will respect the beliefs of a neighbor when they depart from the forms which have become associated with aspiration for a decent neighborly life. This is the illiberalism which is deep rooted in our liberalism. No account of the decay of the idealism of the progressive movement in politics or of the failure to develop an intelligent and enduring idealism out of the emotional fervor of the war, is adequate unless it reckons with this fixed limit to thought. . . . Otherwise we shall have in the future what we have had in the past, revivalism like Bryan, Roosevelt, and Wilson, movements which embody moral emotions rather than the insight and policy of intelligence."[19]

The ambiguities of the new age—sometimes intentional, like the irony of the "lost generation" of writers, and sometimes unconscious, like the posturing of lynch mobs' leaders—deflated all of the ethical certitudes of Pound's generation. Never was the demand for personal self-control so public, and never was it more publicly

17. Smith, *America Enters the World*, 693–736.

18. Pound to Charles W. Eliot, honorary chairman, Boston Committee of the Russian Reconstruction Farms, Mar. 3, 1925, RPP, 32-10. Pound did not know that this was a Communist front organization, nor apparently did Eliot or William Hocking, other supporters from Boston's Brahmin caste, but twenty-five years later, a security check by the FBI classified Pound as a subject for further checks. Using information from the House Un-American Activities Committee, Pound was identified as a member of the advisory board of a front organization (and, worse, a contributor to *New Masses*). J. Edgar Hoover to Loyd Wright, Mar. 15, 1957, FBI File No. 77-74432, Freedom of Information Act Request No. 349815.

19. John Dewey, "The American Intellectual Frontier," 30 *New Republic* 388 (May 1922). But Dewey had much to apologize for—he had abandoned his old free speech positions to argue that wartime dissent should be curbed. David M. Rabban, "Free Speech in Progressive Social Thought," 74 *Texas Law Review* 1001–8 (1996).

flouted. In an era that made the businessman the mirror of Jesus and looked to the values of Main Street, flappers and speak-easies became the icons of a new liberty of personal expression and disobedience to law. Women won the right to vote, but unlike the predictions of the suffragists, empowering the "second sex" did not transform public morals. Political scandals undermined both major political parties. Hedonism seemed to have won the day, or at least shared it with the nihilism of the writers and intellectuals.

In the more ethereal reaches of elite culture, new canons of art replaced realism. Salvador Dali's surreal landscapes and the minimalist expressionism of Wassily Kandinsky joined the swirling, colorful abstracts of Paul Klee and Henri Eduard Matisse. Oskar Kokoschka and Pablo Picasso experimented with new ways to represent the inner torment of the human form. Franz Kafka's vision of a world gone mad was echoed in Adolph Hitler's madness that posed as politics. Thomas Mann captured the emptiness at the heart of the middle class, while Herman Hesse found alternative civilizations more pleasing than the one that crashed in wartime Europe. In America, e.e. cummings and John Dos Passos reminded their readers of the terrible spiritual sacrifices of the war. Social critics like Sinclair Lewis parodied and demeaned the conventions of Main Street. F. Scott Fitzgerald celebrated the lack of values of the idle rich and the would-be rich. Malcolm Cowley, critic and chronicler of the literary expatriates, recalled that, when he arrived at the artists colony in New York City in 1925, he was angry, terrified, and disappointed. There was no soul in the metropolis. "I sometimes had pleasant nightmares in which I fancied that New York was being destroyed by an earthquake: its towers snapped like pine trees in a storm. A tidal wave poured through its streets and swept them clean of lice." [20]

Pound's pessimism took a particular cast. He saw the world turning back to an older, less progressive (in both senses of the word) age. "I do not know what the situation is out west," he confided to his mother in 1920, "but in this part of the world the seventeenth century is repeating itself. Intolerance of opinions on any economic, social, or political question which might in any wise impair dividends is carried to the limit." Pound despised the Puritans and cor-

---

20. Malcolm Cowley, *Exile's Return: A Literary Odyssey of the 1920s* (New York, 1956), 203.

dially hated their ancestors. But behind the intolerance, he saw a bleaker, more mercenary motive: "As near as I can make out the Puritan down here never did believe in liberty for anyone but himself, and just now that means liberty to make enormous dividends." He found the railroad men of his Nebraska boyhood days and the Puritans of contemporary New England bedfellows. "I am constantly reminded of the situation in Nebraska when I was a boy when everything was under the control of the railroad systems. Politically, as you remember, no one could own his own soul. . . . Just now here we have a curious combination of those two types of intolerance. The manufacturers are in exactly the same position in which the railroads were in the west in the [18]70's and 80's. But they carry the thing not merely into politics but into other kinds of mental activity. There are spies in classes and spies in church meetings and spies in forums, and whenever one says something even in a casual conversation it is likely to come back in all sorts of distorted forms."[21]

Not only was Pound disgusted at what he called Puritan New England, but he despised the unreconstructed South as well. From Memphis, two months later, he wrote: "[T]he 'Confederate Dames' have a cast iron table in a park here giving the 'confederate History of Memphis.' I . . . have been lavishly entertained everywhere, but am more doubtful about the South than ever. The South is sure it whipped the Kaiser and [is] held down by a force of a pro-German North. I don't know how I manage to keep so serene a temper with some of these people. They are absolutely intolerable."[22] Of his new summer home in Maine, he wrote sadly, "[T]his region is beautiful, but slowly going to waste. The farmers are dying off or giving up in despair and splendid farms are growing up to alder bushes and thistles."[23]

But Pound was not immobilized by his sadness. Instead, he accepted a series of invitations to give lectures at Dartmouth, at Yale, at Cambridge University, and at the University of North Carolina at Chapel Hill. He was much in demand as a lecturer. John Dewey,

21. Pound to Laura Biddlecombe Pound, Mar. 27, 1920, NSHS, MS 911, box 1, folder S.1, vol. F.3.

22. Pound to Laura Biddlecombe Pound, May 30, 1920, NSHS, MS 911, box 1, folder S.1, vol. F.3.

23. Pound to Laura Biddlecombe Pound, Aug. 2, 1920, NSHS, MS 911, box 1, folder S.1, vol. F.3.

a frequent guest speaker himself in these years (the pragmatists crossed each other's trails on the lecture circuit much as members of the transcendentalist circle had a hundred years before), wrote in 1928: "It is fortunate for the general public that Professor Pound is in so much demand for lectures on various foundations, since by this means it becomes acquitted with his learning and his ideas."[24] All four sets of lectures, published almost immediately in book form, were filled with learning. Indeed, the reader is overwhelmed with the scope of Pound's reading. The allusions spanned all of Western legal and moral thought, aphorisms chasing pithy summaries and wise asides across the pages. All of the lectures rehearsed themes that Pound had introduced elsewhere. One of the series, however, had something quite striking and powerful to say—for in the lecture that concluded the Cambridge series, Pound at last dropped the other shoe. He explained how sociological jurisprudence changed the function of law.

An Introduction to the Philosophy of Law, a compilation of Pound's 1921 Storrs Lectures at Yale, might better have been titled *An Introduction to the Legal Philosophy of Roscoe Pound.* Not that it was didactic or opinionated (not especially, at any rate), for Pound did not write that way. It was quite the reverse, almost stuffy in its balanced opinions. Here were Pound's stages of law, from the primitive, through the statist, to the equitable, the scientific, and finally the social. Here were the rhythmic shifts between legislative law giving and judicial interpretation. Also answering to their names in the roll call were the "schools" of jurisprudence: the purveyors of the metaphysical and the natural law, the analytic followers of positive law, and the historical school, which bet everything on the subliminal pull of custom. The entire cast was assembled. And every path led to the present, Pound's present, wherein "jurists began to think in terms of human wants or expectations rather than human wills. They began to think that what they had to do was not simply to equalize or harmonize the satisfaction of wants, they began to weigh or balance and reconcile claims or wants or desires or expectations." Law became the science of ends, not ideas. But here Pound began to hedge his bets. The law again became passive because the jurist

24. John Dewey, "Review of [Roscoe Pound,] *Law and Morals,*" 28 *Columbia Law Review* 245 (1928).

could assume that there was a way to harmonize the jangle of competing wants. "I do not believe the jurist has to do more than recognize the problem and perceive that it is presented to him as one of securing all social interests so far as he may, of maintaining a balance of harmony among them that is compatible with the securing of all of them." Pound harkened back to his prewar idea of a society in which interests did not compete with one another. The rest of the talks repeated Pound's already expressed views on liberty of contract (bad), the new products liability (good if there was fault, bad if there was none), and the Communists' view of property (unconscionable).[25]

The *Interpretations of Legal History* that Pound shared with his audience at Trinity College, Cambridge, in 1922 were in part a comparison of English and American legal history, in part a song of praise to the common law, and in large measure an attack on mechanical interpretation in case law. The last lecture, however, took a throwaway line from *Introduction* and made it something quite different. In the latter, Pound had offered the hope that legal history would see, in the future, "a continually more efficacious social engineering."[26] It was innocuous—who would not be in favor of more efficiency? Both efficiency and the engineering metaphor were staples of progressive ideology. But in *Interpretations,* Pound changed the meaning of the phrase. He made it present, active, and an obligation of jurisprudence. "Let us think of jurisprudence for a moment as a science of social engineering, having to do with that part of the whole field which may be achieved by the ordering of human relations through the action of political organized society." Jurisprudence was not supposed to just explain; it was also supposed to tutor action. "The engineer is judged by what he does. His work is judged by its adequacy to the purposes for which it is done, by its conformity to some ideal form of a traditional plan. We are just beginning, in contrast to the last century, to think of jurist and judge and lawmaker in the same way." Imagine—the judge as social engineer. But the judge had to be a Cardozo or a Brandeis; that went

25. Roscoe Pound, *An Introduction to the Philosophy of Law* [1921] (rev. ed., New Haven, Conn., 1954), 42, 46, 47. As Brandeis wrote to Frankfurter in 1922: "Pound hasn't overcome all his anti-Bolshevism yet." Louis Brandeis to Felix Frankfurter, June 16, 1922, in Melvin I. Urofsky and David W. Levy, eds., *Half-Brother, Half-Son: The Letters of Louis D. Brandeis to Felix Frankfurter* (Norman, Okla., 1991), 103.

26. Pound, *Introduction,* 47.

without saying (or at least Pound did not ponder whether his thought applied to more "mechanical" judges).[27]

The old idea of balance changed in the new context of social engineering. "Judicial, administrative, legislative, and juristic activity, so far as they are directed to the adjustment of relations, the compromise of overlapping claims, the securing of interests by fixing the lines within which each may be asserted securely, the discovery of devices whereby more claims or demands may be satisfied with a sacrifice of fewer—these activities are collectively the legal order." Note that it was activity, not ideas or rules or the applications of individual fact situations to rules, that Pound praised. He had become a behaviorist. His pragmatism had a new, rough edge. The purpose of law was to reduce these frictions in "the relatively finite store of the material goods of existence." Law had became a zero sum game. Pound had discovered conservation already and praised it, but now he applied the laws of thermodynamics to the legal arena.[28]

Even more important was Pound's proffer of a new theory of law, what may be termed a "demand side" or consumer view of the legal process.[29] Law (and its interpreters, both official and academic) was in the business of "satisfying human demands." It first struck Pound in the 1920s that consumption rather than production, what critics called "consumptionism," had become the chief concern of the market.[30] It was also to be the chief concern of the academics. "Thus it is the task of the social sciences to find out how to make the process of satisfying human claims and demands continually less wasteful." Until then, lawmakers, under the cloak of formalism or conceptualism (the latter a term Pound had introduced nearly two decades before), had "served to cover up what the legal order really was and what court and law-maker and judge really were doing. In fact, as we look at [rights] in action, it is easy to see that they are recognitions of social interests—of the claims or demands involved in the existence of society. . . . In practice the courts continually weighed these and other social interests in the scale by declaring that this or that could not be enforced or that this or that result

27. Roscoe Pound, *Interpretations of Legal History* (New York, 1923), 152.

28. Ibid., 156.

29. I am grateful to Professor Peter Hoffer for suggesting the terminology and pressing the point on me. See his *Law and People in Colonial America* (Baltimore, 1992), 52.

30. William Leach, *Land of Desire: Merchants, Power, and the Rise of a New American Culture* (New York, 1993), 265.

was forbidden. . . ." In each of these calculations, there was no abstract process of reasoning, but a series of compromises of social interests.[31]

Pound had claimed for the progressive-pragmatic jurists the role of lawmaker. The search for an American jurisprudence had led to its progressive-pragmatic conclusion. One would now expect from him a law program, but that was not what Pound wanted to do. Instead, in *Law and Morals,* he rested once again on a pallid pedantry. True, other jurists were "becoming more confident of the efficacy of intelligent effort to improve the law." Projects for " 'restatements of the law' are in the air," and Pound was one of those asked to provide a plan for them. He did not become a reporter for one of the American Law Institute (ALI) Restatements,[32] but did, at the behest of his close friend William Draper Lewis, the first director of the ALI, author a "Draft of a Preliminary Report on Classification of the Law." In it, Pound reminded the would-be restaters that "we must renounce extravagant expectations as to what may be accomplished through classification." The rest was a summary of classification and codification over the centuries—exactly what one might have expected from Pound.[33] But Pound could have done more with the subject of law and morals than he did.[34]

31. Pound, *Interpretations,* 157, 158, 160, 161.

32. Roscoe Pound, *Law and Morals* (Chapel Hill, N.C., 1924), 3–4. On the ALI, see N. E. H. Hull, "Restatement and Reform: A New Perspective on the Origins of the American Law Institute," 8 *Law and History Review* 56–58, 81 (1990). Pound remained very interested in the work of the ALI, however, advising Lewis on the choice of reporters and corresponding directly with reporters and their advisors on a wide variety of topics. See RPP, 4-9, 10; 235-5; 236-1, 2, 3; 236-2 to -9. Pound also began a correspondence with Herbert Goodrich of the University of Pennsylvania, who would replace Lewis as ALI director. RPP, 15-12, 37-1.

33. Pound, Draft of a Preliminary Report on Classification of the Law, 1924, RPP, 236-2, p. 1. A later version was published as "Classification of Law," 37 *Harvard Law Review* 933–69 (1924).

34. Pound, *Law and Morals,* passim. It may be that Pound simply did not want to offend any potential contributors to Harvard's new capital endowment program. Pound had embarked on a building campaign at Harvard. The endowment at the time was small compared to the revenue from student tuition. Space was inadequate for expansion, although Harvard was already large for its time. In 1924, after extensive planning on Pound's part, a campaign to increase the endowment and to expand the school began. The school sought over $5 million, a fivefold increase in the endowment. Part of the funds were allotted for three new professorships. Pound soon went on the hustings. Arthur E. Sutherland, *The Law at Harvard: A History of Ideas and Men, 1817–1967* (Cambridge, Mass., 1967), 262–70. Frankfurter, on the committee to expand the law school, and Brandeis opposed the rush to expansion. Brandeis to Frankfurter, Oct. 9, 1924, in Urofsky and Levy, *Half-Brother, Half-Son,* 175–76.

And an instructor of law at Yale said so, in print. "The presentation of the various views discussed [in *Law and Morals*] is dispassionate, buttressed by ample citations, and accompanied by useful illustrative quotations. At times, as with the historical school's view of legal development as the unfolding of an idea, the author shows laudable patience with a curiously unrealistic conception." Indeed, "[t]he book contains little not already familiar to those who have followed the author's work, but is an excellent introduction for others, and a useful handbook in any event. As a discussion of the relation of law and morals, however, the reviewer finds it lacking, and lacking in a serious matter. The nature of law is discussed at length and with much care. But the nature of morals is hardly discussed at all." If law borrowed from morals in times when law needed aid, there was no distinction made among ethical, moral, and customary origins of non-legal standards. Worse, the argument flowed too smoothly, and the categories—"analytic," "social-utilitarian," and the rest—were too neat and well defined. "We are not used to this in American law, and the unusual arouses not only interest, but suspicion. One accepts this grace and authority from Holmes, for he aimed at simplicity; and from Cardozo, for he wanted to include personal experience, but with Pound, the reader must test the conclusions for himself." Plainly, the review was provocative, and designedly so. The author, Karl Nickerson Llewellyn, wanted to catch Pound's eye, and he did.[35] But why?

Llewellyn was born in Seattle and grew up in Brooklyn, New York. His father was of Welsh background; his mother came from an old New England family. With his father, a businessman of cheery disposition and uneven fortunes, he was affectionate, but his mother, an evangelical reformer, was the real influence on him. "My mother reads Ellen Key, works for birth control, voted for [Eugene] Debs, and distributed peace leaflets at the Democratic Convention in New York last June."[36] Her militancy sparked his irreverence, but her zeal became his ardor. He grew up a New York Democrat—a liberal intellectual partisan. He went to Boys High in Brooklyn, an academy in Mecklenburg, Germany, and Yale Col-

35. Karl Llewellyn, "Review of *Law and Morals* by Roscoe Pound," 34 *Yale Law Journal* 113, 114 (1924).

36. Llewellyn, A Non-Conformist Puzzles over Education, 1924, KLP, B.V.4.c.

lege. His German was excellent, and he formed such strong ties to his schoolmates in Germany that, when visiting them shortly after World War I broke out, he joined them in the service of the Fatherland and the Kaiser. Wounded and decorated, he was brought back to the United States in 1915. There he finished his undergraduate studies at Yale, finally studying hard and doing well.

His earliest intellectual influence, in addition to the discipline of German studies and the comparative laxity of life in New Haven, was Yale's own William Graham Sumner. Sumner's *Folkways* (1906), a combination of comparative anthropology and Herbert Spencer's *Social Statics,* set out to prove that mores and manners were rooted in cultures and that cultures did not change. Folkways were thus deeply rooted, whether in primitive or in civilized societies. Sumner was a sheet anchor on Llewellyn's radicalism, and the latter's later insistence on the importance of custom and established business practices in the law of sales may have owed something to the conservatism of Sumner. Above all, Llewellyn was indebted to Sumner for his views of crime and law enforcement. As Llewellyn told a social work gathering in 1928, "Certainly, I shall insist again, in closing, that law observance is a question of folkways rather than rules; that rules and folkways are not uniform but diversified in our society; and that any problem of law enforcement is a technical job of altering the conduct patterns of specific individuals."[37]

Llewellyn's father suggested a career in the law, and the son enrolled at Yale Law School in 1915. There he fell under the spell of Hohfeld. Hohfeld's attraction to things German appealed to Llewellyn, as did the older man's intellectual rigor. Llewellyn appreciated the breadth of Hohfeld's reading as few students might, for Llewellyn, too, was widely read. When America entered the war, Llewellyn volunteered but was rejected. He was thus one of the few eligible students at the law school who remained to finish the course. With some of the faculty gone and many of the students in uniform, Llewellyn found himself in close contact with the residue of the faculty, particularly Arthur Corbin. Corbin, an early reformer in the field of contracts, particularly stimulated Llewellyn's interest in the field, and the two men commenced a lifelong friendship. Corbin was an

---

37. Karl Llewellyn, "Law Observance versus Law Enforcement," from *Proceedings of the Conference on Social Work* (1928), reprinted in Karl Llewellyn, *Jurisprudence: Realism in Theory and Practice* (Chicago, 1962), 410. On Sumner, see Richard Hofstadter, *Social Darwinism in American Thought* (Philadelphia, 1944), 51–66.

indefatigable scholar. So was Llewellyn. But Corbin was a contracts man who stuck to his last, and Llewellyn thought bigger thoughts. Walter Wheeler Cook was there, too, but Llewellyn was never a Cook follower, in part because Cook was a hard man to follow.

Llewellyn graduated at the top of his class, edited the *Yale Law Journal*, and stayed on for a year as editor in chief and then as a candidate for the J.D.—at that time a postgraduate degree. In the spring of 1919, Llewellyn took on the additional labor of teaching commercial law. It remained, with jurisprudence, his great love. In 1920, he took his ideas to the marketplace, literally, working as house counsel for the National City Bank of New York. When the bank asked the firm of Shearman and Sterling to take over its legal affairs, the firm took Llewellyn on with the job. Llewellyn was apprenticed to William W. Lancaster, a leader in banking law. But a taste of the real world was enough. Llewellyn came away convinced that "the law in the books, at least in the commercial field, was 20 years or so behind the actual work in practice, and I hooked up with the legal work of the National City Bank in the hope of finding out what the law I had been teaching was all about." [38] In 1923, he returned to Yale and was promoted to associate professor. He did not stay long. Marrying Elizabeth Sanford, then a graduate student in economics at Columbia, Llewellyn retraced his steps to New York City, visited at Columbia Law School in 1924, and became an associate professor in 1925, all the while commuting to Yale to teach there as well. He never again held a formal position in New Haven. Although he could be found there many weekends, when offered a position he always declined. After all, he was a New Yorker. [39]

Llewellyn in the 1920s was a striver. Contemporaries recalled his ambition. It was a Faustian drive to understand the inner workings of the world. This made him a sterling teacher. "There were not many hours in a week when a student was not facing him across a desk stacked so high with books that one could hardly see over the barricade. Students were the spice of his life. His excitement came with the growth of their minds and the flowering of their curiosity. He pushed them to the utmost—teasing, taunting, prodding—

38. From an autobiographical sketch Llewellyn apparently prepared for the Yale Law School alumni, probably for the tenth anniversary of their graduation in 1928. KLP, biographical data, red box.

39. For biographical information on Llewellyn, see William Twining, *Karl Llewellyn and the Realist Movement* [1973] (Norman, Okla., 1985), 87–128.

flattering, cajoling, scolding."[40] He never saw himself as a conventional law professor. Llewellyn's first major publication, not surprisingly, appeared not in a law review but in the *American Economic Review*.[41] Llewellyn advocated the reform of commercial law, arguing that the abstract legal principles that dominated late-nineteenth- and early-twentieth-century commercial codes and court decisions were hindrances to modern business. Llewellyn wanted commercial law to use the insights of economics and modern business practices as guides. The arguments in his first article are reminiscent of Pound's comments in 1908. Indeed, Llewellyn publicly acknowledged his admiration for Pound and his debt to Pound's jurisprudence in this article. In the very first footnote, Llewellyn admitted that "[t]he present paper makes little claim to originality in its details. Much of the synthesis too, has been indicated by various writers from time to time." He confessed he was "particularly conscious of indebtedness to Sumner, Holmes, Veblen, Commons and Pound." In other words, he declared himself a bricoleur.[42]

But Llewellyn had hidden a bombshell in the otherwise innocuous call for more attention to commercial practices in the law. In what may have appeared little more than an aside, he suggested, "'Free' competition is rarely, if ever, free in fact, and law is one major instrument of restriction—for a variety of ends." Regulation might be public, to achieve some moral end, or to attempt to level the playing field between unequally situated parties. All of these intrusions were frictions of varying degrees. So was the burden that workman's compensation laid on manufacturers. But the result was a reduction in injuries to workers. The "growing common law tendency [is] to force an insurer's liability on the manufacturer of articles which, like automobiles, are dangerous if improperly made. . . . [A]ll alike recognize the dependence of laborer, bystander or consumer on an industry with which as an individual he cannot cope." The law was adding costs to economic enterprise, and this might be "a potent instrument of reform."[43] In the name of cost analysis of legal rules (a forerunner of today's law and economics school, and very close

40. William O. Douglas, "Karl N. Llewellyn," 29 *University of Chicago Law Review* 611 (1929).
41. Karl Llewellyn, "The Effect of Legal Institutions upon Economics," 15 *American Economic Review* 665 (1925).
42. Ibid.
43. Ibid., 679, 680.

indeed to the work of its liberal leaders, notably Guido Calabresi[44]), Llewellyn had made a powerful statement of the relationship between the formal rules of law, in the form of judicial precedent, and the real world of workers, consumers, and bystanders.

In 1925, the same year in which his *American Economic Review* article was published, Llewellyn, now thirty-two years old and an untenured associate professor at Columbia University School of Law, decided to articulate his general ideas about the new jurisprudence. Like many ambitious younger faculty, he prepared a book proposal for a publisher in the hope of obtaining an advance contract. The book, at least as Llewellyn described it, was neither completed nor published. All that remains is a typescript in the Karl Llewellyn Papers of an outline of chapters and a thirty-three-page introductory essay.[45] That never-published introductory essay is the first expression we have of what Llewellyn meant by the term "realistic jurisprudence" and what he thought were its intellectual origins.[46]

And Llewellyn gave to Pound pride of place in that movement. In 1925, Llewellyn unequivocally stated that "[t]he significant school of jurisprudence today is the sociological, of which Dean Pound has been the acknowledged leader and spokesman." He admiringly proclaimed that "[the sociological school] alone is vital, growing, expanding to meet new needs." The new thinking, a "multiform mass of efforts," came out of the sociological school.[47] In analyzing this "new thinking," the only two tenets Llewellyn identified on which nearly every writer in this movement could agree—"that jurisprudence cannot stand alone; and that the significant aspect of law is law's effect"[48]—were part of Pound's jurisprudential agenda from the very beginning. Llewellyn admitted that most of the breakthroughs and ideas could be traced to Pound. Indeed, in the process of explaining the new jurisprudential movement, Llewellyn called Pound's chapter in the recently published book *The History and Prospects of the Social Sciences* the "best starting place."[49]

44. Compare Guido Calabresi, *The Cost of Accidents* (New Haven, Conn., 1970).

45. KLP, B.I.6.a–c. The draft introduction is entitled "New Trends in Jurisprudence."

46. The date is given as 1925–27 in Raymond M. Ellinwood, Jr., *The Karl Llewellyn Papers, A Guide to the Collection* (Chicago, 1967), 4.

47. Llewellyn, "New Trends in Jurisprudence," 1.

48. Ibid.

49. Ibid. The book was a collection of essays by various authors on all areas of the social sciences published in the same year that Llewellyn penned his unpublished essay

Llewellyn had singled out an obscure essay of Pound's as his "starting place" for explaining realistic jurisprudence. Neither Llewellyn nor any subsequent scholar of Pound or legal realism thereafter cited the piece. Despite the later obscurity of the collection and Pound's essay in it, in 1925, committed as he was to a social scientific approach to law, Llewellyn would have been naturally drawn to read the newly published book. Pound's chapter on "Jurisprudence" was, to some extent, a reworked summary of his three-part *Harvard Law Review* article on sociological jurisprudence, but Pound had strengthened the programmatic impact of his own ideas in the later piece by simplifying the intellectual background and stating his agenda more forcefully. In writing about the "Sociological School" of jurisprudence, Pound had argued that the sociological jurisprudents, including himself, of course, shared a common perspective on the law. He claimed that they

> look to the working of the law rather than to its abstract content; they regard law as a social institution involving both finding by experience and conscious making—an institution which may be improved by conscious human effort; they lay stress upon the social ends which law subserves rather than upon sanctions; they look on legal precepts and doctrines and institutions functionally and regard the form of legal precepts as a means only. *Philosophically they are chiefly positivists or neo-realists.* They employ a pragmatist method which is consistent with different metaphysical starting points.[50]

It is not surprising that Llewellyn found his views resonating so closely with Pound's. All of the characteristics of the sociological jurists that Pound identified in his chapter were characteristics associated with what Llewellyn defined as realistic jurisprudence. Llewellyn outlined in his essay the seven points that Pound had claimed in that chapter as the "program" of the sociological jurists.

    1. Study of the actual social effects of legal institutions and legal doctrines. . . .
    2. Sociological study in preparation for lawmaking.
    3. Study of the means of making precepts effective in action.
    4. Study of juridical method.

---

on "Realistic Jurisprudence." Harry Elmer Barnes, ed., *The History and Prospects of the Social Sciences* (New York, 1925).
   50. Pound, "Jurisprudence," in Barnes, *Social Sciences,* 458 (emphasis added).

5. A sociological legal history; study of the social background and social effects of legal precepts, legal doctrines, and legal institutions in the past, and of how these effects have been brought about.

6. Recognition of the importance of individualized application of legal precepts.

7. In English-speaking countries, a ministry of justice.[51]

These seven points were similar, but not identical, to the characteristics Pound had earlier described in "Sociological Jurisprudence." Llewellyn conceded that "[t]he first, third, fourth and fifth of these points may well be found to cover the bulk of the present paper," but argued that the "differences in emphasis become significant enough to warrant continuing." The primary difference in emphasis, Llewellyn contended through the next several pages, was the integration or confusion of ethics, morality, or prescriptive ideals with juristic science. Llewellyn noted that "[i]t is hard to see how a movement for anything but discovery of objectively verifiable facts and relations between facts can be characteristic of any science." To the extent that Pound and others had characterized jurisprudence as a science, therefore, Llewellyn argued that it was an error to study what "is" and what "ought to be" as one enterprise. The achievement was to open the road, not to traverse its length. "The sociological school, in shifting emphasis from rule and precept to the effect of law, have taken us out of a study of words into a study of deeds." Thus, Llewellyn's conclusion also echoed Pound's own in "Sociological Jurisprudence"—a call for a pragmatic jurisprudential approach. While Llewellyn would temporarily divorce the pragmatic from the progressive, he acknowledged his realistic approach was but a plantlike "shoot" off the "vital" "stock" of Pound's sociological jurisprudence.[52]

If the "New Trends" manuscript began as a somewhat backhanded tribute to Pound, Llewellyn intended it to be a good deal more. "The aim of this paper is to indicate these trends," he wrote in the margin. Llewellyn loved the company of the living almost as much as Pound honored the memory of the dead in jurisprudence. Pound was secretly jealous of the "already considerable and con-

51. Llewellyn, "New Trends," 2a. Llewellyn quoted the list points directly from Pound's chapter in Barnes, *Social Sciences*, 462–63.

52. Llewellyn, "New Trends," 2, 3, 4–5, 6–7, 1.

stantly growing number of American students in the field."[53] Llewellyn was happy to be one of the young turks. He did not name them (after all, "New Trends" was as much a memo to himself as a manuscript, and he knew who he meant). Probably they were a small but energetic and able cadre of empiricists at Columbia Law School—William O. Douglas, Underhill Moore, Leon Marshall, and Herman Oliphant.[54]

Llewellyn began his substantive argument where Pound ended his recitation—with "social control": "We do know that the present aim of jurisprudence as a science is to discover, so far as may be, the ways by which the state machinery can be made to effect men's conduct; that the problem is one of studying the nature, control, and effectiveness of particular means of social control." To do this, one must adapt "the approach of the behaviorists." For "law-on-the-books not reflected in action" was not law "at all," which meant that " '[r]ules of law' ceases to be a term with any meaning, save as being—in the favorable case of a 'well settled rule'—the courts' own statement of how they act." The proper study of law was thus "coming to center on the behavior of officials."[55]

What next? A functional approach does not merely look at the conduct of officials and at "side effects" of law, but also integrates all the new insights. To wit: it turns the law into a group dynamic, fully divorcing it from all previous jurisprudential schemata. Llewellyn did not use group theory as an analogy for the conduct of parties in litigation, or for that of officials of the court; he identified the two as one in the same. By so doing, he could argue—contra Pound—that the institutions of the law did not and perhaps never would reduce friction and satisfy all parties. If Llewellyn's theory is right, the law will always be imperfectly adapted to its function, for social forces and group interests (remember, Llewellyn does not use this as a metaphor—the law *is* a social community) are always beset by internal conflicts and open to the intrusion of unexpected external events. That is what economics and sociology taught.[56]

The jurisprudent must thus become not a student of sociology

---

53. Ibid., 1.
54. Laura Kalman, *Legal Realism at Yale, 1927–1960* (Chapel Hill, N.C., 1986), 68–74.
55. Llewellyn, "New Trends," 3a, 4, 5, 6, 7. Llewellyn anticipated here his famous, or infamous, dictum in *The Bramble Bush.* See pages 171–72.
56. Llewellyn, "New Trends," 8, 9, 10, 11.

and the other social sciences, but a social scientist.[57] Thinking as a social scientist, the jurisprudent will recognize that group structures are invariably complex, fragmented, and changing. The "great society is a composite of lesser societies." How to penetrate the complexity? Easy: "[T]his goes hand in hand with the behavioristic approach described above, whereby the emphasis of jurisprudence is shifted to the behavior of all officials of the state . . . and that, in turn, has other implications. For these officials come to appear not as organs of a general will, but as a group or a host of groups of men, acting in the main like other groups of men within an institutional structure." Look then to the background and attachments of the officials, "a political machine, a trade union, a corporation, a farmers' alliance, and . . . the 'general will' disappears; 'the law' becomes human and inconsistent; the fact of competing group interests becomes evident."[58]

A truly "realistic jurisprudence" (the first time the words appear in the discourse[59]) is one based on "an investigation of the means by which such lesser societies, organized and unorganized, control their own affairs. The corporation, the church, the family, the labor union, the manufacturer's association—their government is not merely a problem interesting in itself, but one which shed infinite light on the generis, limits, general processes of law proper." Pound had talked about "the engineering side of law," a phrase Llewellyn repeated without attribution here, but Pound had not fully credited the way in which "artists in government have for centuries understood the art of educating and controlling such lesser societies[,] . . . of so shaping law-on-the-books as to fit that functioning. And until students of jurisprudence turn their attention to this field, their work will be out of line with living facts."[60]

The next step is to borrow from the other social sciences to help

---

57. Pound in 1925 still insisted that the jurisprudent borrow selectively from the social sciences, including sociology and social psychology, but did not suggest that the jurist become a social scientist. See Pound, Lecture on Sociology and Law, 1925, RPP, 13-10, pp. 11–12. Pound did resent the caricature of sociological jurisprudence as "mere gathering of data," rather than informed adaptation of social science theory. Ibid., 10.

58. Llewellyn, "New Trends," 11–13.

59. Llewellyn would remember this in later years but erroneously relate it to a later article, his 1930 "A Realistic Jurisprudence": "In any event, I claim to have introduced the term 'Realistic Jurisprudence' into the modern literature." Karl Llewellyn, *The Common Law Tradition: Deciding Appeals* (Boston, 1960), 512.

60. Llewellyn, "New Trends," 13.

interpret the data generated by the legal system. True, Pound had called for data gathering, but (despite his participation in the study of crime in Cleveland) he regarded social science methods as ancillary to jurisprudence. Llewellyn wanted adoption of "the theoretical developments" in social science. Perhaps Llewellyn was naïve in this faith, for he either ignored or did not understand that social scientists argue about theory as much as law professors argue about the meaning of cases. But Llewellyn did not mind dissonance of this sort. "For I take it that the new jurisprudence is eclectic, and even acrobatic, and capable of lining up at once with institutional and marginal economists, so far as the views of either serve its needs."

Llewellyn subscribed to the code of the bricoleur. And he tried to deploy the new findings of the economists in a way that Pound did not try to borrow from the sociologists. Llewellyn's treatment of white-collar crime, where the "taboo alone ceases to be effective" and criminal sanctions become necessary, demonstrates the effect of law at the margins of group customs. "Such a hypothesis [indeed, the whole of the project of the new jurisprudence] does more than steer a middle course between Austin and Savigny [that is, between the analytical school and the historical school]. It goes far to clarify not only something of the nature of one major field of law, but also the process of law's operation in that field; not only the process, but also the problem of making that process more effective. And such hypotheses [drawn from the social sciences] together with something of the technique for their verification, the new jurisprudence may be expected to seek and find in goodly number among the sister disciplines." It appears that Llewellyn had married jurisprudence to the other social sciences.[61]

And where did this leave the older, formalist conception of the role of the courts? Llewellyn answered that question by linking Holmes's "Path of the Law" to ideas that would appear in Jerome Frank's *Law and the Modern Mind*: "Yet it may fairly be deemed the fulcrum of all realistic jurisprudence [that term again]. For it means viewing what the court says in its opinion as perhaps only a rationalization of what it proposes to do, on the facts assumed to be before it. Forthwith the focus shifts to 'rules' as worthless except as they are statements of what courts will do."[62]

61. Ibid., 14, 15, 16, 17.
62. Ibid., 33.

Llewellyn did not publish his prolegomenon to the new trends, but (already the careful craftsman) he continued to think and write about his "realistic jurisprudence." Again, the goad and inspiration were Pound: admired and yet the object of attack. In June 1927, Llewellyn found time to write to Pound that he was working on an article on "modern concepts of law," in which he planned to take exception to Pound's eleven-year-old article on the limits of effective legal action. Always careful that he not misquote or mistake someone's meaning, he told Pound that "it occurred to me that it is better to find out what a man means than to speculate in print upon his meaning."[63] Llewellyn dutifully acknowledged his "indebtedness to [Pound's] writings,"[64] but respectfully suggested that Pound had erred in saying that the jurists of the "stage of strict law" had consciously used "rule and form" to achieve certainty and uniformity. Rather, Llewellyn argued, "the process runs other end to: rule and form had come to be and were not subject lightly to men's change; certainty and uniformity resulted, and survived until their survival came to seem somewhat vigorously inexpedient."[65]

Llewellyn's proto-realist critique of Pound's interpretation of jurisprudence emerged clearly in this early correspondence. Pound's historical sketch, Llewellyn thought, was totally ahistorical. Pound, according to Llewellyn, had imposed a design of conscious causal processes on what was undoubtedly an unconscious practical evolution followed by post hoc rationalization. Pound was guilty of what Llewellyn later called in the 1930 article "postmortemizing."[66] Pound's macro-categorization of legal development—in sharp contrast to the emerging realists' interest in studying and collecting individual case data—overlooked the everyday, ad hoc experience of the jurists responsible for that development. "It is hard," Llewellyn told Pound, "to read *Njal's Saga* and believe the rules and forms there involved were built with any conscious aim at either certainty or uniformity of outcome."[67]

63. Llewellyn to Pound, June 27, 1927, RPP, 24-6. Again, anticipating the brouhaha that would arise when Pound accused Frank of misquoting him in *Law and the Modern Mind* and Frank demanded Pound show where Frank had misquoted him. See pages 196–200.

64. Llewellyn to Pound, June 27, 1927, RPP, 24-6.

65. Ibid.

66. Llewellyn borrowed the phrase from his friend Thomas Reed Powell, so he said later. Karl Llewellyn, "A Realistic Jurisprudence—The Next Step," 30 *Columbia Law Review* 437 (1930).

67. Llewellyn to Pound, June 27, 1927, RPP, 24-6.

Llewellyn continued with two additional points. The first was an observation that Bronislaw Malinowski's recently published *Crime and Custom in Savage Society*[68] contradicted Pound's assertion that law in the primitive stage did not distinguish among religion, morals, and rules.[69] The second was a quibble with Pound's claim that, because modern society no longer recognized private actions at law against individuals (presumably men) who harbor disaffected wives who have deserted their husbands, there were no longer any legal (only moral or communal) sanctions against such conduct.[70] Llewellyn queried Pound: "[D]o you not regard divorce for desertion as a sanction of the wife's failure to live with her husband, even though the attempts at specific reparation have gone into the discard?"[71] Llewellyn's letter concluded: "I offer my queries as evidence that your writings provoke to thought."[72]

Llewellyn's query was more than academic. His marriage, despite the passion of his first years with Elizabeth Sanford, was falling apart. Pound's own life was far from serene. His wife had been diagnosed with a heart ailment. We tend to see highly developed intellection as separate from the thousand aches and pains that hobble everyone's personal lives, but that is simply not the case. The realities of human life force themselves into the nooks and crannies of the most apparently abstract systems of thought. Academic jurisprudence was for both men a refuge from the sorrow of personal difficulties. The combat of discourse was a pleasure, for it could be controlled by the power of intellect and was carried on within well-understood rules. The exchange of letters and the cut and thrust of scholarly lectures and articles absorbed their energies and gave them a sense of mastery over words, if not things.

If they kept their personal anxieties out of all but their most confidential correspondence, however, they welcomed the problems of the wider world in their public writing. In fact, both men immersed

68. Bronislaw Malinowski, *Crime and Custom in Savage Society* (London, 1926).
69. Llewellyn to Pound, June 27, 1927, RPP, 24-6. Pound made that assertion in Roscoe Pound, "The Limits of Effective Legal Action," 3 *American Bar Association Journal* 58 (1917). Actually, Llewellyn did not quite get Malinowski right. The latter had said that the Trobrianders did punish crimes, but that there were not the institutional sanctions one ordinarily associates with law.
70. Pound, "Limits," 67.
71. Llewellyn to Pound, June 27, 1927, RPP, 24-6.
72. Ibid.

themselves in the serious challenges to law and order that marked private and public life in the 1920s. Rumors of corruption of the Republican Party became reality when the Teapot Dome scandal scarred President Warren Harding and brought down his mode of "government by crony."[73] Worse still was the widespread belief—exaggerated perhaps, but compelling in its imagery and troubling in its implications—that the public disregarded the Volstead Act and Prohibition. Federal judges and prosecutors saw themselves enmeshed in Laocoön's monsters. So powerful was the public resistance to the law that there was no way to enforce it. Frederick Lewis Allen, writing in 1931, recalled that "[t]his overwhelming flood of outlaw liquor introduced into the American scene a series of picturesque if unedifying phenomena: hip flasks uptilted above faces both masculine and feminine at the big football games; the speakeasy, equipped with a regular old fashioned bar, serving cocktails made of gin, turned out, perhaps, by a gang of Sicilian alky-cookers (seventy-five cents for patrons, free to the police); well born damsels with one foot on the brass rail, tossing off Martinis . . . and the coin of corruption sifting through the hands of all manner of public servants."[74] And then there were the radicals, beaten, but unbowed—but at least quieter. But might not anarchism, communism, and other isms again threaten America?[75] There was still a disposition among the police and the prosecutors to link crime and radicalism (and thereby to place the blame for all crime on foreigners).

In the national law schools, the questions were no longer a matter of philosophical niceties: Was the new jurisprudence any surer guide to action than the old "rules of law?" Did sociological or realistic jurisprudence offer any answers to the dilemma? How much could the law professors accomplish, and to what extent would their ideas influence courts and governments? The power and optimism Pound and his generation felt at the beginning of the decade were staggered in wartime, but that was a national emergency. In the era of "normalcy" that followed, when hysteria should not have overmastered sober intellect so easily, Pound and Llewellyn discovered that reasoned argument and established rules were no match for prejudice and fear.

73. William E. Leuchtenburg, *The Perils of Prosperity, 1914–1932* (Chicago, 1958), 91.

74. Frederick Lewis Allen, *Only Yesterday: An Informal History of the Nineteen-Twenties* (New York, 1931), 210–11.

75. Leuchtenburg, *Perils,* 81, 128.

The case that seemed to capture all of the issues—the excess discretion of the criminal justice system, the powerful xenophobic biases of officers of the law, the lingering fear of all radicalism—was the case of Nicola Sacco and Bartolomeo Vanzetti. On the day before Christmas in 1919, the paymaster of a local shoe company was fired on by three would-be robbers as he transported three metal boxes of cash from a Bridgewater, Massachusetts, bank to his factory in his Ford truck. After the truck hit a telephone pole, the robbers fled in a waiting automobile. No one was injured, and no money was taken. Though the company hired the Pinkerton Agency to track down the would-be robbers, it came up with no positive results.[76] Nearly four months later, on April 15, 1920, another paymaster and a special security officer in nearby South Braintree were gunned down as they walked the short distance between the paymaster's office and the factory, carrying two wooden boxes containing the workers' pay envelopes. The gunmen and their accomplices escaped with the pay boxes in their automobile. The security guard died almost immediately; the paymaster survived him by only fifteen hours.[77] On May 5, Sacco, a shoe factory worker, and Vanzetti, a fish peddler, were arrested while riding on a streetcar at about ten o'clock at night. They had been tracked from a garage where they, with three other men, had tried to recover a vehicle suspected of being used by the bandits. Vanzetti was later indicted for attempted robbery and murder related to the Bridgewater incident the previous December 24, and both were indicted for the South Braintree robbery and murders.[78]

The cobbler and the fish monger were local activists in an anarchist workers movement with ties all over Europe, but particularly in Italy. Anarchists, Communists, Socialists, and dissenters, particularly those who were foreign born, were feared, distrusted, and despised in the postwar atmosphere, but more than Jacob Abrams and those who protested against the war, Sacco and Vanzetti symbolized violent protest. Their friends detonated bombs in public places, killing police and bystanders. It was the bombs, more than the protests, that led to the Red Scare.[79]

76. Louis Joughin and Edmund M. Morgan, *The Legacy of Sacco and Vanzetti* (Chicago, 1948), 26–30.

77. Ibid., 30–31.

78. Ibid., 26–57.

79. Paul Avrich, *Sacco and Vanzetti: The Anarchist Background* (Princeton, N.J., 1991), 105 ff.

Both men were accused and convicted of the South Braintree payroll robbery and murders. Both were convicted and sentenced to death after a long and sensational trial. Defense counsel Fred Moore, whose radical credentials may have exceeded his trial skills, pushed the anarchist evidence to the forefront of the trial, antagonizing the presiding judge, Webster Thayer (a proud and conservative man who needed little urging, as his later remarks proved, to express his distaste for radicals and foreigners), and causing him to overreact, particularly in his closing instructions to the jury. Later interviewed, the jurymen insisted that they took little notice of the radical issue; it neither prejudiced them against the defendants nor convinced them that the police and prosecution had fabricated a case in order to strike at the anarchist movement. They saw the case as a robbery-murder, and the issue for them was the credibility of the eyewitness identifications of the two defendants, compared with the credibility of their alibi witnesses.[80]

The case had drawn widespread attention because substantial questions had been raised about the fairness of the proceedings—were the two radical immigrants found guilty of the crime charged, or had they been prosecuted and condemned for who they were and what they represented? Moore was able to mobilize some of the radical community, but he antagonized others, including his clients, and he was replaced by William G. Thompson. Thompson was paid by a committee of some of Boston's best men and women, none of whose names ended in vowels, for Thayer had acted in inappropriate ways after the trial was over. Not only had he dismissed motions, which was clearly within the official scope of his duties, but also he made private statements indicating that he regarded the defendants as guilty before the trial began. Like the Dreyfus affair less than a half-century before in France, the Sacco and Vanzetti case became a passionate cause célèbre for educated Americans. If a miscarriage of justice was being perpetrated in Massachusetts, then the American system of justice itself was on trial. It was perfectly logical therefore that in addition to literary figures and social reformers, law professors would be drawn into the debate. Who else could better evaluate the judicial proceedings and advise the public on their

80. David Felix, *Protest: Sacco-Vanzetti and the Intellectuals* (Bloomington, Ind., 1965), 153–55.

legality? Who had greater expertise or interest in the fundamental structure of American justice?[81]

Orthodox accounts of the Sacco and Vanzetti case tell us that Felix Frankfurter was the first legal academic to involve himself as advisor to defendants' counsel. Certainly, Frankfurter's participation was the most strenuous and vocal.[82] In fact, Frankfurter was not the first Harvard academic to write to William Thompson, Sacco and Vanzetti's counsel in their appeals, or to comment critically on the legal proceedings. On May 9, 1925, nearly two years before Frankfurter's published defense of Sacco and Vanzetti in the *Atlantic Monthly*, Roscoe Pound contacted Thompson, of whose interest in the case Pound already knew,[83] to suggest a new line of attack on the identification evidence presented at the anarchists' trial.[84] A month and a half later, the Harvard dean wrote to Thompson again with a more forceful expression of his opinion of the case: "At the time of the . . . trial I read the testimony from day to day in the newspapers, and had a very strong feeling that I would not hang a dog on the evidence."[85] He also told Thompson that he was "convinced that the whole trial ought to be written up thoroughly," but personally demurred to do the job, since "just at the moment it would be quite impossible for me to do so." He regretted that his hectic schedule kept him from taking on the task because, he told Thompson, "I feel strongly that somebody ought to have the courage and the sense of justice to speak out vigorously about these cases."[86]

Pound had concluded that the two men were innocent,[87] but for Pound, the real issues concerned the function of the criminal justice system. For twenty-five years, Pound had pondered these concerns.

81. And the debate goes on to this day about their guilt. See, e.g., William Young and David E. Kaiser, *Postmortem: New Evidence in the Case of Sacco and Vanzetti* (Amherst, Mass., 1985), 158–59.

82. Indeed, the Morgan sections of *Legacy* derive in part from the connection between Morgan, a colleague of Frankfurter's at the time and an expert on the law of evidence, and Frankfurter. See, e.g., Joughin and Morgan, *Legacy*, 319 (defending Frankfurter's motives).

83. Pound to William G. Thompson, May 5, 1923, RPP, 32-14.

84. Pound to Thompson, May 9, 1925, RPP, 33-24. But Morgan, in *Legacy*, 319, argues that Frankfurter had "become interested" in the case in 1924.

85. Pound to Thompson, June 28, 1925, RPP, 33-24.

86. Ibid.

87. Pound to Rev. Edwin Lines, Apr. 29, 1927, RPP, 32-14.

His interest was piqued by his first mentor, John Henry Wigmore.[88] At first, Pound thought that not only was the problem of crime susceptible to reasoned solutions, but also it called for the intervention of the academics. Pound had long been concerned by the subject. Even before he arrived at Harvard and was asked by Dean Thayer to teach criminal law, Pound thought long and hard about the social causes of crime and the social consequences of criminal law enforcement. In 1907, he worried about the effects of political corruption on criminal prosecutions, the use of evidence gained through illegal and brutal interrogations, the excessive discretion that judges and juries had in sentencing and verdicts, and, on top of everything else, the public expectation that criminal justice could actually eliminate crime.[89]

Such obstacles to criminal law enforcement were inherent in the system, but they were not the only ones Pound uncovered. The law did not yet take social facts into its cognizance. Legislation that might have been sensitive to such social facts was usually the exact opposite, badly written under the pressure of public dismay with particular kinds of offenses or offenders. "The punishment for selling cigarettes will be as heavy as that for bribery." Worse, both courts and legislatures slighted the administrative solution to crime—its prevention through civil penalties rather than criminal prosecutions. Finally, the courts and prisons were a residue of the "archaic" era—time consuming and inefficient.[90]

Pound's particular bête noire was the use of juries to determine punishment. In the jury box, the "unwritten law" held sway, eloquent counsel could persuade against the clear implications of the evidence, and sentiment replaced rationality. American judges (unlike those in England) could not direct the jury's thinking, although the absence of a bench that specialized in crime hindered the latter development.[91] For a progressive like Pound, the answer was simple. It was the age of the new penology; the reform and professionalization of police forces; the rethinking of sentencing; and the introduction of parole.[92] Pound was intimately involved in these

88. Pound, Untitled Appreciation of Wigmore, Sept. 9, 1941, RPP, 89-25.

89. Roscoe Pound, "Inherent and Acquired Difficulties in the Administration of Punitive Justice" (1907), in Sheldon Glueck, ed., *Roscoe Pound and Criminal Justice* (Dobbs Ferry, N.Y., 1965), 101–7.

90. Ibid., 108–12.

91. Ibid., 113–15.

92. David L. Rothman, *Conscience and Convenience* (Boston, 1980), 43–204.

scientific reforms early in the century, concerning himself with the causes of crime and the likely outcomes of different strategies of its punishment.[93] The way around the "Difficulties" was factual—more data-gathering surveys, "leading to more intelligent legislation and less patchwork." At the same time, he wanted an investment in the sociology of crime, wherein "intelligent, scientific understanding of the problems of criminology is applied to each case."[94]

Pound regarded crime as a social rather than a moral (or immoral) phenomenon. That meant that crime was not deviant or isolated but part of social behavior, albeit at its margins. In 1908, newly installed at Northwestern, Pound had given a talk entitled "Enforcement of Law" to the Illinois State Bar Association. "Law enforcement" did not mean more police in the streets or longer sentences to Pound. Instead, it was a civic issue, in which the rights of the individual had to give way to the rights of the people.[95] In a series of book reviews, talks, and essays thereafter, Pound sought a balance between procedural guarantees—which in the early twentieth century fell far short of the protection of suspects' rights in place at the end of the century—and the rights of the community. He was wary of the criminal jury's discretion, but generally defended it as an institution. He came to reject the idea that crime was simply an immoral choice for which the criminal had to be held responsible.[96]

But Pound refused to be specific. He returned over and over to his stages of law/cycles of law paradigm, describing rather than prescribing. There were periods of repression, he wrote in 1920 (no doubt thinking of the Red Scare, as his audience must have realized), and periods in which the state relaxed its grip. Two years later, he insisted that there must be some compromise, some middle ground, between individual freedom and the demands of the state. Again, he was thinking of the current crisis in law enforcement and covertly may have been arguing against Prohibition. But he did not say so. Instead, he retreated into praise of the new social sciences, and their categorization of criminals. The problem was that the popular mind was still mired in nineteenth-century concepts of blameworthiness. A year later, in a series of lectures later published

93. Thomas A. Green, "Freedom and Criminal Responsibility in the Age of Pound; An Essay on Criminal Justice," 93 *Michigan Law Review* 1951 (1995).

94. Pound, "Inherent and Acquired Difficulties," 116.

95. Roscoe Pound, "Enforcement of Law," 20 *Green Bag* 401–10 (1908).

96. Green, "Criminal Justice," 1991.

as *Criminal Justice in America,* Pound was just as vague but more pessimistic. The police, the courts, and even the prisons had failed in their duty.[97]

By the 1920s, the crisis in enforcement of law was absorbing a good deal of Pound's energy. He and Frankfurter were responsible for one of the earliest attempts to do what Pound had demanded be done a decade before: gather and analyze the data of crime and law enforcement in a particular setting. That setting was the city of Cleveland, whose business elite watched with horror as a municipal judge and numerous policemen were indicted for corruption. The Cleveland Foundation asked Pound to study crime in the city. Raymond Moley, an economist, would handle the administration from the Cleveland end. Pound sought Frankfurter as co-director. In January 1921, the two professors journeyed to Cleveland to present their research plan, and it was accepted by the foundation. Pound hired the field investigators, Moley watched the subvention of $25,000, and Pound and Frankfurter committed themselves to a four-month timetable. The field investigators were all social scientists or psychologists, in support of which a group of statisticians and clerks was enrolled. Almost all were members of the social science professional associations and had published in or served as editors of professional journals. They were also former students of Pound, at Harvard or Nebraska. Most were lawyers as well. Pound the networker had proved how powerful networking could be, summoning the team from their other occupations and pressing them to the new task so promptly.[98]

Pound's crew performed on-site inspections, interviewed officials and criminals, counted references to crime in the newspapers, followed the "life" of criminal cases, and gave personality tests to defendants. They divided up the topics of prosecution, police, corrections, court organization, the newspapers, and the psychology of crime. The researchers were given considerable independence, which resulted in local complaints and Moley's increased supervision (representing the foundation). Pound had editorial control of the report, but Moley interfered with that as well.[99]

Part Eight of the report, "Criminal Justice in the American City,"

97. Ibid., 1995–2007.
98. Michael R. Hill, "Roscoe Pound and American Sociology: A Study in Archival Frame Analysis, Sociobiography, and Sociological Jurisprudence" (Ph.D. diss., University of Nebraska, 1989), 481–503.
99. Ibid., 504–16.

was Pound's, however, and he more than summarized what the investigators had found. His basic thesis was that good intentions and good men were not enough to ensure a fair and efficient criminal justice system. "For good men, if we get them, must work in the social and political and legal environment, and with the legal and administrative tools of the time and place." In every age, and particularly in the 1920s, "[i]t is impossible for any legal machinery to do all which our voluminous penal legislation expects of it." Pound hinted at decriminalization of certain offenses, but did not come out in favor of it, typically. But surely all the laws that tried to enforce a single moral standard crushed the criminal law system under their weight. Yet Pound was a strong proponent of vigorous enforcement of the law. He did not believe that laissez-faire should extend to crime. Once in the criminal justice system, the defender deserved to be treated as an individual, not a cipher; that is what modern psychology and medicine taught.[100] The rest of the summary was just that, with Pound bringing together the comments of the investigators under the rubric of "General Conclusions." All of them supported new technologies to "put this part of the legal treatment of crime upon a modern and effective basis." Supervision, control, training, and modern facilities would ensure speedier justice. A better-educated bar and bench would automatically help. The end of arrest for misdemeanors (a summons would do), more attention to juvenile offenders, and the creation of an office of medical examiner were also recommended. But there was no panacea. There was only effort.[101]

Five years later, Pound sponsored a Survey of Crime and Criminal Justice in Greater Boston; hired Sheldon and Eleanor Glueck and Sam Bass Warner, among others, to manage the data; and later funded an Institute of Criminal Law.[102] The first fruits of the survey, the Gluecks' *One Thousand Juvenile Delinquents* (1934), became an instant classic. Like all of the projects Pound sponsored in the area of criminal justice, it rooted juvenile misconduct in social mores instead of moral defects.

Pound was already busy raising funds for a chair in criminal

100. Roscoe Pound, "Criminal Justice in the American City—A Summary," in Roscoe Pound et al., *Criminal Justice in Cleveland* (Cleveland, 1922), 560, 582, 583, 586, 587, 588.

101. Ibid., 649, 650–52.

102. David Wigdor, *Roscoe Pound, Philosopher of Law* (Westport, Conn., 1974), 246–47.

law and participating fully in the National Commission on Law
Observance and Enforcement (or the "Wickersham Commission"
as it was commonly called after its chairman, former Attorney
General George Wickersham). The commission recognized that enforcement of Prohibition was failing and, in the process, had de-
layed all cases in the federal courts, but declined to recommend repeal of the Volstead Act.[103] Pound was a conscientious and busy
commission member. As he recalled to his biographer Paul Sayre, "I
remember Newton Baker saying in an after dinner speech once that
the way things were done was that I wrote everything, he signed
everything, and Max Loewenthal objected to everything. . . . As a
matter of fact, I generally did draw the first draft which was then
debated and overhauled and sometimes sent back for me to rewrite
and sometimes referred to a committee to revise. . . . The Commission was organized in a number of committees of which the most
important was the Committee on Prohibition. That committee took
a great deal of testimony and it was my job to take down the testimony. Also I worked out an elaborate outline on prohibition which
served as an index to the testimony." [104] Pound continued to give
interviews and write articles on the need for a full survey of crime
as a prelude to a thorough reform of the criminal justice system.[105]

Thus, in the middle of the Sacco and Vanzetti appeals process,
Pound had put Harvard in the forefront of social scientific inquiry
into criminal law. The irony was that too open advocacy of the in-
justice of the case might jeopardize all that Pound had wanted to
achieve. He recounted to Thompson the problems that had plagued
Chafee when he publicly criticized the Abrams free speech trial during the Red Scare of 1918–20.[106] It was one thing to defend a colleague, particularly one so mild and respected as Chafee, and quite
another to jeopardize a decade of institutional planning and alumni
fund raising for two immigrant anarchists. Pound had stood by

103. Sutherland, *The Law at Harvard,* 272–73; *New York Times,* May 21, 1929, at
1, col. 8 (Pound named); *New York Times,* Jan. 21, 1931, at 1, col. 8 (commission
reports).

104. Pound to Paul Sayre, Nov. 16, 1945, NSHS, MS 911, box 1, folder S.1, vol. F.20.

105. See, e.g., "Harvard Dean Warns of Hasty Action on Crime Problem," *Boston
Herald,* Aug. 29, 1925, at 1; "Dean Pound for Court Shake-Up," *Boston Herald,* Dec. 20,
1925, at 1.

106. On Chafee's role in the *Abrams* case, see Richard Polenberg, *Fighting Faiths: The
Abrams Case, the Supreme Court, and Free Speech* (New York, 1987), 272–84, and my
account at pages 117–21 above.

Chafee, saving his job, but local feeling on the Sacco and Vanzetti case was so much more charged that Pound would certainly have jeopardized his deanship if he had gone public with his condemnation of the proceedings.

The result of Pound's understandable caution was that Pound was left in the rear of the reform army. From the beginning of 1927 until August 21, when legal appeals at last ran out and the governor, on the advice of a special commission, refused clemency, supporters of Sacco and Vanzetti stepped up their public appeals and their attacks on the fairness of the proceedings. The law school community was directly drawn into the furor when Felix Frankfurter's strongly worded assault on the legal proceedings appeared in the March issue of the venerable, Boston-based *Atlantic Monthly*. Frankfurter's *The Case of Sacco and Vanzetti* (1927) expanded the argument to book length.

The conservative supporters of the verdict found their champion in the same criminal law and evidence expert who had supported the conviction of the *Abrams* defendants, John Henry Wigmore.[107] His intemperate article attacking Frankfurter and praising Judge Thayer and the legal system of Massachusetts appeared in the *Boston Evening Transcript* on April 25, 1927. Wigmore played on his authority in the field of evidence "to vindicate Massachusetts justice" and assault Frankfurter, Wigmore's old nemesis from the *Abrams* case. Wigmore was free with adjectives: the crime was "cold-blooded," and the protest was "an agitation." Frankfurter's article was "wholly devoid of credit."[108] Wigmore reviewed the evidence in eight columns of newspaper print, but his purpose was more polemical than legal, frankly entering the lists on the right against what had by then become a partisan tourney for the left. He had already privately accused Frankfurter of serving on the defense counsel's team—hence, by implication, forfeiting all claims to impartiality.[109] Judge Thayer was grateful and hoped that "newspaper discussion should cease."[110]

Wigmore's article enraged liberal legal academics, and both sides

---

107. On Wigmore's attack on Holmes's dissent (Brandeis concurring) in *Abrams*, see Polenberg, *Fighting Faiths*, 248–56.

108. *Boston Evening Transcript*, Apr. 25, 1927, at 12.

109. John Henry Wigmore to Felix Frankfurter, Mar. 2, 1927, Wigmore Papers, Northwestern University Library.

110. Webster Thayer to Wigmore, May 4, 1927, Wigmore Papers, Northwestern University Library.

went at it. Frankfurter replied, and newspapers all over the country carried his assertion that "Dean Wigmore could not have read the record; could not have read with care the opinion of Judge Thayer, on which his article is largely based; could not even have examined my little book to which he refers."[111] The *Nation* breathlessly offered proof that Judge Thayer was biased. "The six affidavits in the hands of Governor Alvin Fuller strip Judge Thayer naked of decency and justice. They ought to force his immediate resignation or lead to his speedy impeachment. A comparison between Webster Thayer and Pontius Pilate is all in the latter's favor."[112] Morris Ernst, writing in the same journal, accused the prosecution of deliberately suppressing evidence that would have tended "to affirm the innocence of the defendants" and the Massachusetts Supreme Judicial Court of letting the prosecution get away with it.[113]

Pound privately sided with the protest but refused to allow his private discourse to become public. Before Frankfurter and Wigmore squared off, Pound had approved ex–Ambassador to Italy Richard Child's manuscript article on the trial: "Those of us who had hoped to achieve something for the better administration of criminal justice must feel strongly that to dispose of the Sacco-Vanzetti prosecution on mere technical review of the record and reliance on the discretion of the trial judge is likely to bear much evil fruit in further legal hamperings of prosecution and limitations upon judicial power when presently the public cold fit is succeeded by the inevitable hot fit." Pound was swayed by the views of "newspaper men who have followed the evidence closely and intelligently from the beginning [and] do not think Sacco and Vanzetti guilty." Child was so delighted that he wanted to publish Pound's letter along with his article in the *New York World* and pressed editor Walter Lippmann, a Harvard alumnus, to do so. Lippmann asked Frankfurter to approach Pound on the subject.[114]

111. John Henry Wigmore, "J. H. Wigmore Answers Frankfurter Attack on Sacco-Vanzetti Verdict," *Boston Evening Transcript,* Apr. 25, 1927, at 1, 12 (reprint in Wigmore Papers, Northwestern University Library). Frankfurter replied to Wigmore the next day in the same newspaper and then Wigmore responded in a second article in the *Boston Evening Transcript* on May 10 and 11, 1927 (reprint in Wigmore Papers, Northwestern University Library, labeled as "B Herald").

112. "Judge Thayer Revealed," *Nation,* May 18, 1927, at 547.

113. Morris L. Ernst, "Deception According to Law," *Nation,* June 1, 1927, at 602.

114. Walter Lippmann to Frankfurter, Jan. 19, 1927, and Pound to Richard Child, Jan. 3, 1927, RPP, 23-18.

Pound verbally refused and then explained his actions a week later: "My letter to Richard Washburn Child was written at Professor Frankfurter's request upon a statement that Mr. Child wanted to be sure that the National Crime Commission and those engaged in its work would not criticize him. I looked his article over and dictated my offhand views on the subject. I was told that I was not writing for publication and therefore did not take the pains that I should feel bound to take if I were writing for publication. I have a strong dislike of discussing cases while they are pending in court." Pound's heart was with Child, but "[f]or my part, . . . I cannot consent to write about a case of such importance without very careful study of the record and mature conclusions formed from such first hand study. . . . For these reasons I do not think I ought to allow my offhand letter to Mr. Child to be published, and I should prefer not to say anything publicly about the case unless the ultimate judicial disposition of the case should require it. I am not at all without hope that the dilatory revolution of the judicial machine may yet bring about a right result." Lippmann graciously replied that he fully understood and had asked only because he wanted to tell Child Pound's reasons.[115]

Llewellyn, in 1927 still a mere associate professor at Columbia University School of Law in New York, was either far less vulnerable to assault for public advocacy on behalf of Sacco and Vanzetti or far more vulnerable, for his promotion to full professor, coincidentally processed that same spring, might have been jeopardized by his involving himself in the hotly debated case. But in his draft of "New Trends," Llewellyn had speculated on the causes of crime. "The problem of crime causes seems to be in good part a problem of divergent pulls and patterns derived from overlapping groups. In a complex mass of humanity deterrence becomes one of the great problems of penalty-infliction. And under high and easy mobility of population, extra legal social penalties are relatively easy—and comfortable—to escape."[116] Llewellyn's involvement in the Sacco-Vanzetti case came not from "realistic jurisprudence" but from Llewellyn's own reform impulses. Llewellyn did not weigh his vulnerability. He charged into the crusade for the condemned radicals

115. Pound to Lippmann, Jan. 26, 1927, and Lippmann to Pound, Jan. 29, 1927, RPP, 23-18.
116. Llewellyn, "New Trends," 17.

regardless of the consequences. Llewellyn agreed to spearhead an American Civil Liberties Union campaign to organize the nation's law professors in support of the defendants' appeal. After Vanzetti applied to Massachusetts Governor Fuller for clemency in early May 1927, Llewellyn organized a law professors' petition for Vanzetti on legal grounds. Llewellyn and the ACLU probably hoped that, if an overwhelming number of the nation's law professors publicly expressed their doubt that the trial passed procedural muster, Fuller would have to appoint an independent panel that might recommend clemency and the men would be saved.

Llewellyn's petition barely avoided advocacy, asserting that "only a review by an impartial body can determine whether the widely held belief is true that two issues had been confused in the murder trial—the radicalism of the defendants and their guilt or innocence of the murder . . . [and] the fact there is widespread doubt as to the justice of the result lends color to the possibility that such mistake may have been committed."[117] In other words, Llewellyn, while ostensibly protecting the neutrality of the professors on the merits of the case, actually allied them with those who condemned the proceedings.

With the scheduled execution date only one month away, Llewellyn telegraphed every legal academic he knew and every major law school in the country to obtain signatories for his petition.[118] Sixty-one law professors from twelve law schools signed or authorized acquiescence in Llewellyn's petition.[119] All but two of Llewellyn's own colleagues joined him. The petition was Llewellyn's first major foray into networking, allowing him to reach out to a wide variety of liberal jurisprudents in academe. Three years later, Llewellyn would use the responses as an index not of outrage at the fate of the two defendants, but of sympathy for his own views of law.

Contrary to accounts by Pound's biographers,[120] Pound finally

117. *New York Times*, May 10, 1927, at 9, col. 1.
118. Copies of Llewellyn's telegram and many of the telegraphed responses are in the Sacco and Vanzetti material, KLP, G.II (green box).
119. *New York Times, supra* note 117.
120. Neither of Pound's biographers appears to be aware of Pound's advice to and correspondence with the defendants' counsel on appeal, William Thompson; the Pound petition calling for an independent panel to review clemency for Sacco and Vanzetti; or his letter to the editor about the pardon process. Wigdor explicitly denies that Pound ever engaged in the public debate. Wigdor, *Pound*, 249–50. Sayre simply never mentions any public activity by Pound, and by apologizing for Pound, he implicitly suggests Pound stayed out of the public debate. Sayre, *Pound*, 219–23.

did enter the public debate about the Sacco and Vanzetti case. Pound might have found Llewellyn's petition too forthright on the merits of the case, but shortly after the ACLU-Llewellyn petition was released to the public, Pound wrote and promoted his own petition to Governor Fuller. Pound and several of his Harvard colleagues also called for "'a disinterested board . . . in whom the people have confidence' to report to the Governor their findings of fact, their opinions and their conclusions."[121] But Pound's petition, unlike Llewellyn's, explicitly stated that it was "not intended as an expression of our opinion on the question of the guilt or innocence of Sacco and Vanzetti now under sentence of death, or on the questions of the fairness of their trial or the justice accorded them."[122] Pound's petition was meticulously neutral; it displayed not a hint of his true opinion of the matter. If he had taken a stronger, more partisan stand, such a public declaration by the preeminent law school teacher in the country at that time might have had an enormous impact on the outcome of the appeal.

Though he felt very strongly about the case, Pound still refrained from using his prestige to aid the two men. He had earlier excused himself from taking sides by arguing that it was improper to criticize a case while still on appeal before the courts; that was no longer the situation in mid-May. Pound knew that Frankfurter's involvement had brought the law school into controversy, and any partisanship on the dean's part would have caused serious damage to the school's relationship to the Massachusetts legal community at a time when Pound was trying to launch a drive for funds to enlarge Langdell Hall. It is also possible that Pound's very calculated neutrality may have been a pragmatic strategy. It might be suggested that Pound may have thought that his enormous reputation and professed public neutrality on the merits would lead Fuller to appoint the Harvard dean himself to this independent panel—and if so, Pound could do the two condemned men greater service as an official advisor to the governor than as an outspoken, but officially powerless, public advocate. Pound's description of the qualifications for the men Fuller should choose seems to support such an interpretation. Pound recommended that the "disinterested board . . . be composed of lawyers and laymen of standing in whom the people

121. Undated and unattributed newspaper clipping found in KLP, G.II(S-V) (green box).
122. Ibid.

have confidence." [123] There was probably no lawyer in Massachusetts at that time who had greater standing with the thoughtful public than Pound, and he had demonstrated his disinterestedness, but Pound was not chosen for the panel.

Privately Pound continued to express his reservations about the case to almost anyone who wrote to him about the affair. He wrote to a law school alumnus that "Wigmore ought to be shown up in this matter . . . [his *Boston Evening Transcript*] letters are a disgrace to legal scholarship." [124] Yet, again, Pound would not publicly support Frankfurter's position. Pound confided that he "had thought seriously (when the smoke of controversy had cleared away a bit, and reason on this subject had ceased to be inhibited) of writing the matter up myself . . . [but] I do not see any reason why, after the careful, scientific review of the matter which I know you would make, you should not speak out in meeting your conclusions." [125] He did not hesitate to defend Frankfurter privately to high-ranking members of the legal profession. To Chester Long, ex-president of the American Bar Association, Pound sent a copy of Frankfurter's book on the case in mid-May. "I have looked over the record and can vouch for this as an absolutely reliable statement based on first hand study of the record. . . . Mr. Stimson will vouch for [Frankfurter's] entire reliability in such a matter as this." Frankfurter's reputation was not the only one on the line, however. "You will see that those of us who are urging the intervention of the governor are by no means socialists or irresponsible anarchists but merely citizens who believe on the best of grounds that there has been a miscarriage of justice, and that men ought not to be executed for murder because their economic and political views are obnoxious." It was the same free speech argument Pound had made in his own behalf in Nebraska twenty years before and had then repeated in defense of Chafee and Frankfurter in 1920. Pound wanted the ABA on his side. "I venture to hope that the Executive Committee of the American Bar Association will not allow itself to be rushed into this matter without a full and careful investigation. I am satisfied that if you were able to make such an investigation you would be among the foremost in urging that these men ought not to be executed for a crime which they did not commit." There was no question who was

123. Ibid.
124. Pound to E. R. A. Seligman, May 23, 1927, RPP, 32-14.
125. Ibid.

doing the arguing on the other side. It was Wigmore. "Dean Wigmore has rushed into print twice without examining the record, and without knowing the practice in Massachusetts." Pound took the opportunity to explain why he was upset. It was not just the miscarriage of justice or the need to defend Frankfurter, but a fault in the system. The resolution of the Sacco and Vanzetti case was another example of mechanical interpretation of law. "It seems hard to believe, but it is a fact, that in this commonwealth the Supreme Judicial Court in a murder trial will take the facts as absolutely established by the verdict, and will look simply for errors in the record at the trial. Likewise the Court feels constrained to hold that in case of newly discovered evidence the granting of a new trial is in the discretion of the trial judge, and unless he is so utterly unreasonable that what he does would be idiotic, there is no power to set his ruling aside." [126]

Pound was more circumspect in his only actual publication on the case, a neutrally worded, scholarly letter to the *Boston Herald* in June 1927 about "petitions for pardon and the relation of the exercise of the pardoning power to the administration of justice by the courts." [127] Behind the scenes, he continued to fume to Long, "[T]he commission [to advise the governor,] I understand, has not yet set to work. What the commission will do I can hardly predict. I have a feeling that one member goes upon the commission with a fixed determination not to be affected by evidence, and another member of the commission has had no experience of passing upon evidence, and I am afraid he, also, will be inclined to go on the general proposition that here are two obnoxious persons who have been regularly convicted and that ought to end it. This puts a very heavy burden upon the third member of the commission, who, I am satisfied, intends to give the case very careful and thorough consideration." [128] The "third member" was A. Lawrence Lowell, president of Harvard. Long was noncommittal but friendly in his reply, but Pound did not give up trying to keep the ABA from coming to Wigmore's aid. [129]

126. Pound to Chester I. Long, May 18, 1927, RPP, 24-9.
127. Pound's letter appeared in the *Boston Herald,* June 4, 1927, at 1. The description of Pound's letter comes from a letter of appreciation from Reverend Edward C. Camp, pastor of the Phillips Congregational Church in Watertown, Mass., to Pound, written on the day Pound's *Boston Herald* letter was published. Edward C. Camp to Pound, June 4, 1927, RPP, 32-14.
128. Pound to Long, July 2, 1927, RPP, 24-9. But Pound was mistaken. See note 134 below.
129. Long to Pound, July 14, 1927, RPP, 24-9.

After the commission had made its report in favor of execution of the sentence and the governor had accepted it, he wrote again to Long:

> If the newspapers represent the report correctly it is about the most unsatisfactory thing I ever read. It absolutely ignores what seem to me the vital features of the case. It proceeds upon the theory which has stood in the way of justice in this case ever since the original trial, namely, that public confidence in the institutions of Massachusetts should suffer if it was assumed that a mistake could be made in such a case. . . . My fear is that just as the authorities here have acted upon the assumption that every one who has bestirred himself on behalf of a shoe-maker and a fish peddler must be a radical bent upon destroy-ing institutions (principally because so many foolish radicals have acted in a foolish way in connection with this case) the Executive Committee [of the ABA] might be led to act upon similar assumptions and to do something which ultimately all concerned might very much regret.[130]

Pound's reputation as a progressive reformer and the mentor of the new jurisprudential thinkers was in jeopardy, but Pound would not cross the line from private discourse to public pronouncement. Indeed, his participation in the affair ended with a whimper. Wilbur Bryant, a Nebraska county court judge, wrote to Pound after the executions, asking for a copy of an article Pound had supposedly written on the case. Pound's secretary replied, "I do not know of anything that Dean Pound has written on the Sacco and Vanzetti case."[131] Pound's failure to commit himself in public on the Sacco and Vanzetti case contrasted sharply with Llewellyn's own approach. Indeed, Llewellyn's interest in the case was undiminished even after the executions. He joined the executive committee of the Sacco and Vanzetti National League, the successor to the Defense Committee set up under the ACLU, and began work on a book for the league that would presumably vindicate the dead men. Pound, even after the furor had died down, only encouraged others to protest the in-justice of the case and continued to say nothing in print.[132]

Pound's refusal to join in the public discourse, other than as a

---

130. Pound to Long, Aug. 6, 1927, RPP, 24-9.

131. Wilbur Bryant to Pound, Aug. 26, 1927, and "Secretary to Dean Pound" to Bry-ant, Aug. 30, 1927, copies in Wigmore Papers, Northwestern University Library.

132. See, for instance, Pound's correspondence with Henry Edgerton and Charles Culp Burlingham in the fall of 1927, RPP, 32-14.

neutral, as though he were above the fray, must have annoyed such a fierce partisan as Felix Frankfurter, but Pound's caution was not confined to explosive public causes. He ran afoul of Frankfurter and other liberal members of his law faculty in an in-house postscript to the case.[133] President Lowell of Harvard had been chosen to chair the governor's "independent" panel to review the Sacco and Vanzetti case. Lowell, however, came to the panel predisposed to condemn the two men. Pound and Lowell had been friends and allies, and they respected each other. Lowell had actually confided to Pound, before the former had been appointed to chair the commission, "that he did not care whether they were guilty or not, public confidence in the institutions of Massachusetts required that the sentence be carried out."[134]

During the fall following the Sacco and Vanzetti executions, two law school faculty appointments ran afoul of President Lowell. In both cases, the president was probably using the appointments as surrogates for his anger at his Sacco and Vanzetti "nemesis,"[135] Felix Frankfurter. A young, Jewish assistant professor of law, Nathan Margold, came up for a vote for a permanent position. The law faculty, including Pound, voted overwhelmingly to approve the Margold appointment, but President Lowell vetoed the faculty's recommendation. The faculty suspected Pound "was not as enthusiastic about Margold in his private discussions with Lowell as he was in front of his colleagues."[136] When Frankfurter, Edmund M. Morgan, and Thomas Reed Powell tried to move to resubmit the appointment, Pound opposed the motion. Pound did not carry the law professors' banner. Instead, he acquiesced in Margold's rejection and frustrated Frankfurter and his allies.

Pound's reasons are understandable, if not laudable. Margold

---

133. I take my account of the Margold and Landis appointment disputes from Kalman, *Legal Realism,* 58–61. Kalman recognizes that Pound's difficulties with Frankfurter stemmed from his "appeasement of President Lowell in the 1920s" and that Lowell had been Frankfurter's "nemesis at least since 1927" as a result of their contrary positions on the Sacco and Vanzetti case. Like Kalman, Wigdor attributes the rift between Pound and his faculty to the Margold appointment, but he does not see the connection to the Sacco and Vanzetti case; it is simply a question of Lowell's antiSemitism. Wigdor, *Pound,* 251.

134. Pound did not explicitly identify which of the panel members had expressed these views, but it is a reasonable inference that only Lowell had a close enough relationship to Pound to have made such a confidence. Pound to Long, Aug. 6, 1927, RPP, 24-9.

135. Kalman, *Legal Realism,* 58.

136. Ibid., 59.

was a reasonably strong candidate by law school standards, but he was by no means a rising star of legal scholarship. Lowell may have unfairly rejected the appointment, but Pound did not see the merits of Margold's case as strong enough to jeopardize his deanship. An open challenge to the president of the university on an appointment decision was doomed to failure, and the likely result would then have been that Pound would have been forced to resign. If he wavered over taking such a step for Frankfurter, then it was ridiculous to expect him to make such a suicidal move for Margold. And for Pound, being forced to give up the deanship would have been a kind of suicide. Being dean of Harvard Law School was the position for which he had striven throughout his career. Though tempted with important judicial appointments and the presidency of the University of Wisconsin, he turned them all down to remain where he was. To sacrifice his deanship for a lowly assistant professor was unthinkable.

Later that year, another dispute erupted with Lowell when the president "disregard[ed] the faculty's unanimous support of another Frankfurter protégé, James M. Landis," [137] as professor of legislation. Again, the faculty was unhappy with Pound when the dean sought a compromise with Lowell rather than fighting Lowell on the matter.[138] Pound's actions in the Margold and Landis appointments were not popular with Frankfurter and his friends, and they used their networks to bash the dean. Had he taken a leading role in the Sacco and Vanzetti case, Pound might have been proof against their insinuations, but he was vulnerable. All in all, Pound's role in the Sacco and Vanzetti case and its aftermath helped to isolate him from his jurisprudential heirs because liberal viewpoint was one index of the reformist jurisprudence.

His caution did, however, sit well with many practicing lawyers and not a few judges. Oliver Wendell Holmes, Jr., approached for support by Laski, writing on behalf of Frankfurter, rebuffed the approach, at first by silence, and then directly. "So far as one who has not read the evidence has a right to an opinion, I think the row that has been made idiotical, if considered on its merits, but of course it is not on the merits that the row is made, but because it gives extremists a chance to yell. If justice is the interest why do they not talk about the infinitely worse cases of the blacks? My prejudices

137. Ibid.
138. Ibid.

were all with Felix's book. But, after all, it's simply showing, if it was right, that the case was tried in a hostile atmosphere. I doubt if anyone would say that there was no evidence warranting a conviction, and as to prejudice I have heard an English judge sock it to the jury in a murder case, in a way that would have secured a reversal in Mass." On Frankfurter's role, the justice was charitable, but he reported: "I had a letter . . . saying that Frankfurter will write nothing more about Sacco and Vanzetti for a year. I hope it will be longer than that, as I think all those who were interested on that side seem to have got hysterical and to have lost their sense of proportion."[139]

Pound's status with the legal establishment remained intact as well. His Harvard colleague Samuel Williston, doyen of the contracts professors, celebrated Pound as the leader of the movement to teach social science in the law schools. Williston was proud that Pound had led the way in validating legislation like workman's compensation based on the findings of the social scientists.[140] Though Williston did not mention it, one piece of legislation more than any other required Pound's expertise in 1929—the Volstead Act. Pound lobbied to sit on the National Commission on Law Observance and Enforcement that President Herbert Hoover created to review the effectiveness of the Act and threw himself into its labors. His wife had just died, and though he would shortly remarry, he was lonely. More important, the work closed a decade of interest in criminal law and its jurisprudence. Overwhelmed with violations of the law, Treasury agents could not enforce Prohibition. The federal district courts were overwhelmed with thousands of cases involving smuggled liquor, and civil cases waited years to be processed. All the members of the commission but one recognized the failure of the federal law (the one holdout, Monte Lemann of New Orleans, went further—he called for repeal of the Eighteenth Amendment itself). Pound shuttled between Cambridge and Washington, D.C., filling the void in his personal life with good works.[141]

139. Oliver Wendell Holmes, Jr., to Harold Laski, Sept. 1, 1927, and Holmes to Laski, Nov. 23, 1927, in Mark DeWolfe Howe, ed., *The Holmes-Laski Letters, The Correspondence of Mr. Justice Holmes and Harold J. Laski 1916–1935* (Cambridge, Mass., 1953), 2:975, 999.

140. Samuel Williston, *Some Modern Tendencies in the Law* (New York, 1929), 140.

141. Wigdor, *Pound*, 247–48; National Commission on Law Observance and Enforcement, *Report on Enforcement of Prohibition Laws of the United States*, H.R. Doc. 722, 71st Cong., 3rd Sess. (Washington, D.C., 1931), 159–60 (Pound statement); ibid., 139–48 (Lemann separate report).

But Pound would not be saved from Llewellyn's wrath by Holmes or Herculean labor, not as long as the post was carried twice a day from New York City to Cambridge.[142] For a time Pound was respited by Columbia Law School politics. In May 1928, President Nicholas Murray Butler selected Young B. Smith rather than Herman Oliphant, the leader of the legal empiricists Llewellyn had lauded in his "New Trends," as dean of the law school. William O. Douglas resigned and went to Yale; Underhill Moore shortly followed. Both men tried to induce colleagues to follow them.[143] Llewellyn was torn. He opposed Smith and said so to Butler, but was not really a social science devotee, and if he counted the emigrants as fellow realists, or would in two years' time, they were bean counters, and he was a jurisprudent. He put his manuscript aside and did what Pound had done in 1921. He went abroad in the fall of 1928, to Leipzig, to lecture on American law.[144]

Llewellyn's lectures on the American case law method took as a given what his draft manuscript "New Trends" posited as a program for further research. Some research had appeared in the interim, but Llewellyn's assertions in German lectures had no more foundation than his own powerful intellect. There were, he told his audience, four types of case law. The first arose from a judge's "honest efforts to derive a conclusion from a rule." The second type was based on a "more or less malleable composite in the judges' mind of hundreds of rules." We would call this a category; Llewellyn called it a "legal institution." The third type of case (just as legitimate and, by implication, just as common as the first two) was a "decision based on emotional factors of some kind—ethical, political, sociopolitical, economic, religious, etc." The final kind of decision was "policy-oriented" indeed, "possibly even citing the results of available social-science research." In fact, there were precious few of this

142. Llewellyn to Pound, June 27, 1927, RPP, 24-6. Twining, *Llewellyn,* 104, writes that "[u]ntil 1929 jurisprudence came a poor second to commercial law [for Llewellyn]." This is not quite accurate if one considers the unpublished manuscript of "New Trends in Jurisprudence" and the book proposal that the essay introduced. Llewellyn was, as Twining notes, a craftsman, often slow to publish, but as the unpublished essay shows, he was an endless and fussy reviser of manuscripts.

143. John Henry Schlegel, *American Legal Realism and Empirical Social Science* (Chapel Hill, N.C., 1995), 146–47.

144. Karl Llewellyn, *The Case Law System in America,* ed. Paul Gewirtz, trans. Michael Ansaldi (Chicago, 1989), xi. The first part of the text was finished, according to Llewellyn, in 1928. Ibid., xxxvii. The whole was first published in 1933 as *Präjudizienrecht und Rechtsprechung in Amerika.*

last type, and fewer still of the third—at least that judges owned up to—but Llewellyn hid his personal judgment in objective language. "For," he continued, "a judge is a lawyer; he is also a human being"—and "the sociologist" has demonstrated that such human beings are always subject to "the thought patterns and mental images absorbed from his surroundings; a man is conditioned, limited, and unconsciously constrained to such a degree that his so-called freedom of action seems little more than mechanical." Llewellyn made good his claim that the jurisprudent (here Llewellyn himself) must be a social scientist. His view of the precedential system was not that of a lawyer, even one sympathetic to social science, but that of a social psychologist.[145] When it came to viewing "the facts," they, too, were deconstructed into sense data. Instead of representing some reality out of the court that the law captured, the facts were mutilated in court, made into a story that was legally cognizable. Each side had its own story. Facts became points of view, bent by the prism of the rules of admissibility and the language of the law.[146]

Home from his travels in Germany in the spring of 1929, his lectures finished but not yet ready for publication in Germany, Llewellyn was asked to comment on the state of empirical legal research (and indirectly on the turmoil at Columbia) at the annual AALS convention for 1929.[147] He was joined by two advocates of empirical methods, Felix Frankfurter, who had used them well in his administrative law courses at Harvard, and Edson Sutherland, who was shortly to be named director of the Institute of Legal Research at the University of Michigan School of Law.[148] Llewellyn's paper, read on December 27, 1929, was a belated swipe at the ex-Columbia empiricists: he told the AALS gathering in New Orleans that mere research was useless without sound theory. If the aim of research was practical results—that is, changes in the administration of the law—massive data collection might comfort others, but for himself, he was "helpless in the deluge. There is no end. It is hard to find a beginning." When one turned one's attention to the attempt to construct a "pure" science of law, theory was essential. Llewellyn lastly

145. Llewellyn, *Case Law System,* 10–11.

146. Ibid., 53–54.

147. Karl Llewellyn, "Conditions for, Aims and Methods of Legal Research," 6 *American Law School Review* 670–78 (1930).

148. Elizabeth Gaspar Brown, *Legal Education at Michigan, 1859–1959* (Ann Arbor, Mich., 1959), 340–41.

addressed the problem of conflicting theory within the social science community and dismissed it in a footnote. We have not the time, he said, for such quibbling.[149]

Perhaps the best course was to concentrate simply on what courts did (the conclusion of his "New Trends"). At the very least, such an exploration would lead jurisprudents to examine all the tried and true categories of law. Researchers might test within the law to see if it is consistent and, from within, to see the effects of such classifications on actual outcomes. Overall, however, he was skeptical about the use of research, and he admitted as much. His examples were all negative ones, some of them captious, others amusing. It seems that Holmes, whose call for prediction Llewellyn had made his own, had also captured, for a time, Llewellyn's anima. The result was a return not to the law but to the "lesser groups" and their behavior. For example, "a rule of corporation law is understandable only in terms of what corporation lawyers do because of it." A "long range science of law" must be based on many parallel studies of such extra-legal processes. But even here, "the outlook at first glimpse is discouraging." The data were twisted. The dockets represented only a handful of the actual disputes and then had already changed facts into legal fictions. The dockets or other "book" records ignored the long train of prior abuses that precipitated the litigation. Masses of data might help, but the way through them was not easy.[150]

For himself, research meant borrowing hypotheses from the social sciences and applying them to the law. "Always, it tantalizes. Only sometimes does it satisfy." But here, again, the way was hard. "And it means, I fear, that some of our number will have to turn themselves out good social scientists before any of us can have much comfort in what the social scientists have to offer us." This was a pretty pass—for Llewellyn had finally admitted that there was no rainbow bridge between the social sciences and jurisprudence, that only dual practitioners would be able to move back and forth between the two kinds of disciplines. For example, the masses of data assembled by economists on prices were not accessible to the jurisprudent until the latter understood how those masses of data were assembled. The same was true of psychiatric data for use in court.

149. Llewellyn, "Methods of Legal Research," 670, 671.
150. Ibid., 672, 674, 675.

"An unfamiliar technique cannot be grafted upon a stem it does not fit," and the social science data were not generated for use in court—at least not as a rule. The academic in a law school would have to spend (Llewellyn wrote "waste") a year or two groping before "he learns the first essentials of the game."[151]

The point had been made to Llewellyn sometime between his draft "New Trends" and the talk he gave in 1929, perhaps by his wife, Elizabeth Sanford (whom he thanked in the "Methods" piece), or by one of the social scientists hired to assist Underhill Moore at Yale, Emma Corstvet, whom Llewellyn married in 1933.[152] In a footnote, perhaps not the right place for it, Llewellyn finally named the young men whose research had inspired him in 1925: Moore, Douglas, Hessel Yntema, Herman Oliphant, and Charles E. Clark. But even they "are children at the game. We need to learn long before we can handle it. But when we do learn, we bring to it a child's vigor, and a child's new insight." Llewellyn's counsel: "patience."[153]

But Llewellyn was not particularly patient with his interrogators after the paper. Plainly, he had pleased neither the lawyer-empiricists, whose expertise he had questioned, nor the reformers, whose yearning for usable data he had dismissed. In the end, Llewellyn conceded with ill grace, "If you wish me to state what you already think, I will. I take it what we all have in mind is that the judge has the technique for getting information, but he uses it rarely." Llewellyn did not believe this, for even if judges had access to information, they used it for their own purposes, or misused it for the same reasons.[154] Pound was there but said nothing. He was sixty, still vigorous, but silent. Llewellyn was thirty-seven and full of fight.

What is more, Llewellyn was ready to carry the fight to his own students. In the fall of 1929, he delivered at Columbia a series of ten lectures combining an orientation to law school study, some first-hand reflections on the hard law subjects, and a little jurisprudence. That little went a long way, for a year later the collected lectures were privately published as *The Bramble Bush* (1930) and widely read by Llewellyn's peers. In the first lecture, he told the students

151. Ibid., 676, 677.

152. Twining, *Llewellyn*, 110.

153. Llewellyn, "Methods of Legal Research," 677, 678.

154. "Discussion of 'Methods of Legal Research,'" 5 *American Law School Review*, 726, 727 (1929) (Llewellyn's comments).

something that may or may not have made much of an impression on them, but certainly caught the eye of other law teachers. "This doing of something about disputes, this doing of it reasonably, is the business of law. And the people who have the doing in charge, whether they be judges or sheriffs or clerks or jailers or lawyers, are officials of the law. *What these officials do about disputes is, to my mind, the law itself.*" Not rules or standards or logic, and certainly not concepts or principles—nothing more or less than the conduct of the law-men, that was law. The idea that formal rules of law were right because they were law "contain[s] a truth so partial, so faulty, as to cry out for revision in the light of some such analysis as I have been presenting. . . . Let me say here only this about the rightness of the law. That if most people did not stand behind the officials, however passively, there would be little law to talk about." Law was not logic, nor was it the bare command of the state; it was the consensus of the people. Such a powerful democratic concept of law wedded the instincts of the anthropologist to the aspirations of the democrat, which, of course, Llewellyn was. There could be no mistaking the anti-authoritarianism of this pronouncement, which may have been liberating for students about to undergo three years of subjugation to books and lectures. But as an attack on the stand-alone authority of the traditional sources of law, it was more than liberating. It was downright radical. "The case is clear. The stones speak. What the courts will do means nothing save in relation with how people are to act in the light of the court's doing. For the meaning of the law in life and in the practice of lawyers is its meaning not to courts, but to laymen." [155]

Llewellyn's views are commonplaces (if by no means the only views) in law schools today, but were not when he wrote them. Did he mean to deny the validity of all taught law? He would answer all, he promised, in his forthcoming "A Realistic Jurisprudence—The Next Step." [156]

---

155. Karl Llewellyn, *The Bramble Bush* [1930] (New York, 1951), 3, 15, 16–17 (emphasis in original).

156. Llewellyn, "Methods of Legal Research," 674 n.11. But one must concede that there is an echo of Holmes's *The Common Law* in Llewellyn's tone. See G. Edward White, *The American Judicial Tradition* (New York, 1976), 154–55.

Roscoe Pound, 1904, as dean of the University of Nebraska College of Law. Courtesy of Special Collections, University of Nebraska Archives

Karl Llewellyn, 1918–19, as editor-in-chief of the *Yale Law Journal*. Courtesy of Sterling Memorial Library, Yale University

Wesley Newcomb Hohfeld, Yale law professor who was Pound's protégé and Llewellyn's teacher. Courtesy of Sterling Memorial Library, Yale University

Louise Pound, 1892, college friend of Willa Cather and later professor at the University of Nebraska. Courtesy of Special Collections, University of Nebraska Archives

Lon Fuller, recruited by Pound as his jurisprudential successor at Harvard Law School. Courtesy of Art Collection, Harvard Law School

Pound in his Harvard office, wearing the eyeshade he used to protect his weak eyes. He is standing behind his famous round desk, now used by the receptionist at the main entrance of Langdell Hall, Harvard Law School. Courtesy of Art Collection, Harvard Law School

Llewellyn and his second wife, Emma Costvet, in 1935 on a field trip in Cheyenne country. Courtesy of The Law School, The University of Chicago

"Columbia Law Professor Is Out to Chastise the Tiger; Karl Llewellyn Seeks Hines' Job as Democratic Boss." Thus read the headline of an article accompanying this photo of Llewellyn in the August 14, 1934, *New York World-Telegram.* Courtesy of The Law School, The University of Chicago

Jerome Frank, Llewellyn's Realist ally. Courtesy of Sterling Memorial Library, Yale University

Harvard Law School faculty, October 1948. In the first row is Dean Erwin Griswold (fourth from left). In the third row are Karl Llewellyn (third from right) and Soia Mentschikoff, his third wife. In the fourth row are Paul Freund (second from left), president of the *Harvard Law Review* during the 1930–31 controversy between Pound and Llewellyn, and Lon Fuller (fifth from left). Courtesy of Art Collection, Harvard Law School

To Roscoe Pound
who continues to lead the way
K N Llewellyn

The photograph Llewellyn sent to Pound in the 1930s, with a surprisingly warm inscription indicating the admiration he still held for his Realist adversary. Courtesy of Art Collection, Harvard Law School

CHAPTER FOUR

Llewellyn, Pound, and Their Friends Squabble

The debate between Karl Llewellyn and Roscoe Pound over the future of American jurisprudence, in part a contest of wills between the king and a would-be usurper, in part merely the public continuation of their private discourse, is perhaps the most famous controversy in the history of American jurisprudence. It was a conversation among insiders, eventually drawing in many of the leading law professors. It was also a way station on the road from legal formalism to another, less well defined (or at least less easily caricatured) synthesis, which emerged from the debate as "legal realism." Names evidently did matter, as much as Llewellyn preferred things. As he wrote to Arthur Corbin in the middle of the controversy: "I am, also, with you in general on anti-schooling [that is, refusing to make like thinkers into rigid "schools"]. *But* there is a significant likeness among a whole crew of younger and old legal thinkers: (1) they distrust traditional formulations; (2) they seek to state their baselines of work on law in terms of accurate description and of prediction as accurate as possible. It is useful to have a name for this. 'Realism' will do." [1]

But legal realism itself is still a subject hotly debated not just because legal academics are eager to get their intellectual pedigrees straight or because the commonplace that legal realism is now the orthodoxy of the law schools is still open to question, but because scholars are still trying to get a fix on the concept. Before he died, Llewellyn tried to end the controversy that swirled about realism

---

1. Karl Llewellyn to Arthur Corbin, Apr. 1931, KLP, A.II.65.b (emphasis in original).

throughout his career. Realism, he insisted, "is a method, nothing more, and the only tenet involved is that the method is a good one. 'See it fresh,' 'See it whole,' 'See it as it works'—that was to be the foundation of any solid work, to any end."[2] Llewellyn's art—his lyrical definition—satisfied him but remains elusive to us, not just because of its imprecision (we can duplicate that) but because he could not make his private thoughts public. In effect, he was talking to himself, though two generations of readers have listened in.

Jerome Hall, who began his career in jurisprudence early in the 1930s, was unmoved by Llewellyn's mystical aside and wrote in 1973 that realism did indeed have a central tenet: insisting on "the 'temporary divorce' of the Is and Ought of law and concentration on the Is of law, defined in terms of the behavior of officials."[3] Edwin Patterson, whose office was next-door to Llewellyn's at Columbia, decided that Llewellyn's realism was skeptical of rules, but published his revelation when Llewellyn was no longer his neighbor, the latter having removed himself to the University of Chicago School of Law.[4] Grant Gilmore, who as a young professor joined Llewellyn in drafting the Uniform Commercial Code, believed that a "fundamental shift" in pedagogy had taken place in the early 1930s, but that the debate over the meaning of realism, "which had never been clearly defined, became progressively more confused and more insubstantial as the debate went on."[5]

If the men who lived through the controversy could not define legal realism's central tenets, what hope had the historians? Wilfred Rumble, Jr., the first of the postrealist-era students of the movement, assayed a simple definition of realism's boundaries. "The best answer is that 'realism' meant to them what it has meant in art and literature. It meant the attempt to represent things as they actually are."[6] Thus, Pound was an early realist. The problem with this defi-

2. Karl Llewellyn, *The Common Law Tradition: Deciding Appeals* (Boston, 1960), 510.

3. Jerome Hall, *Foundations of Jurisprudence* (Indianapolis, 1973), 55. Evidently, Hall had not bought Llewellyn's 1960 disclaimer that his remark on law being what lawmen did in *The Bramble Bush* was taken out of context. "This lone sentence became, internationally, *the* cited goblin-painting of realism." Llewellyn, *Common Law Tradition,* 511.

4. Edwin W. Patterson, *Jurisprudence: Men and Ideas of the Law* (Brooklyn, N.Y., 1953), 545.

5. Grant Gilmore, *The Ages of American Law* (New Haven, Conn., 1977), 78–79.

6. Wilfred E. Rumble, Jr., *American Legal Realism* (Ithaca, N.Y., 1968), 44.

nition is that it reflects the aspirations of all jurisprudents. As Patterson remarked, "Everyone, doubtless, wants to be a realist. No one cares to admit that his serious effort to think through to a conclusion any social or legal problem is only shadow-boxing, mere grasping at ghostly unrealities."[7]

More recently, Laura Kalman assayed a sensible short definition from within the canon: "The realists pointed to the role of human idiosyncrasy in legal decision making, stressed the uselessness of legal rules and concepts [in predicting the outcomes of particular cases,] and emphasized the importance of greater efficiency and certainty in law administration."[8] John Henry Schlegel demurred: "*[T]he* story of Realism" is a narrative of a handful of people who tried to make law into a social science. At the center of the circle were Walter Wheeler Cook, Underhill Moore, and others at Yale, Columbia, and Harvard Law Schools. Realism was what they did or tried to do. Brave attacks on formalism were certainly part of the rhetoric of these men, but not the essence of their contribution.[9] Not so fast, argued William Fisher, Morton Horwitz, and Thomas A. Reed, for "[t]he heart of the movement was an effort to define and discredit classical legal theory and practice and to offer in their place a more philosophically and politically enlightened jurisprudence."[10] Fisher, Horwitz, and Reed suggest that the realists were best known by their words. G. Edward White insists that the heart of realism is provocative subjectivism. Robert Summers has proposed a definitional solution reminiscent of Alexander the Great's approach to the Gordian knot. He bid scholars abandon the terminology of legal realism entirely and replace it with his own coinage, "pragmatic instrumentalism."[11]

This is not a book about realism, but in the course of Pound's and Llewellyn's search for an American jurisprudence, legal realism emerged. What gave it substance was not a preexisting, self-conscious school or movement—indeed, those men whom Llew-

---

7. Patterson, *Jurisprudence*, 539.

8. Laura Kalman, *Legal Realism at Yale, 1927–1960* (Chapel Hill, N.C., 1986), 3.

9. John Henry Schlegel, *American Legal Realism and Empirical Social Science* (Chapel Hill, N.C., 1995), 15–21.

10. William W. Fisher III, Morton J. Horwitz, and Thomas A. Reed, *American Legal Realism* (New York, 1993), xiv.

11. G. Edward White, *American Judicial Tradition* (New York, 1976), 273; Robert S. Summers, "Pragmatic Instrumentalism in Twentieth Century American Legal Thought," 66 *Cornell Law Review* 864–65 n.2 (1981).

ellyn regarded as realists either refused to join in the debate or doubted whether there was such a coherent philosophy as legal realism—but the public and private conversations between Pound and Llewellyn, into which Jerome Frank intruded. It was all networks and bricolage, but that is just what one should expect to find.

It was 1930, and the times were out of joint. At Columbia Law School, a simmering dispute over who should be dean, and other internal matters, had led over the course of two years to the resignation of the leaders of the empirical party, notably Douglas, Moore, and Hessel Yntema. Cook had already set up his institute for the empirical study of law at Johns Hopkins and was joined there by Herman Oliphant, the also-ran for the deanship at Columbia. Other apostates took the train to New Haven. Llewellyn had chosen to stay, after a half-hearted attempt to aid the empiricists' cause. He liked New York City.[12]

But the city was in trouble. For a law professor who taught banking and sales in New York City, the precipitous decline of the stock and bond markets at the end of 1929 was a shock to the system. It was the beginning of the Great Depression, and if no one could have predicted it then, for such busts were long a part of American economic life, the crash would fundamentally alter the structure of American government. The expert analysts and respected brokers and bankers, led by the great New York City houses, were discredited in part for their failure to stem the onrushing tide, but more so for their false confidence. As the former president of the National City Bank of New York wrote in 1932, "The present economic disturbance has been so severe that it has made even some changes in our language. No longer is it an apt metaphor to say that anything is 'as safe as a bank.' The word 'securities' has almost become obsolete. . . . [T]he page of stock-and-bond quotations might well be headed Quotations of Risks and Hazards."[13]

The law schools felt the reverberations. Alumni giving declined. Younger and older graduates alike were out of work as law firms failed. Even corporate lawyers, once trusted advisors to the great and near great, found their reputations tarnished, for lawyers had

12. Llewellyn to Emma Corstvet, Oct. 19, 1935, Emma Corstvet Papers, Bryn Mawr College Library.

13. John Kenneth Galbraith, *The Great Crash* (New York, 1962), 111–69; Frank A. Vanderlip, "What about the Banks?," *Saturday Evening Post,* Nov. 5, 1932, at 3.

helped build the facades of the pyramidal holding companies whose fall brought down so many other enterprises. The AALS took advantage of the financial crisis to strike more boldly at the night schools, raising its standards for accreditation and urging the ABA to prod state bar associations to increase the difficulty of their bar examinations. The strategy seemed to work, but Llewellyn was appalled by it. "I say that the honest ambulance chaser does what the 'better' bar does not do. He brings legal services to the man who needs legal services a lot more than the blue stocking man does."[14]

The crash had opened the door that the Palmer raids had shut. Once more, liberal reform was challenged from the left. "In one form or another, liberal pragmatism was seeking means of attaining a stable economy within a framework of free institutions."[15] For advocates of legal reform, the way was blocked, however, by a majority of conservatives on the High Court and an administration in Washington that refused to rethink fundamental conceptions of "free enterprise." It seemed to some liberal professors of law that "the general attitude that pervaded the law at the beginning of the Great Depression, as expounded by professors, lawyers, jurists, and judges, was that property was more important than human rights."[16] The logjam would clear partially during the next decade, with the Democratic victory in 1932 and the New Deal that ensued. The Court would change its mind about deferring to the representative body five years later. But in 1930, all that remained was a clouded and hazardous future.

What were the academics to do to reverse this downward spiral? Thurman Arnold, one of the "Young Turks" at Yale, would later write, "[I]t was out of this struggle that a new school of jurists was born. It went under the name of legal realism. The principal shrine of this new school was located at Yale. Its high priest was Dean [John Maynard] Hutchins."[17] It was true that Hutchins had sponsored the first Yale Law School forays into empirical research, but

14. Llewellyn at the AALS Meeting in 1933, quoted in Robert Stevens, *Law School: Legal Education in America from the 1850s to the 1980s* (Chapel Hill, N.C., 1983), 189.

15. Arthur Schlesinger, Jr., *The Age of Roosevelt: The Crisis of the Old Order, 1919–1933* (Boston, 1957), 200.

16. Thurman Arnold, *Fair Fights and Foul: A Dissenting Lawyer's Life* (New York, 1965), 58.

17. Ibid., 59. Corbin saw it differently: "[T]here were too many self-styled 'Realists' whose eyes were opened and yet saw nothing." Corbin to Llewellyn, Dec. 1, 1960, KLP, R.III.15.

Pound had already done more at Harvard. And as we have seen, Llewellyn had toyed with the idea of a "realistic jurisprudence" four years before the crash. Without meaning to, Arnold had recalled and recorded not the birth of legal realism, but Yale's response to the appearance of a new paradigm from the wreckage of formalism.

But what exactly was that paradigm? It had no name as yet, though Llewellyn had written about "realistic jurisprudence" in "New Trends." In 1930, Llewellyn brought out his long-awaited casebook on sales, in which he stated as a rule (even realism had rules[18]) that "we must recognize that the opinion [of the court] is often a mere justification after the event, a mere making plausible to the legal audience, of a decision reached before the opinion was begun, a decision the real reasons of which we may never learn. And on the other hand, we must remember that the opinion may, in any given case, reveal the true course of decision; and that in any event it will be a factor of power in further decisions of the same or other courts."[19] But he did not dismiss all doctrine or its study as the mask of the law. Indeed, he had plainly hedged the bets he had made in the draft of "New Trends." The casebook's approach was not traditional, for "the book . . . approaches Sales law as a matter of marketing, as a tool of modern business in a credit economy in which future contracts are the rule. It deals with present sale as a peculiar situation of high interest to the consumer as a person, but of relatively little interest to the lawyer in his practice." Nevertheless, Llewellyn included the classic old English cases. After all, no statute would sweep away all the old law, and the basic unit of analysis remained the case, not the market survey. Llewellyn admitted he had added cases to stimulate the second- year student's flagging interest.[20] There was nothing revolutionary about Llewellyn's tactics or his underlying theory, however; Oliphant had done pretty much the same with his casebook on trade regulation eight years earlier.[21]

Llewellyn had hesitated to regard rules as the masks of judicial personality and prejudice, but Frank had no such qualms. Frank was a practicing Wall Street lawyer with a University of Chicago Law School degree and extensive experience in Chicago courts and

---

18. A point Llewellyn emphasized in response to his critics thirty years later. Llewellyn, *Common Law Tradition*, 511.

19. Karl Llewellyn, *Cases and Materials on the Law of Sales* (Chicago, 1930), x.

20. Ibid., xv, xvi, xvii.

21. Kalman, *Legal Realism*, 78.

politics. He also had become a devotee of psychoanalysis and was thoroughly disaffected with large firm practice, even though his firm, Chadbourne, Stanchfield, and Levy, had not suffered from the Depression. Indeed, Frank was hired as a specialist in corporate reorganization, an area much in demand at that time. He wrote *Law and the Modern Mind* (1930) largely without research notes (his biographer reports that he did it while commuting to and from work in New York City).[22]

Frank's quotations were less often from his subjects (the judges and lawyers) and more often from psychologists and other theorists. Frank was a fact skeptic, for to him, facts were psychological constructions, not bricks. There was nothing new in that argument; relativists in the historical profession had argued the same thing throughout the 1920s. He also doubted that rules were made in a legal heaven and discovered by judges, and there was little new in that assertion. But Frank's theories about judging were startling: "Now, since the judge is a human being and since no human being in his normal thinking processes arrives at decisions . . . by the route of any such syllogistic reasoning [as is customarily attributed to judicial opinions], it is fair to assume that the judge, merely by putting on the judicial ermine, will not acquire so artificial a method of reasoning." Of course, that is just what judges asserted they did, even when they conceded that the cloth of policy may have been worn under the judicial robes. Not for Frank, however; not on the train on the way home from a day at the office wondering why such and such a judge had come to such and such an opinion on a case the firm had prepared. Instead, Frank concluded that judges reasoned backwards, from the result they wanted to obtain to the logic for it. Some of these initial "hunches" arose from political and economic opinions, but in the main, they were "idiosyncratic biases" due to unique personal experiences.[23]

Frank was now out on a limb, far beyond the concessions that the most candid of the judges had made in public, for he continued that in the end it was the "personality of the judge" rather than doctrine, policy, or generally shared attitudes that determined the judge's

22. Robert Jerome Glennon, *The Iconoclast as Reformer: Jerome Frank's Impact on American Law* (Ithaca, N.Y., 1985), 20–22.

23. Frank's version of Judge Joseph Hutcheson's far milder "The Judgment Intuitive: The Function of the 'Hunch' in Judicial Decisions," 14 *Cornell Law Quarterly* 274 (1929). Hutcheson had in mind the intuitive leap to the right line of decisions or doctrine.

reading of the facts and decision making. Frank recommended, as therapy for the ills of the judging process, that the judges engage in their own "ventures of self-discovery." And for the poor lawyer or his client—well, for them, "[n]o one can know in advance what a judge will believe to be the 'facts' of a case."[24]

The reaction to Frank's idiosyncratic essay was a mixture of bemused admiration and dismissive outrage. Typical was Felix Cohen's: "In all this, Mr. Frank has missed a large part of human wisdom. . . . Civilization rests upon a vast, intricate complex of expectations and prophecies. . . . A cavalier disdain for the compromises between certainty and sensitiveness which have appealed to legal philosophers like Pound and Cardozo lends a picturesque clarity to our author's assaults upon 'rules of law,' 'legal scholasticism,' 'judicial somnambulism,' and 'Bealism.'"[25] Frank's assertion that those who wanted to see certainty in the law were being infantile in their expectations (buttressed as it was by an array of quotations from experts) made hash of all existing jurisprudential theories, including Pound's, as Cohen, the son of Pound's friend Morris Cohen, noted.[26] So did Llewellyn, in his own review, shortly thereafter, although Llewellyn gently suggested that Frank's treatment of Pound might be a little too harsh.[27]

As a young man, Frank had known and respected Pound. While an instructor at the University of Chicago School of Law in 1919, Frank wrote to Pound that, "when the adaptive aspect of our '*science*' was called to their attention, the students, after the first shock, developed a surprising quantity of creative legal intelligence and nothing helped so much as repeated injections of the Roscoe Pound serum."[28] Over the ensuing decade, Frank must have become dis-

---

24. Jerome Frank, *Law and the Modern Mind* (New York, 1930), 109, 111, 113, 114, 120. Later, when Frank sat on the Second Circuit federal appellate bench, he altered somewhat his choice of psychological models. "Pertinent here is gestalt psychology, the main thesis of which is, roughly, this: all thinking is done in forms, patterns, configurations." No more repressed unconscious; now the whole field came into view. Jerome Frank, *Courts on Trial: Myths and Reality in American Justice* (Princeton, N.J., 1950), 170.

25. Felix S. Cohen, "Review of *Law and the Modern Mind*—Among Recent Books," 17 *American Bar Association Journal* 111–12 (1930).

26. Morris R. Cohen to Pound, Apr. 23, 1933: "[T]his is my opportunity of expressing my indebtedness to you for encouraging me in a line of reflection which, twenty years ago was certainly a very lonely way." RPP, 10-6.

27. Karl Llewellyn, "Frank's *Law and the Modern Mind*," 31 *Columbia Law Review* 85 (1931).

28. Jerome Frank to Roscoe Pound, Apr. 24, 1919, RPP, 221-9 (emphasis in original).

appointed with Pound, for in *Law and the Modern Mind,* he gave Pound a beating that was hardly necessary to make Frank's arguments. Pound was applauded for his views on the law as social engineering and his critique of mechanical jurisprudence, but blasted for his belief that somewhere beneath everything there was "something definite and absolute." It was "a remnant of the scholastic tendency to treat abstractions as independent entities." Worse, Pound was inconsistent. He attacked the rigidities of procedure, yet welcomed the rigidities of certain fields of substantive law, and debunked the myth of judicial discovery of law, while defending some of its uses. It is true that placing different Pound addresses and essays together yielded such inconsistencies, but as Frank admitted in his appendix (Pound got extended treatment in the book), Pound believed that the discordances were a product of alternating or recurrent cultural yearnings.[29] Anyhow, for Frank it was evidently cathartic.

But Frank had removed an obstacle from Llewellyn's path.[30] Now it was acceptable for reformers publicly to attack Pound as it had not been before. Llewellyn's 1930 *Columbia Law Review* article, "A Realistic Jurisprudence—The Next Step,"[31] was published that spring. As an expositor of what the new jurisprudential movement was about, Llewellyn failed to present any coherent analysis of realist thought.[32] The article contained a hodgepodge of legal definition, criticized Pound, offered "some quasi-Hohfeldian ideas about remedies and rules, and ended with a plea for an interdisciplinary approach to legal research, with human behavior as an important focus."[33] The only consistent strains in the article were Llewellyn's

29. Frank, *Law and the Modern Mind,* 221, 222, 224, 229, 317.

30. Schlegel, in *American Legal Realism,* 184, asserts that "[d]espite common assumptions that this was a dispute that, *in print* at least, was between Llewellyn and Pound, it began *in print* somewhat earlier with Mortimer Adler's review of Jerome Frank's *Law and the Modern Mind.*" This cannot be so, for Llewellyn's "Next Step" appeared *in print* in the April 1930 number of the *Columbia Law Review,* eight months before the Adler review in the January 1931 *Columbia Law Review* was *in print.*

31. Karl Llewellyn, "A Realistic Jurisprudence—The Next Step," 30 *Columbia Law Review* 431 (1930).

32. Llewellyn later ruefully recalled that the editor of the *Columbia Law Review* "didn't want to print" the article. "I said 'read it again.' He did. Then he took it." Karl Llewellyn to Emma Corstvet, Dec. 1934, Emma Corstvet Papers, Bryn Mawr College Library.

33. Even a cursory reading of the article cannot help but leave a reader reeling from the juxtaposition of "developing," but unconnected insights. Even Llewellyn's biographer

emphasis on "real rules"—the record of actual court practice, which has no prescriptive value other than to predict "that courts *ought* to continue in their practices"[34]—and his disdain for "paper rules"— "what have been treated, traditionally, as rules of law: the accepted *doctrine* of the time and place—that the books there say 'the law' is."[35] These, of course, were the crux of the difference between Llewellyn and Pound in the earlier correspondence and in Llewellyn's interior dialogue with Pound's work in "New Trends."

Llewellyn had already warned Pound that the article would criticize some of Pound's work. But the 1927 correspondence did not indicate how far that critique would go. It is even possible that the brief but unfruitful dialogue in 1927 exacerbated Llewellyn's disaffection with Pound's jurisprudence and that this was translated into a major attack on Pound in 1930. Scholars have minimized or overlooked the condescending and contemptuous nature of Llewellyn's attack on Pound in this first article.[36] The entire first section of Llewellyn's article is devoted to Pound. Llewellyn began by adopting Pound's summary of nineteenth-century schools of jurisprudence, but quickly turned to a critical analysis of Pound's reliance on "precepts" of law.[37] These in turn, Llewellyn argued, were "roughly synonymous with rules and principles, the principles being wider in scope and proportionately vaguer in connotation, with a tendency toward idealization of some portion of the *status quo* at any given time."[38] Llewellyn's evaluation of Pound was ambivalent: "Only a man gifted with insight would have added to the verbal formulae and verbalized (though vague) conceptual pictures thus far catalogued, such an element *of practices,* of habits and techniques of action, of *behavior.* But only a man partially caught in the traditional precept-thinking of an age that is passing would have focused that behavior on, have given it a major reference to, have belittled

and disciple, William Twining, recognized the problems with the essay. William Twining, *Karl Llewellyn and the Realist Movement* [1973] (Norman, Okla., 1985), 70.

34. Llewellyn, "Next Step," 434 (emphasis in original).

35. Ibid. (emphasis in original).

36. Twining characterizes Llewellyn's comments on Pound as "perceptive" and "quite critical." Twining, *Llewellyn,* 70–71. G. Edward White thought that Llewellyn's criticisms of Pound were "milder" than those of Frank in the latter's *Law and the Modern Mind.* White argues that Frank's "attack on Pound was more personalized and intense." G. Edward White, "From Sociological Jurisprudence to Legal Realism," 58 *Virginia Law Review* 1020–21 (1972).

37. Llewellyn, "Next Step," 434.

38. Ibid. (emphasis in original).

its importance by dealing with it as a phase of, those merely verbal formulae: precepts."[39]

As in the correspondence, Llewellyn's problem with Pound was the latter's refusal to descend from the heaven of generalization to the ground of real life. Indeed, it was in the footnote to the above criticism that Llewellyn referred to Pound's article on "The Limits of Effective Legal Action."[40] Had Llewellyn's appraisal of Pound ended there, Pound might not have felt the need to respond; but Llewellyn's escalating invective in a footnote to his discussion devaluated Pound's entire scholarly corpus:

> Critical reading of Pound's work, it may be noted in passing, and especially the phrasing of any concrete criticism, are embarrassed by the constant indeterminacy of the level of his discourse. At times the work purports clearly to travel on the level of considered and buttressed scholarly discussion; at times *on the level of bedtime stories for the tired bar;* at times on an intermediate level, that of the thoughtful but unproved essay. Most often, it is impossible to tell the intended level of any chapter or passage, and the writing seems to pass without notice from one to another. Now it is obvious that three successive, mutually inconsistent generalizations, though no one of them sustainable as the deliberate propositions of a scholar, may all be illuminating and indeed all true at once—on the level of the after dinner speech, or even of the thought-provoking essay. All of which gags the critic at the same time that it perhaps stimulates his critical faculties.[41]

Llewellyn was understandably taken by surprise when, after the essay appeared, he received a note of congratulation from Pound on the piece.[42] Pound wrote Llewellyn: "Veni fortior me, post me"[43] (whoever comes after me, is stronger for it). Pound may have skimmed the article, noting the flattery and scholarly critique but overlooking the damning footnote. Perhaps it was only after he had written to Llewellyn that the footnote was brought to his attention. Llewellyn, too, may have wondered how carefully Pound had read the piece. In a short handwritten letter thanking Pound for his "gra-

---

39. Ibid., 435.

40. Ibid.

41. Ibid., 436 (emphasis in original).

42. Pound to Llewellyn, Apr. 29, 1930, KLP, III.65.b; Llewellyn noted his astonishment in a footnote added to a reprint of the article in his collection *Jurisprudence: Realism in Theory and Practice* (Chicago, 1962), 14.

43. Pound to Llewellyn, Apr. 29, 1930, KLP, III.65.b.

cious note," Llewellyn remarked that "I note that you withhold comment on its soundness."[44] Then, perhaps not realizing the Pandora's box he might be opening, Llewellyn ingenuously told Pound that he hoped "that sometime you may find leisure to take me over the jumps. Though it would be even better if . . . you could pry loose leisure to show us what skilled irrigation can do to a wilderness."[45]

But a far more likely explanation for Pound's courtesy was his well-practiced false face when he was wounded. To Llewellyn, Pound said one thing, but he thought another. Consider: on July 30, 1929, Burke Shartel of the University of Michigan Law School asked Pound to participate at the end-of-year meeting of the AALS. Shartel was chairman of the Round Table on Jurisprudence and Legal History and wanted Pound to comment on "New Directions" in jurisprudence—in particular, to "get your reaction on the Research Projects proposed at Columbia, Yale, and Johns-Hopkins."[46] In fact, Pound was well aware of what was going on among the empirical data gatherers at those schools. Hessel Yntema, one of Llewellyn's realists, wrote to Pound on June 25, 1928, two years before Llewellyn fired the first shot: "I am writing this because I think you will be gratified to know that I have been asked to join in a group which has been asked to organize an Institute for the Study of Law at Johns Hopkins University. And what should be still more satisfying to you more than anyone else is the fact that this group, as far as I can see, is inspired by ambitions and represents a point of view, which you more than anyone else in this country have stimulated."[47] Pound replied encouragingly, suggesting that the institute men work on conflict of laws.[48] He enjoyed the hospitality of the institute, dining with its staff on shrimp cocktail, squab, and strawberry mousse.[49]

Pound commended himself and the staff to J. S. Ames, president of Johns Hopkins University, some years later: "As you know, I take much interest in the Institute, not only because some of the staff are among my most valued personal friends, but because I believe

44. Llewellyn to Pound, May 1, 1930, RPP, 24-6.
45. Ibid.
46. Burke Shartel to Pound, July 30, 1929, RPP, 5-26.
47. Hessel E. Yntema to Pound, June 25, 1928, RPP, 91-7.
48. Pound to Yntema, July 21, 1928, RPP, 91-7.
49. Menu of Institute Dinner, Mar. 3, 1930, RPP, 21-9.

heartily in the enterprise and have been looking forward hopefully to great results therefrom." [50] But what he said to Shartel was quite different. "Please treat this letter as confidential. . . . I should be glad to do anything for you in reason, but I do not like to comment on the research projects proposed at Columbia, Yale, and Johns Hopkins. Frankly, my friends there seem to me to have chips on their shoulders which makes any such objective discussion of the projects as I should want to make certain of misinterpretation and certain to produce needless controversy." [51]

If Llewellyn had written out of turn, it was no more than he had communicated privately to Pound over the years. Indeed, shortly after the publication of Llewellyn's piece, Pound approached him with a proposition. Alvin Johnson, managing editor of the *Encyclopedia of the Social Sciences* project, wrote to Pound, his editorial advisor on law and frequent contributor, that "we are in a considerable jam over our article on *Contract*." [52] Sometime before, Johnson had asked Pound to write a major piece on contract law for the *Encyclopedia*. [53] Pound had already contributed several articles, including ones on jurisprudence and the American Law Institute. But this time, Pound had had to turn Johnson down. The press of his duties as dean, and his work on the Wickersham Commission, made taking on another scholarly project-for-hire, even for the "handsome" standard rate of $20 (per article), [54] impossible.

Rebuffed by Pound, Johnson decided to ask Llewellyn to take on the task. Pound may have recommended Llewellyn himself, or Johnson might simply have looked up who was teaching contracts on the Columbia campus (the *Encyclopedia* project was headquartered there in Fayerweather Hall, across a campus archway from the Columbia Law School). Llewellyn might have been suggested by either Arthur Corbin or Samuel Williston—the two acknowledged giants of contract law at that time. Llewellyn still affectionately addressed

50. Pound to J. S. Ames, Mar. 9, 1932, RPP, 21-9.
51. Pound to Shartel, Aug. 3, 1929, RPP, 5-26.
52. Alvin Johnson to Pound, Jan. 12, 1931, RPP, 13-9 (emphasis in original).
53. Johnson refers to the earlier solicitation and Pound's response in a later letter. Johnson to Pound, Jan. 12, 1931, RPP, 13-9.
54. Johnson to Pound, Aug. 13, 1929, RPP, 13-9, in which Johnson thanked Pound for two of these articles and mentions he is enclosing a check for $20 for the ALI piece.

Corbin as "Dad."[55] Llewellyn had corresponded with Williston over the years, and the two men respected each other greatly.[56] It is very possible that Johnson first approached either or both of these men to write the piece, but they were both just then engaged in the monumental American Law Institute Restatement project.[57]

However Llewellyn came to Johnson's attention, the former submitted his 7,414-word article (the assignment asked for only 5,000 words) on "Contract" to Johnson in early December of 1930.[58] Johnson's problem was not the length of the piece. He told Pound that Llewellyn "treated the subject dynamically but impressionistically. It seems to us that while his article is excellent as far as it goes, it is weak in its historical and comparative aspects."[59] In other words, Llewellyn had written a realist article on contract law rather than a conventional survey of the field. Johnson told Pound, "I think you will agree with me that the article on *Contract* is so important that we should make some effort to remedy the situation it has created." Johnson pleaded with Pound to come to his aid: "You are the only person who can do an article on the theories of contract within the three or at the very most four, weeks within which we shall require it." Johnson outlined what he had in mind: "Presumably it will deal largely with continental theories although I suppose a com-

55. See, e.g., Llewellyn to Corbin, Apr. 6, 1931, KLP, A.II.65.b. Corbin closed with "Your affectionate" and signed the letters "Dad." See, e.g., Corbin to Llewellyn, May 4, 1931, KLP, A.II.65.b.

56. Samuel Williston to Llewellyn, July 24, 1931, KLP, A.II.65.b.

57. There is no time to go into the relationship between Llewellyn and Williston at this point, though I hope someday to do an article reevaluating Williston, in which the Llewellyn-Williston correspondence will figure. Williston is a curiously more complex legal scholar than he has been portrayed. Consider, for instance, his criticism of Langdell on the sufficiency of mutual promises as consideration for bilateral contracts, Samuel Williston, "Consideration in Bilateral Contracts," 27 *Harvard Law Review* 503 (1914), and his early approval of the doctrine of promissory estoppel, private communication from Williston to Henry Ballantyne, quoted in Henry Ballantyne, "Is the Doctrine of Consideration Senseless and Illogical?," 11 *Michigan Law Review* 493 (1913). Briefly, Williston's correspondence with Llewellyn began when Llewellyn reviewed Williston's treatise on contracts in 1925. Williston wrote to Llewellyn to thank him for his kind words and also to start a friendly exchange over some mild criticisms Llewellyn had made. Williston told Llewellyn that basically he agreed with the younger man and admired his work. Williston to Llewellyn, Feb. 16, 1925, KLP, R.XXIII.7. Llewellyn, of course, later dedicated his casebook on sales to Williston. Karl Llewellyn, *Cases and Materials on the Law of Sales* (Chicago, 1930).

58. A carbon of Llewellyn's manuscript, with the date received, the number of words, and the number of words assigned noted, is in the RPP, 13-9.

59. Johnson to Pound, Jan. 12, 1931, RPP, 13-9.

parison with common law attitudes would be interesting. I should say, perhaps, that we are less interested in the theories themselves which were often doubtless ill conceived than in the sociological factors of which they were a manifestation." [60]

Johnson's request was right up Pound's alley. Pound reveled in synthesizing and comparing Continental thinkers to common law theorists. Johnson asked for something else as well. He suggested, "In doing the article I wonder finally if it wouldn't be possible for you to work in interstitially some of the more technical rules as to the formation and discharge of contracts by way of showing that no theory fits all of them." [61] Apparently, this was another "weakness" (not surprisingly) of Llewellyn's contribution. Johnson told Pound, "These technical rules are also slighted in the article we now have, and while we are not interested in technicalities as such, I think that they are to a certain extent essential to a philosophical grasp of contract law." [62]

Johnson seems to have missed the point that Llewellyn had tried to make, both in his "Next Step" and in the manuscript he submitted to Johnson. Technical rules were unimportant in the abstract. The reality of transactions was the crucial thing to understand about contract law. [63] Johnson instead told Llewellyn that he had asked Pound to help on the article by writing some additional sections, but that Pound had advised him that Llewellyn's piece required more substantive revision. Johnson told Llewellyn that the Harvard dean would phone him about collaborating on the revised contribution. [64] Llewellyn agreed with Johnson's plan and awaited Pound's call. Confusion in Pound's office led to misunderstanding, and Pound never telephoned Llewellyn. [65] Finally, Llewellyn wrote to Pound. [66] Pound, busy as always, reassured Llewellyn that he was willing to help and that "you have the material already in manu-

60. Ibid. (emphasis in original).

61. Ibid.

62. Ibid. Pound's contribution is "Contract," in Edwin Seligman and Alvin Johnson, eds., *Encyclopedia of the Social Sciences* (New York, 1931), 2:323–28.

63. Llewellyn's manuscript is essentially the same as his "What Price Contract—An Essay in Perspective," 40 *Yale Law Journal* 704–51 (1931).

64. Llewellyn recounted his telephone conversation with Johnson in a letter to Pound. Llewellyn to Pound, Feb. 2, 1931, RPP, 24-6. He gave a more detailed chronology of events in a letter to Pound a week later. Llewellyn to Pound, Feb. 10, 1931, RPP, 24-6.

65. Pound to Llewellyn, Feb. 4, 1931, RPP, 24-6.

66. Llewellyn to Pound, Feb. 2, 1931, RPP, 24-6.

script for the bulk of an article and that with a few suggestions I can make, which I hope might appeal to you, it will not be difficult nor take much time to put together something which would satisfy the editor's purposes."[67] Pound suggested that they meet in New York to discuss the matter.

Messages between the two men to arrange a meeting went awry.[68] Pound decided that Llewellyn was avoiding him;[69] Llewellyn wrote Pound to ask "wherein I failed to open the road to collaboration."[70] Llewellyn clearly had doubts about a collaboration; he told Pound that "[i]t is rarely a satisfactory business, at best. . . ."[71] Pound replied that "collaboration is apt to be an awkward matter but [I] had hoped that *our views on many things were so alike* that we could probably give Johnson what he wants after a conference."[72] Since the two men could not agree on a time or place to meet, however, Pound recommended that "if you were willing to let me draw a draft incorporating a good part of yours I would submit it to you and very likely you and I could agree on something to appear as a joint project."[73] Llewellyn overcame his reluctance and wrote back to Pound on February 16 that "I will go with you on any such line of collaboration as you suggest. It would be very interesting to work over the redraft that you speak of."[74] Three days later, Johnson sent Pound Llewellyn's latest version of the article for Pound to revise.[75]

The correspondence between Llewellyn and Pound about the *Encyclopedia* article abruptly ends at this point. Instead of the collaboration on which they had finally agreed, the *Encyclopedia* ultimately published an article in two parts, separately authored by Pound and Llewellyn.[76] What happened? Only a few weeks after

67. Pound to Llewellyn, Feb. 4, 1931, RPP, 24-6.
68. Ibid.
69. Llewellyn to Pound, Feb. 10, 1931, and Pound to Llewellyn, Feb. 12, 1931, RPP, 24-6.
70. Llewellyn to Pound, Feb. 10, 1931, RPP, 24-6.
71. Ibid.
72. Pound to Llewellyn, Feb. 12, 1931, RPP, 24-6 (emphasis added).
73. Ibid.
74. Llewellyn to Pound, Feb. 16, 1931, RPP, 24-6.
75. Johnson to Pound, Feb. 19, 1931, RPP, 13-9.
76. A comparison of Llewellyn's and Pound's independent pieces shows that, while Pound's comparative and doctrinal analysis was more conventional than Llewellyn's, it was neither terribly out of touch with nor contradictory of Llewellyn's. They both approved of modern developments in contract law, but Llewellyn's approach was more imaginative.
Their differing approaches may be illustrated by relating an anecdote from their later

Llewellyn agreed to let Pound rework and rewrite his "Contract" article, Pound published his *Harvard Law Review* critique of the realists. All during the time they had corresponded, Pound had never hinted that he had been working on such a piece. Llewellyn was stunned and probably felt betrayed.[77] He complained to Corbin, "I still can't understand how he could write the article."[78]

Collaboration is an intimate relationship. When one author agrees to collaborate with another, there is, by necessity, a bond created between them not unlike the bond created in marriage. You place your trust in your co-author. You are vulnerable. Betrayal of that trust by public attacks on you by your partner is kin to discovering the infidelity of a spouse. Llewellyn's perceived betrayal by his ostensible collaborator, Pound, enraged him. When Llewellyn wrote his "Some Realism about Realism: A Reply to Dean Pound," when he refused to include Pound in his list of realists, and when he authored the never-published footnote that denied Pound any connection to the intellectual history of the new jurisprudence, it was Llewellyn's way of blotting out all that had been between them and restoring some of his self-respect.[79]

Llewellyn invited a private exchange with Pound but got a surprisingly public rebuke in the March 1931 issue of the *Harvard Law Review*.[80] Pound never mentioned to Llewellyn in any of his letters

---

correspondence. Llewellyn, an amateur poet, sent Pound a copy of one of his poems, "The Common Law Tradition." Llewellyn to Pound, n.d., RPP, 142-6. Pound, no poet, wrote to Llewellyn: "[L]ike everything that comes from your pen, it is lively and pointed. You certainly have the swing of one of Kipling's ballads. I have never been tempted to essay verse. Indeed, I am not adapted to write it. But if I ever did attempt to write in verse about law, I should be tempted to try the style of Lucretius, and the result would, no doubt, fall very flat." Pound to Llewellyn, Nov. 10, 1941, KLP, R.XVI.5 (original) and RPP, 142-6 (carbon).

77. Twining recognized Llewellyn's sense of betrayal but thought it was only because Pound had sent Llewellyn such a nice note after the "Next Step" article. Twining, *Llewellyn*, 72–73.

78. Llewellyn to Corbin, Apr. 6, 1931, KLP, A.II.65.b.

79. Llewellyn's actions—the "Reply" article itself and the unpublished footnote—remind me of a scene in Paul Mazursky's film *An Unmarried Woman*. After Jill Clayburgh's husband, Michael Murphy, leaves her for a younger woman, she tears through their apartment throwing out every item even remotely connected to her unfaithful husband to the extent of tearing off his visage from pictures of the two of them.

80. Twining, who probably did not see Llewellyn's reply to Pound because there was no copy of the letter in the former's papers, speculated in his account of the controversy that as a result of Pound's congratulatory note, Llewellyn may have been "under the impression that Pound looked on him with special favour" and that he was therefore

that he had written and was about to publish an article critical of the new jurisprudence Llewellyn had championed.[81] Pound's forum was a special issue of the *Harvard Law Review* dedicated to Justice Oliver Wendell Holmes, Jr., on the occasion of his ninetieth birthday.[82] In fact, Pound's study, "The Call for a Realist Jurisprudence," was the only solicited essay that did not focus on Holmes's career or jurisprudence. Pound later explained to Paul Freund (then president of the law review) that Pound had not understood that the editors had expected a Holmes piece.[83] The dean was at that time temporarily absent from the law school—serving on the Wickersham Commission in Washington, D.C.—and so a misunderstanding could easily have occurred. Removed as he was from his office, library, and secretary, he may have sent the article on the realists because it was something he had already substantially written and could hastily complete in time for the law review's deadline.[84]

Pound was clearly stimulated by Llewellyn's article and encouraged by Llewellyn's letter to write his essay—the very fact that Pound referred to a "Realist" jurisprudence confirms as much.[85] But most of Pound's specific criticisms of realist jurisprudence were probably not inspired by Llewellyn's published work, or even by Llewellyn's personal challenge to Pound. For one thing, Llewellyn had published fairly little before 1930. For another, the little that Llewellyn had published (and would publish, for that matter) was not the heavily social scientific—statistical and psychological—

"sharply disillusioned in the following year, when 'realism' became the focal point of a bitter and protracted controversy." Twining, *Llewellyn*, 71, 72.

81. Ibid.

82. Pound, "The Call for a Realist Jurisprudence," 44 *Harvard Law Review* 697 (1931).

83. Author's interview with Professor Freund, Feb. 20, 1987. Pound, according to Freund, reproached the student for not informing him that all the contributors were expected to write and, except for himself, had written essays about Holmes—the dean appeared to Freund to have been somewhat embarrassed by his faux pas.

84. Gilmore suggests this in his version of the controversy, and it seems consistent with my reconstruction of events. Gilmore's other assertion, that Pound had neither Llewellyn nor Jerome Frank in mind and had probably never read anything by Llewellyn or Frank before he wrote his critical essay, is totally refuted by evidence from Pound's correspondence. We have already seen this evidence as it relates to Llewellyn; there is also correspondence that irrefutably shows that Pound had read Frank's recently published book, *Law and the Modern Mind*. Gilmore, *Ages of American Law*, 137. Twining's account agrees with this suggestion. Twining, *Llewellyn*, 72.

85. Frank referred specifically to "legal realism" in *Law and the Modern Mind*, 46–52, but it was Llewellyn's creature that Frank meant.

type of scholarship Pound indicted in the second part of his study. Llewellyn's piece became the occasion rather than the cause of Pound's fusillade.[86]

A closer reading of Pound's essay shows that he was caught between admiration for the young empiricists and skepticism about the soundness of their approach. While a great deal has been written—starting with Llewellyn's second article discussed below—about Pound's criticisms of the realists, Pound's sympathy for and understanding of this new jurisprudential movement is rarely emphasized. Indeed, the introduction and first part of "The Call for a Realist Jurisprudence" evidence an introspective empathy for the new approach. Pound admitted, for example, that "our unconscious measure may be that of a philosophy and psychology and legal science of the past, whereas they [the realists] are struggling to put things in terms of the philosophy and psychology of today, and thus to set up a legal science for the twentieth century. Hence I approach the subject of the call for a realist jurisprudence, insistent on the part of our younger teachers of law, with some humility."[87] Pound may have thought he was doing the new breed of jurisprudents a favor by announcing to his own generation the arrival of the new movement: "[H]ere is an important movement in the science of law," Pound proclaimed, "and it behooves us to understand it and be thinking about it."[88] And indeed, Pound's stature in academic and juristic legal circles meant that an article by him, particularly in the Holmes celebratory issue of the *Harvard Law Review,* guaranteed serious consideration of the new movement.[89]

The three parts of Pound's article analyzed the realist methodology in different ways. The first part looked at the realist program generally and is by far the soundest critique. Pound began by trying to define realism: "As I read them, the new juristic realists hardly use realism in a technical philosophical sense. They use it rather in the sense which it bears in art. By realism they mean fidelity to na-

---

86. Even Llewellyn himself saw his work as a moderate, rather than an extreme, example of realist scholarship. See Llewellyn's categories of realists in the manuscript list reprinted in the Appendix.

87. Pound, "Realist Jurisprudence," 697.

88. Ibid.

89. Llewellyn himself admitted in "Some Realism about Realism, A Reply to Dean Pound," 44 *Harvard Law Review* 1222 (1931), that "[w]hen Dean Pound speaks on jurisprudence, men listen."

ture, accurate recording of things as they are, as contrasted with things as they are imagined to be, or wished to be, or as one feels they ought to be. They mean by realism faithful adherence to the actualities of the legal order as the basis of a science of law."[90] Pound seemed to have finally grasped what Llewellyn had tried to convey in their earlier correspondence. Or perhaps, Pound had understood all along and only appeared obtuse as he attempted to convince his young colleague of the value of his own approach. Whatever the provenance of Pound's new insight, Llewellyn's influence on Pound is apparent in the first part of the article.

Once Pound defined the realist approach, he criticized it—as it has been criticized ever since—for lacking any ultimate purpose. For, Pound suggested, "[a]fter the actualities of the legal order have been observed and recorded, it remains to do something with them. What does realism propose to do with them which we had not been doing in the past?"[91] Pound knew firsthand that observation was worthwhile, but the inchoate realist jurisprudence had no program. Having his cake and eating it, Pound also pointed out that what these realists were doing was neither new nor unique. Previous jurisprudential schools—rationalists, historical jurists, analytical jurists, and positivists—according to Pound, had tried to look at the legal system realistically. But "our *new* realist rejects all these conceptions of juristic reality."[92]

Pound expressed skepticism that the new jurists could "find the one unchallengeable basis free from illusion which alone the new realist takes over from the illusion-ridden jurists of the past."[93] Showing sensitivity to twentieth-century relativism,[94] Pound suggested, "If recent philosophy teaches aright, there is no absolute reality" and "no absolute significance."[95] Pound agreed with Llewellyn that "the difference today is one of emphasis."[96] The emphasis of the realists on criticism, Pound conceded, deserved merit, since it "is useful in that it shows us what we have to do in making [the legal

90. Pound, "Realist Jurisprudence," 697.
91. Ibid.
92. Ibid., 698 (emphasis added).
93. Ibid., 699.
94. Paul Johnson, *Modern Times: The World from the Twenties to the Eighties* (New York, 1983), 1–48.
95. Pound, "Realist Jurisprudence," 699.
96. Ibid.

processes] more effective, or in making their workings more in accord with the ends of law, or in finding better instruments to take
their place. The new realists have been doing good work at this
point. . . . But such critical activity, important as it is, is not the
whole of jurisprudence, nor can we build a science of law which
shall faithfully describe the actualities of the legal order and organize our knowledge of these actualities, merely on the basis of such
criticism. There is as much actuality," Pound defended himself and
his generation, "in the old picture as in the new. Each selects a set
of aspects for emphasis. Neither portrays the whole as it is." [97]

Pound concluded that the problem with the "new" realists' insistence on the objective scientific gathering of facts was that "facts
occur in a multifarious mass of single instances. To be made intelli-
gible and useful, significant facts have to be selected, and what is
significant will be determined by some picture or ideal of the science
and of the subject of which it treats. . . . The new realists," Pound
argued, "have their own preconceptions of what is significant, and
hence of what juristically must be." [98] And what did the realists consider significant that Pound found objectionable: "psychological
theories of the behavior of particular judges in particular cases." [99]
Thus, he concluded, "Most of them merely substitute a psychological must for an ethical or political or historical must." [100]

Most of Pound's analysis and criticism of the realists in the first
part of his essay was both perceptive and reasonable. He showed
paternal interest in and approval of most of these younger academics' efforts. Pound attacked neither individuals nor specific approaches until the very conclusion of this first part, when he singled
out psychological methodology. Whom did he have in mind on this
point? Everyone who read the piece knew who it was. One scholar
has speculated that Pound had probably not read Frank's book before writing his article on the realists,[101] but Frank had his publisher
send a copy of his book to Pound as soon as it was released. In a
letter to Pound in which he all but challenged Pound to read the
volume, Frank told Pound, "If you should happen to be interested

97. Ibid.
98. Ibid., 700.
99. Ibid.
100. Ibid.
101. Gilmore, *Ages of American Law,* 137 n.25.

enough to read it, I would be, of course, immensely interested in your reactions."[102] Pound responded by thanking Frank for the book and promising him that he would "read it at the first opportunity" with "much interest and profit."[103] Pound explained that his work on the Wickersham Commission would prevent his getting to it "for the next few weeks."[104] There is no reason to doubt that Pound kept his promise and that Frank's book inspired some of the criticism that appeared in Pound's *Harvard Law Review* article. Pound implied as much to Llewellyn when he wrote Llewellyn after the essay appeared.[105]

Such comments and general criticisms as Pound made in the first part of his article (even his specific disagreement with applying psychology to legal analysis) could have been considered a fair reading of realist scholarship. Neither Llewellyn nor Frank would object to them. But Pound went much further in the second part of his essay. He identified five "items . . . found so generally in the writings of the new school, that one may be justified in pronouncing them, or most of them, the ideas of current juristic realism." The commonalities Pound thought he recognized in the jurisprudence of the "new school" included a "faith in masses of figures as having significance in and of themselves"; a "belief in the exclusive significance or reality of some one method or line of approach"; an insistence on precise terminology or an attempt to fashion "a science of law analogous to mathematical physics," all the while emphasizing "the uncertainties, the lack of uniformity, and the influence of personal and subjective factors in particular cases" and asserting "that the sole valid approach is by way of psychology," or at least "some one psychological starting point is the *unum necessarium*"; an "insistence on the unique single case rather than on the approximation to a uniform course of judicial behavior," leading some "[r]adical neo-realis[ts] . . . to deny that there are rules or principles or conceptions or doctrines at all"; and finally, the conception by "many of the new juristic realists . . . of law as a body of devices for the purposes of business instead of as a body of means toward general social ends." Pound always loved lists. It is not hard to see how Llewellyn and Frank might have thought some of Pound's criticisms were directed

102. Frank to Pound, Oct. 7, 1930, RPP, 14-13.
103. Pound to Frank, Oct. 20, 1930, RPP, 14-30.
104. Ibid.
105. Pound to Llewellyn, Mar. 21, 1931, RPP, 24-6.

at them. Certainly, Frank had laid heavy emphasis on the psychology of judging in his book, and Llewellyn laid equal emphasis in his work on the reality of market and business practices. Nevertheless, the entire tenor of Pound's critique was hyperbolic, a fact that became entirely clear after reading the third and final part of Pound's article.[106]

In the last part of the essay, Pound suggested "a program of *relative-realist* jurisprudence" that could satisfy his criticisms, while furthering the general aims of these younger academics.[107] Pound's positive suggestions sounded like less extreme versions of the positions he had criticized, but Llewellyn, Frank, and the other realists who objected to Pound's criticisms fretted that Pound had, in the second part of his essay, grossly exaggerated their views without citing a single specific example to support his translation and then adopted ideas much closer to their own than to his in the third part. Thus, it was not merely the inaccurate depiction of realism that irked them; it was also Pound's appropriation of their ideas.

This was the kind of intellectual debate Llewellyn enjoyed. He held no grudges and never expected anyone else to hold them. He simply adored the parry and thrust of an intellectual duel for its own sake.[108] In that spirit, Llewellyn did not hesitate to write to Pound to tell him that he had contacted Paul Freund "offering him for the June issue a rejoinder to your paper in the Holmes number."[109] There was no hint of disaffection with Pound himself over what the dean had written; indeed, Llewellyn told Pound that "I found your article quite exciting and only wish that you had put us into the pillory one by one."[110] The reason he gave Pound for writing a reply was that "the realists as a group show up somewhat better than one would gather from your paper. Better in two ways. First, in that the errors and exaggerations that you very properly castigate will prove on a careful examination of the literature to be rather peculiar to individuals than common to the group."[111] (Llewellyn seemed to imply that he agreed that some of his realist brethren might have

106. Pound, "Realist Jurisprudence," 701, 702, 705, 707, 708.
107. Ibid., 710 (emphasis added).
108. Author's interview with Professor Clyde Summers, Jan. 8, 1987, in which the latter recalled that aspect of Llewellyn's personality from his days as a Llewellyn student at Columbia University School of Law.
109. Llewellyn to Pound, Mar. 17, 1931, RPP, 24-6.
110. Ibid.
111. Ibid.

been guilty of the excesses Pound had decried.) "And second, because the positive contributions of the group seem to me to reach
further than comes to clear expression in your article."[112] The
article Llewellyn appeared to contemplate seemed friendly and
unobjectionable.

Pound responded to Llewellyn's letter in the same amicable spirit.
He told Llewellyn, "It did not occur to me that I was pillaring [sic]
anybody."[113] Pound found personal confrontations distasteful. He
even tried to soften his criticism by reminding Llewellyn that he had
been "careful to say that no school can be judged by exaggerations
or eccentricities of particular adherents, and especially so in its early
stages."[114] Roscoe Pound wanted no feud with the realists. He confided to Llewellyn that "[n]ext September when I am back at Cambridge with nothing to do but my school work I wish I could talk
this whole matter of the future of jurisprudence in the United States
over with you. There are very few doing serious work of the first
order in that subject." And, he continued in a conciliatory vein, "I
cannot but think that those who are should be getting together in
the hope of finding a program upon which they can agree. It seems
to me too much of the energy of those who are working in the science of law has been wasted in controversy, and that some really
great things could be achieved through understanding and cooperation." He concluded his letter by offering an unequivocal apology:
"I am sorry if my attempt to understand and set forth a possible
program for a group of thinkers with whom I have a great deal of
sympathy should have appeared to be controversial." And added,
as if to admit he might have been carried away, "I suppose that is
what comes from having to do things in a hurry."[115] The olive
branch was a private gesture; the birch switch had been public.
Llewellyn knew the difference.

Only one thing Llewellyn had said caused Pound even the slightest
alarm, the fact that "Jerome Frank has promised to go halves
with me on the labor."[116] The controversy had always been three-

112. Ibid.
113. Pound to Llewellyn, Mar. 21, 1931, RPP, 24-6 (the original of this letter resides
in KLP, B.65.b).
114. Ibid.
115. Ibid.
116. Llewellyn to Pound, Mar. 17, 1931, RPP, 24-6. According to Llewellyn, Frank
wrote him that on the basis of having seen a manuscript copy of Llewellyn's review of

cornered because of Frank's attack on Pound in *Law and the Modern Mind*. Pound had read Frank's book and wrote Llewellyn: "I must confess I am troubled about Jerome Frank. When a man puts in quotation marks and attributes to a writer things which he not only never put in print any where, but goes contrary to what he has set in print repeatedly, it seems to me to go beyond the limits of permissible carelessness and to be incompatible, not merely with scholarship but with the ordinary fair play of controversy." Pound was not merely critical of Frank; he was indignant: "I cannot afford to discuss anything with one who uses such tactics, and should like to suggest to you whether you can afford to identify yourself with him."[117]

Pound liked Llewellyn and thought he could influence him to give up his association with Frank. But instead, Llewellyn defended Frank: "[C]an you take time out of a busy life to give me a bill of particulars? I am surprised that you have caught him attributing to anyone remarks that have not been made. My impressions have been that he was both too honest and too careful to do that, even in the heat of controversy." Even as he defended his friend, Llewellyn reassured Pound that "[o]ne thing is certain, and that is that this prospective article will not do so [misquote anyone] and also will be free of heat." Whatever antipathy Pound had toward Frank, Llewellyn did not want to chance any rift between himself and the older man. In a hasty postscript to that letter, Llewellyn told Pound that "I have just had Mr. Frank on the phone and he is very eager to learn of the places in which he may have made misquotations, since there is a chance of holding off the second printing long enough to make correction and apology."[118] What Llewellyn actually had done in that telephone conversation was to unleash "hurricane Jerome" on an unsuspecting Pound.[119]

Jerome Frank was incensed by what Llewellyn told him Pound had written. No sooner was Frank off the telephone with Llewellyn

---

Frank's book, Frank thought Llewellyn "showed a curious empathy" with him. As a result of that initial contact, Frank wound up collaborating with Llewellyn on the response to Pound. Llewellyn, *Jurisprudence*, 104 n.aaa.

117. Pound to Llewellyn, Mar. 21, 1931, RPP, 24-6.

118. Llewellyn to Pound, Mar. 23, 1931, RPP, 24-6.

119. When Morris Cohen raised objections to Frank's work, the latter deluged him with dozens of letters, averaging over fifteen pages, refuting Cohen's equally voluminous correspondence point by point. Glennon, *Jerome Frank*, 22–23.

than he checked every reference to Pound in his book and sent a two-page telegram to Pound about the allegations. Frank admitted that he had found misplaced quotation marks on page 208 that "indicated incorrectly that my interpretation of your views is something which you yourself have said." But he attributed the error to bad proofreading rather than deliberate misrepresentation and "humbly apologize[d]" to Pound, telling him that "I greatly deplore and will have [the error] corrected." Suspecting that Pound's criticism might have been as much on behalf of his Harvard friend and colleague Joseph Beale, who had equally been skewered by Frank in the book, he concluded his missive: "[I]f your comments to Llewellyn refer to misquotation of anyone else other than you I shall be glad to have you call any such mistake to my attention."[120]

The next day, Frank followed up his telegram with a letter. Now, having "more carefully examined [his] book and compared it with [Pound's] writings," he had decided that there was no misquotation and enclosed a list of every Pound quote or reference Frank had used for Pound to review. He urged Pound to send him any corrections as quickly as possible, since Frank was holding up the second printing of the book "[t]o the publisher's great annoyance." In a postscript, he listed all of his references to Beale's work, since "[i]t has just occurred to me that perhaps you had in mind some possible misquotations of Professor Beale."[121]

Pound failed to respond to Frank's urgent messages, and Frank sent another telegram three days later, quickly followed by another letter and subsequently a third telegram, when it suddenly occurred to him that Pound might not have received any of his earlier missives because the Harvard dean was in Washington, not Cambridge.[122] Frank was under a great deal of pressure from his publisher and seemed desperate to get Pound's objections before he had to submit his revisions for the second printing. Pound finally sent Frank a brief reply on March 27, in which he told Frank that he was separated from his books and in any event was too busy to proofread and correct Frank's references and that Frank should go ahead with the

120. According to Frank's telegram, Llewellyn had "just phoned" to tell him what Pound had written. Frank to Pound, telegram dated Mar. 23, 1931 (5:22 p.m.), RPP, 14-13.
121. Frank to Pound, Mar. 24, 1931, RPP, 14-13.
122. Frank to Pound, telegrams dated Mar. 27, 1931 (4:47 p.m.), and Mar. 28, 1931 (10:50 a.m.), and Frank to Pound, Mar. 27, 1931, RPP, 14-13. Frank's barrage of telegrams must have made a Depression-era Western Union company very happy.

second printing of the book.[123] But Pound was never vindictive in the private discourse. He conceded, "[V]ery likely in thirty odd years of writing I have written much that I would wish the Statute of Limitations would bar."[124]

Frank took no chances in wiring his reply to Pound; he sent copies to both Cambridge and Washington.[125] Frank also wrote another letter that same day, in which he concluded both apologetically and defensively: "I am sorry that the incident occurred. As I stated in a previous letter, I have never deliberately misquoted anybody and I am glad to find, upon carefully checking my book, that I have not been guilty of even inadvertent misquotation of yourself."[126] Pound coolly repeated that he had no time to reply to Frank's insistent queries about misquotes and attempted to put an end to the entire affair by telling Frank: "I should not think of suggesting to you what you should do in your own book. Certainly that is a matter entirely for your own judgment."[127]

Frank refused to let the matter drop, however, and continued to press Pound to tell him about specific misquotes. Writing in a tone every bit as formal and restrained as Pound's, he defended his conduct and pointed out how fair he had been throughout in giving Pound every opportunity to substantiate his charges and offering to make corrections or clarifications: "I think you will agree that I have done all that was possible in the circumstances."[128] Pound did not reply. Frank persisted. Indeed, as he wrote Pound later that month, now that he had actually seen the original letter Pound had sent to Llewellyn, "The vigorous character of your statements in that letter warrants me, I believe, in asking that, at your very early convenience, you advise me just what you had in mind when you wrote as you did. . . ."[129] Pound fairly begged to be let off the hook: "Won't you please consider that I am doing a full time teaching job

123. Pound's March 27 letter to Frank is missing from the RPP—but a copy exists in the Jerome Frank Papers, Yale University, 4-109. It was a handwritten note Pound sent from Washington. Frank refers to it in several telegrams and letters. Pound subsequently wrote to Frank from Cambridge on April 2 explicitly repeating some of what he said in his earlier note. Pound to Frank, Apr. 2, 1931, RPP, 14-13.

124. Pound to Frank, Mar. 27, 1931, Jerome Frank Papers, Yale University, 4-109.

125. Frank to Pound, telegrams dated Mar. 30, 1931 (1:30 P.M.), and Mar. 30, 1931 (1:36 P.M.), RPP, 14-13.

126. Frank to Pound, Mar. 30, 1931, RPP, 14-13.

127. Pound to Frank, Apr. 1, 1931, Jerome Frank Papers, Yale University.

128. Frank to Pound, Apr. 3, 1931, RPP, 14-13.

129. Frank to Pound, Apr. 24, 1931, RPP, 14-13.

(six hours a week), and doing the administrative work of Dean of the Harvard Law School, and am trying to do my part on the work of this Commission, coming here every Tuesday night and returning Saturday night." [130]

But Frank was neither mollified nor patient. He chided Pound: "I recognize, of course, that you are busily engaged in important work. But a few weeks ago you interrupted your work to write to Llewellyn in most emphatic terms about my alleged improprieties in misquoting you in my book and concerning my character. I think I was, therefore, not unreasonable in asking you to pause for a brief interval to write me, *at least in general terms,* what you had in mind when you made those statements." [131] Frank would brook no excuses: "The lapse of time since you wrote Llewellyn is sufficiently short so that you are surely able to remember, in a general way, to what you were referring. However, I want this effort to cost you as little time as possible. I am therefore sending you two copies of my book—one to your Cambridge and one to your Washington address." In addition, "I am enclosing a memorandum for your convenience, citing each of the passages in my book where you were quoted, and in connection with each such citation, citing (and sometimes quoting) the passages in your writings from which the quotations from your writings were taken." [132] The memorandum he sent Pound was fourteen, mostly single-spaced pages. Frank, a consummate practitioner, had marshaled his resources to produce a completely professional brief, but "Judge" Pound had summarily dismissed Frank's cause. [133] The harassed dean now ignored Frank even though the latter fatuously offered to pay Pound to hire "some student or other person whom you trust, to do for you the more or less clerical work of comparison" and argued that therefore the "plan will involve no labor on your part and no expense to you." [134]

130. Another handwritten note, Pound to Frank, Apr. 25, 1931, Jerome Frank Papers, Yale University, 4-109.

131. Frank to Pound, May 14, 1931, RPP, 14-13 (emphasis in original).

132. Ibid.

133. I have taken up Frank's challenge to Pound. A review of Frank's memorandum, the text of his book, and Pound's works cited or quoted by him indicates Frank was innocent of Pound's charges. I would have to agree with Llewellyn's assessment that Frank "showed [he] could quote Pound against Pound on any point imaginable" and "this riled Pound, especially because [Frank's book] was wide[ly] sold in popular circulation." Clyde W. Summers, Carbon Typescript of Class Notes on Llewellyn's Course in Jurisprudence (hereinafter Summers, Llewellyn Notes).

134. Frank to Pound, May 14, 1941, RPP, 14-13.

It is no wonder after all this that Frank refused to let Llewellyn list him as co-author of the response to Pound.[135] Llewellyn certainly knew that Frank was writing to Judge Julian Mack, Felix Frankfurter, and Thomas Reed Powell, all of whom were closely tied to Harvard, to prod Pound.[136] Frank got nowhere in part because Pound's network could not be tapped into so easily. For his own part, Llewellyn probably wanted no more accusations of misquotation or misinterpretation that seemed to swirl about Frank.[137] If there was any feud among the principals of the controversy, it was between Pound and Frank, not between Pound and Llewellyn.[138]

Although Frank was not to be a public collaborator on the reply, Llewellyn and Frank continued their private collaboration on the response to Pound. Llewellyn's request for space in the June issue of the *Harvard Law Review* had met with a cool response from Freund.[139] He sent a brief formal letter to Llewellyn, informing him that the law review would welcome a submission but could not guarantee acceptance in advance.[140] Llewellyn was outraged and, probably aware of the altercation in progress between Frank and

135. Llewellyn, "Some Realism," 1222.

136. Frank to Llewellyn, March 25–Apr. 25, 1931, Jerome Frank Papers, Yale University, 4-109.

137. A postscript to the Pound-Frank episode: nearly a year after the flurry of letters and telegrams between the two men, Frank wrote to Pound once more, this time in a very conciliatory vein. Frank complimented Pound on the latter's contributions to the reports of the Wickersham Commission and confided that his "admiration for your genius goes back many years, to the time when, about 1908, I was studying political science. That on some points I have ventured to disagree with you does not mean that I do not still humbly endorse the views of the numerous lawyers who recognize your invaluable contributions to legal thinking." He went on to say that "[m]any] times heretofore I have been tempted to write to you in this vein. But I have been deterred by the fact that you have left unanswered my letter to you of May 14, 1931." Frank to Pound, Apr. 6, 1932, RPP, 14-13. If Frank thought he could effect a reconciliation with Pound, he was probably disappointed. The Pound Papers contain no copy of a reply to this letter.

138. A much fuller account of the exchange of letters, memoranda, and other writings among the principals appears in N. E. H. Hull, "Some Realism about the Llewellyn-Pound Exchange over Realism: The Newly Uncovered Private Correspondence, 1927–1931," 1987 *Wisconsin Law Review* 945–53. It is easy to get the wrong impression, however. Schlegel, for instance, following Twining, refers to "Llewellyn's feud with Pound over the existence and content of Realist jurisprudence" in "American Legal Realism and Empirical Social Science: The Singular Case of Underhill Moore," 29 *University of Buffalo Law Review* 250 (1980).

139. This account of Llewellyn's dealings with the law review was related to the author by Professor Freund in an interview on February 20, 1987.

140. Professor Freund commented that, if Pound's "Realist Jurisprudence" article had attacked any specific individuals, the review might have been more amenable to guaranteeing space for a reply.

Pound, suspected the latter of exerting pressure on the journal to keep a Llewellyn-Frank critique from being published.

Llewellyn wrote a scathing letter to his friend Edmund M. Morgan, who, as it happened, was acting dean at the law school while Pound was on leave working with the Wickersham Commission. Llewellyn told Morgan that he would bring Pound's underhanded censorship to the attention of the AALS at their next meeting. Actually, Pound had little to do with the law review even when he was on campus, but after he left for Washington, he did not communicate at all with the review's editors either to bar or to encourage publication of Llewellyn's prospective article. After reading Llewellyn's angry missive, Morgan called Freund to his office to discuss the problem. The acting dean showed Llewellyn's letter to Freund, told the young man not to take the tone of the letter too seriously— Llewellyn, he explained, had a mercurial temperament—and gently suggested that, if he were in Freund's place, he would write Llewellyn to tell him the review would be glad to publish the article in the June issue. Freund took Morgan's advice.[141] Though Llewellyn had asked Pound to write to Freund and later thanked Pound for interceding, the law review president never heard from Pound and says that it was Morgan who convinced him to accommodate Llewellyn.[142]

Llewellyn realized that the only way to refute Pound's charges was to review systematically the corpus of realist literature; but to survey the realists' work, Llewellyn would first have to decide who, in fact, were the realists. His musings on that question in his 1930

141. Ironically, Freund recalled, he had thought that "Some Realism" was one of the best things Llewellyn had written and that, if it had been submitted, as Freund had written to Llewellyn originally, he was sure the review would have accepted it. The entire episode was the result of Llewellyn's misunderstanding of Freund's letter. Freund, looking back on the incident, said that he should have written a less formal letter to Llewellyn.

142. Pound told Llewellyn that he would write to Freund's successor, Schoene, on his behalf. Pound to Llewellyn, Mar. 21, 1931, RPP, 24-6 (original in KLP, B.65.b). Twining, who saw the original of Pound's letter in the Llewellyn Papers and a draft memo from Llewellyn to fellow realists that said—incorrectly it turns out—that the *Harvard Law Review* had refused space for his reply, but that the *Columbia Law Review* would publish the piece (later corrected to say that the *Harvard Law Review* had promised space in the June issue), perpetuated Llewellyn's misunderstanding of the incident. Twining's version, on which later scholars relied, incorrectly states that Llewellyn was flatly denied space for the reply to Pound until "pressure was brought to bear on the Editor by members of the Harvard faculty, including Pound himself." Twining, *Llewellyn*, 73.

"Next Step" article were eclectic. On that first occasion, his purpose was to demonstrate in a genealogical manner the evolution of the new mode of analysis, rather than to define a coherent jurisprudential group. Outspoken critics of the older jurisprudence like Underhill Moore, Samuel Klaus, Charles Clark, Hessel Yntema, and William O. Douglas had been lumped together with older progressive thinkers like Louis Brandeis and even sociological jurists like Eugen Ehrlich who might have inspired the skeptics of the 1920s but resist categorization as members of the realist "movement." [143] Llewellyn admitted that "[t]he work of the different men moves in somewhat different fields, and is uneven in value." He was trying to be as inclusive as possible—"to show that neither a single country nor a single school is involved"—to suggest "that the point of view [of the behavior or realistic approach] has moved beyond the stage of chatter and has proved itself in operation." [144] The list Llewellyn tried to compile in 1931 had to be more clearly defined because he was no longer establishing a pedigree for a new approach, but defending practitioners of the approach from aspersions cast on their work.

Llewellyn was a political democrat with a small "d," as well as a member of the liberal wing of the Democratic Party, and although he carefully avoided politics (other than academic politics) in his first piece on realism, he clearly identified the jurisprudence of realism with political reform. There were no conservative realists. Thus, it is likely that Llewellyn's first take on a list of realists was heavily influenced by the 1927 petition for Sacco and Vanzetti. Without specifically mentioning the Sacco and Vanzetti episode as a criterion for identifying the realists, Llewellyn much later confided to a friend that "he doubted there was any significant connection between the juristic and political views of Realists, except that some, but by no means all, who wanted reform within the field of law were also interested in political reform." [145] Although Llewellyn might later deny that politics was the intellectual impetus for his conception of legal realism, he disingenuously suggested that "Pound's dislike of Realism may have been politically motivated." [146] Notably absent

143. Llewellyn's complete list from the "Next Step" article is reprinted in Table 1 of the Appendix.

144. Llewellyn, "Next Step," 455.

145. William Twining, paraphrasing letter from Llewellyn to G. B. J. Hughes, Aug. 10, 1954, KLP, R.VIII.17. Twining, *Llewellyn*, 522 n.7.

146. Ibid.

from those signing or authorizing support for the Sacco and Vanzetti petition were any of the Harvard Law School faculty, including Roscoe Pound.

Still, in planning for the reply to Pound, Llewellyn hewed to his original design of avoiding politics. His plan for the article, he told Pound on March 17, "was to work through the material of Moore, Frank, Oliphant and Klaus; Cook, Green, Yntema, Clark and Radin and Llewellyn; and to some extent of Corbin, Sturges and Douglas." He would stick to legal stuff. He had decided on these men because this group is the "most vocal . . . , is characteristic, and gathers most of the men who would come in question." Nevertheless, he was uncertain enough of his decision or defensive enough to inquire of Pound: "Do you have any others in mind?"[147] Pound replied, "Certainly I did not have in mind a number of those who you name—for instance, Clark. On the other hand, I did have in mind Bingham and Lorenzen, who had been particularly insistent upon the unreality of supposed rules, principles and doctrines."[148] Curiously, Pound did not group Llewellyn with the Stanford and Yale professors he had singled out even though Llewellyn had been equally insistent on the unreality of rules in his 1930 article. Nor did Pound mention Frank, probably to avoid adding to that imbroglio.[149]

Even more curious is the fact that, although Pound repeatedly referred to the "new realists" as younger academics, part of a new generation of scholars, the only two men he would admit to having in mind when he wrote his critical essay—Bingham and Lorenzen— were actually his contemporaries.[150] Pound, perhaps realizing that the controversy he had always tried to avoid was catching up with him, tried to obfuscate. It had always been Pound's modus operandi to criticize only in general terms, never letting himself be pinned down to specific charges against individuals who might take issue with him. His realist jurisprudence piece had followed the same pat-

147. Llewellyn to Pound, Mar. 17, 1931, RPP, 24-6.

148. Pound to Llewellyn, Mar. 21, 1931, RPP, 24-6 (original in KLP, B.65.b).

149. As Summers summarized Llewellyn's version of the affair heard in class in 1945–46, "The Emperor [Pound] was peeved and wrote about Realism and criticized them [Llewellyn and Frank]." Summers, Llewellyn Notes, 21.

150. Pound was born in 1870, Ernest Lorenzen was born in 1876, and Joseph Walter Bingham was born in 1878. Twining, *Llewellyn*, 76. The three men were thus sixty-one, fifty-five, and fifty-three, respectively. While they might have been considered in their "prime," they could hardly have been called "young."

tern, but now he was being pursued.[151] To refuse to name any names would leave him open to the charge of fabricating his critique. To be more forthcoming could result in an academic feud with the best and brightest of a new and vigorous generation of scholars.[152] At sixty-one, he could not risk offending young men who he had every reason to believe would outlive him. After all, his reputation would be in their hands.[153]

At first, Llewellyn expressed little surprise at Pound's selection of representative realists, except for the categorization of Ernest Lorenzen "as one of us wild-eyes."[154] Also, in the published list in "Some Realism," he would ultimately include Clark despite Pound's disclaimer.[155] Llewellyn consulted Frank about the list and Pound's response. Frank suggested a few additional names: Thurman Arnold, Walton Hamilton, Edwin Patterson, Leon Tulin, and Judge Hutcheson.[156] The two men titillated each other with their dissection of the Pound list and offered one another alternative readings of the work of Sturges, Clark, Douglas, and Tulin. They even arranged to divide up the list.[157]

Even after the two agreed on these men, they probably felt insecure about identifying them in print without acquiescence from the men themselves. On March 27, they composed a carefully worded "general appeal" to the "non-traditionalist" colleagues they had identified, asking them to help with their answer to Pound. They asked each man on the list to write them as quickly as possible as to whether he could "recall any place in your published work in which there appears a statement which more or less coincides with any of the points Pound makes? If not do you hold such positions?" They also asked for citations to published work in which their correspon-

151. Llewellyn thought Pound had "[i]ncluded all modern writers of diverse [views]. Pound brought all the various ideas [together] and called it 'realism' and by grouping them together proceeded to take them apart." Summers, Llewellyn Notes, 21.

152. Pound clearly wanted to avoid a feud with these younger men. His apologetic letter of March 21 emphasizes his distaste for "controversy" and his admiration for the group as a whole. Pound to Llewellyn, Mar. 21, 1931, RPP, 24-6.

153. Actually, Pound would outlive many of this younger generation, including Frank and Llewellyn. Frank died in 1957; Llewellyn died in 1962; Pound died in 1964.

154. Llewellyn to Pound, Mar. 23, 1931, RPP, 24-6.

155. Llewellyn, "Some Realism," 1226.

156. Llewellyn to Frank, Mar. 20, 1931, Jerome Frank Papers, Yale University, 5-118 (acknowledging the latter's list).

157. Frank to Llewellyn, Mar. 23, 1931, Jerome Frank Papers, Yale University, 5-118.

dents might have "taken a stand on either side or in the middle in regard to one of these matters. . . . Of course," they assured their associates, "acknowledgment will be made for any help received." The memorandum delicately concluded with the critical query: "We should also appreciate expression of your opinion as to whether you regard yourself as in general among the 'juristic realists' and as to whether you think that there is any community of point of view among the men whom we propose to discuss and to whom . . . we are sending this letter?"[158]

Responses to the Llewellyn-Frank memo trickled in. Had Llewellyn and Frank simply reprinted them, they might have not only answered Pound but also given new depth to the debate. Unfortunately, none of the men they contacted was willing to join in the public debate. Llewellyn and Frank's attempt to use a private network to foster public discourse had failed, unlike those occasions when Pound had reached out to his peers. Charles E. Clark of Yale, dean of the law school and an energetic empiricist who had known Llewellyn since both men taught at Yale in 1919, responded, "I have your call for help as against Pound. I am not fully convinced whether the game is worth the hunt and whether you are not over-dignifying the article by replying. In any event, I think there probably should be no joint reply from all 'realists,' but perhaps if you and Mr. Frank do it alone, that may be sufficient." There was no way Clark was going into the lists against Pound, although the two schools already had a long and sometimes bitter rivalry, but Clark wanted Llewellyn to know that "I thought Pound's article was in some ways pitiful. Here is a sound movement, of which he himself may almost be claimed to be the originator and certainly a foremost exponent. It seems somewhat as though he were trying to foul his own nest. The points he makes are really only a caricature of the views of himself and others. For example, the suggestions that the realists believe that exact terminology will solve problems. I suppose this goes back to the Hohfeld ideas, and yet Hoh himself and Cook and Corbin have over and over again pointed out the fallacy of this point of view." Clark would have known—he was Hoh's lawyer at Yale in the first decade of this century and shortly there-

---

158. Memorandum to Potential Realists, Mar. 27, 1931, KLP, B.65.b. "Non-traditionalist" was the term they used in the memorandum; "realist" was not a term used by these men to describe themselves, and Llewellyn probably did not want to cloud the issue with an internal dispute about semantics.

after replaced the deceased Hohfeld as a colleague of Corbin and Cook. "I try to be what I hope is realistic in my approach to law and I think there is a general thread of interest in at least most of the men you name of the background of law against which the cases need to be viewed if the entire picture is to be presented, and . . . the existence of a group of this kind seems to me fairly clear."[159]

Despite the fact that he was one of the older members of the group,[160] Arthur Corbin's reply was equally evasive. Corbin told Llewellyn, his protégé, that "[i]t did not occur to me, as I hastily skimmed through Pound's article, that he referred to me at all or that his article affected me in any way. I certainly feel no call to answer it." Corbin also thought that he did not "have much in common with the other men" on Llewellyn's list and that "they have so many and important differences as to make it highly misleading to classify them under a name." Corbin was antipathetic to any jurisprudential classification, and his advice to Llewellyn seems to suggest that for Llewellyn to try to talk about realists as a group would simply lead the young man into the same misguided thought processes as the dean: "Pound has always loved to classify men into 'Neo-Hegelians' and other 'schools.' The men I know do not classify in any such way (if it is a way)." Corbin was more condescending toward than critical of Pound's article. He told Llewellyn that "Pound's article gave me the impression that it was directed at the indefinite group of younger men, partly, at least, at Harvard, who now delight in sneering at Pound. He cannot help being aware of their attitude; and the 'old bull' is making use of his horns." The insight is tantalizing, for Pound was well aware that he was under attack from that quarter, but Frankfurter's younger supporters were hardly realists in the way that Llewellyn was. Corbin was also aware of Pound's penchant for avoiding personal confrontation: "Of course, he can't gore anybody by name; so he creates a straw man and disembowels the straw." Despite his outspoken criticisms, Corbin's remarks were made strictly in confidence. He cautioned Llewellyn that, though he had no objection to Llewellyn using his

159. Charles E. Clark to Llewellyn, Mar. 31, 1931, KLP, A.II.65.b. After the Llewellyn reply was published, Clark wrote to say that he had read it with great interest: "As I read, the more I am convinced as are you, of the all pervading influence of 'realism' as an attitude and an approach, which cant be separated from one's total work." Clark to Llewellyn, July 14, 1931, KLP, A.II.65.b.

160. Corbin was a leader of the first generation of realists. Kalman, *Legal Realism*, 25.

published work to refute Pound's charges, "I don't wish to be taken as answering him in any respect." Corbin, like Llewellyn's other correspondents, was unable or unwilling to suggest names of additional scholars for Llewellyn's list.[161]

Llewellyn's former colleagues at Columbia, William O. Douglas, Hessel Yntema, and Herman Oliphant, were more encouraging, but just as unwilling to join in the fray. Douglas sent a list of corrections and the wisdom that "a couple of careful fact studies will do more to overthrow Pound than a dozen articles."[162] Yntema replied, "I am very glad that you and Jerome Frank are interesting yourselves in the situation raised by Pound's rather banal article and I hope that you and others who are stirred to comment should do so." But Yntema would not. Such a reply dignified Pound's piece and could be easily countered by Pound, for his statements "involve such flexible questions of interpretation that it would be difficult" to pin him down. More important, "there are, of course, differences of opinion among us which I should not like to see ruled out by the development of anything like a formal credo of 'realistic' jurisprudence."[163] No schools, Yntema, an antinomian himself, told Llewellyn. Which left just the name.

Oliphant reported in as well. He urged Llewellyn to write the article, but to confine it to corrections of Pound's misstatements. Oliphant added that Cook was willing to supply a numbered list of the errata. Neither man was eager to sign on to the article's views. Oliphant did offer a private comment that explained why some of the recipients of the memo, however much they might have agreed with Llewellyn's position, were unwilling to attack Pound in print: "In a way I feel sorry for him [Pound], deeply and generously so. He has been able to pontificate on philosophy in such complete immunity from attack by the rank and file of legal scholars for so long, it never occurred to him to be sure he knew what this gang of upstarts was talking about. And what insidious tides of change have carried him into opposition to the group which his own teachings helped to raise up!"[164] Pound was revered, genuinely, by the next generation of scholars, and Oliphant was right: they had gone to school on

161. Corbin to Llewellyn, Apr. 1, 1931, KLP, B.65.b.
162. William O. Douglas to Llewellyn, Apr. 13, 1931, KLP, A.II.65.b.
163. Yntema to Llewellyn, Apr. 2, 1931, KLP, A.II.65.b.
164. Herman Oliphant to Llewellyn, Mar. 30, 1931, KLP, A.II.65.b.

Pound's teachings. Pound might also provide professional help, should the need arise. No need to burn bridges.[165]

Unable to enroll volunteers for a realist network, Llewellyn was forced to turn to Pound again. If Pound would admit that he had certain individuals in mind when he wrote his article, Llewellyn could confront the issue of whether such individuals were actually part of a coherent movement. On April 6, he confided to Pound that "I hate to trouble you again on this matter of the realists, but I can't help it." Llewellyn admitted he was having difficulty in writing the response he had planned because he could not definitively state who the realists were. "It is absurd," he told Pound, "for us [Llewellyn and Frank] to set up our own criterion of who are realists and then demonstrate that your criterion does not fit our group. If the group you have in mind is not the same as the group we have in mind, that is another question, and one easier to handle."[166] Writing the response to Pound was a far more difficult task than Llewellyn had originally thought. By his calculated reticence, Pound was winning the war of nerves and the logical battles in it. Llewellyn could not merely survey the work of a few people he might think were representative of the movement. If Llewellyn had to omit individuals he considered obvious realists because they denied membership in the group, Pound could defend himself by arguing that Llewellyn had overlooked the very individuals whose scholarship Pound had criticized.

Llewellyn developed a plan to circumvent these problems, which he outlined to Pound:

> What we would like to do, therefore, is first, to discuss your criteria with reference to the men you had in mind (and also with reference to those whom we should class as the more notorious rebels)—although we would distinguish according to whether or not you had picked the particular men discussed. And after that we should like to present our own picture of the realistic movement at large. We have to call on you for help because we find extraordinary difficulty in locating passages

165. When Cook's institute at Johns Hopkins began to fail, he turned to his old Nebraska dean. The two men were still cordial. Pound was "sorry to hear" about the collapse of the Hopkins program and offered, "You may rely resolutely on my bestirring myself on your behalf for anything worth while that may open up." Pound to Walter Wheeler Cook, June 25, 1932, RPP, 10-17.

166. Llewellyn to Pound, Apr. 6, 1931, RPP, 24-6.

which would class anybody as being in the group you had in mind; and we figure, therefore, that it must be considerably smaller than we had first thought.[167]

In order to determine who Pound had in mind, Llewellyn enclosed a new list of names, which he asked Pound to annotate "with a *yes* or *no* beside the names according as you either had the man definitely in mind, or were thinking of him as excluded from your discussion." Llewellyn concluded by asking permission to cite Pound's reply in the published discussion.

Llewellyn's first purpose was to outflank Pound's refusal to name names. By giving Pound a chance to tick off individuals, Llewellyn hoped either to trap Pound into specificity and then refute his individual arguments or to simplify his own task in surveying the realist literature by omitting the individuals Pound had not intended to criticize. The list Llewellyn enclosed with his letter to Pound (table 2 in the appendix) was meant to be as inclusive as possible on its face, giving Pound the broadest discretion. Llewellyn noted at the top of the list: "We do not guarantee to discuss all of these; but we shall try to cover at least all you name."[168] The new list dropped Brandeis and the European jurists whom Llewellyn had considered forerunners of the realist movement, but did include Frankfurter, Milton Handler, and James Landis from the "Next Step" article, though these men had disappeared from both his earlier letter to Pound and the memorandum he wrote with Frank. In addition to the three people he had retained from the "Next Step" article, Llewellyn added the two men Pound had mentioned—Bingham and Lorenzen; the five individuals Frank had suggested—Arnold, Hutcheson, Hamilton, Patterson, and Tulin; and sixteen others.[169]

Whether the length of the new list was meant as a courtesy to Pound or an attempt to nail him down, it unveiled a qualitatively different approach to defining realism from those Llewellyn had previously assayed. The intellectual novelty of the list lay in its structure. For the first time, Llewellyn divided his list into categories. These categories were not merely titles grouping names from the old list; here the categories generated names. They conceptualized realism intellectually as well as genealogically.

167. Ibid.
168. Ibid. (emphasis in original).
169. See Table 1 in the Appendix.

The first category included Llewellyn and Frank's "notion of realists who may have taken extreme positions on one point or another."[170] Everyone in this category, except John Hanna,[171] had appeared in the Llewellyn-Frank memo. (Hanna, trained at Harvard Law School, was a colleague of Llewellyn's at Columbia.) Most of them had also appeared on the list Llewellyn originally had sent Pound in March, and two them—Moore and Klaus—had even been included in Llewellyn's 1930 "Next Step" article.

The second category contained the "realists who are thoroughgoing, but probably less extreme in their positions."[172] Again, many of these men had figured in previous lists, though several were new: Adolf A. Berle, Thomas Reed Powell, Young D. Smith, Alexander M. Kidd, Robert M. Hutchins, Joseph Francis, and James C. Bonbright. Of these, only Francis and Thomas Reed Powell would be retained in the published article. Nearly everyone on the private list was a professor at Columbia or Yale—not one Harvard professor had been included. Even Kidd, the only non-Columbia or non-Yale representative, had spent two years as a colleague of Llewellyn's at Columbia in the late 1920s.[173]

These first two categories, though they may have given greater coherence to the names in them, offer no new insights into Llewellyn's concept of realism. The individuals Llewellyn included on the list sent to Pound, in fact, resemble to a great extent the scholars Llewellyn included in the "Some Realism" article. The "extreme" and "thorough-going" realists were almost exclusively part of Llewellyn's inner circle at Columbia or Yale. The apparent intellectual, institutional schism between the realists and Harvard is not contradicted by the addition of the unpublished names. What the private list does tell us is that several individuals whom later scholars thought Llewellyn had omitted from his survey of realists had been included originally.[174] Thurman Arnold, for example, is often men-

---

170. Llewellyn to Pound, Apr. 6, 1931, RPP, 24-6.

171. Llewellyn obviously had doubts about including Hanna, since he parenthetically noted after Hanna's name "perhaps." See Table 2 in the Appendix.

172. Llewellyn to Pound, Apr. 6, 1931, RPP, 24-6.

173. Schlegel, "American Legal Realism," 478 n.92. Only Arnold, of the men in the second category, even studied law at Harvard.

174. Patterson, *Jurisprudence*, 538 n.7, suggests Arnold and Felix Cohen. Arnold's omission is discussed above; Cohen was consulted by Llewellyn on the bibliography of the survey, but probably was not personally included because he had not yet published

tioned as an unexplainable omission from Llewellyn's list. Actually, the explanation is simple: Arnold's response to the Llewellyn-Frank memo indicated his disinclination to be included, and Llewellyn simply honored Arnold's wishes.[175]

The third category is by far the most interesting and suggestive. Not a single name in this third category would appear in Llewellyn's "Some Realism" article. Nevertheless, this category reveals Llewellyn's true vision of realism. Realism was neither an ideology nor a coherent legal philosophy; it was rather a method or technology for looking at the law. The third category contained "examples" of individuals whom Llewellyn considered "realists-in-part-of-their-work." The idea of "in-part-of-their-work" meant that realism was a technique anyone could use, irrespective of their legal philosophy or political orientation. No scholar would have to adopt that methodology as her or his only, or even primary, mode of analysis. Here, embodied in this list of "realists-in-part," was Llewellyn's most effective dismissal of the idea that the realists were a school of jurisprudents. If Llewellyn could show there was no identifiable school of realism—as Corbin and many of his other correspondents wanted Llewellyn to do—Pound's article would have lost all force as a jurisprudential critique of a movement.

Because this third category was such a departure from Llewellyn's previous conceptualizations, it is worth a closer look at some of the men in it. Llewellyn had already cited Frankfurter and Landis's *The Business of the Supreme Court* in his "Next Step" article to show that those Harvard law professors had published work he consid-

---

any of his famous realist articles at the time the list was composed. Llewellyn, "Some Realism," 53 n.34. Wilfred Rumble, *American Legal Realism*, 2, adds Arnold, Cohen, and Rodell. Again, Rodell, a second- or perhaps third-generation realist, had not published anything by 1931. Twining skeptically discusses all the later scholars' realist lists. Twining, *Llewellyn*, 409–10 n.24. Twining himself suggests that Berle, Hamilton, and Arnold were "notable omissions from Llewellyn's list," but the last two had appeared on the list Frank had sent Llewellyn. Ibid., 410 n.32. Berle does appear on Llewellyn's April 6 list. Twining also points to Hutchins, Hale, and Hanna, among others, who he thinks were omitted by Llewellyn, but whose "inclusion would be no more out of place than the inclusion in Llewellyn's list of, e.g., E. W. Patterson or F. Lorenzen or M. Radin." Ibid., 410 n.33. Of course, Twining is right about the fact that the former men seemed to match Llewellyn's criteria, but he was unaware that they had been included on Llewellyn's original list. There is no copy of the extended unpublished list among the Llewellyn Papers at Chicago, Twining's source.

175. Thurman Arnold to Llewellyn, Apr. 18, 1931, KLP, B.65.b.

ered "realistic."[176] Both men had, in addition, displayed their "anti-formalist" inclinations in their teaching of administrative law and legislation, respectively.[177] Except for Frankfurter and Landis, none of the men listed in this category had ever appeared on any of the earlier realist inventories, but this did not deter Llewellyn. He had other criteria in mind. Edmund M. Morgan emphasized actual courtroom practice and a problem approach to teaching evidence in his classes at Yale and later at Harvard and was, "as the realists and Harvardians recognized, perhaps the only professor to lean toward realism in both theory and education."[178] Edgar Noble Durfee was another proponent of reforming the law school curriculum to reflect the real practice of law.[179] Llewellyn's inclusion of George Bogert must come as a surprise to students of realism. Llewellyn, a colleague of Bogert in the National Conference of Commissioners on Uniform State Laws (NCCUSL), however, probably admired Bogert's pioneering work on sales law and thought he recognized a realistic approach in Bogert's work on that subject.[180] Sam Bass Warner, a law professor at Harvard, was a pioneer in collecting criminal statistics and using them to paint a realistic picture of criminal law.[181] Warner's Harvard colleague Sheldon Glueck—a trained sociologist as well as a lawyer—had published a break-

176. Llewellyn cited both Felix Frankfurter and James Landis, *The Business of the Supreme Court* (1928), and Felix Frankfurter and Nathan Greene, *The Labor Injunction* (1930). He may also have been thinking of Frankfurter's work on the Cleveland crime survey. Schlegel, "Legal Realism and Social Science," 496.

177. Kalman, *Legal Realism*, 49–52.

178. Ibid., 54. Kalman states, however, that Morgan "was never a realist." The contradiction between the latter statement and the former assessment of Morgan's work quoted in my text points up the problems that the post–"Some Realism," restrictive definition of who is a realist creates. Had Llewellyn not abandoned the third category, with its expansive conceptualist framework, such contradictory categorizations (like that of Morgan) would not have resulted.

179. Durfee would publish an article on "Broadening Legal Education," 31 *Michigan Law Review* 206–25 (1932).

180. For example, *Commentaries on Conditional Sales* (Brooklyn, N.Y., 1924). On Bogert's career in general, see *Who's Who in America* (Chicago, 1932), 3:336. Twining, *Llewellyn,* 15, 280, notes the connection. Neither Kalman nor Rumble mentions Bogert as a potential realist.

181. Sam Bass Warner, "Survey of Criminal Statistics in the United States," in National Commission on Law Observance and Enforcement, *Report on Criminal Statistics* (Washington, D.C., 1931), 19. Warner was already working on his Harvard Law School–sponsored study of crime in Boston when Llewellyn was compiling his list. Sam Bass Warner, *Crime and Criminal Statistics in Boston* (1934).

through interdisciplinary study of crime and, when Llewellyn compiled his list, was collaborating with his wife, Eleanor Glueck, on their soon-to-be-published studies of crime and delinquency.[182] Llewellyn's Columbia colleague Richard R. Powell was at this time working on an innovative—if ultimately unsuccessful—new comparative-style casebook on trusts and estates.[183] Edson R. Sunderland, University of Michigan professor of law, was active in law reform, particularly procedural reform. His casebooks on code and common law pleading and on trial and appellate court practice may have impressed Llewellyn as realistic.[184] Dean Justin Miller of Duke University Law School taught at Columbia during the summer of 1929, and Llewellyn's talks with him about jurisprudence and social science that term may have convinced Llewellyn to consider Miller a realist-in-part.[185] Charles T. McCormick, dean at the University of North Carolina, may also have become acquainted with Llewellyn during a summer teaching stint at Yale. He may have told Llewellyn about the realist-style research he was doing on the "Parol Evidence Rule as a Procedural Device for Control of the Jury" or his involvement with Charles Clark's study of the federal courts.[186]

It is quite clear that the composition of category three substantially deviated from that of either category one or category two. Harvard's representation, for instance, was considerably higher in the third group, and professors from other, non-eastern schools show up as well.[187] The connecting thread among the members of

182. For biographical information on Sheldon Glueck, see AALS, *Directory of Law Teachers at American Bar Association Accredited Schools* (St. Paul, Minn., 1956), 122.

183. Kalman, *Legal Realism,* 82, 87, 257 nn.55, 56.

184. Sunderland, like Bogert, has never before been associated with realism. Kalman, Rumble, and Twining never mention him. *Who's Who,* 3:2225.

185. Miller was chairman of the AALS committee on surveying criminal law and procedure and served on the advisory committee on crime for the Social Science Research Council. *Who's Who,* 3:1624. Again, Miller has never been mentioned in the standard works on realism.

186. Charles T. McCormick, "The Parol Evidence Rule," 41 *Yale Law Journal* 365 (1932). The realists, on the whole, preferred bench rather than jury trials and therefore applauded any device that could be used to constrain the role of juries in civil litigation. McCormick left Duke to teach at Northwestern the year after Llewellyn's "Some Realism" article was published. *Who's Who,* 3:1554; *Directory of Law Teachers,* 177. Neither of these biographical sources mentions McCormick's summer teaching position at Yale. On the Yale teaching job and McCormick's role in the federal court study, see Schlegel, "Legal Realism and Social Science: Yale," 502 n.203.

187. See Table 3 in the Appendix for affiliations and other biographical details. (The table was modeled after a similar one Twining prepared for the individuals who appeared on the published list. Twining, *Llewellyn,* 76.)

this highly diverse group was method, particularly social scientific, empirical method. This rather than a coherent legal philosophy— or perhaps for Llewellyn method equaled philosophy, since it entails a way of looking at the legal culture that must, by necessity, color one's perception of that system—embodied realism for Llewellyn.

If Llewellyn thought his comprehensive new list would catch Pound off balance and pin him down, he was undoubtedly disappointed. Pound told Llewellyn without the slightest hint of irony: "To use Maitland's phrase, one who classifies tears a seamless web." Pound was not impressed by Llewellyn's compilation of realists. He argued that "[m]any of those you name have done the bulk of their work and all of them some of their work from other standpoints." As usual, he refrained from specificity and dealt with Llewellyn's new categorization evasively. Of the first category of extreme realists, Pound told Llewellyn: "I recognize some. As to others, I haven't seen enough of their writing on jurisprudence to form an assured opinion." While not too helpful, Pound had at the very least not denied Llewellyn's categorization of the first nine men. As to the second category of "thorough-going" realists, Pound admitted that "there is no doubt of some," but who? Pound did not say. "As to others," he told Llewellyn, "I am a bit surprised at your understanding of them." In a congenial vein, he explained, "Perhaps in their case, as in the case of any of us who have been writing for any length of time, there has been a gradual change of front which may have escaped my attention." How maddening Llewellyn must have found such comments; Pound was teasing him with his apparent cooperation, but at the same time lack of specificity. The older man saved his most pithy and devastating remarks for Llewellyn's last, innovative category of "realists-in-part." On that group, Pound chided, "[Y]ou might put almost all of us there. All of us today," after all, "surely have something of what is in the juristic air we breathe."[188]

This last was a powerful rejoinder, for Pound was saying that there was no boundary to the third category. Llewellyn's group could be extended so far as to have no intellectual coherence. Second, if Pound himself could be included in the third category, it lost all analytical utility as a reply to Pound. Third, though Pound had not explicitly said so, anyone (including Llewellyn) could infer that,

188. Pound to Llewellyn, Apr. 9, 1931, RPP, 24-6.

if Pound could be included in the third category, then realism was not so sharp a break with the earlier progressive-pragmatic jurisprudence; Pound's original criticism, in his Holmes essay, that there was nothing very new in what these "realists" were doing would have been correct.

As pointed as Pound's response was, Llewellyn could have maintained the upper hand if he had only adhered to his original concept. Pound may not have realized or simply ignored the full implication of Llewellyn's third category—that realism was only a methodology, not a school of legal philosophy. That definition undercut Pound's rejoinder entirely. Llewellyn might have simply replied that, of course, Pound could be considered a "realist-in-part"—Pound had, after all, prominently called for and participated in empirical studies of the legal process. Such a response would have effectively co-opted Pound into the realist camp. If Pound was clearly wrong that everyone could be included, admitting Pound and sociological jurisprudence to the third category subsumed them under realism, with the result that the latter approach would become the focal point of modern jurisprudence without having to be defined as a school. As such, its practitioners became the new voice of legal thought and analysis without the institutional coherence that could leave them, as a group, open to institutional attacks like Pound's.

Whether as a result of intent or ignorance, Pound treated Llewellyn's entire list, particularly the third category, as if it were only Llewellyn's own stab at classifying realists as philosophical group, rather than the way Llewellyn had meant it, namely, as examples of practitioners, to varying degrees, of a methodology. Only by thus ignoring Llewellyn's definition of realism had Pound maintained the validity of his own critique. In the end, Pound had elusively told Llewellyn: "Why not take me within the four corners of what I have written and go on that as I had to do when I wrote. After all *quod scripsi scripsi.*" [189] Llewellyn, who might have stuck to his guns, fell into Pound's trap.

Llewellyn's "Some Realism about Realism: A Reply to Dean Pound" is probably the most cited, quoted, and reprinted of all articles about the realist movement. In its very structure, it was a model of Llewellyn's view of realism, for it resembled less a discourse on legal philosophy than an empirical study of intellectual

189. Pound to Llewellyn, Mar. 21, 1931, RPP, 24-6.

data. Llewellyn carefully followed the method he identified as realism: he picked his sample realists, qualitatively analyzed their work for the defects Pound had attributed to the movement, and then quantitatively scored the results. The key to the study was, of course, the sample realists Llewellyn chose to survey. Here, however, Llewellyn failed to realize his vision of realism as a methodology. Llewellyn was probably ambivalent about his position at this stage of his career and about the movement itself. While he argued for the methodological definition of realism and was a chief proponent and practitioner of the social scientific, empirical approach all his life, one can sense that Llewellyn wished to stand at the forefront of a coherent legal philosophical movement. His equivocation thus fueled misunderstanding and misinterpretation by contemporary critics and commentators as well as later scholars.

The famous list of twenty realists appears in an extended footnote in Llewellyn's article. Llewellyn exasperatedly suggested that "there are doubtless twenty more," but did not mention the fact that he actually had a list more than twice as long. The names he included were, like the private list, grouped in categories. But these five (not three) categories had no intellectual coherence; they were merely those individuals familiar to Llewellyn and Frank. Llewellyn characterized the fifth category, for instance, as those scholars "chosen partly because their writing has explicitly touched points of theory, partly because their writing was either familiar to us or not too bulky." A closer comparison of the actual names on the published list and the private inventory Llewellyn had sent to Pound reveals the extent to which Llewellyn had retreated in print from his private methodological analysis of the movement.[190]

In the face of Pound's devastating reply to the April 6 list, Llewellyn omitted all of the individuals from the original first two categories who had never been formally associated with the realist inner circle, even though he had obviously thought their work epitomized the realist methodology. Such omissions reinforced the idea that the realists were a small, carping clique. Even worse, Llewellyn had been intimidated into dropping the third category of "realists-in-part" entirely, and that effectively obscured his own definition of realism. The only remnant of Llewellyn's "realists-in-part" was a vague allusion that "[t]he movement, the method of attack, is wider

190. Llewellyn, "Some Realism," 1227 n.18.

than the number of its adherents." He obscurely hinted that "[i]t includes some or much work of many men who would scorn ascription to its banner."[191] One of the latter group was presumably Felix Frankfurter. In what amounted to a surrender to Pound's deconstruction of the list, Llewellyn recanted his private characterization of Felix Frankfurter as a "realist-in-part." He conceded that "Felix Frankfurter we do not include; he has been currently considered a 'sociological jurist,' not a 'realist.' It profits little to show that one one thought a realist does not fit an alleged description of 'realists.'"[192] What was left was a weak denial that the realists were a school[193] and a point-by-point defense of the realists against "Dean Pound's indictment" that effectively dignified the latter.

Llewellyn's reticence, a faint echo of Pound's, denied him the option of defending realism as a working tool of progressive, but non-ideological, law thinkers. The irony was that Llewellyn himself would prove to be just such a law thinker. In denying Pound inclusion among the third category—by electing not to publish it—Llewellyn lopped off his strongest evidence for the constructive, programmatic potential of realism. Left were the bare bones of the first two categories fleshed out by epigrammatic asides. A few individuals from the original third category made their way, without analytical comment, into Llewellyn's footnotes and have resided there unnoticed by subsequent scholars.[194] Although the end of the article pleaded for the positive, constructive intent of realism, Llewellyn's list lacked the names that would have best sustained that claim.

Llewellyn had lost a battle, but not the war. In fact, the controversy itself helped to fabricate "legal realism," although some of Llewellyn's readers did not get the message. Thomas Reed Powell at Harvard thought that the strength of the article was not in the single name, but in the "marshaling of individual views."[195] Cook had objected to the new term from the first: "I don't like the title 'realistic jurisprudence' as the words carry too many ambiguous philo-

---

191. Ibid.
192. Ibid.
193. Ibid.
194. Llewellyn admitted to surveying the work of "a number of others—e.g., Kidd, Maggs, Breckenridge, Morse, Durfee, Bohlen, Bryant Smith and Goble." Ibid., 1242.
195. Thomas Reed Powell to Llewellyn, May 27, 1931, KLP, A.II.65.b. Powell had read the galleys courtesy of the law review.

sophical implications; I much prefer 'scientific study of law.'"[196] Of course, not only was Cook's proposed substitute vague, but also such science was exactly what Llewellyn criticized in "New Trends."[197]

Nevertheless, Llewellyn humbled himself. He wrote to Cook, apologizing for any offense given.[198] He told Yntema, "I myself regret particularly having written the last portion of the article in terms of 'realists' instead of in terms of 'realistic work.'"[199] What's in a name, then? Douglas, Clark, Moore, Cook, Yntema, and Oliphant had all published empirical studies before the exchange between Pound and Llewellyn occurred and continued to do so during and after the controversy. All of them were concerned about the outcomes of cases—the real-world effects of institutions, with or without Llewellyn's articles to guide them. Many of them credited Pound with opening their eyes to the need for empirical research into the products of the legal system long before Llewellyn was Llewellyn.[200] What Llewellyn did was give the loose configuration of legal academics a name, an American name. And such names have magical powers, as every would-be shaman knows.

Llewellyn was not done with the subject of realism. If his prose failed to move Pound, there was always poetry. Llewellyn's first marriage had just come to an end, and he was spending a good deal of time around Yale Law School, in part courting his second wife-to-be, Underhill Moore's research assistant Emma Corstvet, in part holding impromptu seminars long into the night with Jerome Frank and others.[201] What better way to woo a social scientist, refute Pound, and indulge his romantic soul than with poetry?

The poems expressed Llewellyn's vision of law more candidly and movingly than "The Next Step."[202] Llewellyn had written poetry

196. Cook to Llewellyn, Apr. 10, 1931, KLP, A.II.65.b.

197. And the term itself was a bigger minefield than "realism." Cook said yes to a science of law and was gently reproved for it, for law could only be scientific within its own terms. See, e.g., Edwin Patterson, "Can Law Be Scientific?," 25 *Illinois Law Review* 127, 147 (1930).

198. Llewellyn to Cook, Sept. 17, 1931, KLP, A.II.65.b.

199. Llewellyn to Yntema, Aug. 31, 1931, KLP, A.II.65.b.

200. Schlegel, *American Legal Realism*, 56, 67–114.

201. Kalman, *Legal Realism*, 119–20.

202. Llewellyn was hardly the first or only prominent lawyer who had indulged his muse in writing legal poetry. In an interesting but obscure volume edited by Ina Russelle Warren at the turn of the century appear poems by such unlikely authors as John Quincy Adams, "Justice: An Ode," 1; Joseph Henry Beale, "Prescription" (a translation from the

throughout his life, but his two 1931 volumes were obviously influenced by the opening of the realist controversy.[203] Opinion differs as to the quality of Llewellyn's verse. Takeo Hayakawa, while disclaiming expertise in the matter, nevertheless commented that "[s]ome of his poems are regarded as masterpieces in verse that would credit a professional poet."[204] Walter Nelles, who gently and overall favorably reviewed one of Llewellyn's volumes of poetry for the *Yale Law Review,* admitted that his own "aesthetic apparatus" had "grown rusty with disuse."[205] In a section of his book subtitled "The Half-Way Artist," Twining writes that "[Llewellyn] was capable of writing pleasant pieces, but no great talents await discovery."[206]

It is not quite true, however, that "Llewellyn did not take himself very seriously as a poet." While certainly some of Llewellyn's product was intentionally "'art-for-fun,'"[207] other of his output was heartfelt and intended to be taken seriously, particularly by the middle to late 1930s. Hayakawa concluded, apparently from an interview with Llewellyn's widow, Soia Mentschikoff, that Llewellyn "took more pride in poetry than anything else—even jurisprudence."[208] That Llewellyn took the trouble to have two volumes of his poetry privately published, personally promoted their sale among colleagues and friends, submitted his verse (though unsuccessfully) to prestigious magazines, and included his poems in so many of his other writings all suggest that Llewellyn did, to some extent, take himself and aspired to have others take him seriously as poet and artist.[209]

Whatever the quality of Llewellyn's poetry, it defended the juris-

---

German—no original author cited), 148; William Blackstone, "A Lawyer's Farewell to His Muse," 263; Oliver Wendell Holmes, Jr., "A Response at a Boston Bar Banquet," 95 (according to a note to this poem on page 268, at the time this volume was published, "[t]his excellent poem is not found in the collected edition of Dr. Holmes's works"); Sir Frederick Pollock, "The Six Carpenters' Case," 56; and Joseph Story, "Advice to a Young Lawyer," 101. Ina Russelle Warren, *The Lawyer's Alcove: Poems by the Lawyer, for the Lawyer and about the Lawyer* (New York, 1900). In the "Introduction" to this volume, Chauncey M. DePew observed that "[t]here is little poetry in a lawyer's life, but a good deal of romance." Ibid., v. Llewellyn would have undoubtedly seconded this statement.

203. *Beach Plums* and *Put in His Thumb* (Century Co., New York, 1931).

204. Takeo Hayakawa, "Lawman from Japan," 18 *Rutgers Law Review* 718 (1964).

205. Walter Nelles, "Review of *Put in His Thumb,*" 41 *Yale Law Journal* 646–47 (1932).

206. Twining, *Llewellyn,* 119.

207. Both quotation and expression from Twining, *Llewellyn,* 118.

208. Hayakawa, "Lawman from Japan," 718.

209. Correspondence with publisher, KLP, R files.

prudence of realism. In the "Ballade of the One True Road,"[210] Llewellyn focused his attack on the academic legal philosophers whose philosophical exegeses on doctrine promoted the idea of fixed rules of law.

> Over and under the passionate quest,
>   Along the track old skulls are strown,
> school-scholars' skills that none molest—
>   who seeks law's wisdom in a bone?
>   Knight after errant knight o'erthrown;
> Final Perfection still unguessed,
>   Unknowable remains unknown.
> *Ius longum, vita brevis est.*
> School tramples school, and men possessed
>   frenzy their Key to All—or drone.
> Crest swoops to trough, trough sweeps to crest,
>   cross-chopped and harassed. Who alone
>   has chanced upon the Magic Stone,
> Has seen the True Grail of the blest?
>   Mountains in labor: how they moan!
> *Ius longum, vita brevis est.*
> Who toasts with me the cosmic jest
>   that All should be for one to own,
> that men should ween old Law might rest?
>   Surely our simian wits have flown
>   deaf to the ancient organ tone:
> Action is wisdom's only test,
>   sane theory harvests action sown!
> *Ius longum, vita brevis est.*
> Prince, have the addled school-skulls blown,
>   blown like a bird's egg—that were best.
> Judgment by judgment Law has grown.
>   *Ius longum, vita brevis est.*

In another ballad,[211] Llewellyn expanded, in an even more negative tone, on this theme of the destructive influence of fossilized rules in legal tomes.

> Inky-fingered and dust in lung
>   over the parchment scholars pored,
> gathering apples of legal dung,
>   heaping the gatherings on the board.
>   Sparrows that labored before the Lord,

---

210. "Ballade of the One True Road," in *Put in His Thumb,* 43.
211. "Ballade of the Glory of Rules," in *Put in His Thumb,* 45.

filling the tree to which they clung.
   What would they do with the precious hoard?
"The rule is settled," the sirens sung.
O, for the work of the antic throng!
   Kindling splintered by Justice' sword,
hunted wherever it might be flung,
    bundled and packaged round with cord,
    tied into Rules, to be stacked, and stored—
as if it could feed flames high and strong,
   or wedge sweet Justice into a word.
"The rule is settled," the sirens sung.
Dung has virtue where seeds have sprung;
   let us use all that the books afford.
Kindling-gatherers also belong,
   if the rest is at hand, for what is toward—
   who would urge that they be ignored?
But hark to the sparrows give tongue, give tongue:
   "law is known, with the Rules explored!"
"The rule is settled," the sirens sung.
Prince, it is time that the beer was poured.
   Bring on the seidels, and start the bung.
Our wayward Lady! Our strange Adored!
   "The rule is settled," the sirens sung.

But nothing was settled, certainly not the controversy that Llewellyn had started. While Llewellyn composed his poetry and wooed a new love, others were queuing up to enter the lists against him.

CHAPTER FIVE

Legal Realism and Other Ideas Are Put to the Test

Roscoe Pound and Karl Llewellyn had engaged in a public exchange using their law schools' law reviews as fora. To the reader who comes upon these articles afresh, what the two men said in print may seem to be what they thought, but nothing could be further from the truth, for the printed words were only pale reflections of unpublished drafts, private correspondence, and oral exchanges. Apparently at odds, Pound and Llewellyn were searching for the same grail, and their search had taken them in roughly the same direction. Sociological jurisprudence, as modern scholars have recognized, and, more important, as both Pound and Llewellyn knew, was close indeed to legal realism. Why then the controversy in print that distorted the similarities in their views and opened legal realism to a firestorm of criticism? Ironically, the same text that had widened the rift, Jerome Frank's excursus on the psychology of judging, helps explain the way that Pound and Llewellyn got tangled up in their controversy. Personality intruded into the private discourse and thereby bent the public exchange. Llewellyn struck at Pound's writings in "The Next Step" because Llewellyn was bitter at a series of real and imagined slights suffered at Pound's hands. Pound was probably oblivious to these slights (he usually was), but his published reply was the very sort of psychological jousting he used in private correspondence with Wesley Newcomb Hohfeld and others. He was angry at Frank and said so in private letters to Llewellyn, but the article did not take on Frank. On the train to the Chicago meeting of the AALS, he might huff and puff about how to "educate Frank," but the expected "blow up" never came.[1] Instead, Pound chided and reproved Llewellyn. Only this time, Pound did it in public, not in private, and that was a difference that made all the difference for the fate of realism in the public arena. For although Pound's recourse to print did not change Llewellyn's views—indeed, "Realist Jurisprudence" goaded Llewellyn to practice what he preached—it called down on Llewellyn criticism from those who ought to have been his allies as well as from those who might have been more circumspect in their public remarks had Pound smiled on realism in print. For Pound was not just Llewellyn's critic; he was also the mentor of a generation of jurisprudents, the patron of many younger scholars, and the best-placed American academic jurisprudent of his time. He was Harvard Law School's dean.

Another irony was that, up to and even briefly after the battle of the articles, it would have been hard to separate the general tendency of Pound's views from that of Llewellyn's. Llewellyn had found that every discussion of realism had to begin and end with Pound. Were it not for Frank's unprovoked attack on Pound in *Law and the Modern Mind*, an attack that Llewellyn somewhat gratuitously continued in "The Next Step," Pound might well have welcomed the new term without recrimination. After the fray, Llewellyn was contrite (for him, at least), and Pound was gracious. Llewellyn had anticipated that Pound might be offended, and Pound's colleague and Llewellyn's friend Edmund Morgan tried to be sensible about the matter in a letter to Llewellyn: "As to the realism article, I do not think that Pound has any personal malice. Indeed, I think he usually does not bear personal malice. I believe that you will henceforth be regarded by him, however, as a person who speaks without the book, as one who draws more or less rash conclusions from inadequate data, etc., etc., but I do not think you will find that he has any personal animosity."[2]

From Leipzig, to which he had returned to lecture in the fall of 1931, Llewellyn effused to Pound, "As always, it is comforting to have you find [Llewellyn's published work] good." Llewellyn was planning to turn this round of German lectures into a book on so-

1. Karl Llewellyn to Emma Corstvet, Aug. 29, 1933, Emma Corstvet Papers, Bryn Mawr College Library.
2. Edmund Morgan to Llewellyn, Feb. 19, 1932, KLP, A.II.65.b.

ciology and the law, in connection with which he demonstrated that he was still Pound's friendly competitor: "Why don't you take a year off, and beat me to it? Deaning seems to me a sad way to end a scholarly career. Harvard may need a Dean, but the law world at large needs the Sociological Jurisprudence."[3] Llewellyn wanted the rift to heal.

The German language publication of his *Case Law System* provided the occasion for him to mend fences with a number of his peers, including Pound. He set about networking once again, this time without hint of rancor. He fairly begged Morris Cohen, Hessel Yntema, and Max Radin to review the book when it appeared in America.[4] Pound, of course, read it and characteristically praised the work: "It is indeed a great book—worthy of the author. Perhaps one need say no more. I am sure it will have a deservedly wide and great influence." But when Llewellyn pressed Pound to review it, that is, to make the private discourse into public sponsorship, Pound silently declined.[5]

The private praise, followed by a reluctance to repeat in public what he said in private, was pure Pound. "The Call for a Realist Jurisprudence" was uncharacteristic of him. But once again, a Pound comment drove Llewellyn to apply realism to traditional law subjects. Consider two examples from the year after the controversy. American constitutionalism and divorce law seem to have little to do with academic jurisprudence, but Llewellyn deployed realism to explore both topics.

The spur for the first was the United State Supreme Court majority's assault on the first New Deal programs. Constitutional theory is not the same as jurisprudence, at least not in ordinary circumstances. The rules for reading constitutions come in their own wrapping.[6] What Llewellyn did in his stirring "The Constitution as an Institution" was to apply his tenets of jurisprudence to the way the Court's rulings were actually reached. He did not use Frank's theories, for he could not penetrate the individual justices' psyches and

---

3. Llewellyn to Roscoe Pound, Nov. 25, 1931, RPP, 24-6.
4. Llewellyn to Morris Cohen, Dec. 27, 1932, Llewellyn to Max Radin, Dec. 27, 1932, and Llewellyn to Hessel Yntema, Dec. 27, 1932, and Feb. 3, 1933, KLP, A.II.65.b.
5. Pound to Llewellyn, Apr. 12, 1933, and Llewellyn to Pound, Apr. 14, 1933, KLP, A.II.65.b.
6. See, e.g., Robert Cover, *Justice Accused* (New Haven, Conn., 1977) (even anti-slavery federal judges in the 1850s had to credit the Constitution's pro-slavery language).

did not agree with Frank in any case. Instead, he crafted the case against originalism. Assuming the literary pose of "Peck's Bad Boy" (after all, he had written in "New Trends" that the makers of law were sometimes artists), he began by comparing the Constitution to the emperor who had no clothes. "His supposed clothes consist of our now prevailing theory of constitutional law," but they hardly covered the private parts. For the orthodoxy was that the Constitution meant what its framers said it meant and the only additional meanings were supplied by the amendments.[7] "Is this not extraordinary? The Document was framed to start a governmental experiment for an agricultural, sectional, seaboard folk of some three millions. Yet it is supposed to control and describe our constitution after a century and a half of operation?"

The second fallacy (he listed five, but the first two were fatal in themselves) was that the justices of the Supreme Court were the final arbiters of the meaning of the Constitution. Now the clothes might not cover the Constitution, but they did fit the needs of lawyers and judges, giving both "a refuge from responsibility": the Constitution did not change; it was bedrock. Only its interpretation changed. The realist knew that this was not, in fact, what happened. The Court, in fact, did change the Constitution and had done so, to the chagrin of some of the framers, from the inception of the new government. The sense of heritage and continuity that the theory of originalism offered had value, but it obscured how the Court actually behaved and so needed to be replaced. Realism had to be clear eyed.[8]

In a checklist of the way he thought cases were actually decided, Llewellyn anticipated many of the arguments of his *Common Law Tradition: Deciding Appeals* (1960). The essence of the argument was out there: the realists had already proved that rules did not decide cases. Rules might limit the range of decisions, but did not dictate them; rules framed the available choices of terminology for the opinion, but did not fix the actual language. In a code like the

---

7. This is a version of "original intent" that has now been replaced by the more diffuse, and therefore more pliable, "original understanding." In the former, the originalist had to attempt to fathom the motives of the various framers—an effort requiring either historical scholarship or deference to working historians. In the latter, the theorist can supply the meanings from a far broader supply.

8. Karl Llewellyn, "The Constitution as an Institution," 34 *Columbia Law Review* 1, 2, 3, 4, 5, 7 (1934).

Constitution, the language changed its meaning over time, creating a "working Constitution" that shadowed the original document. The "language of original intent" might still be there, but it was there to be manipulated. The result was a process of decision making that was not governed by the original intent at all, being "in good part utterly extra-Documentary." The dramas and dilemmas of the real world, like "white-slaving," were dumped into unreal, artificial categories, like "inter-state commerce," drawn from the document. What was more, all sorts of extra-constitutional institutions, like the political parties, influenced the judges. The real tragedy was that the Constitution, read strictly, did not deal with the real problems of the people. The president was commander in chief of the army, but nowhere did the Constitution explain "the undiscoverability of colored or Jewish West Point graduates." The living Constitution, the Constitution that had authority, had little connection with the dead document.[9]

The realist solution was to regard the Constitution not as a text that spoke in immutable axioms, but as an institution that reflected the customs and behavior of the people. Llewellyn thus did not propose that the symbols of government were shells, although he might have.[10] The idea was to make the real Constitution square with the language of the justices, to end the mystification and obfuscation. He called on the "specialists," the priesthood of professors and lawyers and judges who knew the Constitution best, to admit that he was right. The loyalty of the "general public" to the document and its symbolic functions prevented ordinary people from directing the specialists; indeed, it gave the specialists even more discretion. It was the special interest groups that limited what the specialists might do. The Constitution, Llewellyn implied, was what these three kinds of people actually did. It was not a document but part of the fabric of human political life. Of course, there were still the words, but Llewellyn tried to blur their sharpness: "The penumbra-border of the constitution ranges through practices which are marked with varying definiteness and consistency in individuals, and vary in range as to the individuals who share such practices."[11]

9. Ibid., 13, 15.
10. Compare Thurman Arnold, *Symbols of Government* (New York, 1935), who did just that and opened up Pandora's box thereby.
11. Llewellyn, "The Constitution as an Institution," 21, 24, 25, 26, 28.

Here Llewellyn's hitherto sharp argument blurred. Despite two pages of what today would be called sociograms of the actors and their conduct, he never explained how his living Constitution differed from the day-to-day conduct of government (the same problem that arose with his third list of realists, as Pound had noted). He insisted that the Constitution-as-institution "must consist of or include ways of official office-holders whose action or passivity has real importance." Without this, the conduct in question became part of the "penumbra" of the working Constitution. But if that is all the Constitution was, then it vanished as a rule of reference in cases appealed to federal and state courts. Lower courts were freed to say that the Constitution meant anything at all, the very extreme of indeterminacy that Llewellyn had avoided thus far.[12] He teetered on the edge of the abyss: "a sane theory" rejected the text if "*any relevant practices existed* to offer firmer, more living basis for the ideal picture." But who was to determine what those alternative practices might be? The law professor in her study? The cop on the beat?[13] Llewellyn saw the precipice in time and drew back. "First, there is no disposition, under this approach by way of practice and institution, to disregard the normative and ideal element in constitutional law. . . . Second, there is no quarrel to be had with judges *merely* because they disregard or twist Documentary language or 'interpret' it to the despair of original intent, in the service of what those judges conceive to be the inherent nature of our institutions." Benjamin Cardozo and Louis Brandeis might have sighed with relief when they read these passages. "To my mind, such action is their duty. To my mind, the judge who builds his decision to conform with his conception of what our institutions must be if we are to continue, roots in the deepest wisdom."[14]

To defend realism, Llewellyn realized, one had to apply it. If it worked, then it must be an improvement over its rivals. Llewellyn had always been ambitious and, more than that, combative. At thirty-seven, he was at the peak of his powers. And in the way that

12. Ibid., 29. Perhaps it was the word "penumbra" itself that was so slippery. See David J. Garrow, *Liberty and Sexuality: The Right to Privacy and the Making of* Roe v. Wade (New York, 1994), 245–46 (discussing the origins of Justice William O. Douglas's use of "penumbra" of the Bill of Rights in *Griswold v. Connecticut*, 381 U.S. 479, 486 (1965)).

13. Llewellyn, "The Constitution as an Institution," 31 (emphasis in original).

14. Ibid., 33 (emphasis in original).

the personal always intrudes on the public life, so Llewellyn's life gave him another occasion to prove realism by applying it to the real world. Elizabeth Sanford had left him, and he poured his grief and anger into a classic article, "Behind the Law of Divorce: I." As he admitted in the first note, "This article is, like all of my writings, the expression of personal views. . . . Nothing in the paper purports to have any guaranty more trustworthy than common sense and personal observation. Sample drillings into the available data are offered in the footnotes . . . [but] that of course affords no proof even of the views checked up, still less of the others." Even as he battled personal demons, Llewellyn struck a blow at mindless empiricism, wherein data collection, display, and analysis were always offered as proof.[15]

In law, marriage might be a contract, but lawyers "like other folk find the social reality coloring discussion and thought at every point." Divorce was a legal remedy available from the "law-men," but the end of a marriage was rooted not in law but in life. "The problem before us is description. It is to see, in action, to follow in their interaction, the divergent branches of the paradox, to see them in action as a going whole. To attack that problem means gambling on insight. The scientific data are too meager, too spotty, to serve the need. The pseudo-scientific data are so ambiguous as to make the insight the only warrant for their use."[16]

What could be more realist than a case study that examined events before the law was summoned? Divorce, like all legal proceedings, channeled and bent the real experience, changing words of love and recrimination into legal terms sufficient to bring the desired result in court. Everywhere Llewellyn saw paradoxes in the

15. Karl Llewellyn, "Behind the Law of Divorce: I," 32 *Columbia Law Review* 1281 (1932). Privately Llewellyn was in agony, but he mocked himself as well as wives in general. "I am an enthusiastic feminist insofar as I emphatically and eagerly long for the economic independence of women. I want to marry a girl with an income, not for her money but for my own. . . . Women's success in deriving the principal benefit from men's incomes depends on trickery. Being a wife calls for constant application of practical psychology, to say nothing of the expert, but unexposed, wheedling that wins a man in the first place. . . . I know perfectly well that this is not the whole story and that much of what I may imply to be deliberate is really done instinctively and without malice. (If not much, probably at least some.) Still any philosophy of a change in woman's status must, I think, recognize pretty much the principles I have sketched. Llewellyn, untitled, n.d., KLP, B.V.4.b.

16. Llewellyn, "Behind the Law of Divorce: I," 1281, 1282, 1283. Note echoes of the critique of data mashing in his 1929 AALS talk.

larger world that reflected his own bewilderment. "Law is a going whole we are born into; but law is changing something we help remodel." Could he change the law any more than he could go back and somehow make the marriage work? He limited himself to "bourgeois marriage . . . because the writer's experience is thus limited." And his experience was everywhere apparent: "We know women we call untrue, and others we call loose." Marriage was "one man, one woman, living permanently together, known as belonging together," but each day brought new variants on the norm. "New problems, individual problems, from year to year, from week to week." Back and forth from the anthropological and the legal to the personal he went, from "petticoat marriage" accepted, with grumbling, to "quarrels and suffering, hard to cure with any purely social means of settlement." And always "the facts" (to the realist jurisprudent, to the husband) "press still." For Llewellyn, the personal became the universal: "The drama is clear: the struggle of an older simpler pattern and ideology with the insurgent facts." [17]

Llewellyn as professor reviewed the historical functions of marriage, but the private intruded on the public. He did not discuss the emotional importance of marriage to the wife, but dwelt instead on the value of marriage to the husband: "This woman—this woman beyond any other woman—not only to have her, but to have her around, to know that *she* will stay around." And for infidelity, well, there were "[p]rostitutes, happenstances, girl-friends, poachers," but no boyfriends. This was as close to a confession as Llewellyn came. Consider the treatment of costs: one might assume in a realist tract that this would have to do with family capital, but Llewellyn focused on the emotional costs. All of these strong personal feelings he deployed in the service of the realist credo of regarding law as an institution rather than a set of rules. Law was what the law-men did. But what was the connection between law and social ways, between law-stuff (the term that Llewellyn would later use) and customs? Were the laws against adultery to be taken seriously? Was the licensing ceremony still so important? It all depended on which function of the many that marriage performed. For marriage as comforter, little law was necessary. For the "economic phases" of marriage, law was much more important. So, too, to protect husband and wife against the other's violence, law was vital. Divorce

17. Ibid., 1283, 1284, 1285, 1286, 1287.

was thus the most important legal aspect of marriage, for divorce settled the economic questions and ended the violence.[18]

There was a sequel, as promised, but "Behind the Law of Divorce: II" did not break new ground. Evidently, Llewellyn's sufferings had not abated. He pled in print for changes in the law of divorce, in essence making it easier to obtain, following the changes in the customs of marriage. "The shift in marriage practice has been, like almost any other shift of practice, a result, not a design. When conditions skew, men [read Llewellyn] following old ways unadjusted to the skew will suffer. If the mould will not yield, though the skew spirals, the men endure greatly [women evidently did not suffer from skew of any kind], and may even die." What was to be done? A realist solution presented itself. "Of course men differ as regards these ends to be obtained. Such stereotypes as 'the home' or 'freedom' block analysis, choke off questioning, cripple inquiry into the facts." Llewellyn on the warpath against concepts again: "Yet we have facts that need facing . . . facts as to the increase, prevalence, and routine manner of divorce; especially the fact that free consent divorce is an existing, socially recognized institution in the United States."[19]

Like Pound, Llewellyn saw "ways and desires change." He even invoked Pound's favorite "industrialism . . . the ever bigger city" one-two punch. At the bottom of the page paraded figures and string citations, the march of social science hand in hand with traditional legal sources. There was a price, but factored into the costs of an unsuccessful marriage, these payouts faded. Most important, divorce did not destroy marriage at all.[20] Easy divorce where there was mutual consent did not produce divorce, and the state should recognize as much, as some already had. All in all, the pieces amounted to a monograph on marriage and divorce, a balm to an aching husband, and an exercise in realism, making divorce "an event not too greatly different from any other."[21] Llewellyn did not need outside funding or the support of a university (other than his ordinary affiliation) or an institute to produce results. Llewellyn had not looked at behavior in the legal system and tried to give it

---

18. Ibid., 1298, 1293, 1295, 1297, 1300, 1302, 1306 (emphasis in original).
19. Karl Llewellyn, "Behind the Law of Divorce: II," 33 *Columbia Law Review* 250 (1933).
20. Ibid., 253, 277.
21. Ibid., 283, 294.

meaning by counting it. He had examined a set of mores that had gained sanction within the system. There was nothing skeptical or cynical in his approach (though his personal feelings and his biases did intrude).

Yet in these first realist sallies, had Llewellyn marked a path so far from Pound's own? True, Pound would never have used jurisprudence as a way to probe or express his innermost feelings or to share his woes with the public. Nor did Pound show any desire to sit down, as Llewellyn had, with Jerome Frank and help form the liberal National Lawyers Guild in opposition to the American Bar Association. Llewellyn saw it as a way to provide legal services at low cost to the poor. Pound would refuse, in 1938, when Herbert Goodrich and Alex Frey offered him the presidency of the organization: "I feel compelled to say to you that I should not be willing to accept the Presidency of a National Law Guild, nor indeed to associate myself with that organization." After all, Pound's father had been a founding member of the ABA. He resented the upstart: "It seems to me a serious mistake for the liberally minded who have the advancement of justice and the improvement of the law and the good of the profession at heart to start a rival organization which can only have the effect of impairing the usefulness of professional organizations and lessening the influence which the profession ought to have on matters of law and law reform."[22]

But otherwise? In 1935, Edward S. Robinson, one of Yale's self-proclaimed legal realists (though his field was psychology and he was only a guest instructor at the law school), credited Pound's notion that the jurisprudent must be a "social engineer" with opening the door to the next stage of lawmaking in America,[23] a conclusion that Llewellyn had reached privately a decade before in "New Trends" and had repeated in somewhat different language in *The Case Law System in America*. In the same year as Robinson paid

22. Herbert Goodrich to Pound, Jan. 21, 1938, and Pound to Alex Frey, Jan. 22, 1938, RPP, 147-8; Jerold Auerbach, *Unequal Justice: Lawyers and Social Change in Modern America* (New York, 1976), 199. A decade later, Pound stonewalled T. C. Kirkpatrick, the editor of the pamphlet *Counterattack: Facts to Combat Communism* (1949), when the latter wanted to know if the guild was run by Communists. Pound replied that he had been out of the country for two years and, even before that, had little to do with the guild. T. C. Kirkpatrick to Pound, June 15, 1949, and Pound to Kirkpatrick, June 17, 1949, RPP, 147-8. Pound protected Frank, Goodrich, and Llewellyn.

23. Edward S. Robinson, *Law and the Lawyers* (New York, 1935), 19.

his homage to Pound, Frances Bohlen, one of the realists whom Llewellyn had intended to include in his reply to Pound, but did not, returned to the battleground and insisted that even "the law student today recognizes that many of the most beautifully intricate and subtle of legal theories are merely a particular form of legal fiction designed to make the circle of the assumption of an immutable body of law square with the necessity of making the administration of law accomplish what are recognized as desirable social ends. Theories are now recognized as often a means of justifying decisions rather than as reasons for making them."[24] William Grossman found Pound "at the very center of the liberal thought of his time and subject." What was more, Pound had anticipated the realists' central psychological tenet: "[T]he epistemological aspect of Pound's pragmatism rests on the doctrine of the relativity of thought, according to which every alleged truth propounded by thinking man represents simply an attempt to make an adjustment to the conditions or facts of the time and place and therefore has no claim to universal validity."[25]

Felix Cohen's far bolder attempt to launch a "functional" jurisprudence was criticized by Pound ("Felix Cohen assumes to know a good many things that he has not studied sufficiently to justify his confidence"[26]), but demonstrated that the Pound of 1930 differed little from the Llewellyn of 1931. Cohen judged that traditional legal theory led nowhere, for in it "[j]urisprudence, then, as an autonomous system of legal concepts, rules, and argument, must be independent both of ethics and of such positive sciences of economics or psychology. In effect, it is a special branch of the science of transcendental nonsense. . . . [T]hat something is radically wrong with our traditional legal thought-ways has long been recognized. Holmes, Gray, Pound, Brooks Adams, M.R. Cohen, T.R. Powell, Cook, Oliphant, Moore, Radin, Llewellyn, Yntema, Frank, and other leaders of modern legal thought in America are in fundamental agreement in their disrespect for 'mechanical jurisprudence' [Pound's term, not Llewellyn's,] for legal magic and word-jugglery." Cohen called for an end to meaningless concepts, questions, and

24. Frances Bohlen, "Old Phrases and New Facts," 83 *University of Pennsylvania Law Review* 309 (1935), 309.
25. William L. Grossman, "The Legal Philosophy of Roscoe Pound," 44 *Yale Law Journal* 605, 697 (1935).
26. Pound to Goodrich, Jan. 7, 1935, RPP, 15-12.

fictions, a task begun by Pound's dismissal of the old schools of jurisprudence, though Cohen thought Pound had gone too far. Cohen also criticized Frank for his "hunches" and Llewellyn for his impudence. What he wanted—what Pound and Llewellyn and all the others had not yet produced—was a factual, detailed accounting of the balance sheet of which interests out there were to be favored and which curtailed by the courts.[27]

But the jurisprudence needed for the task (as opposed to its politics) was already in place, and in it, Pound and Llewellyn stood side by side. As Llewellyn himself admitted in 1934, "The needs of the times were there [in the early portion of the twentieth century] and felt. Sociological jurisprudence ought, it would seem, to have found an early echo. . . . But most important of all I suspect to be the fact that leaders in legal practice had fallen hopelessly behind the times. Dominated by bourgeois, business, buccaneering ideology, serving and knowing only, as specialized office counsel, the interests of the 'Ins,' they had no ears for words that betokened change in an existing order. One still meets gentlemen who still voice their profound conviction that such conservative men as Holmes, or Brandeis, or Pound, are 'dangerous.'" But all was not lost, for "[b]eginnings of the influence of sociological jurisprudence can be seen in law-men's actions." The incorporation of the insights of the realists, standing on the shoulders of sociological jurisprudence, could not be far behind.[28]

What, then, did legal realism have to fear, if time and tide were on its side? The answer lay not in the purposes or the ethical concerns of its proponents (for in the main they were mainstream liberals, democrats with a small and often a large "D," who were fully committed to the survival of the republican system and the common law courts). Legal realism became a target because it could be used as a proxy for something else—modernism. Then, as now, modernism was a buzzword, susceptible of many meanings, a charm, a program, an epithet. Its relativism challenged the progressive faith in progress and the conservative longing for stability. It could be cold and heartless, even cynical, in its acceptance of change, but it was

27. Felix Cohen, "Transcendental Nonsense and the Functional Approach," 35 *Columbia Law Review* 821, 829, 843, 847, 848 (1935).

28. Karl Llewellyn, "On Philosophy in American Law," 82 *University of Pennsylvania Law Review* 211–12 (1934).

never without its own ideals and principles. Most of all, modernism rejected cant, smug self-assurance, and unthinking obedience to authority and rules.[29]

Neither Pound, in his mellow criticisms, nor Llewellyn, in his spirited defenses, could have anticipated this outcome. Neither was an extremist, but the fact remained that the Scylla and Charybdis of legal realism were its indeterminacy, on the one hand, and its quest for precision, on the other. Max Radin, a realist himself, captured both in succinct prose: "There is no logical reason why realists should concern themselves with any particular standard or reject one method of valuation [of competing interests] in favor of another. The standard may be a neat and consistent pattern of human actions based on any one of an almost infinite number of arbitrary generalizations. It may be a code divinely sanctioned, or a particular scheme of social utility . . . or perhaps one of these standards is to be used in some situations and another in another."[30] Empirical studies of how courts actually worked did nothing to fill this vacuum of moral guidance. As critics of conceptualism, the realists needed no answer to this puzzle, but their powerful intellectual commitment to overthrow the idols of formalism could easily be misread, or if one had other motives, deliberately mischaracterized, as an indifference to the moral or ethical penumbras of legal rules.

Surely, the flippant tone and cynical spin of some realist pieces, the empiricists' reliance on social science instead of moral verities, and the realist critics' nominalist view of legal language were less dangers in themselves than symptoms of all the other threats to tradition, religion, order, and hierarchy that modernity posed. As Charles Miltner of the University of Notre Dame's law faculty warned early in 1932, "[C]onservatism, opposition to change, the clinging to manners and ideas and institutions, of good standing for even only a few generations, is set down by popular judgment as a sign of incompetence if not of down right failure. . . . The term 'modern' is made to qualify not only what is more recent and me-

29. Sylvia Yount, *To Be Modern* (Philadelphia, 1996), 1; G. Edward White, "Recapturing New Deal Lawyers," 102 *Harvard Law Review* 519 (1988); Allen R. Kamp, "Between the Wars Social Thought: Karl Llewellyn, Legal Realism, and the Uniform Commercial Code in Context," 59 *Albany Law Review* 329–30 (1995). The strongest recent attack on modernism appears in John P. Diggins, *The Promise of Pragmatism* (Chicago, 1994).

30. Max Radin, "Legal Realism," 31 *Columbia Law Review* 825 (1931).

chanically more efficient, which is quite legitimate, but also to connote something more true and beneficial which . . . is often quite absurd." The target was "pragmatism" in the law, "in which truth and justice, and hence also law and right, are never anything absolute and universal, but relative."[31]

Pound was a pragmatist, and some of those who would lampoon realism had already gone after him for it. Walter B. Kennedy of Fordham Law School was respectful of Pound in 1925, for pragmatism was not altogether bad, but Pound had misunderstood what the people wanted. They did not want his pragmatism. They wanted basic truths burnished bright.[32] Later critics of realism would include in their field of fire Pound's sociological jurisprudence.[33] The attack on realism was a continuation of the attack led by Judge Robert Fowler on Pound. But Pound did not see that. He saw instead the personal insults that Frank and Llewellyn had laid on his name, and if he did not publicly join in the calumny to their contribution, he did not raise his hand, as he might have, to stem its flow.

Even so, it would have been a tempest in a teapot had not the 1930s brought a rebirth of the importance and the perils of ideology. Modernism was discerned in the realist art and literature of the 1900s and decried; it was rediscovered in the nihilism of the flappers and the desolation of the poems of e.e. cummings and decried; there was nothing new about the revelations and complaints about modernism in the 1930s. But modernism, with its inherent distrust of tradition, became ominous in the 1930s because other, more violent ideologies were hammering at the door. Europe was engulfed in totalizing ideologies of state control—Stalinism, Nazism, and Fascism. Adherents of the radical left and the radical right were gaining followers in Depression- ridden American cities. The American Communist Party, particularly after the "Popular Front," allied older socialist and splinter far-left groups with the Communists, attracting a small but able group of American intellectuals, artists, and teachers. The supporters of extreme right-wing groups

31. Charles C. Miltner, "The Progressiveness of the Law," 7 *Notre Dame Lawyer* 421, 425 (1932).

32. Walter B. Kennedy, "Pragmatism as a Philosophy of Law," 9 *Marquette Law Review* 68 (1925).

33. See, e.g., Herman Kantorowicz, "Some Rationalism about Realism," 43 *Yale Law Journal* 1246 (1934).

were not so intellectually gifted, but their appeal was even broader, particularly among those whose ethnic sympathies were with Germany and Italy. Radicalism whose inspiration was foreign ideology had counterparts in American syndicalist movements, whose thrust was just as global but whose voices were less philosophical. Baton Rouge's Huey Long and Detroit's Father Coughlin, both brutal in their intolerance of dissent and beguiling in their promises of a better world if only people would see everything their way, reflected a nativist totalitarian instinct.[34]

The arrival of such angry, greedy players at the table raised the stakes of the ideological game, and legal realism was elevated, willy nilly, from a semiprivate, elite, academic subject to a matter of national concern. Actually, Llewellyn was exceedingly vulnerable in this regard if the private discourse of his long love affair with Germany and the German army became public knowledge. In his personal memoir of his days in Germany during World War I, he wrote, "[S]o it throbs through the army: comradeship. And as through the army, so through the people. For you see the army is the Thing of the German people, every family has a part in it and feels with it and works for it. So this crowning glory pulses through the nation, uplifting it, bringing out its best: comradeship. Surely the people have a right to be proud of the way it has stood the test, this Thing of theirs."[35]

Llewellyn meant to describe the Kaiser's army, not Hitler's remade Wehrmacht, but Llewellyn's fondness for Germany was a matter of common knowledge within his circle. As Sam Klaus wrote to Llewellyn in 1934, the Nazis liked *The Case Law System in America* and asserted "that you have been accepted as a true Nazi, fit to be amalgamated into the lifeblood of the new Reich. It also interests me because someone I know who teaches in a provincial law school has called you—and Jerome Frank and others—a fascist and a pillar of the fascist New Deal." Llewellyn rejected the label and the association hotly, but the connection between realism and amorality lingered.[36] German writers praised Llewellyn's work; that

34. John P. Diggins, *Up from Communism* (New York, 1975), 149–59; Alan Brinkley, *Voices of Protest* (New York, 1982), 143–68.

35. Llewellyn, undated manuscript, KLP, B.V.1.j.

36. Sam Klaus to Llewellyn, Apr. 21, 1934, and Llewellyn to Klaus, Apr. 23, 1934, KLP, A.II.65.b.

was ironic because he appreciated the praise but did not like its source.[37] The irony was that Llewellyn was always an enemy to the Nazis, concluding almost immediately after the rise of Hitler that in Nazi Germany, "Law, Mere Law, is Weak."[38] And more irony was to come: a year later, in 1934, Pound accepted a medal from the German government on the steps of Langdell Hall. He even invited (if that was the right word to describe an invitation from the dean) his faculty to come and watch.[39]

Whatever Llewellyn wrote in private and Pound did in public, public attacks on realism linked foreign tyranny and New Deal domestic policies. Legal realism seemed to deny "all the things that make [life] worth while."[40] The very fabric of government was unraveled by the realists' purported cynicism about rules of law. "The danger present in our country today is not that the proletariat, if I may borrow a European term [itself always dangerous, for European terms might bring European maladies], led by some bewhiskered revolutionary [beards were out of fashion in the 1930s in the United States], will seize the government, nor yet that a man on horseback will appear and suddenly and violently impose on us a dictatorship of the fascist type. It is rather that while preserving the *forms* of constitutional democracy we shall have the substance sucked out of them and in fact see our great heritage of freedom destroyed by those to whom the Constitution is nothing but a totem pole and its language immaterial. . . ."[41]

Much of the attack came from the political and jurisprudential

37. Llewellyn to Corstvet, Oct. 13, 1933, Emma Corstvet Papers, Bryn Mawr College Library.

38. Llewellyn, On the Reichstag Trial, 1933, Emma Corstvet Papers, Bryn Mawr College Library.

39. Erwin N. Griswold, *Ould Fields, New Corn: The Personal Memoirs of a Twentieth Century Lawyer* (St. Paul, Minn., 1992), 119. Griswold was upset at the time, and recollection turned his feelings to outrage. In Pound's defense, one must note that in early 1934 Nazism was still allied to the nationalist movement; it had not yet shown all its true colors. Moreover, Pound may have naïvely associated anti-Nazi feeling with World War I–era anti-German feeling.

40. Philip Mechem, "The Jurisprudence of Despair," 21 *Iowa Law Review* 692 (1936).

41. Ignatius M. Wilkinson, "The Lawyer and the Defense of Constitutional Democracy in America," 7 *Fordham Law Review* 308 (1938) (emphasis in original). Wilkinson was dean at Fordham, and his comments, while generally applicable to the realists, were particularly directed against Thurman Arnold and his controversial work, *The Symbols of Government.* Arnold had done for the Constitution what Frank's *Law and the Modern Mind* had done for the courts.

right, and that, too, isolated Pound from his liberal academic constituency. He was a Republican, and by 1933, when the storm of criticism fell on legal realism, it was thoroughly identified as "the leftist movement in the law."[42] From the right came the fear that realism undermined religion.[43] Realism opened the door to European absolutism. Realism espoused dangerous novelties and the useless stockpiling of data. Realism encouraged disrespect for the country. Realism dispensed with the tried and true common law. Realism emphasized efficiency over justice.[44] Behind some of these assaults was open war on the New Deal. Kennedy, whose disdain for the new philosophy of law was repeated in article after article, had the same scorn for the politics of Franklin Roosevelt and his minions. "The New Deal in the law," he told the Bronx County (N.Y.) Bar Association in 1935, "needs a juristic anchor to stabilize the law, to check against the winds of judicial emotion and to rescue the individual against the clamor of the majority. . . . Despite the promises and the tenets of realism, this New Deal in the law, the cure for current evils is not to throw the 'anchor' away nor to permit pseudo-science to hand us untried theories in its place."[45]

Just as Fowler had manipulated the themes of xenophobia in his attack on Pound in 1914, Kennedy chose his symbols and associations carefully. Before an audience of working lawyers, he warned of pseudo-sciences replacing the tried and true science (Cohen's "transcendental nonsense") of the law. So, too, the clamor of the majority must be resisted. How realism became a majoritarian doctrine is not hard to fathom if one links, as Kennedy did, realism and the New Deal.

The most reasoned, and therefore the most powerful, attack on realism came from Lon L. Fuller, a professor of law at Duke. Fuller, like Hohfeld, was reared and educated in a middle-class California

---

42. Walter B. Kennedy, "Realism, What Next?," 7 *Fordham Law Review* 203 n.2 (1938).

43. Edward A. Purcell, Jr., *The Crisis of Democratic Theory: Scientific Naturalism and the Problem of Value* (Lexington, Ky., 1973), 166–72, argues that the Roman Catholic legal scholars and teachers of law took the lead in attacking realism for a variety of reasons, some theological and ecclesiastical, some political.

44. Neil Duxbury, "The Reinvention of American Legal Realism," 12 *Legal Studies* 144–50 (1992); Laura Kalman, *Legal Realism at Yale, 1927–1960* (Chapel Hill, N.C., 1986), 134–35; Purcell, *The Crisis of Democratic Theory*, 159–78.

45. Walter B. Kennedy, "The New Deal in the Law," 68 *United States Law Review* 539 (1935).

household, went to Stanford, and then looked to the great law schools with ambition and avidity. He taught for a time at Oregon; then moved on to Illinois, where he published his three-part book-length study of legal fictions; and then went to Duke in 1931. He visited at Harvard in 1939 and was made a full professor there in 1940. He was prolific in the field of contracts and even more so in jurisprudence, where, again like Hohfeld, he tried to find the deeper meanings of law. Unlike Hohfeld, Fuller eventually came to rest on a kind of natural law jurisprudence. This was not a return to the theology of the eighteenth century, but rather the assumption that in society, in social order, there were the seeds of good law. The law thus had a kind of internal morality.[46] Fuller was not at first a political conservative—that would come in the post–World War II period of his writings—but he was from the first skeptical of the value of thoroughgoing realism. Not that he did not recognize how judges used language to conceal or to facilitate; he was enough of a realist in that sense. He conceded that what worked best of the fictions of the law was retained—a kind of rough-hewn and unsystematic functionalism.[47]

But when it came to Llewellyn's *Präjudizienrecht*, Fuller was troubled. Llewellyn had not even tried to probe the nature of the law. In his first draft of a review of Llewellyn's book for the *University of Pennsylvania Law Review*, Fuller laid "The Next Step" alongside *Präjudizienrecht* to criticize both. "The realist conception, then, seems to demand liberation from the confines of the court room, it calls for application to all kinds of official behavior," Fuller wrote in his draft. "We cannot answer Llewellyn simply by throwing up our hands at his unconventional use of the word 'law.' But we are entitled to this question: Just what is the utility of the word 'law' when it is given the meaning he gives it? . . . [T]he fact is . . . that from the standpoint of a purely observational method, such as Llewellyn purports to follow . . . the word 'law' has no meaning, descriptive or otherwise." Now "law" might describe whatever the lawyer was interested in, and lawyers use the word that way, but Fuller suspected that Llewellyn had a different motive in his work. In a passage not included in the published review, Fuller

---

46. Robert S. Summers, *Lon L. Fuller* (Stanford, Calif., 1984), 2–32; Kenneth I. Winston, ed., *The Principles of Social Order: Selected Essays of Lon L. Fuller* (Durham, N.C., 1981), 11–44.

47. Lon L. Fuller, "Legal Fictions," 25 *Illinois Law Review* 379 (1930).

took a stab at that hidden agenda. "A study of Professor Llewellyn's writings seems to me to make it quite clear that he is an adherent of a fairly definite social philosophy and that this social philosophy colors his whole attitude toward law. In discussing this social philosophy one is under the embarrassment that Professor Llewellyn nowhere makes as distinct and explicit an avowal of it as one might wish [how like the attack on the Critical Legal Studies advocates fifty years later], and never attempts to put it in its historical perspective by indicating its relation to the thought of other writers." Perhaps Fuller had been reading *The Bramble Bush,* for Llewellyn had pretty much given away his social sympathies there, but Fuller insisted that his detective work was conjecture and that to do it he had to look at the entirety of Llewellyn's writings. There followed a list of indicators, all of which added up to a "Teutonic discipline." Here the typescript ended.[48]

The version in print did not include Fuller's animadversions on realism—he was saving those for an article on realism to be published shortly—but closed with Fuller's "personal wish that the Teutonic sense of order which seems to pervade the style and arrangement of the present work may carry over into the English edition. For the book as it now stands offers an irrefutable demonstration of the fact that vigor and originality of thought are not necessarily incompatible with a degree of stylistic discipline."[49]

Fuller kept his word; his "American Legal Realism" appeared in the same issue of the *University of Pennsylvania Law Review* as his book review. It was a blockbuster. Pound loved it, as did Penn's dean, Herbert Goodrich. Pound now thought of Fuller as "one of the most promising of those who are coming forward in Jurisprudence in this country." Goodrich agreed that the essay was an "outstanding piece of work."[50] Pound would later effusively compliment Fuller—in private, of course: "I don't think there can be any doubt where the mantle of Gray and Wigmore and the jurists of the past generation in this country is going to fall."[51] For Fuller had seen what others had missed: realism did not begin with Llewellyn or

48. Lon L. Fuller, The Realist Definition of Law, 1933–1934, Lon Fuller Papers, Harvard Law School, 16-4.

49. Lon L. Fuller, "Review of *Präjudizienrecht und Rechtsprechung in Amerika,*" 82 *University of Pennsylvania Law Review* 553 (1934).

50. Pound to Goodrich, Jan. 7, 1935, RPP, 15-12; Goodrich to Pound, Mar. 1, 1935, RPP, 15-12.

51. Pound to Lon L. Fuller, Jan. 22, 1937, RPP, 65-5.

Walter Wheeler Cook or Frank or Charles Clark. It began with Oliver Wendell Holmes, Jr., and his followers. What is more, he reckoned that realism, called a movement by its friends and its enemies, was not a school. Indeed, its (that is, Fuller's) focus was Karl Llewellyn. At a stroke, Fuller had given to Llewellyn the honor and the burden of defending realism. Frank was left out in the cold.[52]

Llewellyn was the "philosopher" of realism, according to Fuller, and although Llewellyn was antipathetic to formal philosophy, Fuller had a point. Underhill Moore and others were empiricists to whom Llewellyn deferred, when he deferred, but Llewellyn valued law, loved law, in a way that the data gatherers and behavioral observers among the realist corps did not, and this drew Fuller's sympathy (though he never really "got" it when it came to Llewellyn).[53]

Llewellyn understood that the lawyer's "law" was a matter of habits and rules within a system and the layman's "law" was a congruence between a system and a set of vernacular customs. It was a "middle of the road" approach, a wise approach, but it was wrong, for it began by assuming that the formalist credo was the target. As the leaders of the German "free law" movement at the end of the nineteenth and the beginning of the twentieth century realized, but the realists missed, the problem was not the misalignment between

52. Lon L. Fuller, "American Legal Realism," 82 *University of Pennsylvania Law Review* 429, 430 (1934).

53. Llewellyn and Fuller never did agree. Fuller produced a defense of natural law in 1940, his *Law in Quest of Itself* (Boston, 1940). Fuller explained to Llewellyn: "The book's repudiation of positivism, including the positivism of American legal realism, may seem to you like attacking windmills. For me, however, it is something very real [realer than realism—the motto of natural law in the late 1930s] and . . . something tied up with the survival of our civilization." Fuller to Llewellyn, May 13, 1940, KLP, R.VI.6. Llewellyn was kind, in private: "I have been through your book the first time, and find it good. On the negative side, I think there are muffs. The is-lookers are not looking at what you speak of as law, but at their best view of factual conditions, which takes most of the juice out of your criticism. They [the realists] develop not out of the positivists, who were looking for what *law* is, but out of the sociological boys who started to look at what living conditions are, but didn't look hard enough [note the shot at Pound]." Llewellyn to Fuller, n.d., Lon Fuller Papers, Harvard Law School, 4-15 (emphasis in original). They both poked fun, in private again, at "the Great Roscoe." Fuller to Llewellyn, Aug. 9, 1940, KLP, R.VI.6. Llewellyn chortled in return, "What we need is to get on with the job. And school-wise controversy is not the road to that, even when there are schools. Would you especially feel an attack on you, Kennedy, Pound, and Lord Mansfield to have much chance of being significant, rather than merely dialectically defensible—or, indeed, one on Pound as 'Pound' because of his bug on nihilistic absolutistic whatever which left out of account the wisdom he still uses on all others matters?" Llewellyn to Fuller, n.d., Lon Fuller Papers, Harvard Law School, 4-15.

law ways and lay culture, but the narrowness of the formal lexicon of the law, its aversion to social and moral language. The artificial rationalizations of the law (its fictions) were impoverished. "Meanwhile litigants receive arbitrary treatment and legal certainty suffers." The realists had begun the critical examination of the sources of this uncertainty, Fuller granted, giving credit where it was due: "[T]he realist movement has done an immense service to American legal science in inculcating in it a healthy fear of such very real demons as Reified Abstractions, Omnibus Concepts, and Metaphors Masquerading as Facts." The problem was that "American legal science gives evidence that it is on the verge of making an orthodoxy of the sterile and uninspired behavioristic philosophy which has worked such havoc in the other social sciences." No proof of the havoc was forthcoming here, save an approving repetition of Morris Cohen's warnings against the same, but he was a philosopher, not a social scientist. Fuller provided no evidence from the social sciences that a sterile behaviorism was abroad. Instead, the bottom line for Fuller was a "rational and critical evaluation" of the problem because somewhere, he knew, there were principles of law that all would accept. Pragmatism he dismissed out of hand, presumably (he never really made his logic clear on this) because it had no principles.[54]

The realists were tough-minded, Fuller conceded, but in their quest for things rather than words, they had wrongly assumed that facts were concrete blocks instead of mental constructs. They could be imagined, fabricated, or even wished for. Life was not just things. Fuller verged here on the very phenomenology that Pound condemned, but Fuller did not cite any phenomenologists in his support, just as he had not cited social scientists to diagnose ills of behaviorism. Instead, he claimed that Llewellyn was hiding his own cards, for the realist is not a neutral observer. He has a "distinctive ethical bias." Fuller inserted here the passage from his draft review of *Präjudizienrecht* accusing Llewellyn of "nowhere" making this bias distinct and explicit. But it was there, a bias in favor of "the society side" in the polarity of law and society. Of course, Llewellyn must have smiled when he read the article, for he had never believed that law and society were opposites. Law was simply a visible, testable collection of behaviors, statements, and roles within any given

54. Fuller, "American Legal Realism," 431, 432, 434, 435, 437, 438, 443.

society. To have argued as Fuller did was to beg (or rather ignore) Llewellyn's position. But if society and law were opposites, as Fuller claimed, then law could have substance separate from social ways and customs. And this is what Fuller wanted.[55]

There is a sequel to the Fuller intervention, which played itself out at the end of the decade. It does no credit to Fuller. Fuller longed to join the circle of leading jurisprudents, encouraged by Pound and driven by his own ambition. Yet Pound, once upon a time just as eager to leave "this cussed country" of Nebraska, did not stoop so low or bow with so much humility as Fuller did in those years.[56]

Fuller had planned to spend the fall of 1938 in Europe, principally in Paris, with a short trip to Germany. He evidently recalled that Pound had received a medal from the Nazis in 1934 and admitted, "It has occurred to me that it might also be interesting to talk to some of the Nazi legal bigwigs." Fuller wanted to visit with Hans Frank and Karl Schmitt. The former was a barrister turned storm trooper who became the Third Reich's minister of justice and president of the Academy of Law even though he was excluded from Hitler's personal circle of advisors. After the war began, Frank was named governor general of Poland and oversaw the extermination of Polish Jewry with gusto until, realizing the error of his ways, he called for a return to parliamentary government in Germany. Despite his role reversal and his abject contrition at the Nuremberg trials, he was executed for war crimes. Schmitt was a respected jurist before the Nazis took power and joined with them for expedient reasons. He was a conservative critic of democracy and all forms of radical reform, but did not subscribe to Nazi views on race until 1933, after which he defended the Nazi Party as the embodiment of the German sense of order and the strength of the *Volk*. His conversion to anti-Semitism was as convenient and as thorough as his conversion to the Nazi Party line. Internal party rivals forced him from official power in December 1936, but he retained his chair in law at the University of Berlin.[57]

Fuller seemed oblivious to the moral odium of these men's actions, or perhaps found no objections to their views. Positioning

55. Ibid., 447, 448, 451, 452.
56. Pound to Omer Hershey, Sept. 5, 1892, Sayre Papers.
57. Robert S. Wistrich, *Who's Who in Nazi Germany* (London, 1995), 62–63, 225–26. See generally Ingo Müller, *Hitler's Justice: The Courts of the Third Reich* (Cambridge, Mass., 1991).

himself as Pound's client, he concluded, "Needless to say, I would much appreciate anything you might do, of whatever nature, toward getting me properly afloat in the intellectual currents of European legal science, just as I have been deeply grateful for your kind words of encouragement in times past."[58] Pound was pleased to be supplicated and replied as a proper mentor: "It gives me much pleasure indeed to accede as far as I can to the request in your letter. I have come to look on you as the coming man in Jurisprudence in this country, and anything that I can do for you, indeed I want to do." Many of the French jurisprudents that Fuller wished to see were gone from the field, but "[a]s to Germany, I think the man who would be most useful for your purposes is Müllereisert. I am giving you a letter to him. Through him you will have no difficulty in seeing any one that you like. Perhaps Emge would also be worth your while. I am giving you a letter to him. Julius Binder is perhaps the outstanding man just now, and you can probably get next to him through Emge."[59] Pound knew all about Frank and Schmitt and refused to have anything to do with them, a silent rebuke to Fuller, who ought to have known better.[60]

The shots at Llewellyn were fired not only by realism's enemies but also by its friends. The old realists named by Llewellyn, like Felix Frankfurter, wanted nothing to do with the philosophical implications of Frank's doctrines, and Llewellyn suffered guilt by association, whatever Fuller might say to rehabilitate Llewellyn. Frankfurter boasted, albeit ruefully, to Charles Clark that Llew-

58. Fuller to Pound, Jan. 6, 1938, RPP, 65-5.

59. Pound to Fuller, Jan. 10, 1938, RPP, 65-5. Pound's men were all established academic jurists before the rise of Nazism, and although they supported the movement, they were not its mainstays. Herrman A. L. Degener, *Degener's Wer Ist's?* (Berlin, 1935). Information courtesy of Professor John Haag, letter of Feb. 20, 1996.

60. During the war, when a handful of Jews managed to flee the death camps, Fuller wrote to Edwin Patterson of Columbia Law School: "It seems that I am always writing about some refugee or other. This time it is a woman who wants to go through an American law school and would like to finance her legal education by doing stenography and research. Her name is Helen Silving. (Up to about a month ago it was Helga Silberpfennig. It was partly on my advice that she adopted something more maneuverable.) She is a Polish national of Jewish origin. According to [Hans] Kelsen [one of the leading expatriate Austrian jurisprudents] her family was at one time one of the richest families in Poland. She received the degree of Doctor of Political Science from Vienna in 1929 and the Juris Doctorate degree in 1936. . . . She reads the following languages: German, Polish, French, Italian, Hebrew and Latin. . . . Her spoken English is adequate for all ordinary occasions." Fuller recommended her, but without enthusiasm. Fuller to Edwin Patterson, Mar. 6, 1942, Lon Fuller Papers, Harvard Law School, 6-9.

ellyn had blackballed Frankfurter from the realist club because of old fogeyness.[61] Benjamin Cardozo was Llewellyn's close personal friend and mentor, but in 1932, he publicly criticized Llewellyn for underestimating the importance of judicial language.[62]

Other, younger realists went privately to Pound to assure him that the people on Llewellyn's list were not Pound's antagonists. Hessel Yntema, feeling the heat as an untenured visitor at the University of Michigan Law School after the Johns Hopkins institute experiment had folded for lack of outside funding ("liquidation" was Yntema's term), hoped that Pound "will not think that I have put entirely out of mind the suggestions which you made a year ago last winter" about employment at Harvard. After all, Pound and Henry M. Bates, Michigan's dean, were longtime friends (and Yntema was Pound's former student). Cook, who had approached Pound before the institute collapsed, was "not yet satisfactorily placed," and Yntema put in a good word for him (like Hohfeld, perhaps, not realizing that Pound had known Cook for more than thirty years). And just to be on the safe side, Yntema revealed to Pound:

> I am getting a little tired, however, of being stood up in a lump with the other incorrigibles and then being made to stand sponsor for Llewellyn's aberrations as if they were the type, particularly since I did my best to read myself out of the so-called realist group sometime since. And, as you perhaps know, when Llewellyn was working up his statistical anthology three years ago in preparation for the response to your article in the Harvard Law Review, not only did I try to head him off,—which was impossible,—but, with Cook and Oliphant, refused to have anything to do with his activities on the ground that they were quite uncalled for. My own private impression is that the realist school,—or, shall we say the school of real realists?—is composed of two persons, of whom Jerome Frank has indicated that another label would be better, while Llewellyn has recently admitted with inclusive candor that not one of the realists, excepting possibly Underhill Moore, has thought things through.[63]

61. Michael E. Parrish, *Felix Frankfurter and His Times: The Reform Years* (New York, 1982), 227–28.

62. Benjamin Cardozo to New York State Bar Association Meeting, 1932, quoted in Beryl Harold Levy, *Cardozo and Frontiers of Legal Thinking* (rev. ed., Cleveland, 1969), 19.

63. Yntema to Pound, Aug. 9, 1934, RPP, 91-7.

Thurman Arnold was just as apologetic, for he, too, was sensible that "[y]ou have always been more than kind and helpful to me in the past. . . . Add to these very personal obligations my feeling of friendship which leads me to feel that if I have in any way attacked your position I would be very ungrateful indeed." The occasion was a series of rumors that Arnold had dismissed Pound's work, but Arnold wanted nothing to do with the label "legal realist." "I believe that if we become too realistic about jurisprudence the whole thing disappears and we lose the benefit of the ideal." He preferred "legal science" if he had to choose a term.[64] Pound's reply was gracious: "I suppose that the hearsay to which you refer probably grew out of a skit that I wrote which was printed by the Law Review at the time of their dinner. I had not intended it to be published [Pound, again, drawing the line between private discourse and publication] but you saw it on that occasion and know what was in it. I suppose some of the comments made on it, and possibly some of the things I may have said casually and light-heartedly about my good friends the realists have given rise to an erroneous impression. At any rate, do not let the matter trouble you in the least."[65]

The conclusion is inescapable that legal realism was not tripped up, insofar as it was hobbled at all, by the advocates of natural law and American principles so much as by the timidity of the very men who ought to have boosted realism. Realists like Yntema and Arnold feared that Pound would be offended by their arguments, and at the moment, they could not afford that luxury. The job seekers in this time of downsizing of faculties and disappearance of institutes grew day by day. Even established figures like Cook and Yntema needed the reassurance that Pound gave that some place might be found for them at Harvard. Pound held out that prospect to Cook, for example: "I had a caucus with a few of your friends at Chicago this winter who felt as I did that in case the Institute did not continue we ought to bestir ourselves to see that you have a place where you can write your books. . . . [U]nhappily in these days everything is so tentative that we could do nothing more than discuss possibili-

---

64. Thurman Arnold to Pound, July 5, 1935, RPP, 5-20.
65. Pound to Arnold, July 12, 1935, RPP, 5-20. Arnold had nothing to fear from Pound, but why leave enemies around? It is thus an error to use Arnold's view to speak for "the realists," if Llewellyn is supposed to be included. The error appears in G. Edward White, "The American Law Institute and the Triumph of Modernist Jurisprudence," 15 *Law and History Review* 39, 43 (1997).

ties. . . . All that I can say to you at the moment is that I and two or three others have been thinking about this matter, and you can rely upon your friends to do whatever they can find to do." [66]

The asymmetry of the letter was subtle, but Pound clearly was hinting that he might be able to do a favor for someone not quite equal to him in status. Dependency, even if only implied, created obligation. Such homage coursed over the academic networks in the Depression, and Pound's place as Harvard's dean gave him influence (and warded off criticism, at least in public) that others traduced at their peril. Of course, we would not know about this internal hemorrhaging of realism's lifeblood were it not for the availability of the private discourse, nor would we understand why so many law teachers who ought to have come out strongly for Llewellyn held back instead.

In the end, for whatever reason, realism as a thoroughgoing attack on legal certitude was in general retreat. Arnold's brilliant, but stubbornly skeptical, critique of the popular symbols of government was battered by critics.[67] Other realists, notably Jerome Frank, would end up agreeing with many of the propositions of the natural law advocates like Fuller. Frank would fashion a liberal natural law position that borrowed from the moral certitudes of the conservatives, while not bowing to their politics.[68]

The spur was not the internal debate over the applicability of realism, but the rise of "fascist law." The elite law journals welcomed critical articles on the perversion of the idea of law in the European dictatorships. Karl Loewenstein reported in the *Yale Law Journal* that in the Third Reich the line between private law—the law of individual property and domestic life—and public law, the demands of the state, had all but disappeared. Adolph Hitler was the new lawgiver, although the thousands of regulations and ordinances of the national and state legislatures obviously had other sources. In this wholesale revision of the liberal law codes of the previous century, the key concepts were racial purity, collective re-

---

66. Pound to Walter Wheeler Cook, Feb. 10, 1933, RPP, 10-17. Cook could not go back to Chicago, for John Maynard Hutchins, president of the university, was still angry at him for deserting Yale when Hutchins was dean there. Cook eventually went to Northwestern.

67. Thurman Arnold, *Fair Fights and Foul: A Dissenting Lawyer's Life* (New York, 1965), 68. Fuller was preparing notes for a review that was critical, but did not publish it. Lon Fuller Papers, Harvard Law School, 14-7. But other critics had a field day.

68. Purcell, *Crisis of Democratic Theory*, 172–78.

sponsibility, and ideological conformity—the ideology of the National Socialist Party being the only ideology permitted. All rivals and dissenters were criminally punished. Pretrial procedure was abolished; everything happened at the trial stage, which became a performance of political obedience and ritual. Criminal law was harsher, punishment more brutal. Procedural guarantees all but disappeared. This softness of the "Jewish-Roman" law was replaced by the rigor of Germanic law, according to the state's official organs. Although local interests resisted the new national order and the variety of special local courts remained in place, a new regime had its law: non-"Aryans," particularly the Jews, were stripped of citizenship, property, and legal identity. The trade unions were dissolved. Judicial offices were filled with good party members. Private rights were reduced to political privileges.[69]

H. Arthur Steiner published a similar critique of Fascist law in the *Columbia Law Review*. In Mussolini's Italy, he argued, extra-legal violence was married to new theories of the supremacy of the state. The party condoned the former and orchestrated the latter. The state would serve the people, but was to be idolized and obeyed implicitly by the people in return. The individual vanished. The state was all. Rights might be granted by the state, but were not bulwarks against state power. The law was the handmaiden of the state in protecting itself against political and social enemies. Law gave to the state the power to regulate all economic activity. As in Hitler's Germany, the Fascists churned out detailed regulations for employment, prices, and sales. As in Germany, the brooding question in Mussolini's Italy was the relationship between industrial workers and the large businesses, and as in Germany, the Fascist state feared unions, on the one hand, and Communist agitators, on the other. The new laws combined deterrents and benefits to factory workers to ensure their loyalty, or at least suppress their resistance.[70] Loewenstein and Steiner agreed that law without humane principles was tyranny. Relativism had become the handmaiden of dictatorship, as all democrats should concede. The onset of war converted many skeptics into believers.[71]

69. Karl Loewenstein, "Law in the Third Reich," 45 *Yale Law Journal* 779–815 (1936).

70. H. Arthur Steiner, "The Fascist Conception of Law," 36 *Columbia Law Review* 1267–83 (1936).

71. Peter Novick, *That Noble Dream* (Cambridge, Mass., 1988), 253–58, 283–84, 286.

Pound was thus in good company—once again riding with the tide, but his personal influence, as opposed to the general acceptability of his opinions, was slipping. His stature as a jurisprudent was never greater, but it was no longer clear where he stood. He was lionized in the law journals by members of the bar as a new conservative. Typically, George R. Farnum, a Massachusetts lawyer and former federal attorney, lauded Pound's "robust independence and instinctive aloofness from affiliation with any well defined school of legal thought or philosophical movement—phases of his pronounced originality of character and thought—[that] render it impossible to arrange his views within the bounds of any neat and instructive scheme of classification." The great expositor of reforming progressive pragmatism, or more conventionally, of sociological jurisprudence, had evidently outgrown that label. After all, these were troubled times, times of "political uncertainty, economic disequilibrium, and social transition," and the bar needed Pound to be "non-partisan" and to "readjust" the claims of those who laid the cost of litigation to "the failure of the legal profession." This was a Pound who "devoted much attention . . . to the interrelations of law and morals" and "returned frequently to a consideration of the influence of various aspects and schools of natural law philosophy in the thought of the moulders of our legal systems." This Pound took on the realists in the name of "certainty, stability, and predictability in our legal institutions," while gently compromising with them when he wished to nurture their movement. His "fighting spirit was intact," but it was denatured and dispassionate. Pound wanted only more efficient and harder-working administration of justice. His target thus was government itself, with its "bureaucratic regulation of society." Farnum conceded the progressive strains of Pound's thought, but these were less important than the conservative ones. What was needed, and what Farnum found, was a Pound for the times.[72] Farnum did not admire Pound for Pound's real achievement, his dogged progressive pragmatism. Quite the reverse—he admired a Pound-manque, the remodeled Pound, who held excess and unprincipled criticism of the law at bay.

Pound's power to control the public discourse of the elite law professorate was not maintained by such misdirected plaudits because

72. George R. Farnum, "Dean Roscoe Pound: His Significance in American Legal Thought," 1 *Boston University Law Review* 1, 2, 3, 5, 7, 8, 9 (1934).

veteran Pound watchers within the academy knew what Pound had written and how easily they could embarrass him by doing what Frank had done. Conservatives would soon discover that Pound refused to concede all they wanted. "It is no wonder that his jurisprudence gropes along with a blindfold instead of an ethics," one disappointed conservative reported.[73] Liberals were no more pleased with him. In the circled tents of the other camp, Llewellyn drafted a letter to Pound in March 1935: "[S]cientific [that word!] decency demands that a man who can really think and can really write, and has a reputation because he has really thought and has really written, should not be allowed to pass out soothing syrup, without attention being called to the fact." If Pound did not mend his ways, Llewellyn would commission "a set of articles by a lot of men, all testing Pound against Pound . . . for internal inconsistencies, premises contradictory with each other, and meaningless words."[74] It was Pound's formal position as dean of the country's largest and most prestigious law school—a situation he worked mightily to enhance by expanding the size of the faculty, student body, and physical plant of Harvard—that gave him the luxury of moderation and tempered Llewellyn's ire. He never sent the angry letter. You just could not tell where Pound stood in the maelstrom of ideologies.

In fact, Pound's retreat from leadership of the reform party in jurisprudence began quietly in November 1931. "One of the signs of the times in the science of law [a quiet jibe by now, just to remind the empiricists that Pound was still there] is recognition of the significant role of the ideal element, not merely in juristic thinking, but in the everyday administration of justice." Ideals were again influencing human decisions. Such ideals needed the same systematic study as had already been accorded precepts, rules, and other familiar legal authority. Pound proposed to begin with judges' ideals. He noted the resiliency of nineteenth-century natural law morphologies, going back to Sir William Blackstone, but judged them inadequate for the modern world and dismissed religious natural law, for it "never had much currency." In America, a natural law, based on fundamental ideas of rights, was universally established, however,

73. Karl Kreilkamp, "Dean Pound and the End of Law," 9 *Fordham Law Review* 196, 212 (1940).

74. Llewellyn to Pound, Mar. 28, 1935, KLP, R.XVI.5.

and pervaded judicial pronouncements. So, too, did the economics of laissez-faire. Judges had these ideas in their heads as they applied the Fourteenth Amendment to strike down congressional legislation. The formalistic conceptions of the previous century were still alive and well in many judicial chambers. The modern jurist could see that these logical systems were never facts but ideals—"a picture of law as it is conceived it ought to be." Such systems of ideas were "political" at bottom, rooted in a now-gone vision of an individualistic frontier society.[75]

Again, as he had over the course of intellectual career, Pound inched toward a new position. While others were rethinking the need for a modern state, Pound was moving in the other direction—toward the premise that ideals had a value of their own. "To show that these ideals are by no means wholly realized in practice in the course of judicial decision does not dispose of them. . . . [A]n ideal of the end of law, and hence of what legal precepts should be and how they should be applied . . . is too significant a phenomenon to be overlooked in a scientific [that word again, and this time the point was barbed] account of American law."[76] Softly, with dignity, Pound had answered Frank. The answer was bounded by two references to the science of the law, a phrase that Yntema and others had used to describe their work. No one within the circle of legal academics who followed the controversy would have missed Pound's purpose. But Pound had stopped far short of arguing that the ideals commanded adherence, much less that they dictated the outcome of cases. He was still a sociological jurisprudent and a pragmatist. As the latter, he had left the door open to a discussion of what the ideals of leaders should be in these troubled times.

A year and a half later, Pound addressed the Bar Association of the City of New York with a slightly altered message. The "old" Pound opened the address with a eulogy of James C. Carter, late of the New York City Bar, and his historical school–style jurisprudence. In it, "[a]ll attempt . . . to frame new precepts, as distin-

75. Roscoe Pound, "The Ideal Element in American Judicial Decision," 45 *Harvard Law Review* 136, 139, 140, 141, 144, 145, 146 (1931). Pound never cited Frederick Jackson Turner's frontier thesis, but he seemed to have absorbed its basic tenets. Pound and Turner came to Harvard in the same year, 1910, and Turner stayed until 1924. They had similar political views much of the time, and both were leaders in their fields. Frankfurter used Turner's views in public addresses. See Ray Allen Billington, *Frederick Jackson Turner: Historian, Scholar, Teacher* (New York, 1973), 308–90, 446.

76. Pound, "The Ideal Element," 147–48.

guished from a better formulation of old ones, all attempt to work out new premises for legal reasoning, all attempt to give effect to newly pressing interests by reasoned working out of new legal devices or legal institutions, was not merely futile, it was downright injurious to the legal ordering of society." Rather, jurisprudents in 1933 saw that new institutions, like administrative tribunals, were "complementary" with judicial institutions "and think of the apportionment of jurisdiction between them as a matter of the best means of attaining the ends of law in the time and place." In 1933, facts mattered more than abstract reasoning, for law had to take account of the current crisis. Law was no longer autonomous, for "now, on the other hand, we seek a certain unification of the social sciences," in which jurisprudence belonged. Rights were no longer absolute, but grew out of the task "of reconciling or harmonizing conflicting and overlapping interests which were to be discovered, not by deduction from some fundamental ideas, but by an actual inventory of the claims actually asserted by concrete human beings and so pressing upon the law for recognition." In all, jurisprudence "had become relativist."[77]

Thus far, Pound might well have been classed as a realist. But there was a kicker at the end: "Every generation sets up juristic gods in its own image. There is a moral for us in the assured dogmatism of Mr. Carter's address. . . . Realism in jurisprudence has always been a boast rather than a description. Most of jurisprudence has been a putting universally for all the problems of the legal order solutions which have been devised and have worked well for particular problems of the time and place for which they were thought out." Thus, realism was not the next stage of development of jurisprudence at all. The power of this insight was that it changed the course of jurisprudence from a linear progress to curvilinear cycles. Typically, cyclical thinking is conservative thinking, for it denies the philosophical assumption of progress. Was this what Pound meant? Consider what he wrote at the end of 1918: "[M]en's actions are governed largely by the theories they hold as to what they are doing."[78] At that time, such a notion was good sociological jurisprudence. What was it now?

---

77. Roscoe Pound, "The Ideal and the Actual in Law, Forty Years After," 1 *George Washington Law Review* 435, 436, 437, 438 (1933). The title is borrowed from Carter's presidential address to the ABA.

78. Pound, Jurisprudence Seminar Notes, n.d., RPP, 198-4, p. 49.

In November 1933, Pound published "A Comparison of the Ideals of Law," in which he devoted himself to the role played "by ideals by reference to which the starting points for legal reasoning are chosen, by ideals which determine what is 'reasonable,' by ideals by which the 'intrinsic merit' of competing interpretations is determined, and by ideals which lead tribunals to extend one precept by analogy while restricting another to the narrow bounds of its four corners." It sounded like conventional exegesis of judicial language, far from Pound's usual stomping grounds, but Pound had journeyed to a new field for a reason. "I have come to feel and have argued repeatedly that such ideals are largely contained in the law itself. . . . I submit that this is true of all developed systems of law. I submit that it is equally a mistake, on the one hand, to set off the ideal element as something of independent validity above the law . . . as in the old systems of natural law [no retreat into natural law for Pound just yet], and, on the other hand, to set it off in order to ignore it, as did the analytical jurists of the last century." The latter deft twist was a Pound trick once upon a time used to defend legislative activity or some other pragmatic innovation. Instead of coming out and saying it was good, Pound found someone else, a Kohler or a von Ihering, to say that it was good. Similarly, when he did not want to offend, he would find someone else (preferably a dead European academic or someone else) to browbeat as a proxy. Now the ideal was not to be discarded just because the analytical school (that is, the Austinians) had discarded it. The omniscient scholar, with access to all of Pound's earlier public and private writing, looking at the entire run of that writing, can see that Pound had slipped his liberal moorings to sail a new course. Now he was interested in the very ideals that had never before interested him.[79]

From that newfound interest had grown a new commitment to "the ideal of law as reason," for, he now judged, "there is no better antidote to that fear of arbitrary subjection of the will of the individual man to those who wield governmental power with which social control must always struggle. . . . [T]he best assurance of that general acquiescence in legal precepts which obviates problems of enforcement is in keeping those precepts in accord with a reasoned scheme of valuing conflicting and overlapping human demands and

---

79. Roscoe Pound, "A Comparison of the Ideals of Law," 47 *Harvard Law Review* 2, 3, 4 (1933).

in applying them upon a reasoned system." The balancing of interests by social engineers had given pride of place in Pound's new jurisprudence to consensus jurisprudence. "The law of today is turning to an ideal of cooperation." There was a "swing" back to the
"idea of a general law." But Pound courted ambiguity, and his essay
might easily be read as "give the New Deal a chance." [80]

Pound's next foray into the public discourse of jurisprudence was
his December 1933 contribution to the Legal History and Jurisprudence Round Table at the AALS. He expanded his comments for a
February 1934 *Yale Law Journal* piece. The essay is pure Pound.
Fully aware of his audience (fellow academics, many of whom were
committed to New Deal programs, while others were openly opposed to the Democratic administration), fully in command of his
sources, and secure in his place, he did not miss a trick. This was
a bravura public performance, without emotion, wise, balanced,
and sure. There had been a revival of analytic theories, he warned,
this time "on bases of socio-philosophical jurisprudence." Thus, he
gently chided the realists for falling into the trap of the Austinians,
for assuming that what is, by command of the state, is what ought
to be. In this, the realists were no different from those thinkers who
had come before, falling into "the boast of every type of jurist that
he is dealing with reality while those who would apply the label
'law' in a different way are dealing with illusion." Thus, the "realist" was no more than "the realist of the moment," and when he
tells us "that he is a realist because he has found reality in the emo-
tive experience or psychological make-up of particular judges or
officials for the time being, he is but conforming to the settled tradition of jurisprudence [claiming to be reality] for the past two centuries." The insight was a significant contribution (Pound being
gracious), particularly in the 1930s, when the United States was "in
a time of transition [Pound being sensitive to context]. . . . But what
legal precepts ought to be, what decisions ought to be, what the
judicial process in its details ought to be, are questions that have
never wholly disappeared from our books." Again, this was true—
that is, there were plenty of American jurisprudents who were still
trying to weigh competing values, but Pound was not being descriptive. He was tutoring the Franks and Llewellyns that they must be
aware of the importance of value questions. "The fundamental

80. Ibid., 14, 15.

problem of jurisprudence" was the "problem of values." This problem was never more important than it was when Pound spoke, he insisted. Instability, change, growth, and an uncertain future demanded that jurisprudence continue to listen to itself. There were no final answers.[81]

But Pound had not left the field of advocacy wholly to others in order to retire to his study and his books. In the two years before he stepped down from the deanship, Pound was still in the thick of the fight for a child labor amendment. Consider his language and methods then: in reply to Nicholas Murray Butler's objections to the amendment, Pound was happy to prepare a statement for publication. In a letter to William Hepburn of the University of Alabama School of Law (recall Pound's view of all things southern), he lectured: "The time of local economic independence has gone by, there is a complete economic interdependence, not merely in different regions of the country, but among those regions themselves. The consequence is that many things which were of purely local concern even a generation ago have nation-wide effects, and can be dealt with only through the power of the general government. That this power can be wisely exercised seems to me to be demonstrated by the extraordinarily wide powers which have been exercised by the federal executive in the past two years. . . . Child labor is a nation-wide problem. . . . The opposition of the American Bar Association to the Child Labor Amendment seems to me to proceed upon ideals which . . . are quite unadapted to the economically unified country of today."[82] In the *New York Times,* Pound urged the public to recognize that the absolute protection once given to property rights—for example, in the cases of mortgage moratorium—had to be adjusted to fit the crisis.[83]

But Pound's term as dean was coming to a close and, with it, the easy assurance that Pound could control the public discourse.[84] It was this event, so important in his life, if not in the broader course of legal and political events, that turned Pound from a tolerant

81. Roscoe Pound, "Law and the Science of Law in Recent Theories," 43 *Yale Law Journal* 526, 528, 529, 530, 533, 534, 535 (1934).

82. Henry Leach to Pound, Jan. 4, 1934, Pound, Statement in Regard to President Butler's Criticism of the Proposed Child Labor Amendment, and Pound to William M. Hepburn, Feb. 4, 1935, RPP, 9-23.

83. Roscoe Pound, "The New Deal in the Courts: A Changing Ideal of Justice," *New York Times,* Sept. 9, 1934, at 8-3.

84. "Pound Will Resign Harvard Law Post," *New York Times,* Sept. 25, 1935, at 2.

moderate into a sharp critic of legal modernism and political reform. He was still a university professor, but the influence and power of the deanship had passed to James Landis. What was more galling, Pound had retired under fire, or at least he thought so. The first summer after he resigned, at a conference on "The Future of the Common Law" in Cambridge, Pound lashed out at the administration in Washington, D.C., for violating the system of checks and balances. The issue was the attempt by President Franklin Roosevelt to add one justice to the number already sitting for each judge who was over 75 years in age, up to a maximum of 15. Pound opposed the "court packing plan."[85]

His views on administrative agencies had also hardened. He was not opposed to administrative activity, but wanted some curb on the discretion of administrative agencies. The expertise of the administrators was no guarantee of the fairness of their deliberations, he judged, putting himself in opposition to Landis and Frankfurter.[86] But Pound was not a fanatic in his admonitions. He had opposed giving too much authority and discretion to administrative agencies even before World War I, and he forgave the administrative excesses of the New Deal because there was an emergency. But the regulatory agencies had settled down to roost in the "Second New Deal," and they still had no curbs, save Congress and the courts.

Pound granted that the need for "speedy action and treating of each instance as unique" made for administrative initiative, but worried that "reports made by inspectors who act behind the backs of the parties and without opportunity to examine them" were hardly a way to prevent abuse of the regulatory system. Indeed, as a whole, "what governs administrative discretion is seldom as determinate and predictable" as common law or equity. Pound was not "for a minute" seeking a return to the nineteenth century. Instead, "our problem is to achieve a workable balance between the judicial and administrative processes which will be effective for the ends of the legal order." He rooted his concerns in the separation of powers doctrine, a formal concern, and his own experience with the administration of the Volstead Act. More and more boards and administrative agencies did not guarantee fairness to parties, he had found.

---

85. "Pound Pleads for Common Law," *New York Times*, Aug. 20, 1936, at 7; David Wigdor, *Roscoe Pound, Philosopher of Law* (Westport, Conn., 1974), 272–74.

86. Morton Horwitz, *The Transformation of American Law, 1870–1960* (New York, 1992), 220–22.

Preventive—that is, proactive—law enforcement was a perfect task for the regulatory agencies. But giving to agencies the duties and the powers of regular courts would lead only to "administrative absolutism." The danger, then, was that "political pressure on administrative agencies" might lead to "some special advantage" that regular courts might resist.[87]

Pound made the admonitory portions of this argument even stronger in his report for the ABA's special committee on administrative law. The danger was that, just as there was no effective review of the day-to-day decisions of the administrative agencies, there was no way to monitor the extension of their own purview. The science of law (yet again) had now gone too far.[88] Pound (and the ABA) was not alone in this attack. Even Herman Oliphant, then general counsel for the Department of the Treasury, agreed that administrative agencies had to let a person know what was expected by the agency "in order to go about his business with reasonable assurance."[89] Advocates of judicial review of administrative agency decisions had presented a bill to Congress, which the administration fought off.[90] Still, Pound and his allies had history on their side. The Administrative Procedure Act of 1946 did more or less exactly what Pound had wanted eight years earlier.[91]

The enemy was not administrative law in its place or administrative agencies per se; it was absolutism. Whether of a Puritan sort, of a Marxist variety, embodied in Prohibition, or embodied in dictatorships on the Continent, private rights had to be protected against the overweening state.[92] The short cuts that the modern American

87. Roscoe Pound, "Individualization of Justice," 7 *Fordham Law Review* 160, 161, 164, 165 (1938).

88. Roscoe Pound, "Report of the Special Committee on Administrative Law," 63 *Reports of the American Bar Association* 339, 344 (1938). Both Horwitz, *Transformation*, 220, 231, and Wigdor, *Pound*, 270–71, found Pound's language intemperate. They agree that he had changed his mind about administrative law sometime in the middle 1930s as the New Deal gained momentum.

89. Herman Oliphant, "Declaratory Rulings," 24 *American Bar Association Journal* 7 (1938).

90. See, e.g., Felix Frankfurter, "Summation of the Conference," 24 *American Bar Association Journal* 282–86 (1938) (arguing that judicial review was too general to deal with the individuated subject matter of administrative agency determinations).

91. Martin Shapiro, *Who Guards the Guardians? Judicial Control of Administration* (Athens, Ga., 1988), 39–44. Cass Sunstein, *After the Rights Revolution: Reconceiving the Regulatory State* (Cambridge, Mass., 1990), 23, credits Pound with forecasting the whole process of regulation and then curbs on agencies.

92. Roscoe Pound, "The Recrudescence of Absolutism," 47 *Sewanee Review* 18–28 (Jan.–Mar. 1939).

administrative process took to get individual justice might be necessary, given the expense and delay of regular court proceedings,
but "they are characteristic of times of transition when men are
struggling to adapt the machinery of justice to new conditions
imperfectly grasped, and in impatience at the cautious advance
of the courts." Pound was not happy with this impatience, for
"[p]hilosophically [it] is attributable to new modes of thought
which have grown into fashion in an era of post-war disillusionment and cynical acquiescence in a revived absolutism which has
largely grown out of that disillusionment." But Pound, aggravated
as he was, had not entirely lost his historical perspective, for the
new ways "represent a reaction from the extreme tying down of
administration and dogmatic application of abstract individualism
in the last quarter of the nineteenth century." The result was a
yearning for a race of "supermen administrators." It had failed in
the Soviet Union and had destroyed liberty throughout western Europe.[93] There was no law, only symbols to be manipulated and economic interests to be placated. Law reduced itself to a matter of
fooling or bullying people in the service of the dominant class or
group, and the needs of the many (articulated by a special few)
trumped the rights of everyone.[94]

Again, this was a far cry from the Pound of the 1900s, who noted
with approval the subordination of the claims of powerful individuals to the needs of the community, but the context had surely
changed. Then the community spoke through its elected representatives in the idiom of legislation. Now public law was articulated
by independent regulatory agencies. Pound tried to be realistic.

> I recognize the need of administration, and of a great deal of it,
> in the urban industrial society of today. It is needed as an ad-
> ministrative element in the judicial process. It is needed as a
> supplement to the judicial process. It is needed as a directing
> process in a society so organized economically and so unified
> economically that things must be done more speedily, with
> more adjustment to unique situations, with more coordination
> of special skill and technical acquirements than the judicial
> process, looking at controversies after the event, can afford.
> But to admit that development of the administrative process is
> necessary does not involve admitting that it should be free of
> checks such as a due balance between the general security and

93. Roscoe Pound, "Public Law and Private Law," 24 *Cornell Law Review* 476, 478
(1939).
94. Ibid., 479.

the individual life has led us to impose on both the legislative and the judicial processes.[95]

Thus, it was not the New Deal itself that turned him sour; nor was it the court-packing plan, which he opposed in his customary moderation (in public; in private, he was always another man); nor was it the growth of the fourth branch of government. It was the loss of mastery, of formal authority, that made Pound bitter for a time. Was this a matter of personality, the end of his tenure as dean dealing a blow to his ego and self-esteem that caused him temporarily to lose his customary caution? Or did the deanship itself so reinforce his habitual public moderation that its removal simply unbalanced him for a time? Whatever the dynamic, when he fell, it was into the hands of the very forces he had fought with such vigor in the first and second decades of the century. Even the old pleasures seemed to have faded. As he wrote at the start of 1938 to his onetime colleague and longtime friend Edward A. Ross, "I am writing a series of papers on contemporary jurisprudence, and in preparation therefore am going over recent sociological literature. Frankly, I am disappointed in most of it. It seems as if since the [First World War], too many sociologists have been concerned to evade the problems of the social sciences by taking refuge in logical development of abstractions. . . . I do not see any men at work in the subject today doing the things which you and Small and sociologists of that generation did to make sociology worth while for the student of jurisprudence."[96]

Pound had withered into a new kind of truth, questioning innovation, experiment, function, realism, and skepticism, for these had not brought the millennium. He openly pined for the good old days when he and Ross and others led the way. But Pound's old pragmatism had not only survived in the academy, but also reached out its tendrils into government. There no one was a philosopher, and realism meant pragmatic problem solving, not skepticism. Thurman Arnold worked at the Department of Justice, busting trusts; Herman Oliphant was counsel to the Department of the Treasury; William O. Douglas had become the chairman of the Securities and Exchange Commission (SEC), which the young "social engineers" from the law schools had created to manage the markets; and Je-

95. Ibid., 481.
96. Pound to Edward A. Ross, Jan. 4, 1938, RPP, 80-19.

rome Frank, the city boy from Chicago and New York City, the Wall Street lawyer, oversaw the Agricultural Adjustment Administration provisions for managing farm production. Frank, no longer wondering what judges had for breakfast except when they ruled against him, was helping the farmers rebuild their world.

The tumult over the legal realists' agenda, or, rather, what critics perceived to be the flaws and failures in the realists' apparent agenda, may have forced realism as a jurisprudence onto the defensive, but the critique of formalism and the appeal of the underlying experimental and social science tenets of realism were bearing fruit. Pound's seed had blossomed—the realist professors demanded that jurisprudence and the actual making of law thoroughly infuse each other's tasks. And they did in Washington, D.C., under the nurturing of many of the realists on Llewellyn's list. The academic administrative cadre wanted law to serve the people in a new way—through the enlarged social service functions of the modern state.[97] They hoped for a jurisprudence that would be in step with reality—not just a servant of power but its master; not just a recorder of how law was made, but a writer of law. Jurisprudence, filtered through agencies and advisors, would recreate the modern state.

Llewellyn did not go to Washington to join in the exertions of his fellow realist academics. He preferred to stay in New York City, though his support for liberal reform was evident to all. Indeed, in the press, he was regarded as "one of the nation's foremost liberal educators" and publicly defended the New Deal's policies against judicial and jurisprudential attack.[98] Privately he scolded his older friend and mentor Justice Harlan Fiske Stone for docilely allowing the United States Supreme Court to knock down vital New Deal programs.[99] Llewellyn remained a solid Democrat, even running (briefly) for a position on the State Democratic Committee.[100] He

97. Jordan A. Schwartz, *The New Dealers: Power Politics in the Age of Roosevelt* (New York, 1993), 157–94; Peter Irons, *New Deal Lawyers* (Princeton, N.J., 1982), 7, 123–80; Parrish, *Frankfurter*, 244–51, 267–72; William O. Douglas, *Go East Young Man, The Autobiography of William O. Douglas: The Early Years* (New York, 1974), 257–85 (even Douglas agreed with Pound about administrative agency capture [297]).

98. "Conflicting 'Right' and 'Left' Trends in American Life Pictured," *Portland Oregonian*, Sept. 8, 1935, at 1.

99. Alpheus Thomas Mason, *Harlan Fiske Stone, Pillar of the Law* (New York, 1956), 388.

100. "Knickerbocker Fight to Defeat Hines Opened . . . Llewellyn Tells Strategy," *New York Herald Tribune*, Aug. 14, 1934, at 1 (Llewellyn out to "get" the Tammany candidate to show the "hidden cost" of Tammany power to the voters); "Professor Llew-

invited friends like William O. Douglas, head of the SEC, to meet Columbia's "liberal law teachers and law students" and to keep the New Deal on a progressive course.[101]

Retreats are not only withdrawals, however; they may also be places of comfort—refuges. Llewellyn found safety from the storm within himself. His retreat was internal, a going inward. For Llewellyn, retreat in both senses intensified certain self-indulgent tendencies in his thinking. He needed the approbation of others and sought it, but he brooked no foolishness and rejected those accolades not truly won. Truly, as a friend told him, "[W]here I fly, follow storms."[102] He found a refuge in new personas and ribald poetry, a space for himself in which he could use his critical powers to oversee the entire philosophical project while not abandoning it.

Always a romantic at heart in his personal life and his jurisprudence, Llewellyn in his lair was a Romantic. In 1925, he had waxed eloquent on the artists who make the law. In 1935, he called for "an integration of the human and the artistic with the legal. Not an addition, merely, an integration."[103] By the late 1930s, the result was a series of published and unpublished satiric essays and literary ephemera written under the purloined pseudonym Diogenes Jonathan Swift Teufelsdröckh.[104] The published Teufelsdröckh essays took broad swipes at those who engaged in conscious jurisprudential activity—not Llewellyn himself (he could be self-critical, even

---

ellyn Quits State Committee Race," *New York Herald Tribune*, Aug. 30, 1934, at 1 (Llewellyn steps out to aid united front candidates).

101. William O. Douglas to Llewellyn, Dec. 20, 1938, Emma Corstvet Papers, Bryn Mawr College Library.

102. George M. Morris to Llewellyn, May 15, 1940, reported by Llewellyn to Emma Corstvet in a telegram on that day, Emma Corstvet Papers, Bryn Mawr College Library.

103. Karl Llewellyn, "On What Is Wrong with So-Called Legal Education," 35 *Columbia Law Review* 663 (1935).

104. The only piece published by Llewellyn under the Teufelsdröckh pseudonym was "Jurisprudence, The Crown of Civilization: Being Also the Principles of Writing Jurisprudence Made Clear to Neophytes," 5 *University of Chicago Law Review* 171 (1938). Another short piece, "The Universal Solvent of Jurisprudence," appeared in 6 *Harvard Law Revue* 1 (1940), a satirical pamphlet privately published and distributed by the editors of the *Harvard Law Review*. The copies that I have seen were in either the Karl Llewellyn Papers or the Roscoe Pound Papers. Llewellyn's unpublished Teufelsdröckh materials are in a folder marked "Teufelsdröckh miscellaneous" in a suitcase in the KLP file cabinets. Llewellyn also comments on Teufelsdröckh in "On the Good, the True, the Beautiful, in Law," 9 *University of Chicago Law Review* 224 (1942).

morbidly so, but these essays were part fantasy and part play).[105] Yet in them Llewellyn continued to articulate his own view of law and returned over and over, mostly in unpublished minutiae, to his fictional philosopher alter ego to attempt some grand statements about law. It is no coincidence that Llewellyn turned to a literary form—satire—and a literary character—Thomas Carlyle's Diogenes Teufelsdröckh—to express his "jurisprudence" and critical perspective of "jurisprudes." That he specifically chose Carlyle's Teufelsdröckh was no coincidence; Carlyle's work held deep resonances for Llewellyn.[106]

Llewellyn's jurisprudence was always "formbusting"—almost poetic in its license. The opening paragraphs of "Some Realism about Realism" rose to the level of poetry: "Ferment is abroad in the law. The sphere of interest widens; men become interested again in the life that swirls around things legal. Before rules, were facts; in the beginning was not a Word, but a Doing. . . . The ferment is

105. Llewellyn describes his "author" thus:

> The late Diogenes Jonathan Swift Teufelsdröckh, Q.E.D.[5], Nempenusquam, 1930. 1920 (1910 [1900 {1890}]), was Professor of Dialectic Immaterialism at the University of Nempenusquam, and Lord Keeper of the Vault of Themis. He is best known for his exhaustive *Catalog of the Treasures of the Vault* (1900, pp.2); his definitive edition of Lemuel Gulliver's *Laputan Jurisprudence* (1910, pp.22); his *Roots and Powers of the Doctorate* (1920, pp.222); his *Conservation of the Empyrean* (1930, pp.2222). An inexplicable balloon-collapse precipitated his untimely demise. But this Tract, though posthumous, had been worked over by his own hand at least three times, and is so perfect as to warrant unedited posthumous publication.

"Universal Solvent," 171. Later pieces emphasized the persona of Teufelsdröckh over that of Swift. In identifying the author of the 1940 *Harvard Law Revue* piece on the title page of the pamphlet, the Jonathan Swift part of the name was reduced to mere initials: "Diogenes J.S. Teufelsdröckh"; the identification at the end of the piece, however, was the complete name, "Diogenes Jonathan Swift Teufelsdröckh, *Morningside Heights*" (hinting at the author's true identity). In most of the unpublished Teufelsdröckhiana, the "philosopher" is referred to only as "Teufelsdröckh." Llewellyn may have included Jonathan Swift as middle names for his pseudonym to be sure prospective readers realized the piece was satire (Swift's name was undoubtedly better known than that of Carlyle's invention). Llewellyn may have also been in sympathy with Swift, who claimed to have written *Gulliver's Travels* "to vex the world rather than divert it." Louis Kronenberger, ed., *Atlantic Brief Lives: A Biographical Companion to the Arts* (New York, 1971), 753–54.

106. "Jurisprudes" is Llewellyn's term. See N. E. H. Hull, "The Romantic Realist: Art, Literature, and the Enduring Legacy of Karl Llewellyn's 'Jurisprudence,'" 40 *American Journal of Legal History* 115–45 (1996).

proper to the time. The law of the schools threatened at the close of century to turn into words—placid, clear-seaming, lifeless, like some old canal. Practice rolled on, muddy, turbulent, vigorous. It is now spilling, flooding, into the canal of stagnant words. It brings ferment and trouble." [107] This is self-consciously literary prose, and Llewellyn was always conscious of the quality of his writing. Like Carlyle, whose character's name Llewellyn appropriated, Llewellyn pursued Carlyle's "freedom from the usual rules of grammar, its deliberate syntactic dislocations, its coinages, and its vocal pitch, what may be termed his anti-style suggests rebellion." [108] When Llewellyn's critics were baying about him, he answered by becoming the man of letters.

Diogenes Teufelsdröckh was the central character of Thomas Carlyle's novel *Sartor Resartus,* written in 1830–31 and first published in the United States in 1836 and in England in 1838. [109] The title, *Sartor Resartus,* "means the 'tailor retailored,' or the 'patcher repatched,' whereby Carlyle undertakes to refashion common ideas about life and society." [110] The metaphor of tailoring or patching in the title is drawn from the central metaphor of the book, which purports to present to the English reading public the first translation of a great philosophical work on the "Philosophy of Clothes" by a heretofore obscure but preeminent German "Professor of Things in General." [111] The professor's name, Diogenes Teufelsdröckh, translates: "God-begotten Devil's-dung." [112] The essence of Teufelsdröckh's philosophy is that "everything under the sun can be seen as one form or another of clothing: ideas, institutions, manners, aristocracies, religions—all are kinds of outward representations. . . . What Teufelsdröckh's insight means is that all external reality is but the expression of a greater reality." [113] Some postmodern and Witt-

---

107. Karl Llewellyn, "Some Realism about Realism, A Reply to Dean Pound," 44 *Harvard Law Review* 1222 (1931).

108. Albert J. LaValley, *Carlyle and the Idea of the Modern* (New Haven, Conn., 1968), 6.

109. Background on Carlyle's novel is drawn from G. B. Tennyson's "Introduction" to his *A Carlyle Reader: Selections from the Writings of Thomas Carlyle* [1969] (Cambridge, England, 1984), 122–23.

110. Ibid., 122.

111. Teufelsdröckh, according to Carlyle, held the title *"Professor der Allerley-Wissenschaft,* or as we should say in English, 'Professor of Things in General,'" (all quotes and page references from Carlyle's novel are taken from the reprint of the complete novel in Tennyson, *Reader,* 135).

112. Ibid., 122.

113. Ibid.

gensteinian philosophers would undoubtedly find a disembodied language-as-symbol resonance with Carlyle's emphasis on the external representations of reality.[114] For Llewellyn, Carlyle's philosophy of clothes probably resonated more closely with his post–World War I generation's skepticism. Llewellyn partook generously of his generation's conflicts with institutional hypocrisy. His own correspondence reveals him as an active participant in the "roaring twenties" sexual revolution and as a frequent imbiber of bootleg liquor.[115]

Llewellyn rehearsed this skepticism about formal philosophy in a short article entitled "On Philosophy in American Law."[116] He admitted he was "not so much concerned . . . with the philosophers themselves, with whom indeed my acquaintance is but scanty," but nevertheless, he expressed his disdain for philosophers of law who tried to create grand theories rather than focusing on "philosophy-in-action."[117]

Llewellyn himself may have found this effort at philosophizing about legal philosophizing unsatisfactory. Four months after its publication, he tried his hand at satire in a piece he wrote for the *Harvard Law Revue*.[118] Unlike the Teufelsdröckh pieces, his "Equitabillegal Translation—A Reply" was published under Llewellyn's own name. "Equitabillegal Translation" was vintage mid-realist-debate Llewellyn. The ostensible object of derision in the piece was the tendency of legal writers to objectify the people and facts of a case, thereby emasculating its reality for the purpose of deriving a

---

114. A Lexis search for law review articles that mention "Wittgenstein" elicited 421 items. A modified search for "Wittgenstein and Llewellyn" resulted in 115 items. Wittgenstein is very popular; I will not cite all the legal postmodernist Wittgensteinian scholars out there; you know who you are. Llewellyn himself did not have much use for Wittgenstein's philosophy. In a jurisprudence lecture at the University of Chicago on March 28, 1955, he told his class: "[W]ho in hell among the 190,000 lawyers in the U.S. knows what logical positivism is. Not that anybody ought to know what it is, because it's crazy . . . this is the kind of thing that was inflicted upon us by the borrowing of German philosophy." KLP, C.M.1–2.

115. The personal correspondence and memorabilia that document Llewellyn's amorous trysts, parties he attended, and his liquor bills—none of which I am inclined to quote here—can be found in the recently opened X file in KLP.

116. Karl Llewellyn, "On Philosophy in American Law," 82 *University of Pennsylvania Law Review* 205 (1934).

117. Ibid., 206.

118. Most of the satirical pieces published in the *Revue* were originally oral presentations at the annual *Harvard Law Review* banquet. Karl Llewellyn, "Equitabillegal Translation—A Reply," Apr. 28, 1934, KLP, A.I.2.y.

desiccated formal doctrine. Llewellyn explained the idea thus: "*A and B* [the parties in the case] are translated. As by volcanic eruption, we are faced with *A* and *B* no longer. Where they once stood, stand now *V* and *P*; or *S* and *B*. . . . But where does the prevailing doctrine about *A* and *B* give us any slightest indication of *which direction* the inescapable translation will take? Where? I said: *Where?* No. Wholly discrete from those other semi-systematized bodies of pseudo-doctrine which are *supposed* to *follow* on translation has been kept the initial body of rule-stuff surrounding the innovating Aristotle—or amoeba-like transaction-originators *A* and *B*. Myopic. Absurd. And the year is 1934!" [119]

Beyond pointing out the absurdity of the formalist ideological position, Llewellyn's "Equitabillegal Translation" also poked fun at legal philosophy, legal philosophers, the general enterprise of academic law journals, and the realist debate itself—in which he and his colleagues were currently engaged. Llewellyn showed he had a sense of humor about their own *jurisprudery*: "The Realist Hypothesis—more accurately, *one* hypothesis indulged by *so many of* those newer workers as have not seen fit not so to indulge—has been that where terms insist on multimeaningness, closer analysis of the Fact Situations behind the Terms, Worms, worminess may—granted due intuitional correctives (and provided the investigator's psycho-analytic aberrations remain, or are kept, within the range from which they are not, despite attempted trace-jumping, allowed to depart)—give new and fruitful illumination. Let me repeat. (And repeat.)" [120] One footnote within this critical silliness alluded directly to his exchange with Roscoe Pound three years before: "See Llewellyn, *Some Bealism About Realism, Pro-Pounding to Dean Pound*, 44 Morbid Maw Rev. 1222, 1233 *et seq.*" [121] Another foot-

---

119. The text I am using is the edited version of the piece I found in the KLP. I have incorporated corrections added to the text and margins of the printed version in Llewellyn's handwriting. It is not clear whether these were corrections made to page proof or an early edition, or whether these were just Llewellyn's corrections to the published text made for himself in case he should ever publish the piece for general consumption. Either way, the changes were minor and arguably present a more perfect version according to Llewellyn. *5 Harvard Law Revue* 1, 2 (1934), KLP, A.I.2.y (emphasis in original).

120. Ibid., 2–3 (emphasis in original).

121. Ibid., 2 n.10. Also see N. E. H. Hull, "Some Realism about the Llewellyn-Pound Exchange over Realism: The Newly Uncovered Private Correspondence, 1927–1931," 1987 *Wisconsin Law Review* 921.

note mocked both his own genealogy of realist thought in his original reply to Dean Pound and a number of his realist allies:

> At this point my indebtedness to Max Weber, Sumner, W.R. Hearst, the Second Roosevelt, the Only Oliphant, More Moore, the Sears-Roebuck catalogue, Williston's Hörse Major, and Lydia Pinkham's Vegetable Compound will be obvious. But peculiarly to my friend Maltese Peter, whose unceasing attention to the manuscript has produced five several re-writings and needed improvement in both substance and presentation. Furthermore, I have somehow neglected thus far to cite my papers: An Unrealistic Jurisprudence—The Next Trap, But Slice Contract! An Essay for Defectives (The Aims, Conditions and Methods of Wasseal Research. Legal Sedition is Social Science Method). Legal Institutions and Jazz Economics. Raw Enforcement and Law Disturbance. But here they are. They may be irrelevant, but they are good.[122]

In yet another footnote, Llewellyn ridiculed law review footnotes themselves and his own pseudo-philosophizing: "*Ibid.* and into the future. There are MSS. My friend [Julius] Goebel insists that this paper sins throughout, in begnarled socio-jurisprudery. See West, Symbolography; Rabelais, Rabelais; Goebel, Table Talk."[123]

Llewellyn publicly debuted as the resurrected twentieth-century jurisprudential version of Carlyle's nineteenth-century German philosopher in a 1938 article in the *University of Chicago Law Review* entitled "Jurisprudence, The Crown of Civilization: Being Also the Principles of Writing Jurisprudence Made Clear to Neophytes." The article reeks of contempt for academic legal philosophizing.[124] In the years between 1931 and 1938, a flood of criticism of realism poured from the law journals, with no relief in sight. Llewellyn's first outing as "D. J. Swift Teufelsdröckh" might well have been inspired by the very deluge of law review articles he had helped stimulate. The basic theme of the article was a "thoughtful exposition," advice from a master to the uninitiated, of all the ways in which an ambitious

---

122. Llewellyn, 5 *Harvard Law Revue* 3 n.11 (1934). On the Llewellyn genealogy, see Hull, "Some Realism."

123. Llewellyn, 5 *Harvard Law Revue* 1 n.3 (1934). It is interesting to note that this may be the first time Llewellyn used a form of the term "jurisprude," which he would formally introduce in the *University of Chicago Law Review* article four years later.

124. Karl Llewellyn, "Jurisprudence, The Crown of Civilization," 5 *University of Chicago Law Review* 171 (1938).

young scholar might advance his career and bluff his way to a reputation as a wise "jurisprude."[125] In fact, Llewellyn only wanted the
last word. In the process, Llewellyn managed to impale every variety
of jurisprudential activity on the rapier of his wit.

Llewellyn's position, as laid out by his Teufelsdröckh alter ego,
was that jurisprudence contained few original insights and those
few ideas had to be constantly and cleverly reworked and recycled
by the ambitious newcomer who wished to make a name for himself in legal academia. "For where in all the field of burning oil has
callous Nature provided so little oil to burn, so many mouths to
feed? What law teacher, what tired or retired lawyer, what philosopher, what man of politics, what ism-ite, needs not his stake of Jurisprudence? Yet pause to observe the Sahara of Ideas which Nature
gives to work with, to stake out, to hold of right. Consider even that
Great Relation of Law and Justice around which Jurisprudence
turns (and should turn, and must be made to turn) as round a pole.
The available possibilities in natural or real ideas are desperately
limited."[126] Yet Llewellyn's pseudonymous sage counseled hope for
the neophyte. There were tried and true techniques by which "jurisprudes"[127] expanded these few primary insights into an unlimited
palette of pastel jurisprudential colors.

One method favored by experienced jurisprudes was to ally themselves with a "school" of jurisprudential thought.

> Are jurisprudes not legal historians as well? Do they know
> nothing of kneeling, hands placed between other hands? Surely
> he who commends himself to a lord, and swears him fealty, can
> acquire seisin strong and firm, and good legal right to full use
> of his lord's idea, so only due homage be regularly tendered. By
> this Principle of the School, of Teacher and Accredited Dis-
> ciples, this Principle of the Taught Tradition, Jurisprudence
> proudly makes five or ten and can make twenty livings grow
> where but one grew before. Only the lord of the school needs
> to do any thinking at all, or to have had a thought. A sub-

125. My quotation marks around "thoughtful exposition"—it was satire, after all.
"Bluff" is the least vulgar way of expressing this idea—a less acceptable but more common expression would probably be more accurate. The use of the masculine pronoun is
deliberate and historically accurate.

126. Llewellyn, "Crown," 171–72.

127. Llewellyn introduces this term in this article. See Hull, "The Romantic Realist,"
133–40. It makes its first appearance here in the first paragraph of the second page of the
article. Llewellyn, "Crown," 172.

infeudee can hold title to Anything, if he only holds under a first infeudee; and even though the latter may have done no thinking.[128]

As in the earlier "Equitabillegal Translation," some of Llewellyn's most biting comments were left to his footnotes. Llewellyn-Teufelsdröckh's footnote to the "Principle of the School" cut even closer to the bone of organized legal philosophizing.

> This is the positive, or directly creative, and only true application of the Principle of the School. Some have argued also that there is a negative, or dialectic-imputative application, which is more delicate. But this will be seen, on analysis, to resolve itself into a combination of the Hole, of Absolutism in Partiality, and of Non-citation, all discussed *infra*. A School is first set up as a Whole, including at least one man with at least one page of at least one writing capable of being devastatingly interpreted as characteristic of the Whole. Now the values of this are patent, and I should be the last to deny that the method represents a notable production-device for Jurisprudence at large. But it results not in the direct *creation* of any man's Property in Jurisprudence, but only in *enhancement of the value* of a Property created by other means. Eclipse is not creation, and even the neophyte can analyze closely enough to perceive this.[129]

While allying oneself with a "school," with a master on whose original thread of an idea one could weave a seemingly endless tapestry of unoriginal design, was one way of establishing oneself, this obviously would not serve the vast number of aspirants who sought jurisprudential recognition. There was, however, another method that promised to mint riches enough for all.

> Civilization moves from Natural Exchange into the Regime of Money, and then into the Regime of *Credit Currency* which can be held and owned. Jurisprudence, at one step, jumps several steps of Civilization. Observe: By introducing the principle of Multiguity of Terms, *pseudeas* can be produced, and fast enough to meet the need, and added to the theretofore available stuff and also held and owned in the modern world, as perfect currency. A well engraved and handsome *pseu*dea will buy as much as any *i*dea-gold, and more than some, just as

128. Llewellyn, "Crown," 172. Note that Llewellyn personally had few disciples, for he did not cultivate disciples. His *ideas* had adherents—and that seems to have been enough for him.

129. Ibid., 172 n.1 (emphasis in original).

a note may frequently be of more value than a bar of yellow metal . . . a crinkly, well-engraved pseudea will pass in the market, *in the absence of panic,* and never be presented for redemption. And the number of available pseudeas is truly limitless, even our great Masters having only opened up the gates of possibility. Regardless of the barrenness of soil or oil or Nature, in Real Ideas, then, we can see forty acres and a jurisprudential mule ahead for everyone.[130]

Llewellyn-Teufelsdröckh also proffered practical advice about "subsidiary but important principles of marketing" the young scholar's resulting work. Among these was the "Principle of Anonymous Non-Citation [which] [b]y itself, and in isolation, . . . might be well nigh worthless, but when coupled with the Principle of Multiguity of Terms (whose beauties are discussed above) and the Principle of Imputed Nonsense, it leads to results which gratify, and is easy enough, when once truly perceived, to be managed as well by the most untutored finger as by the hand of experience."[131] As an example of how the principle might be applied, Llewellyn, never afraid to mock his friends as well as his enemies, turned to his allies contributing to the realist debate then in progress:

Thus, if some young jurisprude wishes a stake in life, let him cry out loudly against Those who would make Rules the be-all and the end-all of the Law, and shout that Facts are needed. *Facts* has an appealing sound. And every lawyer knows from his own Lawyering that there is more to law than rules. If the jurisprude, emergent or ancient, has read nothing or has not understood what he has read, that is immaterial to his cry, since under the Principle of Anonymous Non-Citation he needs to cite nobody, much less a writing and a page; if he *has* read anything, he has only to add to his Anonymous Non-Citation a proper Imputation of Nonsense, to wit, under the Principle of Absolutized Partiality he will attribute to some, or many, or most among unnamed writers who may have said perhaps that Rules are Important the absurdity that Rules are *All*-important. His adversaries have, of course, only to deal with him in the same way. Having said he wants Facts, he is to be read as Wanting *Nothing But Facts;* having said he dislikes blind following of certain concepts, he is to be read as *Denying all Concepts.* Whom the jurisprude would destroy, he first makes seem mad.[132]

130. Ibid., 172–73 (emphasis in original).
131. Ibid., 175.
132. Ibid., 176 (emphasis in original).

The "philosopher" admitted, however, that the Principle of Anonymous Non-Citation was controversial and an alternative was "extensive citation [which] is the essence of Weight; and *sufficiently* extensive citation can be counted on to block off Inquiry by any but such as are already Initiate."[133] Another alternative was "citation from writers in foreign languages [who] are safe and sounding: no lawyer here reads German, French, Italian or Swiss, much less Chinese, Manchukuon, Hunanois or Peipingsh."[134] (Of course, it was widely known that Pound was multilingual.) The last alternative to Non-Citation suggested by the "Master" again reflected a contemporary trend among his own realist colleagues. "Citations in the more modern fashion also display a pleasing growth among the members of our Mystery, of right feeling. Instead of confining citation to books whose cards in the library catalog include the *Law* in the title, there has been a recent trend into psychology, pomology, embryology, theology, ethics, home economics, economics, politics, the sticks, the realisticks, and symbolic logic."[135]

Llewellyn's first Teufelsdröckh piece remains a classic exposition and critique of academic jurisprudery. It also lays out, in no uncertain terms, Llewellyn's deepest skepticism of and contempt for self-important legal philosophizing. But even as he burst the balloon of jurisprudes of every kind, he alluded to his alternative view of what law and legal thought might be. At one point, he criticized "borrowing" as a technique as "antisocial, *inartistic,* and unnecessary." Later, he suggested that "[i]n Jurisprudence, plagiarism is unnecessary, and therefore inartistic." At another point, he refers to "an artistic pseudea." He concluded that competing principles of citation ultimately fail because "I feel certain that this rests only in our Art's failure to get its Principles into clear consciousness." Admittedly, some of these references to art may have been only to suggest the sly "art" of the poseur, yet it is clear that Llewellyn appreciated even that as literary jurisprudence. Finally, in his "Appendix (A Letter Indicating Professor Teufelsdröckh's Plans for Revision)," he concluded "that Coordination of Principles and Harmony of Tone are the essence of any artistic and satisfying work in Jurisprudence."

133. Ibid. (emphasis in original).
134. Ibid., 177.
135. Ibid. One can only wonder, with so many mocking references to his realist colleagues, whether Llewellyn chose pseudonymous publication to protect himself not from his usual foes but from his friends.

In the last analysis, then, art was a necessary prerequisite to any jurisprudential work.[136]

Llewellyn's Teufelsdröckh inspired a rejoinder by one of the realists' critics, James J. Kearney, a professor at the University of Notre Dame College of Law. Kearney apparently found the article less than amusing. Even as he tried to emulate the light tone of the original, a certain amount of vitriol seeped through. For example, he reluctantly found it necessary to summarize the main points of the article "not because of any intent to make more widespread the ideas contained therein, but simply to render unnecessary a perusal of the article in the original." His main criticism was that Teufelsdröckh "counsels unlimited forgery and inflation [and] nowhere does he suggest one definite protector, one norm, or one factor of stability to be relied upon in the event of the inevitable panic [of the general revelation of these tactics]." Kearney missed the point of the piece, which was not to genuinely endorse these methods so much as to expose their existence and widespread adoption. Obviously antagonistic to the realists, Kearney latched onto Teufelsdröckh's own only half-serious criticism of them: "Who, for instance, even among the uninitiated fails to see the so-called realist as Teufelsdröckh pictures him—possessed of nothing, trying strenuously to crawl out of the 'hole' that threatens to engulf him?" Kearney attacked the author and his colleagues and suggested that the realists were losing the battle of words in the debate: "[A]fraid of defeat in open conflict, Teufelsdröckh counsels his cohorts from the grave to refrain from any definite encounter. In this admonition perhaps he was mindful of his own defeats in such encounters, or remembered the positive rout of Felix Cohen by Walter B. Kennedy."[137]

Perhaps it was because Kearney was able to turn Llewellyn's own work against him and his realist colleagues that Llewellyn later annotated the original typescript of the *University of Chicago Law Review* piece: "Very swell—but query the wisdom of publishing."[138] After reading Kearney's "Comment," Llewellyn wrote to him in polite terms. "I certainly hope that your paper will get into the hands of anyone who may feel tempted to take Teufelsdröckh's advice

---

136. Ibid., 176, 177, 173, 178, 181 (emphasis added).

137. James J. Kearney, "Comment: Posthumous Piffle," 14 *Notre Dame Lawyer* 98, 100, 101 (1938–39). Walter B. Kennedy and Felix Cohen had debated "functional nonsense" in 5 *Fordham Law Review* 272 (1936) and 6 *Fordham Law Review* 75 (1937).

138. Typescript with annotation can be found in KLP, Z.IV.2.

seriously. . . . Even most of those known as realists, including myself, will concur with you that Teufelsdröckh's announced principles
lead to 'jurisprudence' which is not only worthless but likely to be
vicious." [139]

Llewellyn's Teufelsdröckh next made his appearance in another
Harvard Law Revue piece, this one entitled "The Universal Solvent
of Jurisprudence; Or the Riddles Contradicted and the Contradic-
tions Unriddled." [140] This two-page contribution was far less ambitious than the *University of Chicago Law Review* piece and more
conventionally realist in its choice of target. It limited its attack to
the so-called "Truth within the Arcanum" of "high Jurisprudence"
that "[j]udges cannot make the Law, but find it only, and are bound
to follow." [141]

The remainder of Llewellyn's Teufelsdröckh opus can be found
in his unpublished manuscripts. [142] Some of these are incomplete
musings about Teufelsdröckh's life. Others are sustained attempts
to propound serious ideas about jurisprudence and law. Still others are poetic fragments that suggest the depths of Llewellyn-
Teufelsdröckh's feelings about the inherent beauty of law. Llewellyn
wrote and expanded on Teufelsdröckh's life story as though the
character might become the professor's Doppelgänger. Then the
two might collaborate on a grand work on jurisprudence to be published under Teufelsdröckh's name.

One such portrait, entitled "Teuf[elsdröckh].Pref[ace].1," described the "philosopher" as "the greatest jurist of twenty-seven
centuries." The biography conceded that he is "almost unknown in
the Western legal world. . . . Even Dean Pound has failed to give us
an account of his work, actually pretending to ascribe a primacy to
[Hans] Kelsen over Teufelsdröckh which would verge on the laugh-
able if it had been seriously intended." In this same sketch, Llewellyn confessed to being a personal confidant of the late sage: "I count
myself no mean scholar in the law as such things go among us; but
Teufelsdröckh's conversation bogged me regularly within three minutes. That I had the honor to meet him was accident. He was at
work on his American papers, and wanted to listen to at least one

139. Llewellyn to James J. Kearney, Dec. 2, 1938, KLP, R.XI.3.
140. 6 *Harvard Law Revue* 1 (May 1940); I have copies from both the Karl Llewellyn
Papers and the Roscoe Pound Papers at Harvard Law School Library.
141. Ibid.
142. KLP, Z file.

American talk, and I was in Nempenusquam studying the glorious Byzogothic of the cathedral." Llewellyn then admitted to his inadequacy in presenting a coherent jurisprudence for Teufelsdröckh: "I must apologize for not giving a picture of Teufelsdröckh's majestic philosophy of law and legal institutions. The scraps I gathered are inspiration, but I cannot piece them together: chips from the stoneworkers' shed that crouches by the Cathedral." He concluded with an anecdote about Teufelsdröckh's idiosyncratic use of language, suggestive of Llewellyn's attitude toward his own idiosyncrasies: "One thing I did understand, which may give a first glimmering of his range and power. I asked diffidently about the daring of his mixed metaphors. He paused in characteristic and benignant tolerance: 'Young man,' he said, as if talking to a questioning child, 'A metaphor is *mixed* when it is botched. My metaphors are cumulative creative synthesis of overtone, undertone, and connotation.'"[143]

Llewellyn, who never completed an original book of his own on jurisprudence,[144] did outline a grand work that he identified as Teufelsdröckh's. The sections of the "book" look like other outlines Llewellyn wrote without the Teufelsdröckh nom de plume.[145] They include "Keys to J[uris]p[ru]d[e]ns," "Law & Social Science," "Primitive Law," "Sales," and "Phil[osophical] Legal Inst[itutions]."[146] Only a few of the "chapters" show up in any form in the manuscripts. One of these is "Chapter III.v *Teufelsdröckh on the Veil of Jurisprudence.*"[147] The "chapter" is only three pages of text, but it reveals something of Llewellyn-Teufelsdröckh's artistic vision of jurisprudence. He wrote, for example, that "[i]n legal philosophy, as in case-law, the 'holding' or the 'true principle' of an opinion requires art and scalpel before it is dissected cleanly from the surrounding tissue of 'dictum.'" Then, writing as himself talking about the Master, he concluded that "[t]he esthetic received at his hands a devotion matching his ardor for truth, practicality, and

143. All quotes from "Teuf.Pref.1" in KLP, Z file (emphasis in original).

144. Llewellyn never wrote a general book about jurisprudence or realism, though he had apparently made several false starts in an effort to do so. There are outlines and what appears to be a long book proposal for such a work among his manuscripts. Instead, near the end of his life, he collected a number of his previously published essays into a compendium that was published after his death. Karl Llewellyn, *Jurisprudence: Realism in Theory and Practice* (Chicago, 1962).

145. Llewellyn, "New Trends in Jurisprudence" enclosure, KLP, B.I.6.a–c.

146. Handwritten outline on legal pad headed "Teuf: Keys to Jpdns," KLP, Z file.

147. Typescript in KLP, Z file, 3 pp.

the ideal. And not without success. I have myself little love for the styles of Louis Quinze, but this fine tract on the Veil, for all its rococo entitlement, seems to me no unsuccessful venture into the quest for Beauty."

A longer work by Teufelsdröckh entitled "The Nature of the Jurisprudences" may or may not have been intended as part of the larger "book."[148] Here, too, Llewellyn referred to "our art of jurisprudence" and "[t]he judge's art." But the emphasis in this piece, a theme that recurred in Llewellyn's later writing and played a significant role in his *Common Law Tradition*, was the "crafts" of law. Teufelsdröckh argued that traditional jurisprudence slighted the various roles of "craft" in the law and legal system. Yet "craft" for Teufelsdröckh encompassed creation and beauty as well: "[E]ven the neophyte in jurisprudence, and even the general run of craftsmen themselves have also to be sheltered from the too bright sun of truths for which their eyes are not prepared. Some always will find out for themselves some portion, even a great portion of the truth. They are those born to it; they cannot be prevented. Them we must search out, and must take them into the guild."[149]

Llewellyn strongly identified with his creation. Some of the writings as well as other odd remnants attest to this fact. For example, there is a sheet of stationery from the Hotel Sherry in Chicago on which Llewellyn noted "KNL communed with [the spirit of] T at Hotel Sherry, 1960. see Register."[150] There are also two poems Llewellyn signed with either "D.J.S.T." or Teufelsdröckh's name that relate to commercial law—Llewellyn's personal area of expertise not usually associated with Teufelsdröckh. One, "On Construing the Uniform Revised Sales Act, As a Whole, Please, As a Whole," was obviously written in the late 1930s or early 1940s as Llewellyn struggled with his own revision of Williston's act. The other, dated 1949 (long after Teufelsdröckh's ostensible demise),

148. Typescript in KLP, Z file, 8 pp. A note at the end of the manuscript suggests that Llewellyn was moved to write the piece after reading Kearney's comment in *Notre Dame Lawyer*. That would date the typescript around 1938. The aforementioned outline, while undated, lists as one of the proposed "chapters" something on the "Federal Sales Bill and Beyond," which would place the outline in roughly the same time period.

149. Ibid.

150. KLP, Z file. When I consulted the file, it was stored in a suitcase in one of the file drawers housing the Karl Llewellyn Papers. These files may now have been refiled in the drawer without the suitcase. Communing with spirits is again in vogue. See Derrick Bell, *And We Are Not Saved* (New York, 1987), 7 (fictitious Geneva Crenshaw speaks to Bell).

was apparently inspired by a quote from James M. Landis in the *Harvard Law Record:* "The second year was *essentially* dull. *Despite the best teaching,* who can put life into Bills and Notes, Sales, or Wills?" Teufelsdröckh's answer to the question is revealing of Llewellyn's sense of identification with his creation: "Who can put life into Drafts, Notes and Chex / Who can put life into Sales? / Mentschikoff. Let's not be fooled by her sex." [151]

Given the close affinity between Llewellyn and Teufelsdröckh, one wonders if the former's assessment of the latter, in another manuscript entitled "The Jurisprudence of Teufelsdröckh," may have really been an echo of Llewellyn's ultimate evaluation of his own jurisprudential achievement: "Diogenes Jonathan Swift Teufelsdröckh will always remain a puzzle. He cut so deeply, saw so clearly, phrased so shrewdly, gave so much light on things of law and on all the problems of the institution of law—as much in my judgment as any other combined score of thinkers who have written—yet he missed so much." [152]

As his Teufelsdröckh essays suggest, at least in part, by the late 1930s Llewellyn saw the law and legal system as "art." Llewellyn explicitly stated this when he wrote that "the perfect philosopher of law had to be a sound artist; he had indeed to be an eager artist. . . ." [153] To him, "the esthetics of advocacy are closely related to the performing arts—music, drama, dance. . . ." [154] He was devoted to the idea of the literary beauty of law. He wrote, "Beauty in things of law has been slighted as if by law. . . . Law, men have thought, is a thing of words, and literature is the appropriate art to measure by; and how shabby does the resulting measurement appear, when 'art' in things of law is seen or sought in an image or turn of phrase. . . . Such is a common run of thinking among those who have meditated upon law as being thus a matter of words: an illadvantaged distant cousin of belles lettres, too doltish, for the most part, to be hungry for improvement." [155]

151. Both poems can be found in KLP, Z file.
152. Handwritten manuscript on legal pad and later typewritten transcription, KLP, Z file.
153. Llewellyn, "On the Good."
154. Quote from a note Llewellyn added to "On the Good" when it was to be republished in the volume *Jurisprudence,* 167.
155. Ibid., 171.

For Llewellyn, Teufelsdröckh was a temporary retreat, a private world of witticism and parody, though one still rooted in realism. But there was no place to retreat from the spreading darkness of the age. If only he could be free from the strife of the times to think about law. One undated poem, from context almost certainly written in the period between 1936 and 1939, captured this yearning and the ambition behind it. He titled it "A Professional's Prayer at Twilight":

> The Communists march in the streets tonight—
> The Fascists polish their armor bright—
> Away! You joggle my arm as I write.
>
> Follow the left for cosmic relief,
> Follow the Right and banish world-grief
> But let me alone to finish my brief.
>
> Tomorrow the Communists take up their sway,
> Tonight the Fascists arm for the fray
> Leave me! My work must be done today!
>
> Leftist and Rightist, joy in your passions!
> Rightist and Leftist, your power increases!
> But mine is the hand which finally fashions—
> Let me have quiet to pick up the pieces.[156]

Hardly the sentiments of the valiant defender of Sacco and Vanzetti, or even the would-be state Democratic committeeman, this plea for the real world to go away. But Llewellyn would bleed a little and then rise up to fight again, for his retreat had not taken him far from his jurisprudence at all, just into its lusher, more exotic regions. And that only for a brief respite.

156. Undated, KLP, B.VI.2.

CHAPTER SIX

Pound Moves to the Right
and Llewellyn Applies Himself

The controversies of the 1930s among the academic jurisprudents had turned a polite (if not always admiring) circle of acquaintances and friends into snappish cadres of ideologues. Karl
Llewellyn had wanted to stir the broth, but had not counted on the
rise of Nazism or the staying power of natural law theories. Roscoe
Pound had tried to manage the dispute, or at least broker compati-
bility among the disputants, but his power as a mediator declined
with the loss of his office. As a university professor, he retained his
status in the academic world. He still wrote letters of introduction
and gave invited lectures, but he could not promise to find employment for or grant postgraduate fellowships to others.

If events beyond their control had driven Pound's and Llewellyn's
positions apart, at least some of the implications of their two philosophies were conducive to that separation. Sociological jurisprudence
was progressive; it had faith in experts, in the power of well-trained,
well-meaning intellect to sort out and realign the world. Thus, Pound
believed, with good reason, that his later emphasis on reducing friction in litigation was the natural consequence of his sociological approach. He tried to apply that philosophy in his studies of crime,
and if these failed to reduce the crime rate, they did provide an aegis
for major studies like the Gluecks' of juvenile delinquency. Even
Pound's objections to administrative agencies were not attacks so
much on expertise as on expertise concentrated in one set of institutions, unchecked by other institutions. In 1946, Pound would accept the invitation of Chiang Kai-shek to visit China and rewrite its
legal system. Such a task would have daunted another, and there are

those who might conclude that Pound was seduced by the lavish pay. While there is some truth to that charge, a close reading of the reports he wrote demonstrates his continuing faith in objective, dispassionate outside expertise to reform an ongoing system.

Llewellyn's realism grew in a different direction because one of its core tenets was the efficacy of insider knowledge, expressing itself in local custom and action. Llewellyn's now-infamous dictum that "law was what law officials did" gave pride of place to actual behavior over abstract ideas or rules. His rule skepticism was thus never cynical or anarchical. Quite the contrary—he merely shifted the focus of jurisprudence to a microscopic level. In studies he was soon to complete of the Cheyenne criminal justice system and of the way that merchants did business with each other in order to develop a Uniform Commercial Code, he insisted on the legitimate priority of local insider "law-stuff" over outside, overarching expert rules.

Some of the increasingly divergent thinking of the two men was played out in private conversations over the academic networks they created and nurtured. The purpose of the private discourse was twofold: to test ideas and to create ideational alliances. Of course, the personal conversation also buoyed sagging spirits and enervated tired minds. Pound might no longer be a dean and Llewellyn might have isolated himself from some of the patriotic currents of the day, but both men were still cherished academic figures. Networks so long in the making withstood the passage of time and the alterations of fortune of their creators.

John Henry Wigmore and Pound regarded each other with the gruff admiration and fondness of two men who had been through nearly a half-century together. Wigmore was readying a second series of translated works on modern legal philosophy. Once more, Pound's opinion was solicited. Would he consent to supervise the translations?[1] Pound thought that little new of merit had been published, and most of that was "phenominalist or "ultra-skeptical." He was not pleased by recent scholarship, but he encouraged Wigmore.[2]

Herbert Goodrich, not at all offended by Pound's brusk refusal to accept the presidency of the National Lawyers Guild, still courted

1. John Henry Wigmore to Roscoe Pound, Nov. 3, 1939, RPP, 89-25 (enclosing Wigmore memorandum to the executive committee of the AALS dated November 3, 1939).

2. Pound to Wigmore, Nov. 6, 1939, RPP, 89-25.

Pound's goodwill. Goodrich was dean at Penn, and that made up some of the difference in age. "Once upon a time you and I talked a little bit about scientific methods in the law, and its relation to natural science and things like that," Goodrich recalled early in 1940. "You immediately suggested the analogy was not to the things like chemistry and biology and I could see at once that things were starting to go in your active mind as they always do when you have an idea.[3] You told me at that time that you would write a paper about that sometime and I have been watching ever since to see the paper. I hope that you are going to write it and, do more than that, hope that you are going to write it this year and perhaps you will let us publish it in the University of Pennsylvania Law Review."[4] For Goodrich, the offer was the extension of the right hand of fellowship to Pound, who had done little real original work of late. The network was what mattered to both men.

Pound and Llewellyn corresponded, praising each other, encouraging each other, perhaps more out of habit than expectation of real results. Pound opined that Llewellyn's interest in anthropology opened up lines of inquiry of interest to both men. Llewellyn was glad to hear it and urged Pound to take up again his magnum opus, the big book on sociological jurisprudence. Pound replied that he was so busy he could not find the time. Llewellyn rejoined that he and Edwin Patterson, long Pound's admirer at Columbia, wanted to incorporate Pound's most important jurisprudential essays into the class they taught. Would he help them select the pieces? Business as usual, although the correspondence had a formality absent from Pound's letters to others he knew less well than Llewellyn and Llewellyn's letters had a stiffness uncharacteristic of his often flushed frankness.[5] He saw an aging Pound drifting toward certitudes that

---

3. It was an old idea—for by 1919 Pound had likened the biological stage of sociological jurisprudence to the infatuation with Darwinism at the end of the nineteenth century. Pound, Jurisprudence Seminar Notes, 1919, RPP, 184-8, p. 58.

4. Herbert Goodrich to Pound, Jan. 25, 1940, RPP, 65-16.

5. Karl Llewellyn to Pound, May 1940, RPP, 142-6 (KNL likes RP's piece in *Cincinnati Law Review* on ideals in the law; can RP be more specific?); Pound to Llewellyn, May 13, 1940, KLP, R.XVI (RP spoke there off the cuff and does not remember what he said, nor does he have a reprint; wants to get together with KNL sometime); Llewellyn to Pound, Oct. 25, 1940, RPP, 142-6 (KNL has read Pound's paper in *The Creative Intelligence* and will recommend it to students); Pound to Llewellyn, Oct. 28, 1940, KLP, R.XVI.5 (thanks for noticing, and has KNL also noticed that teachers are now regarded as mill hands?); Llewellyn to Pound, Nov. 7, 1940, RPP, 142-6 (encourages RP to bring

the young Pound had dismissed as the conceits of the schoolmen of jurisprudence. What Pound said about the ideals of law had substance, but little weight.[6]

At his specially made circular desk at Harvard (allowing him to put his various projects on and below the desk top and wheel around to them with ease), Pound opened and replied to the letters from other members of his gradually shrinking circle. He still churned out essays, talks, and lectures.[7] With retirement, his teaching load had increased, and he loved it.[8] Pound was called on to bear the administrative burden of staffing courses to replace men gone to Washington or farther afield. With the realities of retirement had come to Pound a different kind of reality, a recognition that jurisprudence did not change the world; that its powers, like his, were limited.

He had time to travel—he always loved travel—and travel still brought honors and invitations. His many Asian students at Harvard Law School invited him to give lectures in China and Japan, which he visited in 1936 and 1937. World War II would not begin in Europe, like the first, but in Africa and Asia, with Italy's invasion of Ethiopia and Japan's investiture of China. Pound never visited the front lines, but everywhere he sensed the coming crisis. He toured in Europe and the Near East shortly before the outbreak of World War II, passing through areas that would become the cockpit of war in a month's time.[9] He made no mention of politics, absolutism, or law in his letters to his sister Olivia, yet he could see the lights going out all over the world once again.[10] His jurisprudence examinations

out his book); Pound to Llewellyn, Nov. 15, 1940, RPP, 142-6 (recalls his days with Hohfeld and how they used to send twenty- and thirty-page letters to each other to thrash out arcane points, but RP is too old for that now); Pound to Llewellyn, Feb. 27, 1942, RPP, 142-6 (congratulates KNL on *Cheyenne Way*); Llewellyn to Pound, Apr. 14, 1942, RPP, 142-6 (wants RP to review the book and asks for Pound's choices for the jurisprudence course).

6. Llewellyn, Lecture on Jurisprudence, Nov. 12, 1941, KLP, C.F.1–3.

7. Pound to E. E. Luther, May 6, 1940, RPP, 175-3.

8. Pound to Olivia Pound, Oct. 23, 1939, NSHS, MS 911, box 1, folder S.1, vol. F.6.

9. Pound to Olivia Pound, Sept. 26, 1939, NSHS, MS 911, box 1, folder S.1, vol. F.6.

10. Two days after Pearl Harbor, he wrote to Olivia: "Many thanks for the pears. They are really wonderful." Regrets on Judge Munger's death. Waiting for his new book on administration of justice. Nothing on the war. Pound to Olivia Pound, Dec. 9, 1941, NSHS, MS 911, box 1, folder S.1, vol. F.6.

obliquely reflected the world situation. The first two questions in 1940 were "What have you to say to the theory of law as an aggregate of threats of exercise of the force of politically organized society?" and "What are the points of contact between law and morals?"[11]

Perhaps jurisprudence still had the power to make these future soldiers (and if they survived the next war, future lawyers) think hard. But Pound could have told his students that sociological jurisprudence, no matter how elegant, no matter how versatile, could not prevent the coming war. As he wrote in 1940, "I remember as a small boy, some sixty-odd years ago, when the memory of the Civil War was still green, being taken by my father to hear one of the great preachers of the time. The sermon made a great impression since the burden [of it] was that we were living in a time and country without parallel in history, and that greater and deeper and more far reaching changes had taken place in our time than at any time since the middle ages. I was full of this idea and told my father what a wonderful thing it was to have been born in such a time and to be growing up in a world where we could cancel all that had gone before and begin anew with a clean slate. Well, said my father, in substance, I shouldn't be too sure of that . . . [T]he past is not so easily disposed of. Civilization is an accumulated experience, ordered and developed by reason, constitutions and bills of rights and our law and judicial application of that law, have behind them the political and legal and judicial experience of government under constitutions for a century and a half."[12]

Pound was tired of trying to change the world, and he refused to put his trust in any "superhuman leader" who saw, when others were blind, "the general good," nor did Pound subscribe to the "superstition" that a "science" of law would save anyone. Had the case for the administrative state sounded in "social utility," he might have been more forgiving, but all he heard now was discourses on hunches and discretion. Unlike the old student of Rudolph von Ihering and Eugen Ehrlich he once was, Pound now would no longer buy into "Continental political and juristic theory" with its "strange political and juristic gods." He preferred "sound Anglo-Saxon sense."

11. Pound, Jurisprudence Examination, Law School of Harvard University, 1940, RPP, 175-3.
12. Roscoe Pound, *Contemporary Juristic Theory* (New York, 1940), 2–3.

If Pound sounded a lot like Robert Fowler had, more than twenty-five years before, he did not admit his backsliding. Instead, he called the "give-it-up" philosophies to account. He conceded that realism had taken as its portion "stimulating us to be zealous and vigilant to increase the effectiveness of the political and legal order" and that the "economic interpretation" was, over the large span of time and place, probably correct. But lawyers and judges had to hold themselves to a standard that was not wholly description. They had to ask and answer questions of values, not just of function and behavior.[13]

Pound tried to do this in his contribution to *My Philosophy of Law*, but admitted to Wigmore that his effort was substandard. He was sick with a grippe the whole time.[14] Instead of a simple summary, Pound tried to squeeze more than a half-century of writing about jurisprudence into a short compass. Bits and pieces of the many Pounds floated on the surface of the essay like the flotsam of a shipwreck after a storm. There was a fragment of "interests" and some "psychology," a paragraph or two on the "give-it-up" philosophies, and an injunction to study the relationship between law and morals. History was no longer a guide. There were ideals to be found, but Pound had nothing specific to say about them. Pound admitted as much in his last sentence: "If we are inclined to scoff at the practitioner, let us remember the warning of William James that the worst enemies of a subject are the professors thereof." Pound's essay is not worth the effort of summary, but his last sentence is full of meaning. He returned to William James, one of his favorite pragmatists, to make the point that the truth of any jurisprudence lay in its applicability to the work of people in the field. A jurisprudence that did not help them was a waste of time. Professors who sought only profundity (as Pound had in the previous thirteen pages) must stumble.[15] It was as close as Pound ever came in his career to confessing error.

As the acuity of Pound's intellectual vision faltered (actually he had complained about his failing eyesight and the need to dictate his papers and letters for the past thirty years), Llewellyn's grew

13. Ibid., 9, 10, 17, 13, 14, 47–48.
14. Pound to Wigmore, Oct. 28, 1941, RPP, 89-25.
15. Roscoe Pound, "My Philosophy of Law," in *My Philosophy of Law* (Boston, 1941), 262.

stronger. It is plain that Llewellyn's retreat into parody had been not a flight from realism at all, but a retreat in another sense. Entire faculties of university departments now go on such retreats to find renewed purpose in a common labor. In two projects, begun during the 1930s but finished in the 1940s, Llewellyn asserted Carlyle's "everlasting yea." The two major projects into which Llewellyn threw himself at the end of the decade were collaborative and in many ways empirical. They even involved data gathering of an eclectic sort.

One of the stories that Llewellyn told about himself and the other realists was that there was a bright line distinction between the realist critics and the empiricists, that is, between men like himself and Jerome Frank and Thurman Arnold, on the one hand, and Hessel Yntema, Walter Wheeler Cook, Herman Oliphant, and Underhill Moore, on the other. That was a line he drew in the years when the fight over Oliphant's deanship was brewing at Columbia. Llewellyn underscored it in his criticisms of academics in the "scientific camp," and they recognized the distinction, although they regarded their work as the more important of the two wings of the realist approach.[16] He did not forbid himself to cross the line, however, and in the wake of the attack on realism, which too often blurred the distinction, he had no need to rationalize his empiricism at the end of the decade. Indeed, in an unsent reply to Walter Kennedy's "Realism, What Next," Llewellyn promised "more realism."[17]

Llewellyn's withdrawal from the storm at the end of the 1930s did not signal a renunciation of realism, then, so much as his determination to reinvent his jurisprudence. The failure of the new "science of law" (for fail it did; the institute researchers scurried off to find regular law faculty jobs or employment with the burgeoning federal government, the Yale empiricists going off to do their magic in Washington, D.C., where they joined the Harvard liberals) actually created a niche for his work. He no longer had to jostle with

16. See, e.g., Hessel Yntema, "What Price Realism," 31 *Columbia Law Review* 925 (1931): "But the essential genius of this interest is scientific and not really 'realistic' or 'jurisprudential' in any precise sense." Two years later, Yntema dismissed Llewellyn's thinking as a "half-way house" between the old speculative philosophizing and the new science. Hessel Yntema, "The Implications of Legal Science," 10 *New York University Law Quarterly Review* 309 (1933).

17. Walter Kennedy, "Realism, What Next," 7 *Fordham Law Review* 203 (1938) (arguing that realism was being replaced by "surrealism"—to wit, Arnold's *Symbols*); Llewellyn, More Realistic Realism Is Next, n.d., KLP, B.II.41.

squadrons of trained surveyors gathering and interpreting data for others. He just needed time and quiet. The task, of course, was to apply realism to understand, critique, and change the law. That was the essence of his search for an American jurisprudence. Just as the younger Pound had assayed the power of sociological jurisprudence to remake criminal law, so Llewellyn was looking for a way to prove that realism was not just sterile intellectual egotism. It had to make a difference, and the right kind of difference.

As he wrote in "My Philosophy of Law" in 1941, "That whole [law] is most fruitfully viewed as a going institution, and a necessary institution, in society. And a going institution is of course never made up of rules alone, nor of ideals alone. It may contain rules as one of its parts. In the case of our own law, the institution contains as one of its parts a . . . tremendously important body of rules, organized (quite loosely) around concepts and shot through with principles. Indeed, companioning these rules and principles of 'law' proper, there are other rules and other concepts: the formulated techniques of 'precedent,' of 'construction' and the like, to guide manipulation of the first. But over and above these, the going institution of our law contains an ideology and a body of pervasive and powerful ideals which are largely unspoken, largely implicit, and which pass almost unmentioned in the books." Llewellyn wanted to expand jurisprudence to cover the life of the law "out beyond the rules."

He was not arguing, as Underhill Moore had, for a close systematic study of everyday functioning of institutions. Instead, Llewellyn was a holist and coined the term "law-jobs" to serve as his unit of analysis. In these law-jobs, it was not the mere behavior that interested him; that would be reductionist, and Llewellyn was not a simplifier. He loved complexity and reveled in it. Jurisprudence was the study of the entire mechanism that any society created to deal with the "trouble-case," or the case of allocation when resources were scarce, or the channeling of behavior in right ways. Jurisprudence was the study of group ways and established traditions, not of rules, but of expectations, not out of books, but out of people's thoughts. "Reaching into the law-jobs takes one at first out into the whole baffling field of the ways and nature of society." And then "the technical ways of law gain pattern because their function can be seen, and each detailed device invites its check-up against experience." But not just for the study of it, or the science of the law—not in

1941 at least and, for Llewellyn, not really before the war either. "The art of building such rules I hold that jurisprudence can recapture and spread, on a democratic scale, among the craftsmen. A long haul it may be, but a good haul to get back and shoulders into. In accomplishing this, jurisprudence also places itself in the world." [18]

First and foremost, of course, realism was a perspective, a way of thinking about law. The watchword was that law was a kind of behavior, an institution. As Llewellyn told his students in his lectures on Pound's "ideals" in the law, the ideal has no substance unless it "is a principle which also makes life-sense." Purely legal principles are meaningless "except in doctrine." Of course, Pound was talking about political principles, but Llewellyn did not tell the students that. He merely used Pound to make the point.[19] What Pound should have done and Llewellyn was prepared to do was to look into the penumbras of the law, into real-life situations, and find those principles. By the end of the decade, Llewellyn began his course in jurisprudence with the law-crafts and the law-jobs. Only after he had instilled in the students the fact that law was an institution did he turn to the more traditional approaches of natural law, positive-analytical law, and the historical and sociological schools.[20] Thus, it was natural for him to search for a quasi-laboratory situation to test his tenets. He wanted to find a legal system that was less complicated and more direct than the common law system. Then the identification of law with law-stuff and law-ways would be easier to spot.

Llewellyn had already cast about for such a laboratory of realism and had found one in the jurisprudence of the plains peoples of North America. His guide was a longtime friend and junior collaborator, the anthropologist E. Adamson Hoebel. The result, published in 1941, was *The Cheyenne Way*.[21] For a bricoleur, such a side-step was hardly surprising. The story began at Columbia, where anthropologists Franz Boas and his student Ruth Benedict

18. Karl Llewellyn, "My Philosophy of Law," in *My Philosophy of Law* (Boston, 1941), 183, 184, 186, 187, 195, 196, 197.

19. Llewellyn, Jurisprudence Lecture, Nov. 12, 1941, KLP, C.F.1–3, pp. 3, 7. But note that in pen, at the top of the typed first page, Llewellyn had written, "[A]dd a solid technical discussion of the use of doctrine." After all, they were law students, and it was a law school course he was teaching.

20. Llewellyn, Jurisprudence Overall Outline '49, Last Desk Pad, KLP, V.IV.

21. Karl N. Llewellyn and E. Adamson Hoebel, *The Cheyenne Way: Conflict and Case Law in Primitive Jurisprudence* (Norman, Okla., 1941).

labored at the center of a revolution in their field. Using their field work among the Native Americans, the German-born Boas and the American-born Benedict connected past to present, showing the adaptivity and persistence of cultures. They treated native religions not as amusing artifacts of primitivism, but as parts of ongoing social customs, a powerful spur to comparative studies. With Alfred Kroeber, Robert Lowie, and Englishman A. R. Radcliffe-Brown, the two Columbia professors invented cultural anthropology. They made the alien familiar.[22]

They also tutored a generation of social scientists in tolerance. As Benedict wrote in the first chapter of her best-selling *Patterns of Culture*, "[T]he study of different cultures has another important bearing upon present-day thought and behavior. Modern existence has thrown many civilizations into close contact, and at the moment the overwhelming response to this situation is nationalism and racial snobbery. There has never been a time when civilization stood more in need of individuals who are genuinely culture-conscious, who can see objectively the socially conditioned behavior of other peoples without fear and recrimination."[23] Llewellyn could not have agreed more. His realism was supposed to have exactly the same effect—not cynicism, but enlightened self-critical reform.

In 1932, Boas and Benedict introduced one of their students, E. Adamson Hoebel (Ad to his many friends), to Llewellyn. Hoebel, born in Wisconsin in 1906 and educated there and in Cologne, earned his master's at New York University in 1930 working on the subject of delinquent boys. For his Ph.D., he wanted to work with the Plains Indians, arguing that the Comanche, long regarded as the most cynical and treacherous of the plains tribes, had a system of laws. Boas and Benedict were not so sure, but brought in Llewellyn to help on the dissertation committee. He was intrigued, as he later wrote. Llewellyn's interest in American criminal law paralleled Hoebel's earlier work. On November 1, 1934, Hoebel walked into Llewellyn's office and expressed an interest in a collaboration—a book on Indians and law. Llewellyn was pleased.[24] This was a chance to revisit the field of collaboration not as a junior partner (as

22. Clifford Geertz, *Works and Lives: The Anthropologist as Author* (Stanford, Calif., 1988), 107; Margaret M. Caffrey, *Ruth Benedict: Stranger in This Land* (Austin, Tex., 1989), 103–15, 124–31, 136–240.

23. Ruth Benedict, *Patterns of Culture* (New York, 1934), 10.

24. Llewellyn to Emma Corstvet, Nov. 2, 1934, Emma Corstvet Papers, Bryn Mawr College Library.

he had been with Pound in 1930), but as the senior author in the new study of the law-ways of the Cheyenne. Unlike the Comanche, hunters from the southern Utah steppe driven onto the plains by the arrival of the warlike Sioux in the eighteenth century, the Cheyenne had been farmers, but they, too, suffered displacement by the great shuffling of tribes in the seventeenth and eighteenth centuries.[25]

The two men became fast friends, as did their spouses. Emma Corstvet went west with Karl and Ad for field work among the Cheyenne in 1935. Llewellyn had strongly supported the Comanche project in a report to the sponsoring agency. This time, it was Llewellyn who was the mentor, and his use of the academic networks and institutional supports to aid Hoebel would have done Pound proud. Of the Comanche and related studies, Llewellyn was pleased to reveal to the dean of the Faculty of Arts and Sciences at Columbia, "So much, however, is already clear: that further comparative study offers promise of value not only in itself, but also in the light it may be hoped to shed on the interrelation of political and legal developments."[26] Hoebel had finished his dissertation on the Comanche that spring and with his first wife was doing field work. Llewellyn was delighted. Here was a true test of the efficacy of local knowledge, for the Cheyenne were quite content with their law-ways.

The two men got to work. Much of their correspondence reflected the mundane concerns of publication and editing, but some of it captured the essence of their collaboration. Hoebel was pleased to report to Llewellyn that after the latter's ten days of field work in the summer of 1935, the Cheyenne had changed his name from "Stump Horn" (a physical caricature of Llewellyn) to "Shimmering, falling as Glass," which Hoebel explained likened Llewellyn to a medicine man who "stands and shakes himself so that all that brilliant stuff showers off of him like snow." For his own part, "Hoebel bows before a greater chief."[27]

25. In a domino-like motion, the arrival of the Europeans had driven the Iroquois confederation to expand west, pushing against the Great Lakes tribes, including the Assiniboine and others. The most successful of these migrants were the Sioux, and they arrived on the plains in time to displace the Pawnee, Kiowa, Cheyenne, and Comanche, among others. See Richard White, *The Middle Ground: Indians, Empires, and Republics in the Great Lakes Region, 1650–1815* (Cambridge, Mass., 1991), 1–49; Alvin M. Josephy, Jr., *The Patriot Chiefs* (New York, 1961), 260–64.

26. Llewellyn to Howard L. McBain, Oct. 9, 1934, E. Adamson Hoebel Papers, American Philosophical Society Library, Philadelphia (hereinafter APS).

27. E. Adamson Hoebel to Llewellyn, Nov. 2, 1935, KLP, R.VIII.13.

Hoebel and Llewellyn expected that Hoebel could plunge into the field work, aided by translators, and reveal the working parts of the Cheyenne legal system. But that was not to be. A year later, a dispirited Hoebel wrote from the trail, "After our first ventures we were all pretty badly worn down, so that I thought it might be most reasonable to cancel the study and return the funds. Now I think a short, intensive study concentrated in effort and focusing of attention on our mainest problems will probably be the best thing."[28] Two weeks later, on the reservation, "the plugging is paying slow dividends. I am afraid our success average in field work was running a little too high. Fortune is determined to scale it down." A drought that stretched from Oklahoma to the Black Hills had withered the Indian grasslands. Grasshoppers and crickets gnawed the stubble. Everyone was on edge. A reality undreamt of in Llewellyn's philosophy was playing tricks on Hoebel. Only the arrival of a Hollywood crew to film Gary Cooper in *The Plainsman* saved the day. Two hundred fifty Indians were hired on as extras at $3.50 a day and then struck for $5.00. The studio anted up, and the Indians finished the job. Meanwhile, Hoebel had to chase all over trying to get his informants to sit down and tell their stories. Lo and behold, it turned out that the incidents described the previous summer to Hoebel and Llewellyn by one set of informants were controverted by another group of Cheyenne. The evidence problem was just as vexing on the reservation as in a New York City courtroom.[29]

Llewellyn remained optimistic. He was not sweltering in the Montana sun. "Sorry about your news, but one can't expect good luck all the time," he replied to Hoebel. Hoebel longed for the perfect conditions, the field worker's paradise. Llewellyn was impatient. He had questions for Hoebel: [W]as "the brother's action on the wife's say-so?" What really happened in the "red-sash" case? "The fact that we have two versions so largely at variance with each other is to be seriously borne in mind." What about the oath that "Stump Horn's buddy took on the medicine hat to free himself from accusation?" The "buffalo robe affair" still worried Llewellyn; was there any indication that the Cheyenne joined with other peoples to hunt the herds? Llewellyn insisted that the story not be the "official" one: "In general, I feel great need for getting at as much as we can of stories about people who are not leading figures, and who corre-

28. Hoebel to Llewellyn, July 18, 1936, KLP, R.VIII.13.
29. Hoebel to Llewellyn, Aug. 11, 1936, KLP, R.VIII.13.

spond less to Al Capone, Benedict Arnold, and J.D. Rockefeller than to the man in the street." More specific questions were on the way.[30]

Llewellyn was aware of the culture-boundedness of his analogy. "The more I think about your universal definition of law, the less I am disposed to like it," he wrote to Hoebel two years later. "I find it very difficult to frame any definition which covers the situation in a non-state, non-authority society, and also has adequate application to a modern society." But there was one constant, one universality: "the presence of these [law-] jobs which need doing." Having denied an ideal universe of law-forms, Llewellyn introduced a universe of law-doers. And the first chapters, which he was already writing, had to focus on the law-stuff of the law-doers.[31] Llewellyn had so far gotten into the spirit of the ethnologist that he offered advice to Hoebel on how to integrate ethnography into Hoebel's own seminar. He suggested that the topics to be covered include "aggression and fraud, disputed right, disputed fact, deliberate arranged change, values and control of official personnel, formulated rules, and law crafts and law craftsmen."[32]

As Llewellyn was remaking himself into the perfect anthropologist, Hoebel was discovering the charms of analytical jurisprudence. "I am having an interesting time on Hohfeld right now," he wrote to Llewellyn at the end of 1940. "I wonder to what extent his concepts might be useful for primitive law?"[33] Hoebel was so taken with Wesley Newcomb Hohfeld that he wrote a manuscript applying the latter's ideas to the Cheyenne. How could Llewellyn ignore an appeal to his old mentor? But Llewellyn knew that Hohfeld did not scan as a realist and gently informed Hoebel, "I do not want to seem either unduly exacting or discouraging. And I welcome your ms. It shows thought, growth, and above all, the translation of both into action." This faint praise was accompanied by three pages of single-spaced exegesis on Hohfeld's schema. Hohfeldian analysis, Llewellyn explained, was best applied to "private" property, not personal relations. What was more, "if the line of law is not clear, neither is any Hohfeldian relation." Next, "the weakest spot in Hohfeld is his approach to secondary rights; and *none* of his thinking carried through to the relations of claimant to official, save in

30. Llewellyn to Hoebel, Aug. 17, 1936, KLP, R.VIII.13.
31. Llewellyn to Hoebel, Jan. 24, 1938, KLP, R.VIII.12.
32. Llewellyn to Hoebel, Sept. 27, 1940, E. Adamson Hoebel Papers, APS.
33. Hoebel to Llewellyn, Dec. 2, 1940, KLP, R.VIII.12.

regard to certain immunities from, say, unconstitutional action."
Hohfeld's ideas might work in explaining one person's claim against
another, but they did not work when the claim reached up or down
in a customary society.[34]

Of such bangs and bumps all collaborations are made, but Llewellyn knew too well what could happen to the expectations of one
or the other of the parties. He recalled later, in what was to be an
appendix to *The Cheyenne Way*, that "[t]he preparation of this
book lasted too long, and the interactions were too continuous, for
any memory to be trustworthy as to responsibility [of authorship].
But I feel one. Books by senior and junior authors are frequently
both misread and miscited, pursuant to a silent convention to the
effect that the senior has provided the ideas and the junior done the
leg work." Not so here. Hoebel was the anthropologist; he had
the "feel" of the Cheyenne "and the value of the described individual case. But for going into law-stuff, there was no technique,
because Law, as a discipline, had not given ethnologists much with
which to work." Thus was Hoebel "[t]rained, eager, and stymied"
by the canons of his own profession. There was no law among the
Cheyenne.

Llewellyn rode to the rescue—and what a ride. Everyone lined
the road along which the bold Llewellyn galloped except Diogenes
Teufelsdröckh. "I hit the law jobs first under the star of Keller and
Sumner (in that order) and then of Hohfeld (the atomizer), Cook
(the logician), Corbin (the combiner of Hohfeld and Cook with
Sumnerlike thinking). I got worried. This must have been twenty
years or so before Ad was getting worried. And I had been studying
boys in boys' camps, and men in faculties, and written records. And
then I had found Ehrlich, and been somewhat crushed in spirit, because he had seen so much, and after that I had found Max Weber.
That was a crisis." If Weber was right, Llewellyn would have to begin again (though he did not say why). Fortunately for this pilgrim's
progress, Weber could be dismissed because his was not an "American mind."[35]

34. Llewellyn to Hoebel, Dec. 7, 1940, KLP, R.VIII.12.

35. Llewellyn, Appendix on Allocation of Responsibility [for *The Cheyenne Way*],
n.d., KLP, I.I.2. Llewellyn did not dismiss Max Weber. In his 1931 Leipzig lectures on
law and society, Llewellyn distinguished legal activities from non-legal activities within a
culture. He used Weber's notion of a "law staff" (*Rechtsstab*), the same language he used
in *The Cheyenne Way*. Llewellyn was thus referring in this draft appendix to his 1933

Then on down the road to where the ethnologists were busy rejecting the legal thinking of "Holmes, Cardozo, Hohfeld, Cook,
[and] Corbin." This was a crucial passage of arms for Llewellyn
because in print Llewellyn had already argued that the law was
what officials did, and if (as he assumed) the Cheyenne had law, one
had only to identify the officials and find out what they did in crucial
disputes. From his manuscript appendix, it is clear that it did not
matter to him that the weight of current anthropological opinion
was against his assumption. Bronislaw Malinowski, who had virtually invented the concept of anthropological field work in his New
Guinea studies during World War I, insisted that primitive societies
had no "crystallized" legal institutions. Law was but one of the
"several systems of social control" that different peoples deployed.
Custom was not law, nor law custom. The difference was clear: in
law, the sanctions for a violation of a code were official, imposed by
officers of some court. But in his draft appendix, Llewellyn suggested that the Columbia anthropologists understood and accepted
the Llewellyn approach—that what the Cheyenne law-doers did
was law.[36]

It is obvious why the appendix was not published—it was unpub-
lishable. Indeed, even to those with access to the private discourse,
it is almost impenetrable. But one omission stands out from all the
names. There is no Pound. In the same year that Llewellyn privately
urged Pound to publish his indispensable treatise on jurisprudence,
Llewellyn left Pound out of his confessional. The omission was dou-
bly odd because Pound would have agreed with Llewellyn. Law
went everywhere. Unfortunately for realism, however, Pound would
have based his concurrence on his newest line of argument—that
every society had legal ideals. Llewellyn wanted none of this.

In the book, Llewellyn simply begged the problematic question of
primitive law by assuming that the Cheyenne had law. Among
them, organized force was used to compel or to punish those who

manuscript *Recht, Rechtsleben, und Gesellschaft,* based on the 1931 German lectures.
That manuscript was published in 1977, fifteen years after Llewellyn's death. Michael
Ansaldi, "The German Llewellyn," 1993, 43–44 (manuscript courtesy of the author).
Llewellyn chose not to mention the unpublished *Recht* in the appendix and was left with
a series of oblique references to Weber instead.

36. Llewellyn, Draft Appendix; Bronislaw Malinowski, "A Scientific Theory of Culture" (1941), in Bronislaw Malinowski, *A Scientific Theory of Culture and Other Essays*
(Chapel Hill, N.C., 1944), 129, 6.

had violated norms or expectations. He regarded the warrior societies and the chiefs as officers, for they were the ones who determined the penalties in consultation. If his logic was circular, his argument seemed to fit Cheyenne society, for the perpetrators accepted the authority of the punishment and behaved accordingly. The book began with a series of case histories of such individual misconduct, "cases of trouble," the elucidation of which was Llewellyn's long-awaited chance to discourse on law-stuff and law-jobs in an anthropological vein.[37] The result was a triumphant end run around the conventional language of jurisprudence.

"Law has as one of its main purposes to make men go round in more or less clear ways," Llewellyn introduced his chapter entitled "A Theory of Investigation." Law functioned; it acted. "Law has the peculiar job of cleaning up social messes when they have been made. Law thus exists also for the event of breach of law and has a major portion of its essence in the doing of something about such a breach. By its fruits is it to be known." Thus, the "law-stuff" of a culture not only includes norms or rules for proper behavior, right-ways, but also deals with grievances, disputes, and troubles. These right-ways and mechanisms for settling disputes were fused in custom, but for Llewellyn, the rule was not nearly so important as what happened *"in the pinch."* By emphasizing the latter instead of the former, Llewellyn proposed that the observer could see the "play" in legal structures, or what he called "the ranges of leeway." For not all rules were enforced. If disregarding a norm led to little of consequence, the norm is social, but when organized force was brought to bear on the suspected misdoer, then the norm is legal. Llewellyn rejected Malinowski's concept of "neutral custom," for neutrality was not a thing in itself. A violation was neutral only if, in retrospect, one could see that nothing came of it. Thus, the study of cases of trouble revealed a world of law that the overly tutored eye of the veteran ethnographer might miss, so close was he or she to the cul-

37. In the anthropological literature, this technique is associated with Hoebel and not Llewellyn. Llewellyn backed away from it in later studies. In 1953, he told his students, "You do not get a picture of how an outfit operates by seeing it in crisis. You get a picture of how it operates in crisis by seeing the background out of which it approaches a crisis." Llewellyn, Jurisprudence Lecture, May 6, 1953, KLP, C.L.1–20, p. 11. Currently, the case of trouble approach is out of favor among the ethnologists, for it emphasizes the singular case, rather than the long duration of more normal operation of legal institutions. See Peter Just, "History, Power, Ideology, and Culture: Current Directions in the Anthropology of Law," 26 *Law and Society Review* 379 (1992).

ture ways. "The trouble cases [not the day-to-day life], sought out and examined with care, are thus the safest road into the discovery of law. Their data are most certain, their yield is richest. They are the most revealing." [38]

Llewellyn had a not so ulterior motive in all this theory. He was delighted with the Cheyenne system and boasted of his conversion experience: "It might bear a surface appearance of romanticizing for us to attribute legal genius to a people of those aboriginal American plains which have long been thought to be so relatively barren of legal culture, if the data had not been laid before the reader." The Cheyenne possessed a rare and "utterly clean juristic intuition, individualized yet moving with singular consistency whither tribal welfare demand that it shall move." They were the jurisconsulti of the Plains. In case after case, the Cheyenne proved that precedent could be creatively bent by common sense or, rather, that other precedents could be brought to bear to take into account the facts of individual cases. Llewellyn called this "feeling the way through to a solution." [39]

The word "equity" is nowhere mentioned in the book, though that is exactly the Anglo-American analog for the Cheyenne practice. Of course, the maxim that Llewellyn and every chancellor in equity knew too well was that equity does not extend to crime, yet the Cheyenne, unhindered by codes, book law, and judicial decisions, had done just that, and very nicely. It was "a regime of implicit principle and case work, both attuned to the net dynamic need of the people. This the Cheyenne had, rather than a regime of letter or of rule or of form." [40] They even handled divorce and remarriage with a deftness that was so subtle as to be almost uncommunicable to the outsider. If there were cases where the Cheyenne system broke down (frequently in matters of religious observance) and violence sometimes outran the law's reach, such episodes were

---

38. Llewellyn and Hoebel, *The Cheyenne Way*, 20, 21, 22, 23, 24, 25 n.6, 26, 29 (emphasis in original). Malinowski got some of his own back. In a posthumously published review of the book, he praised the authors but asked them to "accept the anthropological position" (a nice touch that) that law was not just what happened when a transgressor was called to account. In missing this point, the authors "have hardly done justice to their own scholarship." Bronislaw Malinowski, "A New Instrument for the Interpretation of Law—Especially Primitive," 2 *Lawyers Guild Review* 9 (1942).

39. Llewellyn and Hoebel, *The Cheyenne Way*, 310–11, 317.

40. Ibid., 323.

rare. Overall, the Cheyenne system of "pleading by action" was a model.[41]

But a model for whom? Against what? Llewellyn knew the answer to that question when he began the work nearly a decade before. "If there be one central problem of legal philosophy, it is that of the relation between law and justice." The give-away was the reference to legal philosophy. The Cheyenne had none, by Llewellyn's own admission. They felt their way to solutions. But Llewellyn had been thinking about legal philosophy in 1932 when he reached out to help Hoebel. "The relations between law and the general health of society and, on the other hand, among law, the general regulation, and the individuated need of the particular case" were not issues that troubled the Cheyenne. But they were the bane of modern academic jurisprudence. "This is because the law [no longer the Cheyenne law, for Llewellyn was moving toward his own objective now] tends, as few other institutions do, into fixity. . . . [C]ultures which have developed the regularity side of law and procedure have rarely managed to avoid having the major emphasis of their technique and theory turned to the development and manipulation of these tough, slow-yielding regularities. In such a situation (which has been that of Western Europe and of these United States) machinery to give any leeway has been so hard to manage that getting a measure of justice into the individual case has tended to swamp effort to handle justice's broader aspects."[42]

The problem was the specialization of law-men in America, the domination of individual cases by uniform, expertly engineered rules. "Individuation" could come only from a more primitive (in the generic sense) type of law, a law closer to the people. Leeway and the law-ways must come together in individual cases for justice to be served. And the inevitable by-product of empowering local law-ways was the persuasiveness of the outcomes. Consent would come from the same local, intimate sources as the decision itself.[43]

This was an important point for Llewellyn to make at this moment, for he was deeply involved in what would be his most famous legal project—the drafting of the Uniform Commercial Code (UCC). Llewellyn taught commercial law throughout his career. His 1930

41. Ibid., 325.
42. Ibid., 331, 332.
43. Ibid., 334, 337.

casebook on sales was a model of the new style of real-world pedagogy. More to the point, he used it to attack the 1906 Sales Act that
Samuel Williston of Harvard Law School had drafted. The old Act
failed on two counts. Most sales transactions of any size no longer
followed the pay-and-take-away model that informed the 1906 Act.
The new mode was a "nationwide indirect marketing structure," in
which paperwork replaced face-to-face dealings and for long periods of time, neither the seller nor the buyer had complete control
over the goods in question.[44]

More important to Llewellyn's mind, the Act itself was wrongly
cast in rules-and-principles form, instead of allowing the courts to
use the customs of the trade as the measures for remedies.[45] From
the middle of the 1930s, he was busy trying to modernize the Uniform Sales Act, an effort that grew out of his membership on the
NCCUSL. When his efforts on that front stalled, he pushed for a
federal Sales Act. That project, too, fell short, and Llewellyn began
to campaign for a new code that would include sales, secured transactions, and other commercial transactions. For others, the issue
was uniformity across state lines. For Llewellyn, it was a test of legal
realism. Courts tortured the old law to make it fit new facts or
mangled the facts of cases to make them fit the old law. He reached
out to the merchant community, tried to organize support in the
academic world, and found an ally in William Schnader, chairman
of the executive committee of the NCCUSL.[46]

What he wanted was a law that would capture the "feel" of commercial transactions.[47] In a confidential memorandum to the other
members of the Uniform Commercial Acts section of the NCCUSL,

44. Karl Llewellyn, *Cases and Materials on the Law of Sales* (Chicago, 1930), xvi.
45. Zipporah Batshaw Wiseman, "The Limits of Vision: Llewellyn and the Merchant
Rules," 100 *Harvard Law Review* 476 (1987).
46. Ibid., 477–89.
47. "Feel," Llewellyn wrote to his therapist Max Mayer at the end of 1941, was at
the root of Llewellyn's problems and his successes. He knew where he had erred by "feel."
Llewellyn to Max D. Mayer, n.d. [Sept. or Oct. 1941?], Emma Corstvet Papers, Bryn
Mawr College Library. But feel was not just a matter of emotional self-exploration. It
was a way of knowing about the world. Llewellyn had felt the rhythms of Cheyenne law
and then saw how the Cheyenne felt their way through cases of trouble. Merchants had
a "feel" for the course of business, which nineteenth-century German commercial lawyers felt as well, and that feel echoed in Llewellyn's writings on commercial law. James
Whitman, "Commercial Law and the American *Volk*: A Note on Llewellyn's German
Sources for the Uniform Commercial Code," 97 *Yale Law Journal* 164–65 (1987).

he urged the deletion of the term "custom" from the draft Sales Act of 1937. It recalled the power of the English king to supersede the law merchant. "The words 'usage of trade' on the other hand call up and attempt to find out what the parties meant by what they said. I am therefore in favor of striking the word 'custom' entirely out of the statute."[48] He urged that business practices be codified and consulted the New York "Merchants Association" on their handling of various problems.[49] But Llewellyn had no intention of enacting the usages of the trade. He refused to follow local customs, preferring instead Continental business-stuff. In the memorandum and throughout the drafting process—nearly a dozen years until the report in 1949—he told the businessmen what they ought to do, and such law was hardly mimetic of actual practices.[50]

Llewellyn had no intention of passing the strings of his program into another's hands. He wanted to be the draftsman, the "reporter" in technical parlance, of the new code. He lobbied for the post in a memorandum to Schnader. Llewellyn's staff would have to be full-time people "who have ambition, brains, energy, and some understanding of what I happen to think it is all about."[51] (In fact, he did get the people he wanted, and they formed a loyal cadre of workers. He bonded to them over the years and demanded loyalty from his "team" in return. To his drafting team, in private, he offered a bit of doggerel set to the tune of "Old Ninety Six": "Now all you reporters, you must take warning / From this time now and on / Never speak harsh word to the dear chief reporter / he may leave you and never return."[52]

Two months after the bargained-for control of his staff, he informed the executive committee of the NCCUSL section on Uniform Commercial Acts that "large portions of this body of law can be put into terms which afford material guidance to the layman [i.e.,

---

48. Llewellyn, Memorandum re Federal Sales Act and the Uniform Sales Act, Sept. 3, 1937, KLP, J.I.3, p. 4.

49. Ibid., p. 11.

50. Ibid., p. 13. Llewellyn here substituted his notions of fairness for local custom. See generally Ingrid M. Hillinger, "The Article 2 Merchant Rules: Karl Llewellyn's Attempt to Achieve the Good, the True, the Beautiful in Commercial Law," 73 *Georgetown Law Journal* 1141–84 (1985).

51. Llewellyn to William Schnader, Memorandum on Code, May 19, 1940, KLP, J.II.1.a.

52. Llewellyn, untitled, Jan. 24, 1946, KLP, X file.

the non-lawyer] in the *doing* of his business. . . . A democracy needs law which is friendly to the people . . . neighborly law." [53] Llewellyn, working simultaneously on the law of the Cheyenne and the law merchant had found (or rather imputed to them) similar themes: local knowledge was the most effective source of law, and law was what officials do. In both projects, however, Llewellyn imposed on the "stuff" that he found his own powerful organizing vision and set of priorities. He would improve on reality by harmonizing, simplifying, and explaining the law.[54]

But there were too many audiences to please, and Llewellyn's vision "demanded sharp changes from the past." [55] He promised Emma that he would be very cautious, but his letters to her from the drafting sessions revealed how exhausted he was and how every item seemed to bring a battle over wording, rules, and his role.[56] Llewellyn drafted three versions of the Sales Act, in 1940, 1941, and 1943. In the end, none was completely successful from his point of view, although the sales provisions of the UCC and the UCC itself were major achievements for which he deserved and gained much credit. His effort to treat merchant sales differently from non-merchant sales survived, but his reasoning was lost with the amendment of his draft by the oversight committees of advisors in the NCCUSL and the ALI, with the ABA looking on closely. It should have been Karl Llewellyn's greatest triumph, this Uniform Commercial Code. He had worked hard to become the reporter, and even harder to make his ideas of merchant rules into its centerpiece.[57]

However, he had reckoned without the "interests" that Pound had long before warned against—for the law was not the consensus

53. Llewellyn, Memorandum to Executive Committee, Aug. 30, 1940, KLP, J.II.1.b, p. 1 (emphasis in original).

54. Ibid., p. 2.

55. Wiseman, "Vision," 501.

56. Llewellyn to Corstvet, May 20, 1940, Sept. 26, 1941, and Dec. 29, 1945, Emma Corstvet Papers, Bryn Mawr College Library.

57. Wiseman, "Vision," 520–38. Initially, Schnader was overjoyed that Llewellyn was willing to make the Sales Act and the code a joint project of the ALI and the NCCUSL. William Schnader to William Draper Lewis, Aug. 22, 1941, American Law Institute Archives, Philadelphia, 116-3. By the fall of 1945, Llewellyn was restive and said so to Lewis ("Uncle Billy"): "I am seriously vulnerable on the matter of the Sales Act comments . . . you were utterly superb, and, as I had expected, I needed you . . . Soia and I salute you." Llewellyn to Lewis, Nov. 30, 1945, American Law Institute Archives, Philadelphia, 58-1. I will tell this story in greater detail in my book *The New Jurisconsults: The American Law Institute and the Restatement of the Law.*

of a homogeneous society, but the broker of the demands of competing interests. Llewellyn, in heated pursuit of a new integration of law, had forgotten that basic truth. In 1951, Schnader, a one-time ally turned critic, explained why "interests" mattered in an angry letter addressed to Soia Mentschikoff but meant for Karl.

> If your purpose is to start a feud which will result in bitter recriminations between the drafting staff, . . . and the Bankers Association for Foreign Trade, I think you are starting out in the right way to accomplish your purposes. . . . One thing that I am sure of is that if in Pennsylvania the important bankers of Philadelphia and Pittsburgh . . . were to let the legislature know that they disapproved of a part of the Code, there would not be a Chinaman's chance of obtaining enactment. Also, what you said about Wall Street may be perfectly true, but I am satisfied that if the New York State Bankers Associations . . . were to express opposition to the code, it would not be enacted in New York.

Schnader believed that Karl, Soia, and Grant Gilmore were pushing for a reform of the law, not its codification, and that put him in an awkward situation. "I have never said, and am not now saying, that the Code should be framed for the advantage of banks to the prejudice of depositors; but, after all, the purpose of the Code is to facilitate commerce, including banking, and I cannot for the life of me understand how anyone can take the position that the code should be unworkable from the bankers' standpoint. They are the people who will work under the code day in and day out, and it seems to me that it just must be legislation which they believe practicable and feasible." Llewellyn should have conceded the point—banking law should be, realistically, what bankers do, but Llewellyn's realism was here, as elsewhere, closely tied to reform, as Schnader recognized. "I do not think that anybody entered upon the code undertaking with the idea that it was to be a piece of reform legislation and that the persons who should be consulted about it should be the social service agencies."[58]

Schnader was right; confirmation came from within the team. Gilmore chaffed at the fact that "[m]ost commissioners and most members of the Institute were conservatives—not only in politics but in jurisprudence." The "irony" that Llewellyn was the chief reporter was a tribute to his reputation as the leading academic au-

58. Schnader to Soia Mentschikoff, Nov. 8, 1951, KLP, X file.

thority on sales, but his intent to do away with "obsolete rules" had to overcome the opposition of just about everyone.[59] While Gilmore fumed and Mentschikoff kept the critics at bay, Llewellyn fulminated to Herbert Goodrich, head of the ALI, with a copy to Schnader, "I do not let down my people." Llewellyn resigned from the NCCUSL, but he remained the head of the ALI drafting team.[60]

During the early stages of the UCC drafting sessions, Llewellyn's second marriage, to Emma Corstvet, slowly collapsed. It had survived her living in New Haven and his in New York City; their long struggle and final success in adopting a little boy, Nial; Karl's many trips to conferences and to Washington, D.C.; and Emma's employment at Sarah Lawrence. But it could not survive his drinking and his constant need to control her life. And now there was another woman. Soia Mentschikoff had been his student and had become his collaborator on the UCC project. She wrote to him in May 1946 that she could not marry him, for he did not love her as she loved him and her "self-respect" could not survive such an inequality. Yet she advised him as a friend, "You are making a great mistake in not plunking for divorce. So long as I was around, it was a barely livable marriage. Now that I'm gone, it will be intolerable. . . . You both will be happier and less strained living apart from each other."[61] Llewellyn shortly thereafter made financial provisions for Emma and his son, which Soia oversaw, and he married Soia. Llewellyn continued to correspond with Emma, but appointments to spend time with Nial always seemed to go astray. There was always the work, of course, and, increasingly, the balm of spirits.

Llewellyn found a kind of peace in the Cheyenne law-ways, a completeness and fulfillment that he would never find in the UCC. Both efforts to explain and rationalize law through application of jurisprudential principles, at close range momentous and consuming, soon paled in the face of international lawlessness. Shortly after *The Cheyenne Way* was published and Llewellyn completed his second draft of what would become Article Two of the UCC, America entered the war raging in Europe and Asia. This time, no right-thinking American jurisprudent publicly defended the Ger-

59. Grant Gilmore, *Ages of American Law* (New Haven, Conn., 1977), 84–85.
60. Llewellyn to Herbert Goodrich, Nov. 1951, KLP, X file.
61. Mentschikoff to Llewellyn, May 26, 1946, Emma Corstvet Papers, Bryn Mawr College Library.

man cause. Young lawyers had signed up for the duration as well, as sons and lovers were off in faraway places, in uniform. Law schools again emptied. Professors took on additional teaching and administrative assignments. Dr. New Deal had become Dr. Win the War, and the eager realists who went to Washington to save the economy now labored in agencies that put labor and agriculture second to the army and war production. The businessmen were back, too, offering their services and ensuring that their former (and future) companies did well by doing good. Some of the characteristics of fascism were in evidence as well—central planning, exultation of the laborer, a culture of communal sacrifice, and strong patriotism. Sometimes this took the form of racism, as in the internment of Japanese Americans. There were race riots in Harlem and Los Angeles. Meanwhile, the Federal Bureau of Investigation hunted spies with foreign-sounding names.[62]

Pound had no love for any of the ideologies of totalitarianism, whether they were posed by Axis spokesmen or erstwhile Allies. Speaking at Holy Cross College in the middle of the war, he condemned the arrogance of the age and tied it to a hardening of philosophy. "There are abundant signs of a significant change from the ideas and ideals and values which governed in the immediate past. . . . Whatever the confident self-styled advanced thinkers of today may be looking forward to, the immediate actual result is a cult of force . . . a realism which in law and in politics takes force to be the reality and those who wield the force of politically organized society, as the representatives of force, to be the actualities of the legal order and of the political order. . . . The significant things in the world are force and the satisfaction of material wants. Education must be shaped to the exigencies of these. Nothing else is to be taught or learned. Such a doctrine carried into practice, a regime to that pattern, would indeed give us a new world." The result was not a critical pose, but a political repose, in which men turn to "absolute political ideas" and autocracy. Ordinary people lose interest in self-government. Such philosophies "must be wonderfully heartening doctrine for dictators."[63]

62. Richard S. Kirkendall, *The United States, 1929–1945: Years of Crisis and Change* (New York, 1974), 205–18; John P. Diggins, *The Proud Decades: America in War and Peace 1941–1960* (New York, 1988), 14–34.

63. Pound, The Humanities in an Absolutist World (Speech at the Classics Association of New England Conference), Mar. 26, 1943, RPP, 170-12, pp. 3, 6, 7.

Had Pound changed, age bringing conservatism? Had the world changed, as he so often noted now, becoming too depersonalized and materialistic, forcing him to adjust his values? Or was he saying much the same thing in the early 1940s as he had nearly three decades before? Pound paused to reflect on the changes he had seen in his lifetime in his lectures on "Social Control through Law" to the Mahlon Powell Foundation at Indiana University. The year was 1942, and the war against the Axis powers was consuming all of the country's energy. The end was not in sight, but for Pound, the new endeavor showed how little academic jurisprudence had done and could do to change the world for the better. "To speak only of my own special field, it is certainly true as we look back that the judges and practitioners of fifty years ago were well in advance of the jurists and teachers in what have proved to be the significant movements in law. Everywhere the science of law [an unconscious dig at the empiricists perhaps] lagged behind the actual course of legislation and judicial decision." This is the exact opposite of what Pound wrote with such fervor in the first two decades of the century, and Pound may well have been sitting in judgment of himself. Even in the formulation of a sociological jurisprudence, "the teachers have been going their way with too little knowledge of the problems with which the administration of justice has to wrestle and often with too little grasp of the experience developed by reason which is formulated in the traditional element of legal systems."

Pound's apology for his earlier arguments was not total, for he recognized that the "failure of the received ideal to furnish satisfactory adjustments of conflicting and overlapping interests as they are presented to the courts today" ruled out any simple-minded formalism. And the persistence of the notion of "the self-sufficient individual in an economically self-sufficient neighborhood and freely competing with his neighbors" clearly annoyed him. But he had to admit that "we cannot see an exact picture of that society to take the place of the old picture." The danger, then, was that, "[w]ith no authoritative ideal to guide it, exercise of [political force] becomes a matter of individual wish and prejudice and predisposition—the very things law seeks to repress. A regime of force tries to do the work of a regime of law." That is what had happened in Europe, with catastrophic consequences. "It is a paradox, no doubt, but so it is: absolute ideas of justice have made for free government, and skeptical ideas of justice have gone with autocracy." Pound did not attack any realists by name, but the implication was clear to anyone at all acquainted with the old controversy: "[S]keptical realism puts nothing above the ruler or ruling body."[64]

If the realists complained that Pound was being unscientific, he answered that "we are not dealing with physical nature . . . we are dealing with phenomena under the control of human will and what is does not tell the whole story. Here the ultimate question is always what ought to be." Twenty years before, Pound had suggested that jurisprudents who held to such opinions as he now expressed ought to read the latest in social psychology, proving that the idea of a un-fettered free will was nonsense. Not this Pound: for him, "[c]iviliza-tion rests upon the putting down of arbitrary, wilful self-assertion and the substitution of reason." This reason sounded much like the metaphysical school that Pound belittled in his former works, but now he had seen the face of the enemy in a different light. Legal rights existed. Social engineering through law was dead. "This idea that there are no rights, that there are only threats announced by the ruling organ of a politically organized society, from which, if exe-cuted, individuals may obtain certain advantages, is a symptom of the rise of political absolutism all over the world."[65] Pound had be-come the "anti-realist." It was Oliver Wendell Holmes, Jr., who was the father of realism now, not Pound.[66]

Llewellyn had not succumbed to such global *Weltschmertz;* in fact, he had found his second wind. The unrepentant realist had no heartening words for dictators. Indeed, Llewellyn was fierce in his defense of democratic principles and his condemnation of fascism. The problem was how to draw the line between exercise of rights and liberties, particularly free expression of political opinion, and suppression of doctrines that would undermine the existence of those rights and liberties. Llewellyn wrestled with the issue. He could expect no help from Europe. "The thesis is this: That the Con-ditions of Effective thinking require—and so much I hold to be in-evitable—that your country take the leadership in the Jurispru-dence of the World for a Decade and perhaps for a Decade and a

---

64. Roscoe Pound, *Social Control through Law* (New Haven, Conn., 1942), 2, 6, 7, 14–15, 28, 29.

65. Ibid., 32, 87, 96.

66. Frances E. Lucey, "Natural Law and American Legal Realism: Their Respective Contributions to a Theory of Law in a Democratic Society," 30 *Georgetown Law Journal* 494, 496 (1942).

Half following." The war had driven jurisprudence to cover in Europe, the home of traditional legal theory. Totalitarian aggressors twisted law to rationalize oppression. Democratic victims bent law to save themselves. "Thus, for the moment, new jurisprudence issuing from the non-absolutist Countries is doomed to insolidity."[67] It was up to American jurisprudents to find the middle course. Llewellyn's handwritten few pages were never meant to be published (he said so on the first page), but now who could doubt that the star of empire had indeed gone west, over the seas? It is the only statement that he or Pound made about American leadership in jurisprudential thinking, and it was private, not public.

A year later, in 1942, Llewellyn accepted an invitation to contribute to the first number of the new *Journal of Legal and Political Sociology*. He was ready to answer the question he had posed for himself, and all of Western jurisprudence, the year before. Although the first few pages of the piece bristled with an almost impenetrable display of social science jargon, the jargon soon gave way to a powerful think piece on the connection between "American Common Law Tradition and American Democracy." He was honest, almost confessional: "The unspoken [surely a Ciceronian touch] background which informs this paper is local, contemporary, and largely bourgeois 'intellectual.'" Llewellyn was consistent—he rooted his views in local knowledge, or, rather, local values, from the start. He had Pound on his mind as well, for he feared that Pound did not reveal to his readers all he should. It was the one time in the public discourse that Llewellyn openly referred to the private discourse. "Thus when you read Pound in praise of 'the common law tradition' you get little inkling of the hitches and blindnesses which are, also, one past and present part of that tradition." Pound knew better, of course, but confined that knowledge to private communications within his circle. Llewellyn, on this occasion at least, tried to give the public a peek into the otherwise closed world of the jurisprudents.[68]

For Llewellyn, even in wartime, democracy implied "a political regime whose pervading accepted or dominant values are carefully left open to modification or displacement." In other words, democracy wanted and needed freedom of speech, assembly, and press and

67. Llewellyn, West and East in Jurisprudence, n.d. [1941?], KLP, B.II.4.

68. Karl Llewellyn, "American Common Law Tradition and American Democracy," 1 *Journal of Legal and Political Sociology* (1942), reprinted in Karl Llewellyn, *Jurisprudence: Realism in Theory and Practice* (Chicago, 1962), 282, 285.

all the other guarantees of ordered liberty. He wryly noted that such guarantees applied "differentially with regard to persons, groups, classes." "One thinks of the Negro messman who needed Pearl Harbor to get his chance to serve a machine-gun and a public; or of interned loyal Japanese citizens; and one thinks then of the peacetime analogues." But there was a limit—there had to be—when the guarantees of liberties "cease to serve the end" of liberty. An attack on particular values or ways of governing, such as that posed by the Communists, could be tolerated, even though it is was a "noisome irritant," because "none of it has come within howling distance of being an active danger" to democracy. Fascism was another matter because there was much in the American character to which fascism appealed, particularly the "knock-em-out and run-em-out" psychology of "Know-Nothingism, the Klan, and Red-hunts." But this was special pleading, and Llewellyn knew it.[69]

The ideal was restraint, not suppression, and that is where the common law mattered. In America, rule of law meant adherence to bills of rights. But as Llewellyn had written about the Reichstag trials in Germany, liberal law was weak without official commitment to its underlying precepts. How, then, to restrain those who endangered the democratic process itself, while allowing the refreshing challenges that democracy needed? "I grope here for ideas as well as for words," Llewellyn admitted, but he made a brilliant distinction nonetheless. The danger to "primitive democracy, with its mass participation and its minimalist state, was the demagogue," but the danger to the modern administrative state, with its "expert governmental staff," was "non-participation, and . . . first allowing, then demanding that things be done for one, without individual or folk participation." It was an abandonment of local knowledge in favor of centralized expertise and the replacement of local action by central action. In other words (though his reader was unacquainted with the private debate between Pound and Llewellyn), it was the surrender of realism to progressive expertise. The brilliant twist in the argument was that Llewellyn was accusing Pound of fostering the very administrative elitism that Pound had criticized in public in 1938.[70] Democracy could survive the administrative state if it truly brought a redistribution of power and wealth from the few to the

69. Ibid., 287, 289, 290.
70. Ibid., 295.

many, a proposition that Pound would have found unappealing at the very least.[71]

Judges had a special place in this process, for they were the last line of defenders of the bill of rights. Llewellyn well knew that the Japanese relocation cases were working their way through the federal courts, with four lead defendants represented by the American Civil Liberties Union.[72] He reminded his readers that the judges were bound not just by rules (the realists' first tenet), but also by a "craft-tradition" that enforced a "high duty not only to The Law but also to Justice." This did not mean the intrusion of an uninformed "judicial 'intuition.'" Instead, Llewellyn introduced a historical model. In the 1830s and 1840s and again in the 1920s, 1930s, and 1940s, a craft tradition that "shapes men, makes men" allowed judges like Benjamin Cardozo "to shape a legal epoch." In what Llewellyn called this "grand style" of judging, "the reason must make life sense. . . . Law is thus daily tested for its sense in life, and the huge leeway of doctrine which the accepted seven-wayed [i.e., multiple or discretionary] techniques for handling or 'reading' accepted authorities afford is to be used, (in the main cautiously, but always to be used) to make law for today and tomorrow accomplish sense in life."[73]

If appellate courts follow Llewellyn's prescription (note how easily description became prescription in his hands; the same sleight of hand marked his draftsmanship of the UCC), "if appellate courts can make sense and talk sense for people, serving as the residual general horse-sense organs of the people in any and in every type of manner, then such courts are a most appropriate body of review to determine whether other governmental agencies (torn between politics, favoritism, enthusiasm, specialized expertness, woodenness, lopsidedness, ambition, and vision) can give persuasive reasons that

---

71. Ibid., 298.
72. Peter Irons, *Justice at War: The Story of the Japanese American Internment Cases* (rev. ed., Berkeley, Calif., 1993), 112 ff.
73. Llewellyn, "American Common Law Tradition," 301, 303, 305, 307, 306. Clearly, Llewellyn was rehearsing in this essay the main lines of his 1960 book, *The Common Law Tradition*. Note that he has anticipated the "indeterminacy" thesis of the Critical Legal Studies (CLS) movement. See Mark Kelman, *A Guide to Critical Legal Studies* (Cambridge, Mass., 1987), 12–13 (realists focused on the indeterminacy of language of legal decisions, a posture that CLS copied). But Llewellyn was not stymied by the possibility of indeterminacy, for in his preferred "grand" style of judging, the "life-sense," the situation, the facts grounded the judge's decision, or ought to ground it.

what they do is both reasonable in aim and reasonably regular in method."[74] Thus, Llewellyn's solution neared Pound's own, but the convergence was only apparent, for Llewellyn held out for local knowledge ("horse-sense"), while Pound wanted the review courts to seek the ideals behind the claims.

In time of war, the epigram goes, the laws are silent. Much the same could be said for the jurisprudents. Pound labored away on the "Big Book,"[75] now grown to more than one volume, and taught classes by memory. Llewellyn continued to race from lecture halls to seminar rooms, to consultations in Washington, to the meetings of the NCCUSL, ALI, and AALS in the nation's hinterlands, fleeing from a failing marriage, protesting his love and his need for love along the way. Both men had lived through so much, they ought to be forgiven for failing to anticipate the perils of peace. The end of war brought not concord among nations, but a colder conflict of ideologies between the victorious Western powers and the Soviet Union. It was an old warrior, now private citizen come to visit and receive an honorary degree, who gave the Cold War its defining metaphor. "From Stettin in the Baltic to Trieste in the Adriatic, an iron curtain has descended across the continent [of Europe]," Winston Churchill told an audience at Westminster College in Fulton, Missouri.[76]

Llewellyn warned lawyers returning from the war that there would be "the spread of a new series of problems" in commerce and domestic relations. Lawyers, particularly sole practitioners, must draw on their wartime experiences to counsel their clients in dispute resolution.[77] He worried to himself (another of his pen-and-ink soliloquies, never published): "These are days in which a problem opens ahead, with the atomic bomb. That problem takes on an uncomfortable appearance, the appearance is that of an alternative: *Either* produce new and effective law with new and international

---

74. Llewellyn, "American Common Law Tradition," 309.

75. Llewellyn to Pound, Apr. 14, 1942, RPP, 142-6.

76. Winston Churchill, Mar. 5, 1946, quoted in Herbert Feis, *From Trust to Terror: The Onset of the Cold War, 1945–1950* (New York, 1970), 77.

77. Karl Llewellyn, "The Modern Approach to Counseling and Advocacy—Especially in Commercial Transactions," 46 *Columbia Law Review* (1946), reprinted in Llewellyn, *Jurisprudence,* 326. Llewellyn's note in the later publication recalls that the paper was planned for a volume on developments in the law during the war years. Ibid., 323.

scope and authority, *or* see existing nations gamble as to whether all or most and if most, which, will be wiped out or thoroughly suppressed." For this challenge, "[j]urisprudence has also assumed an immediate practical and fighting aspect, if you will take time off to look at a bothered world . . . it becomes plain that jurisprudence is no matter of light fancy; it cuts, or tries to cut, to the guts of what law is, what law is for." Llewellyn could not decide—or so he wrote in his final uncompleted paragraph—whether to name the jurisprudents who refused to recognize the new reality. He closed with a whimper: "[L]et me remind you of the climate of opinion when the realists appeared. . . ."[78] But his voice was raised loudly when Columbia was prepared to grant an honorary degree to Churchill. At a protest meeting he chaired in March 1946, he praised Churchill as a noble war leader, but reminded the audience that the time for peace and healing had come, and Churchill, fresh from his Iron Curtain speech, seemed disposed to further neither of those goals. Llewellyn took the opportunity to plead for a new regime of international law based on an association of nations.[79]

Pound was more cautious about assessing blame and revising international moral standards through law. He told philosopher Ernest Hocking, an old friend, that visiting the sins of the leaders of the defeated countries on their people was unacceptable. Moreover, "I do not see how international law can, as you put it, strike through the outer shell of the nation-state and light on the individual person to punish him. He certainly can be punished for what he does as an individual. But for what he does as an official of the state in accordance with the laws of the state it may be that the person to be reached is the lawmaker who made the law and the lawmaker is pretty hard to locate in a democratic state."[80] On trial at Nuremberg were the German judges who had advised, aided, and then abetted the Nazis in their extermination of the Jews, and Pound was obliquely questioning the tribunal's proceedings.

At Harvard, Pound continued to shoulder a "heavy teaching load," but paused long enough to tell Llewellyn that his views "ought to be brought before both sociologists and jurists in more

78. Llewellyn, Natural Law, Realism in Law, and the Problems Ahead, 1946, KLP, B.III.25 (emphasis in original).

79. Llewellyn, Address to Meeting of Veterans and Students at Columbia, Mar. 18, 1946, KLP, B.V.3.i.

80. Pound to William Ernest Hocking, Mar. 29, 1946, RPP, 67-13.

thorough-going fashion and I should like to be the one who does it."[81] Llewellyn was pleased by the compliment, but saddened by the fact that the "pressure of the Code" kept him from readying his planned contribution to a volume in Pound's honor. Pound understood. With the death of two long-term colleagues, he was forced to teach the first-year course in property.[82] Llewellyn was more "playful," but just as committed to legal education and the lawyer's craft as Pound. "Thinking of myself as wild-eyed helps me keep one foot on the ground." If there were rebels at Harvard or Columbia Law School, and they were "looking for something to rebel against," that was not altogether a bad thing.[83]

But two months later, to his Catholic University Law School audience, Pound complained that an "[o]rdering of conduct and adjustment of relations according to law and a separation or distribution of the powers of government, whereby a legal check is imposed on authority, seemed to Aristotle [and to Pound] the significant things; where the realist of today sees only a pulling and hauling of conflicting desires rationalized by traditional formulas." Where once he had welcomed the intercourse of the social sciences—indeed, reached out to them and bid them contribute to legal education—now Pound warned that "we have economic determinists and psychologists and positivists and realists with us in increasing number, with mouths speaking great things and challenging the significance and reality of what we have taken to be the chief agency in this harnessing of internal nature to the tasks of civilization. . . . Jurists must cast about how to meet these challenges."[84] The two men were still sparring—in private, gently reminding one another how hard they worked and how craft-minded they were; in public, firing off salvos that made them seem much farther apart in their thinking.

It was business as usual for Pound and Llewellyn in these private letters; there is no hint that they saw a fundamental shift in the political scene that would make liberal jurisprudence an act of per-

81. Pound to Llewellyn, Feb. 1, 1946, RPP, 142-6.
82. Llewellyn to Pound, Feb. 4, 1946; Pound to Llewellyn, Feb. 7, 1946, RPP, 142-6.
83. Llewellyn to Pound, n.d. [Mar. 1946?], RPP, 24-6.
84. Pound, The Future of American Law (Address to Catholic University Law School), May 31, 1946, RPP, 167-12, pp. 2–3. Pound's message was simple: "A few fundamental ideas of justice are common to civilized peoples. A small body of axioms of justice we share with the civil law. . . . More may be said for finding unity and continuity in legal institutions." Ibid., p. 10.

sonal courage. Neither man sensed that the tensions and the competition for diplomatic and military advantage between the United States and the Soviet Union would bring domestic recrimination. But within the next few years, a new Red Scare would challenge jurisprudents in ways even more profound than in 1919. Once again, law was bent to ferret out the malign intentions of people who were somehow different, and whose difference was dangerous. The enemy this time was the Communists rather than the anarchists, and the supposed enemy had become harder to discern. In 1919, a handful of anarchists, most of them poor immigrants, was the target of federal prosecutors. Most of these anarchists made no bones about their aims. In 1949, the objects of investigation were men and women who had been loyal Americans, often serving in important posts or in a professional capacity. There were a few actual members of the Communist Party, and some of them were prosecuted, but that was not the end of the story. The House Un-American Activities Committee (HUAC), the Federal Bureau of Investigation, and numerous private, ideological vigilante groups beat the bushes for Communists and Communist sympathizers. Informal "black lists" of former radicals were used to discredit scientists, performers, and professors who had associated themselves with Communism decades before. Loyalty oaths became mandatory in many professions, and local watchdog committees busied themselves with rumors, gossip, and denunciations. The allegations that Alger Hiss, formerly a high-ranking State Department official and in 1948 the head of the Carnegie Endowment for Peace, had been a Communist agent in the 1930s put the defenders of the First Amendment on the defensive. Prosecutions of members of the Communist Party under the Smith Act for espousing the overthrow of the government received the imprimatur of the Supreme Court, Justices Hugo Black and William O. Douglas alone dissenting. But the worst came from the person of Joseph McCarthy, senator from Wisconsin, who used innuendo, false claims, and bluster to terrify the Truman and Eisenhower administrations into partial compliance with his witch hunt.[85]

Liberal intellectuals toed the new line. School history textbooks were rewritten to conform to the new orthodoxy. Conyers Read, the president of the American Historical Association in 1949, warned

85. Diggins, *The Proud Decades*, 110–17, 157–76; David Halberstam, *The Fifties* (New York, 1993), 49–59.

that "the liberal neutral attitude . . . will no longer suffice." Yale historian Ralph Henry Gabriel used his textbook *Exploring American History* to urge young readers to report any suspicious activity: "The FBI urges Americans to report directly to its offices any suspicions they may have about Communist activity on the part of their fellow Americans."[86]

Pound had absented himself from the first rounds of the battle, retiring to what remained of Nationalist China to help Chiang Kai-shek rewrite the law. The invitation came from Nationalist Chinese Minister of Justice Kwan-Sheng Hsieh in 1945. The first trip was to take place over the summer of 1946. Pound was to return for a longer period in 1947, after he retired at Harvard. Pound had picked up some Mandarin and was to advise the ministry on "matters of judicial reform." But Pound had other ideas. In accepting the invitation, he offered to supply a plan for reorganization of the courts. The minister was concerned about Pound's advanced age and wanted him to conserve his strength. Pound huffily replied that he was teaching a full load and doing more besides in Cambridge. The financial arrangements may have invigorated Pound—he was to receive a total of $37,500 for his pains.[87]

Pound's labors were strenuous. He compiled data sets on the courts, studied the draft for a new constitution, and worked on an "Institutes" of Chinese law. A comprehensive collection of the statutes and commentaries would fill seven volumes, he guessed. The materials at the Harvard Law School Library were probably better than any collection he could find in China. His model, plainly, was the Institutes of Justinian. The comparison was not far-fetched at all, for between 1911 and 1930 Roman law was made the basis of a Chinese code. Pound could read the code in the original, and using it, he fashioned a tentative table of contents for his compilation.[88] In addition, he provided letters of recommendation for the sons of leading Koumintang politicians to study law at Harvard.[89] He gave interviews and talks in the United States denying that the troubles

86. All quotations from Stephen J. Whitfield, *The Culture of the Cold War* (Baltimore, 1991), 54, 58, 102.

87. Kwan-Sheng Hsieh to Pound, Oct. 28, 1945, RPP, 58-10; Pound to Chao Lung Yang, Dec. 1, 1945, RPP, 58-12; Receipts on Bank of China, n.d., RPP, 58-13.

88. Pound, Report, Feb. 27, 1947, Roman Law in China (enclosure), Table of Contents (enclosure), RPP, 191-4.

89. Pound to Hsia Ching, Nov. 7, 1946, and Pound to Judson Nyi, Jan. 17, 1947, RPP, 58-13.

in China amounted to anything, "not a little speaking on behalf of the Chinese Government which as seemed to me to be important in view of the general misinformation current in this country and what persistent hostility of a section of the press and some of our periodicals."[90] The counsel-general to the Republic of China asked Pound to reply to criticism of Nationalist China, and Pound promised to help.[91] "There is No Real Civil War in China," he was reported as saying on another such occasion.[92] Perhaps unwittingly, he had become a paid lobbyist for the Nationalists. Indeed, one wonders, looking at the record, whether Chiang and his ministers were sincere in hiring Pound to reform anything. Pound was an American jurist whose status and connections provided a perfect cover for their propaganda.

But Pound took his stated duties seriously. His major effort was a survey of criminal justice and law in eastern China along the lines of the Cleveland Crime Survey and the Wickersham Commission report. He requested statistics from the Ministry of Justice and the Ministry of the Interior. Some questions would have to be asked in the countryside, but Pound knew there would be slippage in the results. He wanted to know, in advance, "[i]s there any way of corroborating the results of investigation of the typical localities chosen, perhaps by questionnaires addressed to competent persons in other localities: Judges? Procurators? Members of the bar? Clerks of courts?" He would begin with criminal justice and then turn to civil procedure if he had time.[93]

In an addendum marked "confidential," he was bolder. He proposed to use the survey to determine the extent to which village chiefs usurped or evaded the orders of the local courts. He was also concerned about corruption—civil and military. Plainly, Pound was aware of both, but could not confront them directly.[94] The survey itself was to be centrally administered by the minister of justice, with Pound acting as an advisor. All the ministers were to cooperate in gathering data as well.[95] The design was progressive. It assumed

90. Pound, Report, Feb. 27, 1947, RPP, 191-4.

91. P. H. Chang to Pound, June 2, 1947, and Pound to Chang, June 6, 1947, RPP, 58-14.

92. *Portland [Oregon] Press Herald*, July 19, 1947, at 12.

93. Pound, Request for Information in Preparation for the Survey, 1947, RPP, 191-9.

94. Pound, Confidential General Scope, Plan, and Method of the Survey, n.d., RPP, 191-9.

95. Pound, Sketch of a Program for 1947–1948 and Preliminary Draft of Project of Survey, n.d., RPP, 191-9.

that the cure for ills was the amassing of data. Pound expected expert help and was confident that his and the ministers' expertise would allow the government to see the problems and make appropriate adjustments.

Nothing could be farther apart than Pound's approach to the Chinese criminal justice system and Llewellyn's to the Cheyenne way. Pound distrusted local knowledge; Llewellyn (most of the time) reveled in it. Pound wanted to stay at the center and manage the project; Llewellyn loved the time he spent with the Cheyenne, and although he was able to make only one visit to the reservation, he stayed in touch with his local informants through Hoebel. Pound believed in disinterested expertise; Llewellyn preferred subjective "feel." Pound drafted and wished to impose a Western-style social science survey on provincial officials; Llewellyn listened to local "law-men" and tried to see the world through their eyes. Pound wanted to generalize through extensive comparison and categorization; Llewellyn wanted to particularize through the stories of individual cases. Pound planned conferences and Chinese law centers at Harvard; Llewellyn never expanded his interest beyond his immediate circle.[96]

Pound was aware that the Nationalist government had persecuted its political opponents. "Dear Professor Pound," one wrote, "do you think you can in any way tell my rulers that torture and improper detention or execution of political opponents are condemned by civilized government?"[97] Pound, unmoved, continued to travel in China, not gathering data but making appearances at high-level functions and giving invited lectures at universities. At home, he defended the Nationalist cause.[98] In the winter of 1949, he was not sanguine about his project or the prospects for the Chiang regime. "If our government persists in abetting the Chinese Communists I suspect there will not be much use in Americans going [to China]," he wrote to Paul Sayre in March 1949. "If you could have seen China under Nationalist rule with the high type of public men whom I found there, it would have been worth your while." Later, Pound reported that he had actually begun the introductory volume of his Institutes of Chinese law.[99] The end was near, but Pound was

96. Pound, Second Report for 1947, Sept. 27, 1947, RPP, 191-9.
97. Y. H. Tseng to Pound, Apr. 8, 1948, RPP, 191-10.
98. Pound, Report on Work of 1947–1948, Oct. 6, 1948, RPP, 191-4.
99. Pound to Paul Sayre, Mar. 8, 1949, and Pound to Sayre, Mar. 23, 1949, Sayre Papers.

still loyal. In April, he told Herbert Goodrich, "If anything could be done to help the Nationalist government at this time I would want to go out of my way to do it." Unfortunately, Pound believed, the State Department was busy undermining the Nationalists.[100] Pound blamed the Nationalists' collapse not only on American cupidity, but also on the intrigues of the Soviets. They had armed the Chinese Communists, he wrote to his sister Olivia.[101] And Pound had not lost sight of the fact that "the nationalist government was overthrown by exactly the methods which have threatened to overthrow the government in South Korea."[102] Everywhere the Communist menace was on the march.

While Pound was gone, the Red Scare came to Harvard Law School. Dean Erwin Griswold remembered the pressure that Hiss's conviction put on the school, for he was one of its most distinguished recent graduates and other Harvard luminaries like Zechariah Chafee, Jr., had initially come to Hiss's defense. So had Griswold, which led to an FBI investigation of him. Closer to home, Griswold had to fight to prevent expulsion of students associated with the National Lawyers Guild. Griswold again took the lead in defending the Fifth Amendment rights of those accused of disloyalty, while Chafee battled against everyone from Harvard's President James B. Conant to Joseph McCarthy and Richard Nixon.[103]

When he returned to America, Pound was no longer the defender of free speech. He settled down in the heart of China lobby country, accepting a professorship at the University of California at Los Angeles School of Law (with a visit at the Hastings School of Law), where he stayed until 1953. After a year in India, he settled again in Cambridge. Always willing in the past to give a public lecture, he not so artfully dodged an invitation from Anton-Hermann Chroust to join a seminar at Notre Dame on "congressional committee tyranny" in the interrogation of witnesses.[104] Moved, he wrote, by his

100. Pound to Herbert Goodrich, Apr. 12, 1949, RPP, 61-2.

101. Pound to Olivia Pound, Aug. 16, 1950, NSHS, MS 911, box 1, folder S.1, vol. F.21.

102. Pound to Kenneth Colegrove, Aug. 16, 1950, NSHS, MS 911, box 1, folder S.1, vol. F.21.

103. Erwin N. Griswold, *Ould Fields, New Corn: The Personal Memoirs of a Twentieth Century Lawyer* (St. Paul, Minn., 1992), 189–94; Donald L. Smith, *Zechariah Chafee, Jr.: Defender of Liberty and Law* (Cambridge, Mass., 1986), 248–66; Ellen W. Schrecker, *No Ivory Tower: McCarthyism and the Universities* (Oxford, England, 1986), 202.

104. Anton-Hermann Chroust to Pound, Aug. 28, 1953, RPP, 39-2; Pound to Chroust, Oct. 13, 1953, RPP, 39-2 (Pound was tired and "the matter is controversial").

experience in China, he found the defense of American liberties required strong medicine. The State Department, he now believed, "systematically undermined the Chinese Nationalist Government and promoted the taking over of China by the Communists." [105] Quietly, he lent his aid to the Red Scare by supporting the Freedom Clubs. "It takes some courage to speak out for Senator McCarthy to American college professors who seem to have been thoroughly indoctrinated in State Department pro-Communism," Pound wrote in 1952. [106]

But this was private correspondence. In public, Pound had become, if anything, more oracular in tone and distant from current events than he was in the 1940s. In lectures given at Westminster College (the same site where Churchill had proclaimed the descent of the iron curtain), Pound declaimed on justice. Justice was an ideal relationship among men, an ideal "in the natural law and the eternal law behind the regime." Unfortunately, "[i]nstead of defining justice some today seek a theory of values by which to measure competing, conflicting, or overlapping expectations." Pound did not mention that he was once such a searcher in the 1920s. Now he had discovered a new faith. The control on the misuse of power was not investigation and experiment; it was a return to the deal of justice. Those who wanted to reconcile competing values had to concede that values "were purely subjective. Objective valuations cannot be reached. I dislike to surrender to this give-it-up philosophy." Pound's targets were "[p]ostwar theories of futility" unnamed by him, but there all the same. In what must be regarded most charitably as absent-mindedness, Pound called to his aid the shade of William James, no longer the exponent of pragmatism, to prove his point. "William James tells us that there is a continual search for the more inclusive order. This is illustrated by the history of ideas as to the end of law. Thinkers have continually gone behind an idea of the past to a more inclusive one." The violence that Pound did to James's thought was no less than to his own earlier writings. Pound had turned about, rejecting sociological jurisprudence. His search had led him to what he regarded as a higher ground of law, from which he now saw that every jurisprudent seeks the ideal in law. [107]

From his hilltop, he could see the perversions of the realists, who

---

105. Pound to David W. Angevine, June 3, 1952, RPP, 240-7.

106. Pound to James W. Fifield, June 3, 1952, RPP, 240-7.

107. Roscoe Pound, *Justice According to Law* (New Haven, Conn., 1951), 19, 21, 22–23, 30.

claimed that "[a] science . . . does not trouble itself about subjective ideas of balance and of guaranteed liberties and rights. Rights [to them] are no more than inferences from exercise by state officials of the force of a politically organized society. Law is no more than what those officials do." [108] Llewellyn was right; his comment in *The Bramble Bush* had become the goblin of the conservative jurisprudents. [109] Pound pressed on: "[T]he menace [note, not the "error" or some other soft word, not in 1951] in the so-called [always a storm warning when something is "so-called"] realist theory in action is that from assuming that we do not in practice attain a high degree of objectivity, or indeed any at all, it leads to an idea that we need not try to attain it and ought not to try to attain it because the attempt would be only pretense." But this was wrong, for "[t]o judges well brought up in the common-law tradition the main body of its precepts speak alike no matter what their individual social or economic backgrounds or temperament." [110]

Pound had only considered the first of the four potential motivating factors that Llewellyn had outlined in *The Case Law System in America*. But Pound was no longer trying to come to terms with realism; he was trying to destroy it. By insisting that all sound common law judges relied on the precepts of the law to reach their decisions, Pound dismissed Frank's *Law and the Modern Mind*. The blow came late, however, for Frank himself had moderated his earlier views and, as it happened, at that moment was carrying on a war with fellow Second Circuit Court Judge Charles Clark over a whole range of common law precepts. If Pound's rule was correct, one of the two men must not have been "well brought up" at all. [111] But stubborn facts no longer moved Pound. It was "the ideal element" that was decisive. [112]

And Pound no longer had any patience for "legislative justice."

108. Ibid., 35.

109. He knew it would be almost as soon as he wrote it, and by 1941, he was fed up with apologizing for it. "Not an inch do I head-hang," he wrote that year to Lon Fuller. "I find nothing (Well not much) in my earlier writings to retract. Even Bramble Bush p. 3 carried its own correction in ch V." Llewellyn to Lon Fuller, n.d. [1941?], Lon Fuller Papers, Harvard Law School, 4-15.

110. Pound, *Justice*, 35, 36, 37.

111. Marvin Schick, *Learned Hand's Court* (Baltimore, 1970), 219–46. Frank explored the issues from his new perspective in *Courts on Trial* (New York, 1949). He was still a fact skeptic, but no longer believed that judging was so uncertain or driven by personality. The fact that learned judges disagree about common law is the substance of common law, of course.

112. Pound, *Justice*, 55.

In this country, he warned, it has "showed the influence of personal solicitation, lobbying, and a corruption far beyond anything charged against our courts by even the most bitter opponent of our judicial system in the course of a long history." Even without its corruption, legislation "has always proved highly susceptible to the influence of passion and prejudice," and on top of everything else, "it has been disfigured everywhere by party politics, partisanship, and often crude 'deals'. . . ." Pound even accused the legislatures of granting too much discretion to that most unjudicial of all tribunals, the administrative agency. Even the Administrative Procedure Act of 1946, for which Pound had campaigned, did not go far enough to check "highhanded and one-sided administrative action." [113] His jurisprudence reflected his new politics. He had always been a Republican, but now Dwight Eisenhower seemed too liberal to be the party's standard bearer. "When I see the enormous amount of money being spent by the General's followers and the enthusiasm with which extreme left-wing Republicans enlist under his banner . . . I have a feeling . . . that Eisenhower as President would give us four years more of what we have been having for the last twenty years." [114]

Pound must have realized that he had an FBI file; everyone of any substance who traveled abroad did. His applications for passports were scrutinized, and his casual contributions (for Pound was always willing to help the needy) to radical organizations in the 1920s and 1930s were now deemed suspicious. More so was his subscription to *New Masses* in 1947. Was he perhaps "another Harvard Professor . . . allegedly among those who were critical of U.S. government action against Communists" in the 1920s? The FBI confused the anarchists with the Communists (a confusion no Communist or anarchist would have made), but Pound had, in fact, signed a petition against the HUAC in 1947. Yet all this happened before the trip to China, before Pound's eyes were opened by Chiang Kaishek to the insidious ways of the Chinese Communists. Pound had traveled extensively, but the Central Intelligence Agency reported "no derogatory information." The FBI had no objection to Pound keeping his passport, and Pound, for his part, joined the crusade against Communism. [115]

113. Ibid., 68–69, 76, 82–83.
114. Pound to Olivia Pound, Apr. 7, 1952, NSHS, MS 911, box 1, folder S.1, vol. F.8.
115. Roscoe Pound was the subject of FBI File No. 77-74432. Information was obtained from Freedom of Information Act Request No. 349815/190-73105, received

Llewellyn, still an iconoclast and, more important, a devoted Democratic liberal, had no patience for the FBI and its antics. For that, he became the focus of an active investigation in the early 1950s. The FBI had a list of those "hostile to the bureau or critical of its work," and Llewellyn made the list without trying hard. Interviewed on January 21, 1952, about a potential employee for Voice of America, he "told the Agent that he objected very strenuously to any inquiry by the Bureau regarding character, reputation, associates or loyalty to the United States regarding any individual. He also said he disliked very much any inquiry as to the trust and confidence which could be placed in an individual under consideration." Llewellyn was not content with general objections to the procedure. He "gave the Agent a lengthy lecture" on his lack of preparation for the interview, as if the agent were one of his students. "He added that for an Agent to ask any such questions of an interviewee was meaningless unless the interviewee were given a complete description of the duties to be performed by the subject of the investigation." What else could one expect from a realist—how could one judge fitness without knowing the "job-stuff?" The agent attempted to defend the FBI (or so he said in the report), but Llewellyn was "obviously not interested." What the agent and Llewellyn both knew was that the FBI had already begun an investigation of Llewellyn. Llewellyn had recommended civil rights legislation to President Harry Truman, and "the letter was obtained from a building occupied by organizations under control of the Communist Party." He was "present at the initial meeting at which the National Lawyers Guild was founded. The House Committee on Un-American Activities has called this guild 'The foremost legal bulwark of the Communist Party.'" Llewellyn was on the mailing list of the League for Mutual Aid in 1942, later listed as a Communist front by the HUAC. He had even supported the ACLU "to defeat proposed legislation in Congress against Communists." The agent recommended that the FBI open a full-fledged "security investigation." [116]

May 4, 1995. On Pound's anti-communism at UCLA, Hastings School of Law, and Harvard in the 1950s, see David Wigdor, *Roscoe Pound, Philosopher of Law* (Westport, Conn., 1974), 278.

116. The file on Karl Nickerson Llewellyn was FBI File No. 100-388288; Freedom of Information Act Request No. 349816/190-73105, received May 23, 1995. As usual, in materials provided in response to Freedom of Information Act requests, the names and identifications of confidential informants are blacked out. In this file, whole pages are so treated. The names of Llewellyn's first two wives are included, but Soia Mentschikoff is

There was already a file. "Reliable informants" confirmed that Llewellyn was affiliated with Columbia University until June 1951, that he visited at Harvard Law School in 1948–49, and that he left Columbia to teach at the University of Chicago in the fall of 1951. Special agents confirmed that he was married to Soia. They uncovered his name on ACLU documents. Another informant of "known reliability" reported that Llewellyn had attended the 1951 National Lawyers Guild convention in Chicago and had given a seminar there. More accusations followed, but they were "not specified." Mere suspicion and guilt by association were evidently enough. Special agents at the New York City, Boston, and Chicago offices were mobilized. An agent at the Seattle office was instructed to check on Llewellyn's birth records. The agent, R. D. Auerback, discovered that Llewellyn was indeed born on May 22, 1893, in West Seattle. The file grew in size as all through 1952 agents confirmed and documented the obvious, cited one another's reports, repeated the pronouncements of the HUAC, and wrung their hands. Another nugget appeared to reward their efforts: Llewellyn had been "a member of the Communist Sacco-Vanzetti National Executive Committee." Unfortunately, the informant could not remember whether the Llewellyn under investigation in 1952 was the same Llewellyn who tried to save Sacco and Vanzetti from execution. Someone thought to look at the Edmund Morgan–G. Louis Joughin book and found that the two Llewellyns were one and the same. They might have asked Llewellyn, of course, but no one was allowed to approach him.[117]

In the winter of 1953, agents began to close the net around Llewellyn. "On January 9, 1953, the writer [a Chicago agent] observed subject shoveling snow from the walk in front of the residence located at 4920 South Kimbark Avenue, Chicago, Illinois. Upon completion of the work, subject entered instant residence. On this same date the writer observed a 4 door dark green Ford Sedan, bearing license tags number 5T1317, parked in front of instant residence." The university cooperated. So did the Chicago police. His associates were interviewed. Security checks were run on his ex-wives and on Soia. But here the inquiry lost momentum. People who knew Llew-

---

referred to only obliquely. It may be that she was an informant herself. She was a Russian émigré from an anti-Communist family as it happened.

117. Ibid.

ellyn agreed that he was "100% loyal American." On July 3, 1953, the FBI decided not to place him on the "Security Index." [118]

But Llewellyn had some parting shots of his own to deliver. He called the FBI on February 11, 1954, and demanded to speak to J. Edgar Hoover, with whom Llewellyn had shared a speaker's platform in days past. Hoover was not in and did not return the call. Nor was Llewellyn deterred from liberal political activity by the investigation. In 1958, the FBI was informed that Llewellyn was again helping a suspicious organization, this time the National Association for the Advancement of Colored People. The file was reopened, the old allegations were briefly repeated, and then the file was closed, this time for good. [119]

Other ex-realists, even those on the bench, spoke out against the new witch hunt. Thurman Arnold defended those accused of un-American activities. Charles Clark and William O. Douglas spoke out from federal appellate posts to protect lawyers who defended accused Communists. [120] Llewellyn did not seek a public forum for his objections in part because he divorced realism, qua "sound technology," from politics. As he wrote to an English correspondent in 1954, it was only a "temporal accident that the rise of realism coincided with the Roosevelt Administration. . . . [F]rom the beginning many of the most effective contributors to Realism have been Tory in outlook." [121]

But Llewellyn was a realist and a liberal, and he was unhappy with his treatment at the hands of the FBI. He recalled the original interview in a paper he wrote for his own amusement, but left in his files, titled "Llewellyn to the Salt Mines." Max Ascoli, dean of the New School for Social Research where Llewellyn had taught for a time, was up for a job with the United States Information Agency, and Llewellyn had been interviewed as part of a background check. "No, I cannot say that Max Ascoli never discussed Communism with

118. Ibid.

119. Ibid.

120. Thurman Arnold, *Fair Fights and Foul: A Dissenting Lawyer's Life* (New York, 1965), 204–27; Jerold Auerbach, *Unequal Justice: Lawyers and Social Change in Modern America* (New York, 1976), 231–62.

121. Llewellyn to Graham Hughes, Aug. 10, 1954, KLP, R.VIII.17. Llewellyn did make one exception to this rule in the letter—Thurman Arnold was a realist whose views on law were inseparable from his politics. Was Llewellyn right, however? He was there, and autotopic authority should count for something. And he knew that he had written about realism in 1925.

me.—Yes, he was anti-Fascist. Yes, communists are anti-fascist.—Yes, I knew that at all times.—Yes, in my judgment he was vigorously anti-Fascist—even more so than I. . . .—No, I do not know whether he was a Fellow-Traveler—No, I do not know whether he followed the Party Line." So it went, in Llewellyn's recollection. "No. I said before that I have no evidence that—No. You are right; I said before only that I do not know that this Ascoli is undermining—Yes, I must agree: What is 'Evidence' depends a good deal on who is doing the judging.—Yes, that means, I suppose, partly on what he would like to see.—Yes, my views about Communism and these united States are very close to this Ascoli's. . . . Yes, I would almost certainly interpret all circumstances in his favor.—Yes, that would be in my own protection, too—No, that would not be prejudiced evidence. Now—May I make a statement, now that I know what this Investigation is about, and how it is being conducted? No? Am I permitted to 'record exceptions,' as I might if I were in a court operating under some type of established control? No?—*No*. No. And yet, even as all of us of goodwill labor to improve it, *and even as we need to*—how much better it is than any regime which simply blacks out talk." That was the lecture that the agent (perhaps a lawyer himself because the FBI liked to recruit lawyers) resented and recorded in his report.[122] But Llewellyn had the last word. In 1955 he gleefully told his students, "[The FBI] is the most amazing machine in our particular government, the world is full of ex-FBI men, and by and large they are the most passionately loyal alumni that anybody ever saw."[123]

His students never forgot these lectures. After all, as he told the father of a student at the University of Chicago Law School, seven years after he and Soia went there in 1953, "I am Llewellyn."[124] Mary Ann Glendon recalled her first year at Chicago and the spell that Llewellyn cast. He taught an "elements of law" class and had a "tent meeting voice" when "he wanted to implant something permanently in our gray matter." He told the novices that their forthcoming professional duties "'do not sit easily with one another. You will discover, too, that they get in the way of your other obliga-

---

122. Llewellyn, Llewellyn to the Salt Mines, n.d., KLP, B.V.3.g (emphasis in original).

123. Llewellyn, Jurisprudence Lecture XII, 1955, KLP, C.M.11–12.

124. The chance meeting took place in a hallway in Llewellyn's last year of teaching. The anecdote is told by Professor Charles A. Heckman and was related at the New York University School of Law Legal History Seminar in the fall of 1992.

tions—to your conscience, your God, your family, your partners, your country . . . you will be pulled and tugged in a dozen directions at once. You must learn to handle those conflicts.'" For Glendon, today a chaired professor at Harvard Law School, the message was inspirational, and Llewellyn seemed "a tremendous moral and intellectual force."[125] Llewellyn knew, firsthand—true local knowledge—that the way to change the law was to win over the hearts of the next generation of lawyers. Glendon had the privilege of seeing Llewellyn try to do this.

His jurisprudence lectures were part indoctrination, part reminiscence, part program for the future, and all Llewellyn. They were stream of consciousness, more often tracking Llewellyn's current projects than any systematic exposition of the great thinkers or signal movements in jurisprudence. Only sometimes were they concerned with scholastic categories because for Llewellyn jurisprudence was anything and everything. Thus, advocacy, appellate practice, lawyering, and, of course, Llewellyn's personal experiences took up most of the class time. Occasionally, an Ehrlich or a Kohler would appear, but the only name Llewellyn consistently raised was Pound's. Pound was like the ghost of Banquo at Llewellyn's feast. The shade accompanied Llewellyn everywhere. Llewellyn told Harvard's men, in the fall of 1948, that jurisprudence was not a philosophy. It was not a science. These misapprehensions were the result of expecting rules to govern legal outcomes. Whose misapprehensions? Pound's, of course. Pound had slid into this mistake, recognizing that law was craft, but insisting on precepts and ideals and a legal order as well. Pound wanted the law to control and guide men—wanted it and so believed it did.[126]

Llewellyn told the men of Harvard, and later the men and women of Chicago, that they made a great mistake in lumping jurisprudents into schools. "[Your] papers are full of schools. Those of you who don't read Pound and get schoolified . . . get schoolified by nature. . . . I ought to have a passage in the syllabus somewhere called the Theory of Schoolifying." The virtue of schoolifying is that it

125. Mary Ann Glendon, *A Nation under Lawyers: How the Crisis in the Legal Profession Is Transforming American Society* (New York, 1994), 177, 18–19.

126. Llewellyn, Jurisprudence Lecture IX, 1948, KLP, C.H.1–40. Llewellyn arranged for many of the lectures to be recorded, and his secretaries transcribed the results. Unfortunately, no complete set exists, although transcriptions of the majority of the Harvard lectures of 1948–49 and the Chicago lectures from 1953 and 1955 survive.

makes attack easier. "If you put 7 or 20 people into a lump and call them a school or a something, you can pick on the most outrageous characteristics of any as characteristics of all. . . . [T]he most flagrant example of that has recently occurred in the attack on the so-called realists. A beautiful job of confusion of thought and effective invective." [127] And who had masterminded that? Pound again. The ghost smiled and shook its gory locks. But Pound was still the leader, for "of all the twentieth century jurisprudents, Pound was the only one, the only one, who had sense enough to see that each of these outfits [jurisprudential approaches, that is] had its contribution and to attempt to gather them into a whole—a great contribution indeed." [128]

Five years later, the phantasm was still hovering somewhere near the lectern, having traveled with Llewellyn to Chicago: "And Pound is, after all, a terrific figure. You can get mad as hell at him, as I do, and you can regard him as four times of a self-made s.o.b. in many ways, which he is, and none of that detracts from the greatness and from the power that is there. . . . I do not think we have ever grown a jurisprude like him." Llewellyn had at last realized that all his criticism of Pound did not murder Pound's reputation at all, and Llewellyn could at last put Pound in his proper place. "In a sense Pound's faults are the faults of our own law, he is a kind of impersonation and embodiment of the common law. . . . He gives you two inconsistent ideas to which, when you ask him to reconcile them, he adds two more equally inconsistent ideas, inconsistent with both of the first two—but each valuable in the field to which it applies—is not that the common law? You ask Pound to put it together, and he envelopes you with words, he will never put it together. He looks out over the water, and where you just see a waste of waves, he sees a current. This is greatness." [129]

Why Pound, though? Surely there was a limit to the utility and the pleasure of pounding Roscoe—even in his old haunts. The answer was that Llewellyn needed to play off Pound, needed Pound as a brilliant son needs to rebel against an august and distant intellectual father. Llewellyn had never lost his admiration for Pound's achievements, nor his insight into Pound's unwillingness to push

127. Llewellyn, Jurisprudence Lecture XI, 1948, KLP, C.H.1–40.
128. Llewellyn, Jurisprudence Lecture IX, 1948, KLP, C.H.1–40.
129. Llewellyn, Jurisprudence Lecture XII, 1953, KLP, C.L.1–20.

those achievements to their limits. Llewellyn's lectures often began with Pound. In 1945, Llewellyn told his students at Columbia that "Pound went flat from overloading of activities and overload of work. He hit his first real criticism in Frank's Law & Modern Mind. . . . This riled Pound, especially because it was widely sold in popular circulation. The Emperor was peeved and wrote about Realism and criticized them. . . . He then swung into attack on administrative tyranny and grouped his opponents as tending in that direction. Pound has now settled down to rework and mature his ideas and put them in ripe form. Exceedingly good. He is able to spot currents in the law, but doesn't chart it accurately." [130]

In 1949, while Pound was recovering from his trip to China, Llewellyn was still on Pound's case. In an essay on law and the social sciences, he held up Pound's work as a model: "Pound, for instance—one of the shrewdest [observers of law]—has for some three decades been insisting on a number of things on which most men of sociology and government still turn a stubborn back. Rules he sees as an important part of law, and he sees them as rules *for* conduct ('precepts') not as that queer confusion which persists in the literature (both legal and non-legal) as 'rules *of* conduct.'" That was the kiss; it was followed by the slap: for all of his "phrasings simplify more than is wise. . . . No less striking is the degree to which Pound's work in its most original and fruitful phases still goes unused and above all undeveloped; as also, in its exaggerations, and errors, uncorrected." There was no one technique that allowed the judge to find the ideal behind the law. There were many, crossing over each other over time. The technique was not a process, a mark of the "legal order," as Pound implied, but an "institution," a collection of behaviors.[131] Llewellyn had made this point before, and in making it again—that is, promoting himself as both Pound's successor and his revisor—Llewellyn demonstrated his ambivalence toward and admiration for Pound.

In opposition to the new Pound, Llewellyn's pitch was that law was an institution, "not a single purpose institution," but one that had many heads. Law was the conduct of officials—the same sermon that Llewellyn had preached in *The Bramble Bush* two decades before; the same sermon that Pound rejected every chance he got, in

130. Clyde W. Summers, Llewellyn Notes, 21.

131. Karl Llewellyn, "Law and the Social Sciences," 62 *Harvard Law Review* (1949), reprinted in Llewellyn, *Jurisprudence,* 354–55 (emphasis in original).

public at least. But Llewellyn was not a philosopher—he was not interested in an analytic refutation of Pound. Instead, he was Llewellyn, and what interested him was Llewellyn's world. That year, 1948, Llewellyn was suffering through a crucial stage of the drafting of the UCC, and that labor became the central theme of his lectures. Within the institution of law, Llewellyn insisted, the most important behavior was "teamwork." He could not overstate the importance of "making the team run . . . the leadership of the team . . . and the holding of the team together against centrifugal tendencies." Hardly a coincidence this reference to team play—for his UCC "team" was flying apart under the pressure of competing interest groups. Llewellyn never drew a line between hard law and jurisprudence, even if he did not tell his students what was really on his mind that day. (But he did leave a clue. His next example was barter and sale among primitive merchants.)[132]

But if Llewellyn had looked out the window across the arms of Langdell Hall to the other great lecture room, he might have sensed that the debate over realism was on the wane. It had been replaced at Harvard by something called process jurisprudence. The new ideology started by taking Pound and Llewellyn at their word: legislation was a full equal of common law. Indeed, for Harvard Professors Henry Hart, Albert Sacks, and others who championed "legal process" theories, thinking about law began with statutory interpretation, rather than case law and precedent. It was a brave new world of legal thinking, and it reached out, just as Langdellian dialectics had some fifty years before, from Harvard Law School. The new emphasis was on structure, coherence, and legislative intent—fully realist in one sense, for it accepted the axiom that law derived from policy, but closed to the local knowledge and behavior that Llewellyn stressed and indifferent to the ideals that Pound still sought behind the acta. Instead, good law was law that was procedurally correct—duly arrived at by those institutions commissioned to make the law. Such law was neutral and reasoned, and its very existence reinforced the legitimacy of the organs of government.[133]

In the consensus-seeking intellectual world of the 1950s, the

132. Llewellyn, Jurisprudence Lecture III, 1948, KLP, C.H.1–40.
133. Morton Horwitz, *The Transformation of American Law, 1870–1960* (New York, 1992), 254–55; Robert Stevens, *Law School: Legal Education in America from the 1850s to the 1980s* (Chapel Hill, N.C., 1983), 270–71; G. Edward White, "The Evolution of Reasoned Elaboration: Jurisprudential Criticism and Social Change," 59 *Virginia Law Review* 279 (1973).

process-oriented analysis of law struck a responsive chord. Hart and Sacks, whose teaching materials were circulated in draft early in the 1950s and finally bound for use in other schools in 1958, were influential missionaries of the process approach. The karma of the materials was that law is good, a rational aid to identifying and furthering the goals of a democratic society. Hart had worked in New Deal programs; Sacks was his student at Harvard after World War II. Both men saw law as the glue of community. Thus, the process approach updated Pound's often expressed wish for a law that reduced friction among interest groups and gave a realistic coating to Lon Fuller's belief that law should foster harmony. Both men were supporters of civil rights for minorities, but both took the Warren Court to task for failing to provide a reasoned defense of *Brown v. Board of Education*.[134] When it came down to cases, the ideal reasoned elaboration allowed the law to work itself pure. The plain truth was that Hart and Sacks adopted Fuller's language.[135] But Fuller presumed a basic consensus, and although the clamor of the interests was quieted in the 1950s, the competition for material advancement and social equality among Americans simmered just below the surface.

For a younger Pound, the rise of process jurisprudence might well have stimulated a series of thoughtful articles and talks—Pound trying to appropriate the new ideas into his own corpus—but now he was tired. As he wrote to Sayre in September 1958, "Between January and July I had taken on seven speaking engagements which called for lectures which have since been published, and five minor speaking engagements which have not called for publication. . . . In the meantime I revised and completed the manuscript of a book on jurisprudence, 1344 pages of text and 900 pages of notes, which went to the printer July 3."[136]

The last was his magnum opus, a five-volume essay on jurisprudence, but apparently there was no room in it for Lon Fuller or process jurisprudence. True, he had begun it in 1911 and continued

134. William N. Eskridge, Jr., and Philip P. Frickey, eds., *Henry M. Hart, Jr., and Albert M. Sacks, The Legal Process: Basic Problems in the Making and Application of Law* [1958] (Westbury, N.Y., 1994), li–cxxxvi.

135. Neil Duxbury, "Faith in Reason: The Process Tradition in American Jurisprudence," 15 *Cardozo Law Review* 665 (1993).

136. Pound to Sayre, Sept. 8, 1958, Sayre Papers.

it in fits and starts until 1958, but he had known Fuller for a long time, much of that time intimately, and had told Fuller that he was the coming giant in American jurisprudence.[137] Hart's tenure at Harvard overlapped with Pound's in the war years, and Hart's legal process materials circulated at Harvard for many years before 1958. Pound mentioned Frank in the treatise and gave high marks to Llewellyn. There was much to be done to complete the program they had begun, Pound judged, though he preferred what he called "logical positive realism" of the sort that Cook and other outright devotees of the social sciences pursued.[138] On legal process, there was only an obscure reference to the "marked tendency toward a synthesis of the philosophical approaches" among the moderns.[139]

The reason for the exclusion of the legal process writers was simple: Pound was not writing about current theory; he was ruminating, in print, about the meaning of his own journey through academic jurisprudence. That introspective quality (insofar as Pound allowed himself the luxury of introspection) is what makes *Jurisprudence* so unique and so exasperating to read. Pound had written and revised it over so long a course of years that it had become a part of his personal experience. The pages of text went everywhere with him, in the form of notes, unfinished chapters, and preliminary drafts. It was almost as though he had kept an intellectual diary. The published version, for all its wonderful erudition, often talks to itself. Once upon a time, Pound tried to impress his readers with abstruse citations and vast learning; now Pound did not mind if the reader could follow him or not. Typically, key figures in the story, like Rudolph von Ihering, are never properly introduced. Pound had known them so long that they needed no introduction in his mind— and let the reader beware.[140]

In the first two volumes, Pound introduced a third generation to his schools of jurists and his categories of theories. The parade of

137. Roscoe Pound, *Jurisprudence* (St. Paul, Minn., 1959), 1:xi–xii; Pound to John Wu, Nov. 21, 1955, RPP, 54-5.
138. Pound, *Jurisprudence*, 1:274–76.
139. Ibid., 1:190.
140. Frank Bayley, an old student of Pound's, recalled in 1958 that Pound always ran ahead of his audiences. At a twenty-fifth reunion, the toast to Pound went: "Here's a toast to Roscoe Pound / Whose mind exceeds the speed of sound. / When we sat under him we could hardly / understand a thing he said; / We are older now, but if the truth be told—/ And we sat once more under him / We would hardly understand a G.-D. Thing." Bayley to Fuller, Feb. 24, 1958, Lon Fuller Papers, Harvard Law School, 13–15.

familiar faces he mustered marched by with measured tread. They would never pass this way again. Here were the cycles and stages of analytic and historical jurisprudence, a Ptolemaic universe of legal stars and planets. Throughout the volumes, he cited himself, sometimes reprinting four- and five-page excerpts from his old articles, which was fair, considering that he had said it all before. As Dean Erwin Griswold later wrote in a volume commemorating Pound's ninetieth birthday, "Some ideas are worthy of repetition, and Dean Pound has done much to make his ideas effective by reiteration, at appropriate times, and on suitable occasions."[141] Nevertheless, in his *Jurisprudence,* sometimes he simply did not bother to look up and notice that the world had changed. For example, in a long discursive ramble about the unchecked growth and unpoliced procedure of administrative agencies in America, based largely on his articles and reports from 1938 to 1943, Pound forgot to mention the Administrative Procedure Act of 1946, which altered the rules for agency hearings in ways that he had wanted.[142]

The middle volume returned to his theory of interests. Law quieted the clamor of interests. Pound bowed to Llewellyn's account in *The Cheyenne Way*—the law need not be written so long as it was available and answered the needs of a people. Pound's law did not create interests; the interests were already there. It was only necessary, then, to enumerate (more lists) the kinds of interests, match the law to them, and explore the fit.[143] What was advertised as a treatise on jurisprudence overflowed the confines of theory, becoming a sampler of substance, a companion to the comparative law of libel, privacy, religious toleration, domestic relations, real property (an overview of two thousand years of Western theory on possession followed this heading), labor contracts, and servitude and concluding with an extensive essay on public interest law. As he wrote to John Wu, a former student, in October 1958, "I have always had serious doubts of the profitableness of teaching jurisprudence as an abstract subject . . . in the everyday professional curriculum in the Law School."[144] But there was a kicker at the end. Because law followed interests rather than creating them, "[t]here is a serious limi-

141. Erwin Griswold, "Introduction," in Ralph A. Newman, ed., *Essays in Jurisprudence in Honor of Roscoe Pound* (Indianapolis, 1962), xiii.

142. Pound, *Jurisprudence,* 2:407–46.

143. Ibid., 3:15, 21.

144. Pound to Wu, Oct. 9, 1958, RPP, 54-5.

tation upon the possibility of social progress through law. To a large extent law . . . must express progress rather than immediately bring about progress." [145] This was quite the opposite of what the younger Pound thought, in print at least, about the role of legislation and the workplace. Perhaps Pound had forgotten, though that is unlikely, given his use of his earlier publications throughout the text. No matter—he had come a long way.

The last two volumes read as though Pound tried to marry Sir William Blackstone's categories of law to Hohfeld's schema. Rights, powers, duties, and liabilities opened the volume, followed by persons, acts, and things. There were proprietary rights and obligations as well—jurisprudence again wore the mask of the substantive headings of the law. Did any of it matter? Pound had lived through wars and civil insurrections; he had taught law to the barbarous nations and to the most civilized of audiences. All that he could summon at the end read at first like a cliché: "Laws are easily made instruments of dictators. Law, by which a reasoned technique is applied to laws in order to achieve an ideal relation among men, is the arch enemy of dictators." [146] Pound had worked directly for one, Chiang Kai-shek, and had accepted honors from others. Was he seeking absolution? In the end, the many pieces of his thought far exceeded in value the whole, as, once again, Llewellyn promptly noticed.

For Llewellyn, the publication of Pound's *Jurisprudence* was a final chance to assess the work of a man who had been his inspiration and his tribulation throughout his career. Llewellyn had the critique finely honed by now, the result of years of practice, but privately Llewellyn was troubled by the five volumes now before him. "For it is unmistakable that the author's love lies not in results, nor yet in process, but in abstract thinking about abstract thoughts. Yet even there it is a touch horrible to find this father of my mind devoting endless pages to 'the' theory of the corporate person—each several 'theory' being exploded as insufficient because it cannot handle *every* point of doctrine—when single cause thinking in social matters has been off since this author's youth." In the end, Llewellyn was puzzled. "So here we have a queer book. . . . Always learned and sometimes shrewd . . . which does not touch the most troubling

145. Pound, *Jurisprudence*, 3:373.
146. Ibid., 5:715.

modern aspects" of governments, corporate activity, management, and, most of all, application of jurisprudence to real life.[147]

In print, Llewellyn praised the work as a unique compilation of jurisprudential theories infused with "the powerful and critical home-grown insight about us-folk, our legal problems, and our legal ways, which has been the foundation of Pound's greatness." In it were echoes of his masterworks, his attacks on mechanical jurisprudence and spurious interpretation. It was also full of clichés, going everywhere (except into public law) and yet arriving nowhere. Pound's judgments of men and contributions were sound, but he cared little for their methods and nothing for their results. Such analysis was not beyond his reach: "*Nothing* was beyond his reach." He simply preferred "gathering, observing, portraying, arranging" to process.[148]

And like Pound, Llewellyn in his last years had withered into a kind of wisdom, a balancing of demands and expectations. He was still a staunch liberal, but he had learned, as Pound had when he retired from the deanship, that the law had its limits as a vocation as well as an ideal. He had left his beloved New York City to live and teach in Chicago, just as busy and hardly new to him (he spent many convention hours and much time drafting the UCC there), but change at such an age is never easy. The retreat motif of the late 1930s reappeared in some of Llewellyn's later, unpublished poetry. Many reflected his deepest inner struggles, pains, and joys, perhaps because they never were intended for publication. He wrote love poems, poems about and for his young son, poems about his own mental health.[149] Because Llewellyn's unpublished poetry was so personal, so self-revelatory, he may have revealed some of his deepest and strongest feelings about law in these poems as well. In a 1955 effort, Llewellyn displayed in verse a contempt for philosophy that came close to self-loathing. The refrain went: "I say to Hell

147. Llewellyn, Draft of Review of Pound's *Jurisprudence,* n.d., KLP, A.II.4 (emphasis in original).

148. Karl Llewellyn, "Review of Roscoe Pound, *Jurisprudence,*" 28 *University of Chicago Law Review* 174–82 (1960), reprinted in Llewellyn, *Jurisprudence,* 495, 503 (emphasis in original).

149. "O I want to be a manic depressive" is disturbing in its revelations of Llewellyn's pain over his mental state, though ostensibly written as humorous. Another poem, "I have grown weary of the world" (handwritten and dated 1932) had apparently been written at one of the low points of his life and reflects a deep despair. KLP, B.VI.1.

with Philosophical 'Poetry' / I say to Hell with people who yell in 'verse' / when or because their prose is dull / null / dead / lead." [150]

But there was still the good fight to be fought, if not won. In a talk at Villanova that is not usually included in Llewellyn's canonical works, he thought out loud about "What Law Cannot Do for Inter-Racial Peace." The civil rights movement was churning through the Deep South. Martin Luther King, Jr., and the bus boycott were only the beginning. Segregationists had formed citizens councils, die-hard southern congressmen and senators had pitched their defiance of the Supreme Court's rulings into the wells of the Houses of Congress, and hooded violence had escalated.[151] But Llewellyn's judgment was sure and wise. He did not concede that law is helpless before customs. He had abandoned the Spencerian conservatism of William Graham Sumner. "The machinery of law-government has no need to lag behind or to lag with or to uncreatively just fit into the existing ways of people in their race relations, whether inside a nation or between nations. On the contrary the machinery of law-government can be built (as has been done in part by our Constitution and by our Supreme Court and by our system of armed services and of elections) to set up an ideal still far from full attainment, to set up tension, steady or sudden, in the direction of those ideas, and in some degree to block off or to beat down obstruction." Pound might have been pleased to hear Llewellyn at last concede that the job of law was to find and hold up a people's ideals. "But the second thing is no less clear: put tension on too suddenly, too sharply, too hard, and your wire can snap, even snap back into that devastation called destruction and reaction." But even the softest, most cautious forward movement would bring results if people were willing to keep on working for those results. "My faith in jurisprudence as in legislation has always rested on the need for seeing the facts straight. . . . A hard-eyed view of what the law-government craftsman is up against is thus of the essence of his coping with the problems of his necessary, nay, his noble craft. This approach I have been preaching for more than a quarter century. I called it realistic. It is realistic." Where to fight for equality then? In hospitals, yes, and in hotels and restaurants as well. And in colleges

150. Llewellyn, To Hell with Philosophical Poetry, Mar. 9, 1955, KLP, B.VI.2.
151. Numan V. Bartley, *The Rise of Massive Resistance: Race and Politics in the South during the 1950s* (Baton Rouge, La., 1969).

and schools, for they, too, must be integrated. What the law-man needed was inventiveness.[152]

In such talks, Llewellyn reached toward a summing up of his views, a proof that his unflagging powers could triumph over failing health. His classic, *The Common Law Tradition: Deciding Appeals,* was thus a valedictory. Like Pound's *Jurisprudence,* it was the work of many years. What looked like an exegesis on judging was, in fact, the last application of realism. Of course, there was a contradiction—as Frank, had he lived, would have noticed—in applying realism to that most unreal of acts, the appellate court opinion. For the appellate courts did not have the reality before them, as Llewellyn long before had admitted. They had the record, the final distillation of many prior squeezings of reality out of the legal process. But Llewellyn had never dealt directly with reality. Instead, his realism was a set of instructions for a learned, specially trained elite—law students, lawyers, lawmakers, and judges. Even when he spent his ten days on the Cheyenne reservation, he was a tourist in someone else's reality. The Cheyenne were not gifted, intuitive lawmakers. They were a people with a long tradition of negotiated settlements, gestures, scripted mini-dramas, and well-versed oral lore. Llewellyn's romantic inclinations and his breathless prose made them into something else, as his craftsmanship (the same "craft-tradition" he attributed to the great judges) transformed the humdrum of business transactions into an ideal world of usages and fairness.

The Common Law Tradition had two powerful themes. Both were taken from Llewellyn's jurisprudence lectures over the course of years. Like Pound, Llewellyn had used the lecture room as a rehearsal hall. The first theme was that judging was not always or inevitably a formalist exercise in matching fact situations to established rules of law. There were judges, of course, "who feel it's [their] duty to disregard such things as sentiment, fireside equities, a sense of justice which has to be referred to the political sense, and the recognition of new interests and the like. It's [their] duty to stand on the law."[153]

But there was another style, which he termed a "grand" style, in

152. Karl Llewellyn, "What the Law Cannot Do for Inter-Racial Peace," 3 *Villanova Law Review* 30–36 (1957), reprinted in Llewellyn, *Jurisprudence,* 481, 483–84, 485–86.

153. Llewellyn, Jurisprudence Lecture XVI, 1948, KLP, C.H.1–40.

which judges tried to fit their decisions to the felt needs of the time. In effect, in a period when the grand style predominated, the judges reached down from their pedestals to incorporate local knowledge into their opinions. In no period was one style universal, but various periods were characterized by the force of important judges' thinking.[154] Llewellyn tested that thesis in thoroughly realist fashion in his jurisprudence classes. He required the students to go to any state appellate reporter and follow two hundred pages of opinions in the years 1830 to 1840. They were to do the same for the period 1880–1900 and then again for the 1930s and 1940s. "Now I'm interested in how courts decide cases and how doctrine goes round in these United States, something that you can apply to a case that you never heard of before and a body of law which will not come into existence until 15 years from now, and it's going to work just the same, just the same."[155]

The second theme came out of Llewellyn's sales casebook. Moving through the cases, Llewellyn became aware of how judges altered their reading of precedent to fit the facts of the case and how they presented arguments to get to a result they wanted. When he went to Germany and gave his lectures on the case law system, he reproduced selections from the cases, pointing out "what he is doing here; and pointing out what he was doing."[156] Thus, the opinions were no longer oracular discoveries of law, but evidence of judicial work. The craft of the judge, as well as the art of writing a convincing opinion, became evident. Llewellyn had laid out these revelations in his *Präjudizienrecht*, but the work was still not available in English.

One would, then, expect *The Common Law Tradition* to be an updated, domesticated *Law and the Modern Mind*, less psychoanalytical and more anthropological perhaps, but just as averse to the canons of formalism. But Llewellyn still had the power to surprise. His purpose was not to trash the ideals of consistency and precedent (what he called "reckonability," for he still loved to coin new terms), but to prove to the "moderately successful lawyer in his middle years" that appellate courts were bound by their own craft canon.[157]

154. Llewellyn, Jurisprudence Lecture XVII, 1948, KLP, C.H.1–40.
155. Llewellyn, Jurisprudence Lecture XI, 1948, KLP, C.H.1–40.
156. Llewellyn, Jurisprudence, May 6, 1953, KLP, C.L.1–20, p. 2.
157. Karl Llewellyn, *The Common Law Tradition: Deciding Appeals* (Boston, 1960), 4, 5.

There were fourteen steadying factors, all of which Llewellyn had explored in his lectures. The judges were lawyers, trained to think in legal categories. They accepted the notion of doctrine controlling cases (at least easy ones) and employed conventional ways of reading and espousing doctrine. When "the interests of justice" diverged from doctrine, they tried to reconcile or distinguish precedent. Most appellate judges no longer believed that "one right answer" was always available, but they still looked for the right answer. This tendency, of all those he found, troubled Llewellyn the most, for it was the one great relic of formalism. The appellate courts had to write opinions, however, and this required consensus building, constraining the "leeways" (i.e., discretion—"leeways" was another Llewellyn coinage) of individual judges. The record itself, with its factual content frozen and its pleadings formalized by rules, encouraged steadiness over time. The adversarial process ensured that the judges had just about all the relevant precedent laid before them. Most judges took into account the opinions of their brethren and were honest about their own motivations. What is more, the professional observer (herein the lawyer) could pretty much tell which way any particular judge or panel would bend after watching for a number of years.[158] But above all, there was the professionalism of the modern appellate judge, the sense of duty, the high regard they sought and retained among the public, the "honesty, reasonable effort, and reasonable dignity" that protected the bench and gave it moral force.[159]

Then, of course, there was the "period style" of judging in that time, much like the dominant architectural or musical style. The extent to which policy considerations would move a court depended on the style of judging the court had encouraged. The grand style constantly reexamined precedent, fitting the past to serve present needs. The first such period in American juridical history Llewellyn found in the work of Lemuel Shaw and others.[160] In the Gilded Age, formalism returned, demanding "large scale Order." The grand style returned in the 1930s, save in the United States Supreme Court, which "was indeed amazingly slow in responding to the

158. Ibid., 19–35.
159. Ibid., 48.
160. Indeed, Llewellyn ended with a paean to "Lemuel Shaw's noble dream of American law and decision made plain, made warm and near, made proud." Ibid., 520.

tide."[161] Style, like professionalism, created traditions, a kind of local knowledge of appellate judging: "Tradition grips [the judges,] shapes them, limits them, guides them; not for nothing do we speak of *ingrained* ways of work or thought, or men *experienced* or case-hardened, of *habits* of mind."[162]

The rest of the body of the book was example, the example of cases from state reporters, the example of realistic "horse-sense" analysis. Most of the cases were commercial transactions—drawn directly from the archives of the UCC drafting team. Thus, Llewellyn once again tried to link the academic to the real-world practice and his personal experience to more general subjects. And again, typically, Llewellyn was not recording reality, but arguing for his vision of what reality should be. The book is a not-so-covert brief in favor of the Llewellyn plan for the UCC, discarded in part by the bankers and the lawyers of the NCCUSL and the ALI, but never surrendered by its author. With the sounds of his battle over the UCC with the New York commissioners still ringing in his ears, Llewellyn was telling the judges who would hear cases under the UCC to obey "the pressure of fact and feeling."[163]

This was positively Machiavellian on Llewellyn's part, using all the arguments of princely prerogative to convince the prince to behave like a republican magistrate.[164] "I am going to waste little time on those objectors who can be heard growling or sneering that our appellate judges are a bunch of hypocrites, or are dishonest, or lack the sense to sail an even course, or are sacrificing all principle to expedience, and to pressure, political or popular [i.e., from the lawyers] or what have you more."[165] Above all, his advice was this: Stick to the facts. Do not be afraid to overrule or to admit error. Trust situation-sense. Avoid procedural hang-ups. See the case as a whole. Do not be afraid to take a *fresh* look, which brought Llewellyn back to the beginning—the facts.[166] There was more, of course, and the message was in the details. There was even a musical

161. Ibid., 41.

162. Ibid., 53 (emphasis in original).

163. Ibid., 128.

164. On Machiavelli's subtle stratagem, see Frederico Chabod, *Machiavelli and the Renaissance* (Cambridge, Mass., 1960). Of course, it did not work. Princes, whether they be dullards or swifts, are hard to fool.

165. Llewellyn, *Common Law Tradition*, 129.

166. Ibid., 134, 259, 261, 268, 283, 285, 293.

version of "The Common Law Tradition," whose chorus went "Rowdy, dowdy, doodle-ee-o, In the Common Law tradition." [167]

But Llewellyn did not want the frivolity to spread too far. He would not be misread to say that the great judges could or did decide whatever they wanted to decide. He wanted instead "the application of reason and sense to spotting the significant type-situation and diagnosing the sound and fair answer to the type-problem. This leads to *rules* of law, not to mere just or right *decisions,* much less to decisions merely according to any personal equities in individual cases." If the judges would only follow Llewellyn's instructions, there would be an "*on-going and unceasing judicial review of prior judicial decisions* on the side of rule, tool, and technique." [168] In effect, Llewellyn would have the judges act as teachers of law (to put the matter plainly, Llewellyn clones) as well as judges of law cases. [169] Then, once dissected (by Llewellyn, of course) and laid out in what amounted to a handbook for judges and their professional audiences, the common law tradition would be defined for good and all.

Of course, it was not. Llewellyn sent a copy to Arthur Corbin, still living in a New Haven suburb and still intellectually active. Corbin was frank and almost wistful. He had only read the first one hundred and sixty pages and dipped into the rest when he wrote first, at the beginning of December 1960. But he could not wait, for Karl and Soia were his fourth pair of children (figuratively, of course), and he, at age eighty-six, had to "hurry, hurry." He was delighted to report that so much in the book was "strikingly new" to him, but he approved of most of it. Llewellyn's style "is the best you have shown," and though Corbin had no truck with the empiricists and the psychologists, "I can join cheerfully with you in your kind of 'Realism.'" For there was a law, a law that had to be learned by students who would practice. He had always believed that a court had to begin with the type of situation and work its way up to the law. But here was the rub—how do you know which types fit which cases? "Where do you go to find them?" Corbin had practiced before the appellate courts, particularly before the Second Circuit. He had lost cases he felt he should have won when the judge

---

167. Ibid., 400. Sung in class as well. Glendon, *Nation under Lawyers,* 178.

168. Llewellyn, *Common Law Tradition,* 401, 402 (emphasis in original).

169. Which Llewellyn just about admitted in his confessional and autobiographical "Appendix B" on "Realism and Method." Ibid., 516.

(Jerome Frank) had a different "type-situation" in mind than the one Corbin presented. "Do the above anecdotes shake my confidence in your conclusions? Not a whit."[170]

Corbin told Llewellyn that "your book will be welcomed by the judges and will sharpen their minds as to their own style and method."[171] Charles Clark, who lived a few blocks away from Corbin, still lectured at Yale, but spoke with the authority of a longterm federal appellate judge (and a realist). He was more critical of the book, both in print and in private. Clark used the Yale celebration of Cardozo's career to strike at *The Common Law Tradition.* In a review he co-authored with his clerk, David Trubek, Clark conceded that much of Llewellyn's work was brilliant, and "in its Gothic encrustations the book reminds one of a great cathedral, whose very structure is the lack of a mechanical plan."[172] But Clark and Trubek had the same objections to the work as Corbin. How was the judge to know what a "type-situation" or "situation-sense" was, and even if the judge had an innate "situation-sense," how was this to be applied in any particular case? In effect, Llewellyn had created a new set of legal categories just as "immanent" and compelling as the old set but even more metaphysical. By comparison, Cardozo was far more realistic than Llewellyn, for Cardozo recognized the signs of "judicial subjectivity" when he saw them.[173]

Llewellyn was generous in responding to the barbs in the review, but Clark was not deterred from a few more private remarks. He had known Llewellyn as a student and a colleague, for young Clark (three years Llewellyn's senior) replaced Hohfeld on the Yale faculty in 1919. In January 1962, Clark wrote to Llewellyn that one of Clark's new colleagues on the bench regarded the book "as a desk guide." Clark was not amused. He thought that Llewellyn had given away the game to the conservatives: "I feel sure I am right that you are orienting the judge toward conservatism, which, in my view, is the last thing our craft needs or should get from distinguished legal philosophers. The trend toward dodoism is overstrong in any event."

170. Arthur Corbin to Llewellyn, Dec. 1, 1960, KLP, R.III.15.
171. Ibid.
172. Charles E. Clark and David M. Trubek, "The Creative Role of the Judge: Restraint and Freedom in the Common Law Tradition," 71 *Yale Law Journal* 258 (1961). If the comparison was apt, it was not fair to cathedrals, which invariably had precise formulae for their construction.
173. Ibid., 260, 262, 263, 265.

Clark was still a New Deal realist (New England men did not change their views easily) and remained convinced that "most judges are already so conditioned by their past, as, for example, their long period as Wall Street lawyers, that they are not going to change."[174] Llewellyn never did reply.

Karl Llewellyn died suddenly on February 14, 1962. His collection of essays on jurisprudence was complete; Soia saw it through the proofreading and publication. Like Pound, he had gone the distance. But Pound still lived when Llewellyn passed away, and the *New York Times* obituary page editor asked Pound for a quotation to close the obituary. Pound was happy to oblige: "[Llewellyn's work was] the most basic and thoroughly thought-out *sociological* theory of law which has yet appeared."[175] Pound had graciously ceded pride of place to Llewellyn and in the process slyly reduced legal realism to a variant of sociological jurisprudence. If Pound was right, then Llewellyn's *Common Law Tradition* was the long-sought-after treatise on sociological jurisprudence that they had discussed for so many years.

174. Charles E. Clark to Llewellyn, Jan. 19, 1962, Charles E. Clark Papers, Yale University.
175. *New York Times,* Feb. 15, 1962, at A32 (emphasis added).

The Romantic and the Encylopedist

O n his notepad, found on his desk after his death, was the last thing Karl Llewellyn wrote about law. There is a certain poignancy in the final sentence. Almost predictably, he used the powerful metaphor of birth and creativity to express his deepest feelings in a few lines reminiscent of his verse. "Law is a bursting thing, and has the pains and dangers of childbirth. And when new law is born it is that tender and sometimes that helpless. I suppose that some of what is eating in me is to give form and bones to this beauty which is to be, and is beyond me."[1]

Perhaps it was, for what was important in the end was not the realization of the law but the admiration of its beauty. As he told his jurisprudence students during his visit at Harvard Law School in 1949, "I am hopelessly on the romantic side, both in substance and in form."[2]

Roscoe Pound did not meet his end so dramatically. He spent the last year of his life in the Harvard infirmary with a broken hip from a fall. "As you know I do not give up easily," he had written to his sister a few years before, but his decline was now irreversible.[3] As Llewellyn's last words were, characteristically, poetry, so Pound's last major judgment on law was prose: "As I have argued in other

---

1. Karl Llewellyn, Last Desk Pad, 1962, KLP, V.IV.
2. Llewellyn, Jurisprudence Lecture XXI, 1949, KLP, C.H.1–40.
3. Roscoe Pound to Olivia Pound, Nov. 16, 1960, NSHS, MS 911, box 1, folder S.1, vol. F.10.

connections, law is experience developed by reason and reason tested by experience. The experience comes through decision of concrete controversies in which working solutions are found for problems of adjusting relations and ordering conduct. . . . Laws are easily made instruments of dictators. Law, by which a reasoned technique is applied to laws in order to achieve an ideal relation among men, is the arch enemy of dictators."[4] Not bad for a man of eighty-nine years—wise, sober, thoughtful, and still idealistic. Pound did not try to soar over the terrain. He walked through it with measured tread.

Pound and Llewellyn had spent much of their careers in a search for an American jurisprudence, but if I am right about where and how they looked, their exploration never discovered a single over-arching answer. What mattered was the search itself. In the process of looking, they formed and reformed networks of academic peers. The networks themselves took on an institutional life. Network mores, to coin a term, governed what one could and could not do. Jerome Frank, never fully integrated into any of the networks, violated these norms. Pound and Llewellyn, for all the vigor of their dispute, conformed to network expectations. This is what the private discourse reveals. They even encouraged each other in private to disagree with each other in public. And then they used private channels to patch up whatever soreness the print controversy might have caused.

The search was also a grand exercise in bricolage. The two men were constantly shifting positions and forms of argument as they incorporated and discarded bits and pieces of other disciplines. Pound was a great listener and synthesizer, as Llewellyn was the first to admit. Llewellyn's speed of thought and intuition made him the perfect point man for novelties, as Pound fulsomely observed. In different ways, their class lectures were pure bricolage—Pound's a stately synthesis, Llewellyn's a chaotic intellectual bazaar. Did the bits and pieces add up to a "jurisprudence?" Hardly. But the process of assembling the bits and pieces was uniquely American, and it continues to this day. American jurisprudence is a bricolage, a "law and . . ." par excellence.

Pound and Llewellyn could not have anticipated this concordance

4. Roscoe Pound, *Jurisprudence* (St. Paul, Minn., 1959), 5:715.

over time. It is better for historians to leave such acrobatic leaps through time for the jurisprudents. But I can say that both were searching for something more than a pat intellectual formula. Pound wanted to gain knowledge, to see inside the law. He concluded that law was best left in the hands of an elite, experts whose training and neutrality allowed them to reduce interest-group friction. Llewellyn needed art to feel the law. He valued local knowledge, the expertise that came from living.

Both were readers, but read the law differently. They shared a passion to get it right, but Pound was both inspiration and target for Llewellyn. Philosopher Richard Rorty recently wrote: "When I was young, I watched A.J. Ayer replace A.N. Whitehead as the most widely imitated Anglophone philosopher. Whitehead stood for charisma, genius, romance, and Wordsworth. Ayer stood for logic, debunking, and knowingness. He wanted philosophy to be a matter of scientific teamwork rather than of imaginative breakthroughs by heroic figures. He saw Whitehead as a good logician who had been ruined by poetry."[5] Rorty's elegy on the dynamics of "dryness" and "knowingness" and their polar opposites, romance and intuition, fits Pound and Llewellyn. Llewellyn was never content with the aims or the claims of knowingness, with an empirical science of the law, whoever might be its purveyors. Pound was never content with a piece of the story. He had to have all the rest, the stages and cycles, the schools and great thinkers.

But to leave the account here is to lose its history once again, just after we have found it. For the search made all the academic politics, all the polemics, all the false starts and failed negotiations worthwhile. The bricolage was nothing more than the wonder and delight of getting the chance, in the words of the modern educators, to read all over the curriculum. The networking was nothing more or less than the joy of reaching out to others working in the same fields, to savor all the potential replies one might make before choosing one's words. Pound never put it in a flight of fancy, but one can read the pleasure in his letters; his support for younger scholars like Wesley Newcomb Hohfeld, Llewellyn, and Lon Fuller; his sharing with John Henry Wigmore and Herbert Goodrich; his trips to the conventions; and his lectures on circuit, invited and sponsored.

5. Richard Rorty, "The Necessity of Inspired Reading," *Chronicle of Higher Education*, Feb. 9, 1996, at A48.

Llewellyn revealed the joy of all this to his students, laughing while telling them the lecture was no laughing matter. "And jurisprudence is for the purpose, not only of making lawyers better lawyers, but of making each lawyer have more fun."[6] He even put it in poetry:

> Among our folk, as among the nations,
>> Justice is never a thing, but a quest.
>> The measure is always a little messed.
> But a man must manage without vacations
> and, if he must, on shortened rations,
>> when questions press and press and are pressed
>> For Justice is never a thing, but a quest
> among our folk, as among the nations.[7]

6. Llewellyn, Jurisprudence Lecture 1, Mar. 31, 1959, KLP, C.P.1–5.
7. Karl Llewellyn, *Jurisprudence: Realism in Theory and Practice* (Chicago, 1962), 214.

Llewellyn's Lists of Realists

Table 1   Evolution of Llewellyn's List of Realists

"Next Step" (1930)	KNL to RP[b] 3/17/31	KNL/JF Memo[a] 3/27/31	KNL to RP 4/6/31	"Some Realism" 6/31
Moore	Moore	Moore	Moore	Moore
	Frank	Frank	Frank	Frank
	Oliphant	Oliphant	Oliphant	Oliphant
Klaus	Klaus	Klaus	Klaus	Klaus
	Cook	Cook	Cook	Cook
Green	Green	Green	Green	Green
Yntema	Yntema	Yntema	Yntema	Yntema
Clark	Clark	Clark	Clark	Clark
	Radin	Radin	Radin	Radin
	Llewellyn	Llewellyn	Llewellyn	Llewellyn
	Corbin	Corbin	Corbin	Corbin
	Sturges	Sturges	Sturges	Sturges
Douglas	Douglas	Douglas	Douglas	Douglas
		Arnold	Arnold	
		Bingham	Bingham	Bingham
		Hutcheson	Hutcheson	Hutcheson
		Hamilton	Hamilton	
		Patterson	Patterson	Patterson
		Tulin	Tulin	Tulin
			Francis	Francis
			T. R. Powell	T. R. Powell
			Lorenzen	Lorenzen
Frankfurter			Frankfurter	

[a] Source: University of Chicago Law Library, KLP, A.65.b.
[b] Source: Harvard Law School Library, RPP, 24–6.

Table 1 *continued*

"Next Step" (1930)	KNL to RP[b] 3/17/31	KNL/JF Memo[a] 3/27/31	KNL to RP 4/6/31	"Some Realism" 6/31
Handler			Handler	
Landis			Landis	
Brandeis				
Ehrlich				
Lambert				
Hedeman				
Nussbaum				
Moley				
Ishizaki				
			Hanna	
			Morgan	
			Kidd	
			Smith	
			McMurray	
			McCormick	
			Miller	
			Sunderland	
			R. R. Powell	
			Berle	
			Glueck	
			Warner	
			Bogert	
			Durfee	
			Bonbright	
			Hutchins	
			Hale	
			Turner (Steffins)	
			Bohlen	

Table 2   The List Llewellyn Sent Pound, April 6, 1931[c]

"Our notion of realists who may have taken extreme positions on one point or another":

[Walter W.] Cook
[Joseph W.] Bingham
[Jerome] Frank

[c] Source: Harvard Law School Library, RPP, 24-6.

[Underhill] Moore
[Herman] Oliphant
[Samuel] Klaus
[Wesley] Sturges
[Joseph C.] Hutcheson
[John] Hanna (perhaps)

"Our notion of realists who are thorough-going, but probably less extreme in their positions":

[Arthur L.] Corbin
[Max] Radin
Walton Hamilton
[Adolf A.] Berle
[Ernest] Lorenzen
C[harles] E. Clark
[Karl N.] Llewellyn
Leon Green
[Edwin W.] Patterson
[Hessel E.] Yntema
T[homas] R[eed] Powell
Y[oung] B. Smith
[Alexander Marsden] Kidd
[Milton] Handler
[Leon A.] Tulin
[Robert Maynard] Hutchins
[Thurman] Arnold
[William O.] Douglas
[Joseph] Francis
[James C.] Bonbright

"Our notion of realists-in-part-of-their-work (examples)":

[Felix] Frankfurter
[James M.] Landis
[Edmund M.] Morgan
[Edgar Noble] Durfee
[George G.] Bogert
[Sam Bass] Warner
Sheldon Glueck
R[ichard] R. Powell
[Edson Read] Sunderland
Justin Miller
[Charles T.] McCormick
[Robert Lee] Hale
[Roscoe B.] Turner [Steffins]
[Orin Kip] McMurray
[Francis] Bohlen

Table 3 Llewellyn's Additional Realists, April 6, 1931

Name	Birthdate	Education	Occupation 1930–31
[John] Hanna	1891 (d. 1964)	Harvard, LLB	Prof. of Law, Columbia
Walton Hamilton	1881 (d. 1958)	Univ. of Michigan, Ph.D.	Prof. of Law, Yale
[Adolf A.] Berle	1895 (d. 1971)	Harvard, LLB	Prof. of Law, Columbia
Y[oung] B. Smith	1889 (d. 1960)	Columbia, LLB	Dean, Columbia Law School
[Alexander Marsden] Kidd	1879 (d. 1955)	Harvard, LLB	Prof. of Law, California (Berkeley)
[Milton] Handler	1903	Columbia, LLB	Prof. of Law, Columbia
[Robert Maynard] Hutchins	1899 (d. 1977)	Yale, LLB	President, University of Chicago
[Thurman] Arnold	1891 (d. 1969)	Harvard, LLB	Prof. of Law, Yale
[James C.] Bonbright	1891 (d. 1969)	Columbia, Ph.D.	Prof. of Economics, Columbia Univ.
[Felix] Frankfurter	1882 (d. 1965)	Harvard, LLB	Prof. of Law, Harvard
[James M.] Landis	1899 (d. 1964)	Harvard, LLB	Prof. of Law, Harvard
[Edmund M.] Morgan	1878 (d. 1966)	Harvard, LLB	Prof. of Law, Harvard
[Edgar Noble] Durfee	1882 (d. 1958)	Chicago, JD	Prof. of Law, Michigan
[George G.] Bogert	1884 (d. 1977)	Cornell, LLB	Prof. of Law, Chicago
[Sam Bass] Warner	1889 (d. 1979)	Harvard, LLB	Asst. Prof. of Law, Harvard
Sheldon Glueck	1896 (d. 1980)	National Univ., LLB; Harvard, Ph.D.	Prof. of Law, Harvard
R[ichard] R. Powell	1890 (d. 1982)	Columbia, LLB	Prof. of Law, Columbia
[Edson Read] Sunderland	1874 (d. 1959)	Univ. of Berlin, LLB, A.M.	Prof. of Law, Michigan
Justin Miller	1888 (d. 1973)	Univ. of Montana, LLB	Dean, Duke University Law School
[Charles T.] McCormick	1889 (d. 1963)	Harvard, LLB	Dean, U. of N.C. Law School
[Robert Lee] Hale	1884 (d. 1969)	Columbia, Ph.D., Harvard LLB	Prof. of Law, Columbia
[Roscoe] Turner [Steffins]	1893 (d. 1976)	Yale LLB	Prof. of Law, Yale
[Orin Kip] McMurray	1869 (d. 1945)	Hastings College of Law (Calif.)	Visiting Prof. of Law, Columbia
[Francis] Bohlen	1868 (d. 1942)	Univ. of Pennsylvania, LLB	Prof. of Law, Penn